RECONSTRUCTING JUSTICE

About the Author

Franklin Strier is a professor of law at California State University, Dominguez Hills, and the editor of the *Journal of Business and Management*. He has been a senior policy analyst with the United States Department of Commerce and a practicing attorney. He is a co-author of *The Adversary System*. His articles and essays have appeared in publications such as the *ABA Journal*, *Judicature*, *Barrister*, the *American Journal of Forensic Psychiatry*, *The National Law Journal*, the *Los Angeles Times*, and *The Humanist*.

RECONSTRUCTING JUSTICE

An Agenda for Trial Reform

Franklin Strier

With a new Preface

The University of Chicago Press
Chicago and London

To my wife, Pat; son, Zachary; and daughter, Casey.

RECONSTRUCTING JUSTICE: An Agenda for Trial Reform, by Franklin Strier, was originally published in hard cover by Greenwood Press, an imprint of Greenwood Publishing Group, Inc., Westport, CT. Copyright © 1994 by Franklin Strier. This edition published by arrangement with Greenwood Publishing Group, Inc. All rights reserved.

The University of Chicago Press, Chicago 60637
The University of Chicago Press, Ltd., London
Copyright © 1994 by Franklin Strier
Preface © 1996 by Franklin Strier
All rights reserved. Originally published 1994
University of Chicago Press Edition 1996
Printed in the United States of America
02 01 00 99 98 97 96   6 5 4 3 2 1

ISBN 0-226-77718-9 (pbk.)

Library of Congress Cataloging-in-Publication Data

Strier, Franklin D.
    Reconstructing justice : an agenda for trial reform / Franklin Strier.
        p.   cm.
    Originally published: Westport, Conn. : Quorum Books, 1994. With a new pref.
    Includes bibliographical references and index.
    1. Adversary system (Law)—United States.   2. Jury—United States.   3. Dispute resolution (Law)—United States.   4. Justice, Administration of—United States.   5. Legal ethics—United States.   6. Law reform—United States.   I. Title.
    [KF384.S78   1996]
    347.73'9—dc20
    [347.3079]   95-46979
                                                                CIP

♾ The paper used in this publication meets the minimum requirements of the American National Standard for Information Sciences—Permanence of Paper for Printed Library Materials, ANSI Z39.48-1984.

CONTENTS

ACKNOWLEDGMENTS

I am indebted to several people whose cooperation and assistance made the writing of this book possible. Dr. Yoram Neumann, Dean of the School of Management at California State University, Dominguez Hills, graciously (and wisely!) provided the released time and resources which facilitated completion of the book. The technical expertise of Dr. Patricia Vacca was immeasurably helpful in producing the final copy. Law librarian Naomi Moy supplied valuable research assistance in compiling the extensive references. Last but not least, Stanley Prentice, M.D., was a welcome source of inspiration and exhortation over the years.

PREFACE

THE TRIAL OF THE CENTURY: REASONABLE DOUBT FOR AN UNREASONABLE PRICE

Since *Reconstructing Justice* was first issued in 1994, public discourse about the trial system has been dominated by one case, O. J. Simpson's. Whoever coined the "Trial of the Century" appellation in reference to the Simpson trial displayed remarkable prescience: the trial threatened to become the "Trial That Lasted a Century." Over a year elapsed between the preliminary hearing and the closing arguments. Live television coverage provided nearly round-the-clock publicity, while the hapless jury was sequestered for a record nine months.

For all the fluff and theater associated with it, the Simpson case taught Americans a great deal. The case was a public tutorial on the adversary system of justice, and drew unprecedented public attention to many fundamental weaknesses and inequities of the trial system. Our new awareness of the problems, however painful, was a first step to the good. This book takes the next step by addressing these problems with specific reform proposals. The key to the reform scheme is this: the trouble lies in the trial *system*—not in any specific attorney, judge, or jury.

In the American courtroom, there is reality and there is illusion. One pervasive and enduring illusion is that we have a trial system optimally suited to the discovery of truth. In reality, the adversariness of that system is just as likely to hide or corrupt the truth. If the adversarial trial is optimally suited for anything, it is for fomenting hostility and rancor, as the Simpson case amply and vividly illustrated. Most prominently, this case has demonstrated the untoward influence of attorneys over the courtroom search for truth.

Many surveys will be taken using the Simpson trial as a model of the system in action. I strongly suspect the results will reveal a decidedly low level of approval by the general public. By the same token, I believe a poll of judges and lawyers would conclude just the opposite.[1] Attorneys and judges will tend to perceive the Simpson trial as: a) well-lawyered (the attorneys played the game well) and b) fair (the judge was impartial and passive). The general public, on the other hand, will probably regard the trial as excessively contentious, unacceptably protracted, and presided over by a judge patently flustered by his own inability or unwillingness to control the proceedings. Many judges probably share Judge Ito's apparent belief that when in conflict, a defendant's right to due process (as largely conceived by the opposing attorneys) supersedes his right to a speedy trial.

The most lasting memento of the Simpson trial, for me, will be Judge Ito's internal struggle. Obviously bright and sedulously scrupulous, Ito was nevertheless riven by conflicting allegiances. He clearly showed a humane sensitivity to the limits of the jurors' physical and psychological endurance, frequently grumbling about the time consumed by attorney bickering and pettiness; nonetheless, he hewed to the traditional non-interventionist model of the judge. To Judge Ito—and doubtlessly to the vast majority of kindred spirits on the bench—the trial belonged to the attorneys.

Practitioners and academics hailed the Simpson trial as perhaps the finest demonstration of the adversary system in practice—two highly competent teams of opposing attorneys plying all their skills and resources to battle it out, with minimum interference by the court. When the dust settled, however, the exposure served more to liken trial procedure to sausage-making: You don't want to know what goes into either.

Another prominent illusion suffuses our image of the jury. Historically we have seen juries as protecting us against government overreaching and law administered without benefit of the common person's judgment and sense of fairness. The grim reality is as ignoble as the illusion is high-minded. As the Simpson case confirmed, trial attorneys shamelessly yet routinely manipulate juries. Moreover, juries are captives of an antiquated and byzantine procedural mechanism which at once keeps them ignorant of much of the relevant evidence and restricts their ability to independently investigate the facts.

Together, the adversary system trial and the jury fact finder often combine to deliver a witch's brew of injustice. Operating separately, each would do better at seeking the truth. Remove the jury and the flavor of the trial changes markedly. In a nonjury trial, where opposing attorneys argue their case before a judge, attorney theatrics and emotional pandering are rare. Put the same attorneys before a jury and the trial metamorphoses: Raise the curtain and strike up the band.

Alternatively, a lawyerless tribunal using a jury factfinder, even an all-lay jury, would seek the truth more effectively. Freed of the current restrictions on independent jury inquiry, the jury could directly investigate the facts. Now, jurors must passively view the evidence through the attorneys' partisanly filtered prism.

Eliminating the attorneys or limiting their roles would also remove another profoundly corrupting impact upon jury decision making: a mismatch
in the skills of the opposing attorneys. The central message of this book is
that the outcome of the Simpson trial and many other trials under the adversary system are too dependent upon the relative skills of the opposing attorneys. Chapter 1 argues this contention through a comparative analysis of the
two Rodney King trials. The Simpson case reaffirms the point.[2]

The so-called "Dream Team" of defense counsel had in Simpson a client
with means and motive for murder, and with no presented alibi. DNA and
other circumstantial forensic evidence (exceeding that which had sent other
defendants all the way to the gas chamber) implicated him, without a trace of
any possible third-party culprit. Simpson also had a history of physically
abusing one of the victims, his former wife Nicole. Confronted with this challenge, the defense counsel adroitly countered with two theories, contaminated
evidence and police conspiracy, creating sufficient reasonable doubt for this
jury. A few minor tactical errors did not detract from the defense's virtuoso
performance. Conversely, the prosecution committed fatal errors. In particular, calling Mark Fuhrman as a witness irretrievably doomed their case. Given
Fuhrman's past and his propensities—both presumably known to the prosecution—his testimony opened up a Pandora's Box. When his lack of credibility was added to the ill-advised change of venue and the abortive glove demonstration, the prosecution's defeat was inevitable.

The opposition of competent and roughly equal attorneys is the theoretical cornerstone of the adversary system. Nevertheless, yawning disparities in
success rates and fees among litigators attest to the mythology of this presumption. Notwithstanding the inspirational words "Equal Justice Under
The Law" carved into the facade of the U. S. Supreme Court building, justice
is for sale in the United States. The only thing equal is that anyone with five
or six million dollars to spend, not just a celebrity like O. J. Simpson, can get
the very best legal representation.

Despite all the post-verdict journalistic hysteria, racism is not the bogeyman unearthed by the Simpson verdict. African American juries have long
been more disposed to acquitting an African American defendant, just as
white juries have been more prone to acquit white defendants. Rather, the
more telling indictment of the verdict is the obscene privilege of wealth in
our society, especially in the legal system. Take the Simpson trial—the same
defendant, crime, evidence, and jury—and simply substitute for the Dream
Team a typical public defender or private defense counsel. Few would argue
that you would get an acquittal, or even a hung jury. The difference is money,
not race.

This book prescribes a reallocation of power in the American courtroom, away from the attorneys and to the judge and jury. Throughout the book, I suggest ways of doing this without impairing the integrity of the attorney's role. Much of the jury's empowerment must be mediated and facilitated by the judge. For example, consider two paradoxes attending the "reasonable doubt" standard of proof for a criminal conviction. A cardinal tenet of criminal law is that a crime must be well-defined by statute; if it is vague or overbroad it will be held unconstitutional. Yet the reasonable doubt standard is so vague as to be practically meaningless. (Many contend the Simpson jurors held the prosecution to an extraordinarily high standard of proof.) Judges must give more precision to this and other instructions and guidance to jurors if we expect them to implement the law with anything remotely approaching objectivity.

Even more paradoxical is the corruption of the reasonable doubt standard by operation of the adversary system. A reasonable doubt standard impliedly asks jurors to use their reason. But the adversary system freely permits trial attorneys to enflame the emotions of the jurors, even to call upon the jurors to follow their emotions. In the Simpson case, the closing arguments of the defense and prosecution were fire and ice, respectively: the incendiary emotionalism of Johnny Cochran's summation versus the prosecution team's calm, cool appeal to reason. Emotional and rational decisions correspond only by coincidence.

The Simpson trial illustrated the folly of presenting highly technical and complex evidence to an all-lay jury, especially through the testimony of partisan expert witnesses. Such evidence frequently overwhelms jurors. Particularly dismaying was the account of a dismissed Simpson juror who could not (or would not) distinguish DNA from ordinary blood typing; this notwithstanding that DNA evidence was the linchpin of the case, painstakingly explained by experts for both sides over months of testimony. Unfortunately, experts often compound rather than ease the jury's task: How is a lay juror to know if the most persuasive expert is the most authoritative? Also troubling is the degree to which the experts' hefty fees flavor their testimonies. The book proposes a remedy to the expert testimony problem.

The trial also raised the thorny issue of jury nullification: intentional disregard of the law by the jury. After nine months of evidence, just three hours of deliberation implies that the jury may have been playing by its own rules. *Reconstructing Justice* explains how our current treatment of jury nullification is akin to feckless fence straddling, and suggests either of two preferable alternatives.

The Simpson case prompts reexamination of two other practices. First, trial venues should no longer be changed because of pretrial publicity. In the age of mass media and instant communications, everyone not residing in a

closet hears about a high-profile case immediately. The first Rodney King trial
was moved from a minority community to a predominantly white one; the
resulting jury had no African Americans. Deadly riots followed the verdict.
Now it has been bruited about that Los Angeles District Attorney Gil Gar-
cetti moved the Simpson trial from the predominantly white west side of Los
Angeles—its original venue—to the more racially mixed downtown area because he feared a conviction by a predominantly white jury would "lack credibility," possibly leading to another Rodney King–type riot. If true, this was a
purely political judgment, having little to do with the law. It certainly contra-
vened the ideal of a jury representing a cross-section of the community where
the crime occurred. In effect, a venue change is a peremptory challenge of an
entire community.[3]

Secondly, the many witnesses in the Simpson case whose testimony appeared suspect gave me pause. Perhaps no other practice of the adversarial
trial impairs the search for truth more than witness-coaching. It would betray
great naiveté to deny that attorneys routinely rehearse and stage the testimonies of their witnesses. The dangers of coaching are clear: attorneys can orchestrate a common story among the client and all friendly witnesses; attorneys can suggest "better" answers that subtly but effectively shade, dissemble,
or distort the truth.[4]

Most importantly, attorney coaching inappropriately enhances the credibility of the coached witness' testimony with the jurors. The more witnesses
are rehearsed, the more confident and detailed they become in their recollec-
tions.[5] And the more confidence displayed by the witness, the more juries treat
the witness' testimony as accurate, despite the absence of any relationship
between confidence and accuracy.[6]

A related phenomenon occurs with regard to *consistency* of recollection.
Rehearsing begets consistent recollection. The more potential witnesses are
questioned and rehearsed about a past event, the more they dredge up details—often inaccurately—to fill in the blank spots of their memory. Psychological research tells us they will "remember" details which reinforce their
general recollection. The resulting consistency also unduly influences jurors.
Contrary to popular (and therefore juror) belief, studies show that witnesses
who change their initial recollection are generally *more* accurate than those
who do not.[7]

We probably cannot eliminate pretrial contact between attorney and potential witnesses without violating a client's right to effective assistance of
counsel. But we can require that all attorney contacts with anyone who is later
called as a disinterested witness would have to be *recorded*, and that opposing
counsel be given the opportunity to be present during the conversation. In the
eyes of jurors, corroborating witnesses, particularly disinterested witnesses,
immeasurably reinforce a witness' testimony. Reasonable limitations on pre-

trial indoctrination of disinterested witnesses would substantially inhibit the trial attorney's coaching scheme without impinging upon the sanctity of the attorney-client relationship.

The personalities and intense drama of the Simpson trial should not distract us from the larger problems of courtroom justice. The Simpson case and other sensational trials come and go. But the need for reform of the trial system remains. To that end, this book is devoted.[8]

NOTES

1. As the Yankelovich survey discussed in Chapter 1 found, the public holds a distinctly less favorable view of the courts and their performance than does the legal profession.
2. To be sure, both cases also suggest the preemptive effect of racial bias upon jurors when there is a defendant of the same race and a victim of another race. In the first King case, a jury with no African Americans acquitted the white assailants of an African American victim in the face of ostensibly undeniable evidence of guilt. In Simpson, a predominantly African American jury acquitted an African American defendant of the murder of two white victims notwithstanding apparently overwhelming forensic evidence of guilt, albeit circumstantial.
3. George Fletcher, *With Justice for Some: Victims' Rights in Criminal Trials* (New York: Addison Wesley, 1995), p. 252.
4. Coaching is virtually absent in the English and continental trial models. In England, the barrister who tries the case does not even meet with clients or witnesses before the trial. Under the inquisitorial system trial procedure followed in continental Europe (and much of the rest of the world), attorneys and witnesses rarely meet before the trial; if they do, the court assigns a commensurately low probative value to the witness' testimony.
5. Elizabeth Loftus, "The Truth, the Whole Truth and Nothing but the Truth?" *Los Angeles Times*, 8/25/95, B9.
6. See Gary Wells and Elizabeth Murray, "Eyewitness Confidence," in G. Wells and E. Loftus, eds., *Eyewitness Testimony: Psychological Perspectives* (Cambridge: Cambridge University Press, 1984), pp. 155, 159–65; Kenneth Deffenbacher, "Eyewitness Accuracy and Confidence: Can We Infer Anything from Their Relationship?" *Law and Human Behavior, 4* (1980), pp. 243, 257–58.
7. James Marshall, Kent Marquis and Stuart Oskamp, "Effects of Kind of Question and Atmosphere of Interrogation on Accuracy and Completeness of Testimony," 84(7) *Harvard Law Review* 1620, 1637 (1971).

8. The new interest in jury trial reform will undoubtedly spur many studies
    on the subject. Three recent books which I recommend are Jeffrey Ab-
    ramson, *We the Jury: The Jury System and the Ideal of Democracy* (New
    York: Basic Books, 1994); Stephen Adler, *The Jury: Trial and Error in
    the American Courtroom* (New York: Times Books, 1994); and George
    Fletcher, *op. cit.* See also Michael Dann, "'Learning Lessons' and
    'Speaking Rights': Creating Educated and Democratic Juries," 68(4) *In-
    diana Law Journal* 1229 (1993); Dann, an Arizona trial judge, has imple-
    mented important innovations in his courtroom.

CHAPTER 1

THE BATTLE OF CHAMPIONS

I think we must be aware of the societal interests being sacrificed in pursuit of providing an adversary forum for the vindication of claims of individual right. . . . We ought to judge each situation carefully to make sure that the game is always worth the candle.

—William Rehnquist[1]

We were horrified. My wife and I listened to the car radio in stunned silence as the jury foreman intoned the execrable verdicts. With each "not guilty" in this, the first Rodney King trial (hereafter "King I"),[2] a sense of surrealism escalated, eventually giving way to benumbing incredulity. This couldn't be happening; everyone saw the beating on television. In shock, I heard myself muse, "People are going to die." They did. Fifty-two died in the riots which erupted in the wake of the verdicts. Violence and arson spread across much of Los Angeles, destroying ten thousand homes. Total property damage exceeded one billion dollars.

Few were prepared for the verdict. The infamous videotape of King being kicked, stomped and beaten with metal nightsticks had been shown *ad nauseam* to a national audience. They watched him writhe on the ground, absorbing fifty-six blows. At times King lay prone and still, apparently susceptible to handcuffing, only to be struck again and again. The defendants charged with assault and excessive force were the three officers who administered the beating—Laurence Powell, Timothy Wind and Theodore Briseno—and their sergeant, Stacy Koon. Koon shot King twice with a 100,000 volt taser stun gun, then supervised the beating. Fifteen other officers witnessed the action nearby and were available to assist in King's arrest.

At trial, the defense attorneys faced an ostensibly insuperable problem. They had to convince the jury that nineteen police officers were incapable of subduing one unarmed man without first doling out the ferocious thrashing seen on videotape. Conjuring a more implausible interpretation beggars the imagination. Yet that is what the acquittals implied.

What can explain this gross miscarriage of justice? What forensic sorcery could induce the jury to deny what the rest of us clearly saw on television? Intensive search is unnecessary: The defense was masterful, the prosecution inept. After the suit was filed, defense counsel immediately moved for a change of venue based on the extensive pretrial publicity. They claimed a fair trial—one heard by "unbiased" jurors—was impossible in Los Angeles. When an appeals court ordered the trial moved out of Los Angeles, the trial judge selected Simi Valley, a predominantly white suburb in neighboring Ventura County.

The prosecution's first mistake was in failing to strongly protest and appeal the judge's decision. Simi Valley could not have been more unfavorable for the prosecution. It had a distinctly conservative, law-and-order, pro-police bent and was filled with retired police. All the defendants were white police officers; King was African American. Post-trial juror interviews fueled the belief that racial bias harbored by at least some of the Simi Valley jurors (none African American) was instrumental in the verdicts. Several of them were quoted as saying that, by his behavior, King "asked for" the beating he received.[3]

Although a judge has discretion as to whether and where to move a trial, there are constraints. Ideally, juries represent the values of the community where the alleged crime occurred. King was beaten in the Lake View Terrace section, which had a substantial minority and low-income population. Its community standards as to police-dispensed street justice were hardly the same as those of Simi Valley.

The venue change to Simi Valley was unconscionable; it was insensitive to the belief—supported by ample evidence—that white juries are more prone than integrated juries to convict an African American or Hispanic. Transfer to Simi Valley also markedly reduced the number of minority individuals available for jury service, which probably affected the outcome. Charles Lindner, past president of the Los Angeles Criminal Courts Bar Association, said the venue change reflected a callous disregard of the rule that the jury pool from which the jury was to be drawn should represent a cross-section of the community where the alleged crime happened. "An integrated jury pool is necessary," he writes, "not because it will be unprejudiced . . . but because putting minority group members in the jury room hopefully *offsets prejudice* by suppressing its expression."[4] (Emphasis supplied.)

Both legal theory and past practice indicated that if the trial was to be moved, it should be to a community demographically similar to that where the beating took place. Alameda County, in the San Francisco Bay area, roughly fit the description. Nevertheless, it was rejected by the judge in favor of Simi Valley. The judge never indicated the basis for his venue decision, but moving the case to Simi Valley allowed him to continue presiding over the case. Litigation experts scored District Attorney Ira Reiner for not vigorously protesting the judge's venue ruling.[5]

Twelve years earlier, a remarkably similar incident in Miami, Florida, graphically demonstrated the danger inherent in such venue rulings. Before Rodney King, there was Arthur McDuffie. McDuffie, an African American, was beaten fiercely and repeatedly by four white police officers after he lead them on a high-speed chase through the streets of Miami. In this case, however, the victim did not survive. After a change of venue out of Miami, an all-white jury acquitted all four police officers. Devastation ensued. Riots lasting three days claimed eighteen lives and caused $100 million in damages.[6] Whether in ignorance or wanton disregard of the striking parallel of the Miami lesson, Judge Weisberg's decision ultimately redounded to even graver consequences—in lives lost and property damages—for Los Angeles.

Once the King trial was moved to Simi Valley, the prosecution faced another strategic decision. Its main prosecutor, Terry White, was an African American. If racial bias was operative in Simi Valley, it would not likely stop with King. The district attorney's office nevertheless chose not to replace White, who admittedly had strong reservations about remaining on the case after the venue change.

Other differences in approach by the prosecution and defense surfaced during the critical pretrial phase. The defense hired jury consultants; the prosecution did not. Jury consulting is a litigation support service increasingly employed by trial counsel in major cases because of the strategic importance of jury selection. Prosecutors felt jury consultation would be a waste of taxpayer money.[7] Given the national attention focused on the trial and the considerable resources the district attorney's office had already spent on the case, an additional fee for the help of behavioral scientists in selecting a favorable jury was arguably worth the price. In the subsequent King federal civil rights case held in Los Angeles the following year (hereafter "King II"), there were two African Americans and one Hispanic on the jury. It was racially, ethnically, and economically diverse.[8] In contrast, the Simi Valley jurors were near-homogenous: eleven whites and one Filipino. Further, several had close ties to law enforcement. Arguably, the die was cast before the first witness was heard.

During evidence taking in King I, glaring omissions marked the prosecution's handling of the case. It failed to call outside (civilian) witnesses. It failed to mention that one of King's car passengers, Freddie Helms, was also injured by the police while in custody.[9] It failed to tell jurors that Powell regaled his colleagues with war stories of the arrest instead of transporting King to the hospital. It failed to use expert testimony (as did the defense) on what constitutes excessive force until—later and with less effect—the rebuttal stage of the trial. Legal scholars faulted the prosecution for not vigorously contesting in the first place the admission of the defendant's expert testimony on use of force. The prosecution could have argued that this was an issue for the jury to decide; expert analysis is usually reserved for technical or scientific questions. Once the defense brought this issue within the domain of experts, its job became immeasurably easier. It only had to raise a reasonable doubt as to the propriety of the force used. All but the most incredible expert testimony was sufficient for that.

The prosecution also failed in its case-in-chief to offer expert testimony that King's facial injuries were caused by baton blows from the defendants, a violation of LA Police Department policy. Two doctors so testified for the prosecution in King II; neither was called in King I.[10] One of the most successful tacks of the defense was convincing the jury that King's behavior prior to the videotaped action justified the subsequent beating. Significantly, the prosecution failed to point out that the pre-tape behavior was irrelevant.

Perhaps most controversial was the prosecution's decision not to call King himself as a witness. Prosecutors in King II reversed that strategy by calling King. Well-dressed, slimmed down and obeisant on the witness stand, King defused the image constructed of him earlier by the defense as a "PCP-crazed giant." Many people in Simi Valley had moved there precisely because they feared the likes of Rodney King. His absence as a witness allowed the defense to play on the jurors' worst fears and stereotypes.[11]

One of the benefits of King's testimony in King II was that it provided the opportunity for him to explain why he lurched to his feet at the start of the videotape. The state's inability in King I to explain this contributed to its decision not to call King, possibly crippling its case.[12] But on the witness stand in King II, King said the officers threatened to kill him and then told him to run for his life. When he complied, the police used that move to justify the escalation of force. John Burton, an attorney who represented one of King's passengers in a suit against the city, said the videotape confirmed King's allegation.

The tape clearly shows King stretched out in a prone position, and [defendant] Powell's already in a batter's stance. King gets into a running position, and Powell hits him. I think it's the last piece of the puzzle and fills out the whole picture.[13]

The prosecution's ineptitude was not limited to omissions. Testimony of several of the witnesses it called backfired. When it finally called a use-of-force expert, that expert was ineffective. He was successfully attacked by the defense as a high-ranking officer with little street experience. The jurors later criticized him as dull and unpersuasive.[14] Then there were the testimonies of Tim and Melanie Singer, the California Highway Patrol officers who first pursued King by car. Although they were witnesses for the prosecution, Tim Singer compared

King to a "monster," while Melanie claimed King grabbed his buttocks and shook them at her.[15] Indeed, so feckless was the prosecution in King I that in King II the defense sought to call several of the state prosecutors as witnesses in order to attack King's story. Commenting on this ploy, Burton said, "Since no one helped the officers get off in the state case more than the prosecution, I'm not surprised the defense would try to get them to come and do it again."[16]

In the aftermath of the King I verdict and the ensuing riots, a widespread angst suffused public discourse about the quality of our court system and jury justice. Social and political leaders alternatively condemned the justice system and searched for palliatives. Central to the dialogue was the question of whether King I was an aberration, albeit one amplified by unprecedented media coverage. That is, was the outcome dictated by a mere chance convergence of three factors—skillful pretrial maneuvering by the defense, a questionable venue ruling by the trial judge and an inept prosecution? Or, disturbingly, was the verdict indicative of far-reaching defects all too common in American trials?

In seeking the answers we must assess the two King trials. Rather than vindicating our trial justice system—as many claimed after King II—the inconsistent results starkly revealed its abject weaknesses. King I illustrated two implacable verities of trials: First, juries are unpredictable; second, a mismatch in the skills of opposing attorneys can affect the outcome of even the most apparently open-and-shut case. On the other hand, King II reached what most people in and out of the legal profession would consider the "true" or "just" result. Although neither trial was commonplace, King II was certainly the more extraordinary. The prosecution's disadvantage in King II vis-a-vis King I was that it had to prove specific criminal intent. But that was far outweighed by its advantages: a battery of attorneys, headed by two of the best prosecutors in the federal government; virtually unlimited resources in preparation (investigation, expert witnesses, etc.); and the availability of the entire King I trial on videotape from which to plan strategy. Moreover, only a handful of state assault charges had ever been retried under federal civil rights laws. In short, King II was the anomaly.

The prepotent reason for the different outcomes was the disparity in the quality of the prosecution in the two cases. This is not to discount the effect of different juries. Any analysis of the verdict must consider the attorney-jury chemistry. But it cannot be overemphasized that selecting and "conditioning" prospective jurors was and is the province of the attorneys. Rather than being an analogy-corrupting variable, the considerable disparities in the King I and II juries directly reflected a disparity in the skills of the prosecutors in each case.

Comparing King I and II dramatically illustrates how capricious is our notion of American jury trial "justice." Here, we had two trials with the same defendants (and defense counsel) accused of essentially identical crimes arising out of the same actions. How can they have reached contradictory verdicts and still both deemed to have "done justice?" The answer, according to the law, is that both trials were conducted according to the adversary system and without any breach of procedural due process. Yet if this is the only justice the law requires in a trial, then the law's justice is either meaningless or so esoteric that it deviates profoundly from popular conceptions of justice.

Some of the most prominent stalwarts of our government acknowledged similar misgivings about our trial system. One was John Quincy Adams, attorney and sixth president of the United States. "[L]aw logic," he notes in his diary, is "an artificial system of reasoning exclusively used in courts of justice, but good for nothing anywhere else." Adams continues:

The source of all this pettifoggery is, that out of judicial courts the end of human reasoning is truth and justice, but in them it is law. . . . Hence it is my firm belief that, if instead of the long robes of judges and the long speeches of lawyers, the suitors of every question debated in the courts between individuals were led blindfolded up to a lottery wheel and there bidden to draw, each of them one or two tickets, one marked Right and the other marked Wrong . . . more substantial justice would be done than is now dispensed by courts of law.[17]

Oliver Wendell Holmes, Jr., too, noted the disjuncture between trial justice and law. Reprimanding the rhapsodizing of a youthful attorney, the Supreme Court Justice said, "This is a court of law, young man, not a court of justice."[18]

When considering the inequities of our trial system, it is facile and convenient to blame individuals or particular circumstances, and then move on. That leaves unsettled, even unexplored, the issue of whether the system within which these individuals and circumstances operate is fundamentally rational and fair. I contend that our system of trial court dispute resolution is gravely flawed; that it has, as Adams, Holmes and others have averred, much irrationality and injustice; and that it, not simply its practitioners, is greatly in need of thoughtful and future-oriented remediation. In the duality of this culpability, I concur with Charles Dickens:

The system! I am told on all hands, it's the system. I mustn't look to individuals. It's the system. . . . I mustn't go to Mr. Tulkinghorn, the solicitor in Lincoln's Inn Fields, and say to him when he makes me furious by being so cool and satisfied—as they all do, for I know they gain by it while I lose, don't I?—I mustn't say to him, "I will have something out of someone for my ruin, by fair means or foul!" *He* is not responsible. It's the system. But, if I do no violence to any of them . . . I will accuse the individual workers of that system against me, face to face, before the great eternal bar![19]

We all take certain things for granted. In decreasing degrees of certitude, for example, we assume: Night will follow day, the mail will be delivered, and Democrats and Republicans will differ on budget priorities. When it comes to the legal system, we also have expectations. One is that the fundamental mechanisms of our trials are rational and fair. So ensconced is this expectation that it receives little critical attention. That is not to say that trials *per se* have been neglected by the public or the media. Trial lawyers, judges and juries have all been the subject of celebrated TV shows, books, articles, movies and plays.[20] Rather, it is the foundational philosophy of trial procedure as a whole—known as the adversary system of justice—which, like a legal forest, has escaped scrutiny due to our preoccupation with its trees.

Rather than encouraging rationality and fairness, the adversariness of our trials frequently conduces rancor, irrationality and inequity. Nonetheless, the legal profession sedulously guards the system from change and nurtures the "hardball" attorney tactics which characterize it. Walter Olson writes in his popular 1991 book *The Litigation Explosion*:

> Gratuitous belligerence and cost infliction, witness coaching and information control, may to some degree be inevitable in any system of justice. But they have been made much worse than they need to be by rules that encourage the pursuit of litigation as total war. It would be a mistake to imagine that the answer is simply to exhort lawyers to be more considerate and conscientious. Within the American legal profession, probably a solid majority already would like to see the fighting de-escalate. Even many lawyers who are doing well financially out of the strife would be happy to make a bit less money if a more rational and civilized style of practice could result. Those who like the system the way it is, however, are rapidly coming into their own as leaders of the profession.[21]

So unreserved is the legal profession's commitment to trial adversariness that its ethical codes and many of its spokespersons suggest that anything less than zealous advocacy is a breach of the attorney's responsibility sufficient to invite a malpractice suit. "You can all go pick up your 'being a nice guy' medals the same day you turn in your law licenses," sniffs Sanford Dranoff, president of the Texas chapter of the American Academy of Matrimonial Lawyers.[22] Responsibility for this state of affairs is not confined to the bar. Judges condone it by their passivity on the bench, and the law schools ensure a continuous supply of courtroom gladiators by glorifying the adversary ethic.

Despite its combative nature, the adversary system has achieved institutionalized, even sanctified, status. But that is not surprising. Adversariness has become an enduring thread in the fabric of American life. As a distributive process, it is not confined to the law. Economic competition, politics and sports[23] are also contests decided by battles conducted in accord with prescribed rules.

But what is ingrained is not necessarily what is right. A dynamic society must continually and dispassionately reevaluate its institutions. They exist at the pleasure of society. Their function is to serve us, not to be served. Their legitimacy is never a tenure to be presumed. As with court precedents, they must continue to be fair and rational in application and practice. When instead they become obdurate and self-serving, they must either reform or risk overthrow. The implosion of communism in the former Soviet Union bears witness to the capability of even a totalitarian society to rid itself of the yolk of dysfunctional institutions.

In stating the purposes of this book, I borrow some themes of others. Few writers discern the modern role of institutions in our society more ably than Robert Bellah *et al.* in *The Good Society*. This widely acclaimed book issues a clarion call: Our institutions are in trouble. They are decaying from within, neglected and adrift. According to Bellah *et al.*, the source of the problem is our preoccupation with the ideal of Lockean individualism. We view maximization of individual freedom, rights and economic gain as the *summum bonum*. Institutions are valued only to the extent they serve this desideratum. Institutional problems are perceived as technical; thus the solutions require only fine-tuning. Correct as this may be for certain problems, many other problems require a fundamental reassessment of the operative values of the institution. We need to ask not simply whether something is effective, but *effective for what purpose?*[24] In Los Angeles, for instance, the historic response to traffic congestion has been adding lanes to the freeways and occasionally building a new freeway. Now, Los Angeles' nascent light rail system demonstrates a sorely needed new approach.

Just as traffic congestion can be addressed in more than one way, so can court congestion. The traditional answer to court congestion has been expediting trials. (Rarely is the construction of more courthouses funded.) This tunnel vision approach, embodied in legislation such as the federal Civil Justice Reform Act of 1990 (CJRA) and parallel state efforts, ignores other answers that follow from re-evaluation of the justice system. Although justice delayed is justice denied, justice hastened is not necessarily justice served. We obsess over accelerating trials while neglecting to embrace viable alternatives that go to the core of the problem. For example, many disputes should not be adjudicated by trial. Instead, they should be diverted from the court system to more felicitous dispute resolution mechanisms and fora. More importantly, those cases going to trial should not be and need not be as adversarial as they are. In trials, contentiousness begets prolongation.

Bellah *et al.* say we must eschew the prevalent institutional paradigm—that institutions exist to serve the short-term private ends of individuals—as largely dysfunctional. "All-out pursuit of individual or group advantage, which is one consequence of institutional failure in the polity, quickly becomes not only pathological but threatening to the survival of all."[25] Rather, they suggest we put our institutions to the service of common purposes and the common good in the long run. We must "concern ourselves with the larger meanings of things in the longer run, rather than short-term payoffs."[26]

The Good Society rightly focuses on the future. Our institutional policies should be redirected to what psychologist Erik Erikson called "generativity," the care that one generation gives to the next. It behooves us to consider what kind of society we will bestow upon posterity. We give appallingly scant pause to reflect on the social and economic consequences of our decisions to our children and their children. But if not us, then whom? If we are not the fiduciaries of the future, does that office simply devolve to Divine Providence?

Appreciating the problem is but the first step. The next is reshaping our institutions in pursuance of revised goals. To do so, Bellah *et al.* advocate cultivating our institutions rather than exploiting them per the dicta of Lockean individualism. This, in turn, requires the active participation of the citizenry. No option to do otherwise really exists, for our institutions can cripple our capacity to be the persons and society we want to be just as surely as they can enable us.

In this effort, process itself is salutary. Mobilizing our citizens to think about the values and roles of our institutions in light of the realities of modernity will revivify democracy. But democracy, our most important institution, demands special cultivation. It requires continuous and broad-based involvement. As with individuals and groups, some institutions in our pluralistic society dominate our thinking at the expense of others. (Economic and budgetary problems in the courts, for example, have come to overly influence jurisprudence.) Bellah *et al.* caution, "If we want a democratic society, we need to maintain a plurality of institutions; we need to avoid economic as well as political totalitarianism."[27] The dialogue that ensues from a reinvigorated institutional pluralism is invaluable. It can break obsolete constructs and reveal different perspectives.

Whereas *The Good Society* addresses all institutions, this book focuses on just one: the adversary system of trial justice. More than any specific reform proposal, reshaping our perception of the trial justice system is my paramount objective. Any individual proposal recommended herein may prove less than optimal in practice. I hold with far greater certitude the value of alerting the body politic to fundamental problems of the trial system and the need to rethink our approaches to solving them.

The adversary system is the infrastructure of our system of trial justice. Proponents often claim it to be the world's best. As our chosen method of trial court dispute resolution, it has far-reaching consequences for individuals, organizations and society. Yet it has in large measure escaped the probing scrutiny usually directed at public institutions. It has certainly received remarkably spare literary treatment. Only a few books cover the adversary system as their exclusive subject.[28] Higher education similarly accords it short shrift. Most undergraduate business law texts devote no more than one page to it. And although trial strategy and tactics are commonly taught in a law school trial advocacy course, you will not find a course on the adversary system in the traditional law school curriculum. Thus the first purpose of this book is to fill this breach and put trials on trial. My fond hope is to disabuse the reader of the belief that the adversary system is a legal or moral axiom. We should not maintain it for its own sake, and certainly not for the sake of those who prosper by it, but for the virtues we hope to realize by its use.

Critical analysis, however insightful, is not the ultimate desideratum here. Reform is. Fault-finding is easy, amelioration is not. Any systemic critique is an inchoate exercise without suggesting the direction and means of change to rectify the flaws exposed. That is the second objective of this book.

A subtext of the reforms proposed herein is reclaiming our dispute resolution system. It has become the near-exclusive province of attorneys, compounded by a general complacency of the bench. Americans tend to think of the system as basically immutable: We take it as we find it. This is wrong. Consider, as illustration, health care—another major societal institution generally thought immune to change. Radical reconfiguration of health care services were proposed by the Clinton Administration. Although its sweeping initiatives were not adopted, many in Congress and the public endorse the need for reform. Whatever the outcome of the health care debate, the medical profession will not have been an agent for change. To the contrary. The vested interests—doctors, hospitals, insurers and drug companies—have been the inertial forces to be overcome. By the same token, the bar stands to gain the most—in power and financial gain—by preservation of the *status quo* in the courtroom. Consequently, needed change will not come about without greater involvement by reform-minded members of the bench and legislatures, court administrators, opinion leaders and community-minded citizens. Without the salutary engagement of institutional pluralism, reform will founder.

The bar is self-policing. Nonattorneys do not ordinarily populate its policy-making or disciplinary committees.[29] Given this state of affairs, more and better oversight by nonattorneys of the administration and delivery of courtroom justice is necessary to ensure that the public interest, that is, the common good, is accorded a higher value in court proceedings. In this regard, University of Chicago law professor Albert Alschuler observed:

Although the adversary system may need a watchman, the task need not be assigned to the watched. Lawyers simply are not the appropriate figures to correct the defects of our adversary system. Their hearts will never be in it, and more importantly, it is unfair to both their clients and themselves to require them to serve two masters.[30]

One way of gauging the public's receptivity to court reform is through opinion surveys. A national survey by the Yankelovich organization indicates that the bar and bench may be significantly out of touch with public expectations of the court system. This is suggested by two of the survey's major conclusions:

1. There is a profound difference in view—between the general public/community leaders on the one hand, and judges/lawyers on the other hand—with respect to what the courts do and should do in our society.

2. The general public and community leaders are dissatisfied with the performance of courts and rank courts lower than many other major American institutions.[31]

The specific survey findings validate these conclusions. While 37 percent of the public reported low confidence in the courts, only 5 percent of judges and 17 percent of lawyers shared this view. Conversely, only 23 percent of the public had high confidence, as compared with 63 percent of judges and 45 percent of lawyers.[32] Behind the public's concern are three basic unmet expectations of the courts: protection of society, equality and fairness, and quality performance by court personnel (including lawyers and judges). Survey data illustrate the disparity of views regarding these expectations:

Only 2% of judges and 3% of lawyers believe that court decisions influenced by political considerations is a major problem. This contrasts with 26% of the public . . . Delay is seen as a major problem by 10% of judges and 12% of lawyers compared to 36% of the public.[33]

Those who would discount the study accurately note that it found the general public's knowledge of and direct experience with the courts to be low. The rejoinder is this "sobering" conclusion of the study: "[T]hose having knowledge and experience with courts voice *greatest* dissatisfaction and criticism. This contrasts sharply with research we have conducted on other institutions and organizations."[34] One would be hard put to find a more damning datum.

What is the basis of these inconsistent opinions held by the public and the legal profession about the courts? Interpretations vary. If the differences are attributable to mere mistaken perceptions (by either group), then the gap can be closed—or at least narrowed—by educational programs. On the other hand, if the divergence of views is due to fundamentally incompatible values, then the chasm is unlikely ·to be bridged soon. As the Yankelovich study observed, "Value conflicts are not readily resolved; indeed, many value allegiances are non-negotiable."[35] If the dissension of views between the public and the legal profession is indeed due to conflicting values, the case for reform is all the more compelling.

EVOLUTION OF THE TRIAL

Our means of dispute resolution do not remain static. The adversary system as practiced today is only the current version of a process that has been evolving for a millennium. If the reforms proposed here are to endure, they must contemplate some vision of the future. To know where we are going, we need first look at where we have been. In this way, the evolving pattern of the trial may reveal itself.

Two salient transitions emerge from trial history. The first begins with the concept of natural law. That people could judge their fellows in formal trial was a foreign concept to the Europeans of the Middle Ages. Their faith reposed in

God as the actual decision maker; people only established the tests by which God's decision was interpreted. These tests were commonly known as *ordeals*.

There were ordeals of fire, hot water, cold water, food and poison. Common to each was some physical trauma visited upon an accused, followed by an evaluation of the resultant bodily reaction. One reaction indicated God's determination of guilt, the opposite reaction innocence. For example, in the ordeal by hot water, the accused's hand was plunged into a cauldron of boiling water and wrapped in cloths by the presiding judge or priest. After three days, the cloths were removed. If the wound was clean, the verdict was innocent; if not, guilty.[36]

Ordeals were thus trial truth-telling devices. They were elegantly simple. No gray areas clouded the decision. However primitive, they were arguably an improvement over the *hue and cry* practiced in England, whereby alleged wrongdoers were identified by townspeople, hunted down and killed on the spot. Trials by ordeal had a ritual flavor. Families attended and a sense of community prevailed. "The trials were a time of holiday, of priestly pageant and popular drama, for villain and serf."[37]

In one form or another, *oaths* always accompanied ordeals. Divine intervention was summoned via these imprecations (usually avowing the veracity of the oath-taker). A modern vestige of the oath is the one taken by witnesses before testifying. Oath-taking was also the basis of *compurgation*, another means of old English trial justice used by upper-class criminal defendants. These defendants could defeat the claims against them by obtaining a required number of compurgators (usually twelve) who would back the defendant's sworn denial by their oaths. They did so upon their faith in the accused, irrespective of total ignorance of the facts in issue. To be effective, the oath had to be sworn without any errors, which were interpreted as the divine sign of guilt.[38] (In disputes between individuals, the side whose oath-takers made the fewest errors prevailed.)

The most famous predecessor of the modern trial was *trial by battle*. Commonly practiced in continental Europe, it was brought to England as part of the legacy of William the Conqueror. Unlike the false oath, trial by battle brought down prompt and unequivocal retribution upon the perjurer. For private disputes, litigants could hire mercenaries, or "champions." Thus arose a profession of "hired guns," roaming the country for clientele. But trial by battle never became popular in England, partly because it was hard to see God's hand in it, and partly because it was foisted on the populace by the hated Normans.[39]

As people became skeptical of oaths and ordeals, the so-called rational mode of trial grew in popularity. Its novelty was that *people*, not their God, judged the veracity of oaths and testimony.[40] Litigants looked to *peers* for redress, rather than divine retribution or reward.[41] Nevertheless, trial by ordeal and battle lasted until the thirteenth century.[42]

A second major historical transformation was the evolution of jurors and witnesses. Jurors in the early Middle Ages were not proof-takers, i.e., hearers of evidence, as they are today. In the courtroom, they were reconnaissance agents for the king. The Norman conquerors needed an effective system for gaining accurate information on the holdings and doings of their Saxon subjects. Individuals who had personal knowledge of these matters (again, usually twelve) were selected from the neighborhood. They reported to the king their knowledge of communal affairs affecting the king's rights. These jurors, as they were called, had to swear to the truth of their reportage. The role of the juror is seen in the derivation of the word *juror* from the French *jure*, meaning "sworn." Hence the oath shifted from the party or compurgator to the juror.[43]

In this form, jury trial was imported from France to England via William the Conqueror. It spread in competition with trial by ordeal and battle, which it eventually displaced. But it was not until the fifteenth century that the jury had transformed from a body of witnesses to a body which *hears* witnesses.[44]

Before going further, thumbnail sketches of the characteristics of the adversary system and the inquisitorial system, to which the adversary system is generally contrasted, are in order. This is followed by a chapter-by-chapter preview of the remainder of the book. Readers with particular needs, such as researchers, can thus select their area of interest. As a polemic advocating reform, however, the book is best appreciated if read in full.

CHARACTERISTICS OF THE ADVERSARY SYSTEM

The distinguishing general characteristics of the adversary system are as follows:

A. *Presumption Of Conflict.* The trial must be conducted as a contest of opposing interests. With the rare exception of declaratory judgments, no adjudication of rights, duties or liabilities can be made unless presented to the court as an existing dispute.[45] Although the law requires a conflict (albeit a legally synthesized one) before parties can avail themselves of the courts, *it does not perforce follow that the courts must always employ adversarial dispute resolution.* Yet that has been the *modus operandi* of our trial system. Nonadversarial conciliatory dispute resolution methods are not the province of the courts. Case disposition is by rigidly prescribed procedures. No systemic goal obliges the court to inquire if the underlying problem is thereby solved or even embraced.

B. *Party Control.* Two distinct principles compose party control. The first is party autonomy. That is to say, the parties have the right to pursue or dispose of their legal rights and remedies as they see fit. They define the scope of the adjudication by deciding which dispute to litigate. If they want the judge to decide one dispute, the judge will not insist on resolving another even though she* perceives the latter to be the real cause of the conflict. Similarly, the judge will not expand the parameters of the trial by raising related issues, notwithstanding her belief in a compelling need for the articulation of public policy relevant to those issues.

The second principle of party control is party prosecution. Under this principle, the parties choose—without interference from the judge—the manner in which they pursue their case and the proofs (evidence) they present. The parties control the flow of information to the decision maker. Testimony and all other evidence is ordinarily introduced exclusively by the litigants. And although the judge has authority to independently research the applicable law, the court usually adopts the legal argument of one of the parties. Party prosecution is the connotation most people have of party control, autonomy seeming to be taken for granted.

C. *Zealous Advocacy.* In a judicial (as distinguished from administrative) tribunal, litigants are usually represented by attorneys.[46] The Preamble of the American Bar Association's (hereafter, ABA) Model Rules Of Professional Conduct prescribes the traditional nature of that representation: "As advocate, a lawyer zealously asserts the client's position under the rules of the adversary system."[48] Simply put, the lawyer not only can but *should* do everything he can to further his client's interest, or risk being deemed in breach of the fiduciary obligation to his client. Another ABA publication states:

Advocacy is not for the timid, the meek, or the retiring. *Our system of justice is inherently contentious in nature*, albeit bounded by the rules of professional ethics and decorum, and it demands that the lawyer have the urge for vigorous contest. Nor can a lawyer be halfhearted in the application of his energies to a case.[49] (Emphasis added.)

There are few limitations on this injunction. The lawyer's behavior cannot be illegal or in contravention of the rules of professional conduct. But those rules are decidedly vague. They lend themselves to idiosyncratic interpretations based on the particular values of the individual attorney. Given the several distinct allegiances of every attorney, issues of priority often surface in practice. The Model Rules admit as much: "Virtually all difficult ethical problems arise from conflict between a lawyer's responsibilities to clients, to the legal system

---

*In trying to observe gender neutrality, I find awkward the "he or she," "him or her," and "his or hers" usages. Instead, I will use the masculine pronoun when referring to attorneys, and the feminine pronoun when referring to judges. No conclusion should be drawn from this convention; it was a purely random allocation.

and to the lawyer's own interest in remaining an upright person while earning a satisfactory living."[50]

D. *Judicial Impartiality*. The judge must maintain her neutrality vis-a-vis the litigants. Even the appearance of partisanship is expressly proscribed under the codes of judicial conduct,[51] and U.S. Supreme Court dicta.[52] The adversary system judge is essentially a referee whose principal function is to oversee the advocates' adherence to the rules of procedure. In stark contrast is the role of her inquisitorial system counterpart. As noted in the next section, the inquisitorial system judge is imbued with the authority to take proof, call witnesses and otherwise conduct the trial.

Judicial impartiality can be executed with varying degrees of involvement. The styles of individual American judges run the gamut—although under party control none actually conduct the trial, as this is the bailiwick of the litigants through their attorneys. The preponderant stylistic choice of the American trial judiciary has been passivity. Two constraints pressure judges in this direction. The first is purely political: Elected judges want to distance themselves as much as possible from unpopular decisions. To the extent that their activism is perceived as influencing the jury or any other key aspect of the proceeding, they risk adverse publicity.

The other constraint is also political. It is axiomatic that no trial judge wants to be reversed on appeal, that is, have the decision of her court overturned by an appellate court because of her procedural error during the trial. Activism by the trial judge is frequently interpreted by the appellate courts as reversible judicial interventionism. Who knows how often this consideration has tempered the desire of a trial judge to pose her own questions or call her own witness? Whether the resultant abstinence serves or inhibits justice is debatable. What is clear is that the trial judge's role in the adversary system is characterized by passivity.

E. *The Lay Jury*. Not all cases are tried before juries. But the Sixth and Seventh Amendments provide a broad right to jury trial for criminal and civil litigants. Regardless of the complexity of the facts and law of a case, responsibility for the verdict depends upon a jury of individuals almost always untrained in the law,[53] and with no special fact finding skills. Blue ribbon (expert) juries are used infrequently because they are thought to violate the requirement of "a jury of one's peers," that is, jurors representative of the community.

Juries, as we know them, are peculiar to the adversary system. Trial by jury is a concept held dearly by many Americans. During jury selection, prospective jurors whose prior experience or prejudice may render them incapable of or unwilling to make unbiased judgments are excused. In some states, this ferreting out process is the job of the attorney. In other states and the federal courts, jury selection is conducted exclusively by or jointly with the judge.

In the vast majority of cases, a general verdict is used, as follows. The judge instructs the jury on the law and the jury applies the law to the facts as it finds them. The jury conducts its deliberations in secret. It need not explain its findings of fact or application of the law. Nor is it obliged to explain its methods of deliberation or decision making.

F. *Zero Sum Remedies.* The conflict model of the adversary system presumes the litigants want the same thing. Therefore, what is awarded one party tends to be exactly the loss of the other party. In civil cases, the object of contention is property or personal rights. In criminal cases, it is the defendant's freedom or life.[54] Our image of justice, the Goddess of Justice holding scales, underscores this perspective:"[The] symbolism of the scales expresses a deep-rooted tendency to see no shades between black and white, to admit no degrees of right and wrong, to allow no distribution of loss and gain among several litigants, to send a party away either victorious or defeated."[55]

THE INQUISITORIAL SYSTEM

Inured to the adversary system, we pay little heed to the relatively nonadversarial process used in continental Europe and much of the rest of the world. This is the inquisitorial system, so called because the trial conducted under its aegis is considered an inquest by the state. Theoretically, the trial is a vehicle for the enforcement of state policies.[56] The most salient difference in an inquisitorial system trial is the role of the presiding judge. As the state's representative, the judge controls and conducts the court's investigation, calling witnesses and establishing the scope of the inquiry. The attorney's courtroom role is limited primarily to proposing additional questions for the judge to ask.

Adversary system proponents find inherent fault with the role of the judge in inquisitorial system trial procedure. By such pervasive involvement with the prosecution of the case, they argue, the judge cannot hope to maintain her impartiality: The greater her participation in the case, the greater her likelihood of developing an unconscious bias. Defenders of the inquisitorial system concede this possibility. They contend it is nevertheless worth the risk of some latent judicial bias to avoid having control of the proceedings devolve to those openly biased—the attorneys.

An understanding of the inquisitorial system trial is essential to a broader appreciation of the adversary system. Each system puts the other in context, setting a baseline for comparison and contrast of their representative features. Further, the inquisitorial system's prevalence among nonAnglo-American postindustrial countries should prompt us to reflect upon the wisdom, suitability and fairness of the adversary system.

CHAPTER PREVIEW

Let us now look in-depth at the adversary system. The analysis begins in Chapter 2, which examines the justifications and putative benefits of the system. The focus is on the advantages said to issue from four characteristics of the adversary system: party control, zealous advocacy, judicial impartiality and jury trial. We should ask whether the underlying premises of the system remain valid. Clearly, some of the claimed advantages are illusory.

Chapter 3 turns to the criticisms of the system. This is the foundational chapter of this book, and the basis for the reform proposals in the last chapter. These problems of the adversarial trial are explored: truth-finding defects, jury incompetence, unsuitability for many disputes, inadequate remedies, incompatible attorney-client goals, adverse consequences of mismatched attorney skills, drawbacks of judicial passivity, role-based immorality of the attorney, and the length and cost of trials. The chapter concludes by proffering the ideal qualities of a just trial, noting how the adversarial trial does not meet these standards.

Chapters 4 and 5 focus more intensively on two of the system's most prominent criticisms. Chapter 4 evaluates the jury. Some say this historical icon is the most redeeming feature of the trial; others contend it is its Achilles heel. The chapter first examines the evolution of the jury and its development within the adversary system. We see that some limitations of the jury are intrinsic, others imposed. These limitations materially impede the ability of juries to find the facts, understand the judge's instructions on the law, and apply the law to the facts. Lay jury incompetence will undoubtedly increase with the growing number of trials involving technical and complex issues. The notorious unpredictability of juries is also addressed. It acts as a disincentive to out-of-court settlements: If juries were more predictable, there would be more out-of-court settlements. How courts respond (or don't respond) to this problem will greatly influence the future role of the jury. Lastly, the chapter raises issues concerning the jury selection process. The bench-bar territorial dispute over who should control this key element of the trial continues unabated. A new phenomenon in this area is systematic jury selection—the use of "scientific" techniques such as community demographic surveys by behavioral consultant teams to assist attorneys in exercising their challenges of prospective jurors. Is this too radical a departure from the basic intent of jury selection? Whatever the answer, only wealthy litigants can afford this service, which raises a fairness issue.

Chapter 5 considers two cognate features of any trial: truth-seeking, justice and advocacy ethics. Is the adversarial search for truth rational? Significant problems beset this most fundamental of trial functions in the United States. More than other court systems, our trials compromise the search for truth by according equal weight to various nontruth values. For example, extensive exclusionary rules intended to protect privacy or the integrity of certain relationships limit the admissibility of much relevant evidence. Pretrial discovery, once thought a boon to factfinding, has instead become the greatest source of cost, delay and attorney abuse of the system. The chapter limns other attorney practices that corrupt the determination of truth during trial, such as witness coaching and dirty tricks. And expert witness testimony, a growth industry, tends to confuse more than aid factfinders.

Issues of justice interlace the search for truth in the adversarial trial. The claim that trial attorneys, in pursuance of their special role, are exempt from censure for otherwise immoral conduct has long been used to justify questionable attorney tactics. This assumption and the related professional rules are threshed out. Another justice-related issue discussed is the maldistribution of legal services in the United States. Finally, the role of the judge is reviewed. The chapter probes the constraints that induce or deter judicial intervention in the name of justice.

After scrutinizing the adversary system, this book refers to alternatives in Chapter 6. In so doing, it breaks with convention by including trial procedures of foreign systems as a form of alternative dispute resolution (hereafter, ADR). When disputants look to the government or other third parties for a hearing and resolution of their disputes, the source of the conflict-resolving mechanism would seem to matter little to them. Instead they care about whether the mechanism effectively addresses their problems and provides reasonable remedies. Equally important for many is the quality of the process. One that is costly, lengthy, and characterized by excessive hostility is repugnant. In this regard, foreign trial methods have much to offer. The chapter first reviews domestic ADR mechanisms and discusses their respective pros and cons. This is followed by a description of the inquisitorial trial model and a comparison with the adversary system. The advantages and disadvantages of each are weighed.

The final chapter presents specific reform objectives and proposals. (Those familiar with the problems and issues discussed in the intermediate chapters may wish to go directly to this chapter.) Several of the reforms are adoptions of foreign trial procedures, including those of the English system. Where diversion of disputes to ADR is advocated, it is in the context of an expanded paradigm of courthouse justice by way of a multi-door courthouse. But the intent of this chapter transcends the mere enumeration of reform proposals lacking an ideological framework. Rather, the overarching objective is to systematically rethink and redesign the adversarial trial where it can still be constructive.

Outright abandonment of the dysfunctional shackles of the past may be preferable to the mechanistic fine-tuning we tend to engage in now. The roles of the key trial players—judge, attorneys and jurors—must be reevaluated in light of the needs of modernity. In particular, the judge and jury who, as neutrals, are the only ones capable of seeking classical, "blind" justice, should be further empowered. Conversely, the prerogatives of the partisan attorneys to influence trial outcomes should be selectively curtailed.

ISSUES TO PONDER

If we are to progress as a society, we must continually monitor and reevaluate our institutions, including our court system. Public dissatisfaction with courts and with trial attorneys mounts. As our primary instrument of justice, the trial court system must withstand ongoing scrutiny. We should inquire: Do the theoretical premises of trial procedure remain valid? Are trial procedural practices felicitous in light of current problems and issues? Can trial attorneys justify the ethics of their actions?

Several derivative issues need also be addressed. First, is the trial method, rooted in conflict, optimal for the resolution of any problem which can now be resolved in court? It must be remembered that conflict is what brought the problem to the court in the first instance.

Second, what is the ultimate purpose of the trial? Presumably it is more than simple disposition of disputes. Rather, the trial is assumed to be the most effective means of implementing the law and our standards of justice. If so, is the optimal method of conducting the trial the adversary system—a vestigial, sclerotic, and largely irrational mechanism whose forerunner, trial by battle, was based on the premise of seeking divine enlightenment? If the answer is still affirmative, we must ask further why the adversary system is perpetuated when it is contrary to all other contemporary forms of problem resolution? Why do judges, attorneys and court administrators labor to rationalize and ameliorate a system which is essentially counterintuitive?

Third, do we accept a trial system whose decisions and ultimate justice are significantly dependant on the relative skills of the representing attorneys? Consider this syllogism:

A. *Only the closest cases go to trial.* Of all disputes, only a small fraction end up as filed lawsuits. Of these, less than 5 percent are litigated.[57] Untoward results would follow if people took frivolous, insupportable cases to court. In civil cases, there would be far more summary judgments (the case does not go to the jury because the facts are not contested; the judge delivers the verdict); more litigants would be charged with abuse of the judicial process. In criminal cases, guilty defendants would lose their chance for shorter sentences via plea bargaining; more prosecuting attorneys who brought unwarranted prosecutions would be removed by the voters. And in all cases, attorneys would have to be more discriminating in the cases they bring to trial.

B. *Attorney skill and strategy make the most difference in close cases.* Given the closeness of most litigated cases, that is, the relative weight of facts and law supporting each side, much depends upon the variable of attorney strategy and forensic skills. The attorney's role pervades the entire process, from pretrial investigations, motions and discovery, to "preparing" witnesses, to jury selection, to selection and interrogation of witnesses and, finally, to summation. The significance of the attorney's role is also suggested by the mushrooming litigation support and jury consultation industries, and by the proliferation of trial advocacy and technique courses.

A. plus B. strongly suggest C. *Attorney skill and strategy exert an undue effect on trial outcomes.* If this is true, it plays havoc with our notions of equal justice. For ordinarily, only the wealthy and privileged have access to the best practitioners in a field marked by as much disparity of individual skills as any other.

NOTES

1. William Rehnquist, "The Adversary Society: Keynote Address of the Third Annual Baron de Hirsch Meyer Lecture Series," 33 *University of Miami Law Review* 1, 16 (1978).
2. The first trial was held in a California state court. The second trial was held in federal court in February 1993 largely as an anodyne to mollify those enraged by the state verdict. The charge was violation of King's federal civil rights.
3. Charles Lindner, "Lesson of the King Case: The Risk of Shuttle Justice," *Los Angeles Times*, 4/25/93, pp. M1, M6.
4. Id.
5. This and other criticisms of the prosecution subsequently led Reiner not to seek re-election.
6. Miles Corwin, "How Good a Student is Los Angeles?" *Los Angeles Times*, 4/12/93, p. 1.
7. Gail Cox, "Experts Helped Pick King Jury," *National Law Journal*, 5/25/92, p. 3 at 28.
8. Laurie Levenson, "The Trial is Ended: Now Ours Begins," *Los Angeles Times*, 4/19/93, p. B7.
9. Jim Newton, "Prosecutors Say Officers Hit Passenger in King's Car," *Los Angeles Times*, 3/6/93, p. B1.

10. Jim Newton, "King Struck on Head by Baton, Expert Says," *Los Angeles Times*, 3/12/93, pp. B1, B10.
11. Jerome Skolnick and James Fyfe, "A Case for Federal Prosecution," *Los Angeles Times*, 4/19/93, p. B7.
12. Id.
13. Martin Berg and Susan Seager, "King Testimony Seen Helping the Prosecution," *Los Angeles Daily Journal*, 3/12/93, pp. 1, 26.
14. Susan Seager, "King Testimony Is Symbol of New Prosecution Plan," *Los Angeles Daily Journal*, 3/9/93, p. 1. In contrast, the use of force expert chosen by the prosecution for the second (federal) King case had seventeen years experience as a patrol officer. He testified that he witnessed the use of force on one hundred occasions. Jim Newton, "Beating of Downed King Broke Policy, Expert Says," *Los Angeles Times*, 3/4/93, p. B1 at B10; Susan Seager, "Prosecution Admits Flaws in King Case," *Los Angeles Daily Journal*, 2/26/93, pp. 1, 5.
15. Seager, "King Testimony Is Symbol of New Prosecution Plan," *op. cit.*, p. 4.
16. S. Seager and M. Berg, "Prosecutors in First King Trial Subpoenaed," *Los Angeles Daily Journal*, 2/18/93, p. 1.
17. Diary of John Quincy Adams, Vol. IV, quoted in Charles Warren, *A History of the American Bar* (1911; reprint, Buffalo, N.Y.: William S. Hein, 1980), p. 382.
18. Quoted in Laurence J. Peter, *Peter's Quotations: Ideas for Our Times* (New York: William Morrow Co., 1977), p. 276.
19. Charles Dickens, *Bleak House* (New York: New American Library, Signet ed., 1964), p. 228.
20. *LA LAW* is currently one of the most successful television shows about trials and trial lawyers. Equally popular predecessors were *The Defenders* and *Perry Mason*, still in syndication. And for sheer dramatic entertainment derived from real-life adversary proceedings, few who watched them on television will forget the Army-McCarthy hearings, the Watergate hearings and the Iran-Contra hearings. In literature, Perry Mason's creator, Erle Stanley Gardner, is the best selling author in American history. Several literary classics depict fictional or real trials, for example, *Anatomy of a Murder*, *The Caine Mutiny*, *Inherit the Wind*, *Witness for the Prosecution*, *To Kill a Mockingbird*, *Twelve Angry Men* and *The Andersonville Trial*. All became famous movies and plays. Often attorneys and the trial process are the literary symbols expressing deep-felt aspects of the human condition: Stephen Vincent Benet's *The Devil and Daniel Webster* has the lawyer victoriously battling for fallible, mortal man in a struggle between good and evil; Camus' *The Fall* and *The Stranger* portray the attorney as the alienating, judgmental and judged everyman;

and in Kafka's *The Trial*, legal procedures and personnel personify everyone's guilt.

21. Walter Olson, *The Litigation Explosion* (New York: Dutton, 1991), p. 244.

22. Id.

23. The analogy of a trial to a sporting event was made by Roscoe Pound in 1906. In an article that marks the starting point of modern critique of the adversary system, Pound disparagingly referred to the system as "the sporting theory of justice." Roscoe Pound, "The Causes of Popular Dissatisfaction with the Administration of Justice," orig. 29 *ABA Reports* 395 (1906), reported in 35 *Federal Rules Decisions* 241 at 281 (1964).

24. Robert Bellah *et al.*, *The Good Society* (New York: Alfred A. Knopf, 1991), p. 289.

25. Id., p. 271.

26. Id., p. 273.

27. Id., p. 292.

28. (Excluded from this category are the many instruction texts on adversarial tactics and strategy.) The most significant books on the adversary system are: Jerome Frank, *Courts On Trial: Myth and Reality in American Justice* (Princeton, N.J.: Princeton University Press, 1949); Marvin Frankel, *Partisan Justice* (New York: Hill and Wang, 1978); Monroe Freedman, *Lawyers' Ethics in an Adversary System* (New York: Bobbs Merrill, 1975); Anne Strick, *Injustice For All* (New York: Penguin Books, 1977); and Stephen Landsman, *The Adversary System: A Description and Defense* (Washington, D.C.: American Enterprise Institute, 1984). Several other works give substantial attention to the adversary system, but focus primarily on lawyers, the legal profession or legal ethics. See for example, Charles Wolfram, *Modern Legal Ethics* (St. Paul, Minn.: West Publishing, 1986); and David Luban, ed., *The Good Lawyer* (Totowa, N.J.: Rowman and Allanheld, 1983).

29. Consumer-oriented states are the exception. California is illustrative. It recently moved to make nonattorney members the majority on the Complainants' Grievance Panel, which reviews state bar discipline actions. *Cal SB* 645 (1993).

30. Albert Alschuler, "The Preservation of a Client's Confidences: One Value Among Many or a Categorical Imperative?" 52 *University of Colorado Law Review* 349 at 354 (1981).

31. Yankelovich, Skelley and White, Inc., *The Public Image of the Courts: Highlights of a National Survey of the General Public, Judges, Lawyers and Community Leaders* (Williamsburg, Virg.: National Center for State Courts, 1978), p. 1.

32. Id.

33. Id.

34. Id.
35. Id., p. 46.
36. Bernard Botein and Murray Gordon, *The Trial of the Future* (New York: Simon & Schuster, 1963), p. 25.
37. John Guinther, *The Jury In America* (New York: Facts on File, 1988), p. 6.
38. Sir Frederick Pollock and Frederic Maitland, *The History of English Law*, Vol. 2 (Cambridge: Cambridge University Press, 1895), p. 601.
39. Guinther, *op. cit.*, pp. 6-7.
40. However, ordeals were still used in cases without eyewitnesses. In such cases, the omniscient God was still the judge of truth. Frank, *op. cit.*, p. 45.
41. The Greeks developed such a system around 400 B.C., but it fell into disuse after the Roman conquest.
42. Botein, *op. cit.*, p. 24.
43. Id., p. 26.
44. Frank, *op. cit.*, p. 109. For further discussion of the development of the jury, see Chapter 4.
45. The vast majority of all filed cases are actually resolved by compromise. Ninety percent of criminal cases are plea-bargained. Roughly the same percent of civil cases are settled out of court. At first blush, this seems a nonadversarial exercise. But the preceding negotiations are conducted "in the shadow of the court." The subsequent agreement is affected by this "what-if-trial" scenario.
46. Exceptions obtain in small claims courts and other statutorily created courts of specialized jurisdiction.
48. ABA, *Model Rules Of Professional Conduct* (Chicago: Author, 1989), p. 5.
49. *The American Bar Association Project on Standards for Criminal Justice-- Standards Relating to the Prosecution and the Defense Function* (Chicago: ABA, 1971), at 174.
50. Id.
51. Canon 2A of the *ABA Code of Judicial Conduct* states: "A judge should . . . conduct himself at all times in a manner that promotes public confidence in the . . . impartiality of the judiciary."
52. In legal proceedings, "justice must satisfy the appearance of justice." *Offul v. United States*, 348 *U.S.* 11, 14 (1954).
53. In the states that do not exempt attorneys from jury service, they still are rarely selected. An attorney is likely to have an inordinate influence with other jurors. It is improbable that *both* opposing trial counsels will be willing to risk that this influence will redound to their benefit. Thus, the attorney's prospective jury service will probably be precluded by a peremptory challenge.

54. The current trend of sentencing celebrities to "community service" work appears a positive sum alternative: The defendant avoids jail, and the court exacts a penalty. It could be argued, however, that the community service requirement is a loss of the defendant's freedom, albeit in a loose sense.

55. David Daube, "The Scales of Justice," 63 *Jurid. Rev.* 109 at 109 (1951).

56. Mirjan Damaska, *The Faces of Justice and State Authority* (New Haven, Conn.: Yale University Press, 1986), p. 11.

57. T. R. Tetzloff, "Four Urgent Questions," *Litigation*, *18* (1991), pp. 1 at 2.

CHAPTER 2

AN ADVERSARY SOCIETY

The fact that our society has so many competitive institutions . . . does suggest that the adversary system of justice reflects the same deep-seated values we place on competition among economic suppliers, political parties, and moral and political ideas. It is an individualistic system of judicial process for an individualistic society.

—Robert Kutak[1]

In the final analysis, few choices distinguish us more as a society than how we define and dispense trial justice. Present and future generations will judge us by the trial system we use to judge others. For as a secular society, our judicial system's means and pronouncements of justice are the closest we come to articulating a moral philosophy. Some would say our laws alone serve this function. But the democratic constitutions and laws of totalitarian states demonstrate that legislation is just words on paper until it is interpreted and enforced by the courts.

All individuals, organizations, even governments, are subject to the decrees of a trial court. Given the import and resonance of trial court decisions, it behooves us to select the most just and effective trial procedural mechanism. How then do we justify an adversarial system of trial court dispute resolution? It is certainly not universally prevalent, as evidenced by the wider use of a relatively nonadversarial (inquisitorial) procedure in most other industrialized countries. Yet from its inception, the United States has embraced the adversary system. In a sense, we have grown up as a country and as a culture with it. This chapter analyzes the traditional rationales for the system. Most have been theoretical. Twenty years ago, however, a group of University of North Carolina law and psychology professors began publishing the results of a series of comparative studies which ostensibly confirmed the long-claimed assertions of adversarial trial superiority. These studies are critiqued at the end of the chapter.

The law's resistance to change is legendary.[2] As a cornerstone of the law, the adversary system seems equally impervious to all but incremental tampering. More than mere historical inertia accounts for the glacial pace of change. Over the years, advocates have claimed an imposing array of advantages for the system. Most of them are unverified or unverifiable; they remain part of the adversary mythology. Proponents of the adversary system say it is the best means of trial court dispute resolution. Presumably, the vast majority of the legal profession—if not the general public—would echo this sentiment. Exclusive use of the system with no fundamental change since the beginning of American legal history is testament to the durability of that belief. Discussed below are the most commonly cited justifications and putative benefits of the adversary system. They correspond to the characteristics of the system identified in the first chapter.[3]

PARTY CONTROL

Party participation in and control of the proceedings is perhaps the most distinctive feature of the adversary system. One set of justifications for this feature relates to party satisfaction. Proponents believe litigants are satisfied by their control of the procedure. This derivative satisfaction can come from (a) sublimation of the battle instinct, and (b) perceived procedural fairness and justice.

Sublimation of the Battle Instinct

Popular belief has it that psychological benefits inhere in the "battle atmosphere" of adversary litigation, particularly in civil suits.[4] The adversary system may sublimate more direct forms of hostile aggression. Famed lawyer, legal scholar and iconoclast Charles Curtis so argued in his book *It's Your Law*:

The law takes the position that we ought to be satisfied if the parties are; and it believes that the best way to get this done is to *encourage them to fight it out*, and dissolve their differences in dissension. We are still a combative people not yet so civilized and sophisticated as to forget that *combat is one way to justice*.[5] (Emphasis supplied.)

Echoing similar sentiments was James Marshall, who was both a practicing attorney and prolific writer in the field of law and psychology. "The adversary process serves the social purpose of offering to litigants a legitimized channel for the expression of their hostility and thus acts as a stabilizer of society."[6] Thus the adversary system's greatest value may be nonlegal or supralegal: By relieving tensions and aggressions that would otherwise find more destructive outlets, it may be the agent of catharsis. Reasoning from this premise, the trial has more profound psychological connotations than "self-vindication of one's cause by valor or might. It expresses the animosity factor in litigation."[7]

Few things are more embarrassing than the genealogy of one's most cherished ideas. The adversary system's genealogy suggests it is used to satisfy primeval urges. In the view of some, the ancestry of the modern American trial is trial by battle and individual or group acts of vengeance.[8] The truth of a controversy was arrived at when armed bravos hired by the respective litigants fought each other until the skull of one was smashed or he "cried craven" before the sun went down. As Roscoe Pound, eminent jurist and one of the early critics of the adversary system, observed: "[American adversary procedure] is probably only a survival of the days when a lawsuit was a fight between two clans."[9]

Other historical instances of battle sublimation abound. Sporting events are the most common illustrations. The original Greek Olympic Games were instituted in part to avoid battle among the city states.[10] The palio in Sienna has, since the Middle Ages, been an arousing but dangerous horse race in which men and horses were sometimes killed. Each section of the city had its own entry as part of a ritual geared to the displacement of intracity hostilities.[11] The Eskimos had colorful battle substitutes. When an Eskimo man found another man had taken his wife without consent, he had several nonviolent options for channeling his hostility. The most distinctive was a marathon song contest in which he vilified the malfeasor in every way he could.[12]

The adversary system of trial court justice mirrors the male model of dispute resolution. Whether innately or by socialization or both, women typically avoid conflict as a means of dispute resolution. At the risk of oversimplification, women are more likely to be compassionate, nurturing and sensitive to the feelings of others. These qualities lend themselves to dispute resolution by more conciliatory methods. On the other hand, men are prone to aggression, confrontation and verbal if not actual physical hostility—traits congruent with courtroom battle.

As litigators, men puff, bluff, strut and generally "play the game" more easily than women. Of course, women can and do become skilled litigators. But in so doing, they generally adopt male behavioral models and play by men's rules. Men are also more facile at detaching themselves emotionally from their clients or their clients' cases, a cardinal tenet of effective advocacy.

In one celebrated case, however, defense counsel successfully employed a twist on these tactical norms. In 1993, Eric and Lyle Menendez went on trial for the shotgun killings of their parents. During the trial, Eric's attorney, Leslie Abramson, conspicuously "mothered" Eric: constantly touching him with affection, removing lint or hair from his clothing, and so forth. Eric, it would seem, had a surrogate mother, one who would fight unreservedly before allowing the jury to take "her boy." The strategy worked. Notwithstanding obvious motives—the boys had been sexually molested by their father and stood to inherit millions—and clearly evidenced premeditation, the jury hung.[13]

Perceived Procedural Fairness

Landmark empirical research by John Thibaut and Laurens Walker of the University of North Carolina concluded that, compared with the nonadversary (inquisitorial) procedure, the adversary procedure was judged fairest and most just by experiment subjects in the role of litigants.[14] Thibaut and Walker hypothesized that their subjects' preferences for the adversary procedure may have been due to its fulfillment of an important metaphorical criterion of justice: structural balance. This criterion is symbolized by the "scales of justice." The physical separation of the advocates in the adversary procedure may add to the aura of balance essential for this perception.[15]

In analyzing the reactions of their subjects, Thibaut and Walker found *disputant control of the proceedings* to be the key feature of the adversary model that engendered perceived fairness and satisfaction. In the study, this control was exercised by allowing the subjects the opportunity to present evidence, the major component of party prosecution.[16] (To simulate the nonadversary inquisitorial system proceeding, evidence was presented by an impartial third party.)

Thibaut, Walker and their associates (hereafter TW&A) conducted several follow-up studies confirming the perception of procedural fairness.[17] Some studies tested whether this was culturally based, that is, if American subjects preferred adversary procedure because of familiarity with it. They examined the reactions of French and German subjects (the main inquisitorial system countries in continental Europe) to the adversarial and nonadversarial (inquisitorial) models. When a procedure called for a binding third-party decision (as is the case in courtroom procedures), both American and European subjects perceived the adversary procedure as fairer, and registered greater satisfaction with it.[18]

One follow-up study specifically tested for the determinants of perceived procedural fairness. TW&A took what they believed to be the three characteristics distinguishing adversarial from inquisitorial procedure and integrated them into their studies. First, the inquisitorial system uses a single individual to investigate the facts and a judge or magistrate to present them in court. In the study, this was represented by having a single attorney present the evidence for both cases, whereas adversary procedure was represented by having two separate attorneys present the cases of the opposing sides. Second, adversary attorneys were aligned with their clients, whereas the single attorney (representing the inquisitorial system) was neutral. Third, parties in the adversary procedure were given a choice of attorneys, whereas the neutral single attorney representing the inquisitorial procedure was appointed by the court.

All three characteristics of adversary procedure were required to produce maximum satisfaction and perception of procedural fairness in the study subjects.[19] The perception of fairness and justice may be founded on the involvement and freedom of creativity enjoyed by the participant in the adversary proceeding. Party prosecution guarantees the affected parties the right to prepare the representation upon which their dispute will be resolved. By doing so, they participate in the solution to the dispute. This nexus heightens the rationality of the procedure, an element of justice.[20]

Adversary system exponent George Adams observed that if the law is to command allegiance, it must keep pace with social change; hence, the application of the law must be a creative enterprise.[21] By allowing party prosecution, the adversary process decentralizes dispute resolution. Those whose interests are involved—the parties—identify the relevant necessities. With this adversarial input, the resultant decision should be comprehensively and creatively fashioned.[22] In this way, Adams said, "[T]he fabric of the law will be continually stretched and shaped to best resolve human conflict."[23] In contrast, the inquisitorial process is said to suffer in its relative inflexibility and lack of creative remedies. Without feedback from the parties, the creativity of the adjudication is constrained. Any one judge, even the most brilliant, is unlikely to better consider the most effective legal arguments and remedies than the attorneys for two interested parties.[24]

Procedural fairness may be perceived in economic terms. Adams claims that the adversary process results in a great cost saving to society and individuals by facilitating negotiated settlements.[25] This provides a dollop of social justice to those unable to afford the greater expense of full formal adjudication. Most nascent disputes have predictable outcomes. That is why approximately 90 percent of all cases are settled beforehand. Through their attorneys, disputants can evaluate the probable outcome, time and expense of full adjudication and elect voluntary settlement instead. By comparison, Adams says, the inquisitorial process eliminates the vast majority of negotiated settlements because the parties are essentially unrepresented and must rely exclusively on the decision maker to determine the merits of their case.[26]

Adams' factual assertions, if not his reasoning, are suspect. In actuality, the wide availability and use of legal insurance in European countries permits their citizens greater access to legal representation. Furthermore, disputants in inquisitorial system countries tend to litigate less—in part because the absence of juries renders the outcome of civil litigation more predictable.

Reinforced Traditional American Values

Beyond satisfying the individual litigant, proponents claim that society at large is benefitted by the party control feature of the adversary system. It does this by reinforcing certain enduring cultural values. Specifically, it is argued that party control best reflects the American values of laissez-faire, individualism and competition.

Some say the adversary system is the legal counterpart of laissez-faire,[27] the theoretical foundation of capitalism. Both models stress competition and arguably reflect the political and economic ideology of classic English liberalism in three ways: (1) by emphasis upon self-interest and individual initiative; (2) by apparent distrust of the state; and (3) by the significance attached to the participation of the parties.

Judge Jerome Frank was one of the first to associate the adversary system with classic laissez-faire theory and unbridled individualism. More recently, legal scholars have examined the linkage between ideology and procedural choice. Yale comparative law scholar Mirjan Damaska writes:

[W]here the issue of rival ideologies has squarely been faced, collectivistic values and benevolent paternalism were isolated as preconceptions of the non-adversary model, while traditional Lockean liberal values, with distrust of the state and freedom from its restraints were found to be in the ideological matrix of the adversary model.[28]

Legal historians Marion Neef and Stuart Nagel add:

[A]t the base of the adversary proceeding we encounter the old laissez-faire notion that each party will (or indeed can) bring out all the evidence favorable to his own side, and that if the accused is innocent (if his is the best case) he can "out-produce" the presentation made by his competitors.[29]

Liberal political philosophy is premised on a distrust of the state and public officials. Party control decentralizes power. In a liberal state, the adversary system can be seen as a means of preventing abuse of state power in the trial by the state's representative, the judge. The fact that some rules of trial procedure were originally based on a felt concern over centralization of power in the judge supports this view. During the Jacksonian period, for example, a serious effort was initiated to remove many of the judge's prerogatives, including the rights to comment on and summarize the evidence to the jury.[30]

The adversary system coincides with our prevalent political philosophy because it affords the parties the opportunity to participate in decisions affecting their interests. In the political arena, this opportunity is manifested by the franchise: Whether in a presidential primary, on a ballot initiative, or in a local judicial election, the individual as voter is empowered to inform his or her political and legal environment. Similarly, in the trial, the opportunity is realized through party prosecution: By proffering favorable evidence and law during the trial, the individual as litigant has direct input into the decision makers' calculus.

Defenders of the adversary system insist that adversarial trial court dispute resolution is appropriate for a predominantly adversarial society. Just as Japan is characterized by consensus seeking and informal problem solving, America is distinctively competitive and litigious. No other large country has as many *per capita* attorneys. Thus, rather than a court trial being a forum of last resort, it is for many the dispute resolution mechanism of choice. "I'll see you in court" becomes the refrain heard not after all intermediate steps have failed, but when a disagreement first escalates. This is illogical as an initial dispute resolution norm. A trial immerses the parties into an environment where conflict must be presumed, precluding forms of remediation less innately hostile. It may, nonetheless, be the manifestation of a profound and ingrained cultural preference.

A society can emphasize either compromise or winner-take-all. Its consensual values dictate the choice. The United States is a prominent (but not the sole) example of winner-take-all flourishing in a country where the ideal of conflict rather than cooperation prevails.[31] Game Theory psychologist Anatol Rapoport casts the relationship between societal values and choice of legal system this way: "The adversary system of legal procedure faithfully reflects many aspects of the ethos that attends the 'free enterprise' conception of social justice. It reflects the primacy of competition."[32]

Increased Acceptance of Judicial Decisions

According to adversary theory, if parties are intimately involved in the prosecution of their cases and feel they were given fair opportunity to present their evidence, they are more likely to accept the results, whether favorable or unfavorable.[33] This, in turn, would decrease postlitigation friction and increase compliance with judicial decrees. Empirical support comes from the TW&A experiments. Adversary representation produced greater satisfaction of the parties with the judgment, irrespective of case outcome or the party's belief concerning the issue under adjudication.[34] Although several follow-up studies confirm the TW&A findings, others dispute them.[35]

The legitimacy of governmental authority derives from public acceptance. Court adjudication as a means of social ordering would be nugatory without such consensus. Many of the putative benefits of party control previously discussed—perceived procedural fairness, sublimation of the battle instinct and consistency with prevalent societal values—also contribute to public acceptance of judicial decisions. This helps stabilize society.

In much of the previously noted empirical research, public acceptance was measured by the responses of observers—study subjects who watched the experiments but were not given a stake in the outcome. Although there was not a one-to-one correlation between the adversary trial elements necessary to satisfy both participants and observers, the common element is the one most descriptive of party control: separate presentation of evidence by two attorneys. Indeed, separate presentation was the *only* adversary element necessary to increase observer satisfaction.[36]

Ritual theory suggests another basis for public acceptance. Under this theory, the adversary system is retained because the public ritualism of the adversary trial wins consent for difficult societal decisions.[37] Ritualism may have particular appeal in securing popular approval of criminal case decisions.[38]

ZEALOUS ADVOCACY

Nothing epitomizes the American trial more than the ardent attorney plying his trade: indignantly objecting to (vulnerability-exposing) questions by opposing counsel; ferociously cross-examining hostile witnesses; rendering impassioned pleas to the judge and jury; and searching ever-vigilantly for weaknesses in the opposition's case or for reversible errors by the judge. From this flow several putative benefits to client and society.

Superior Factfinding

Perhaps the most common argument for the system is that courtroom truth is best revealed through the clash of opposing views (rather than through investigation by the judge or other neutral third parties). It is assumed that the personal motivation of the parties' attorneys will generate the most assiduous search for favorable evidence. Consequently, more evidence will be found than in an inquisitorial proceeding. As Monroe Freedman, former Hofstra Law School dean and prominent adversary system proponent, explains:

The adversary system presupposes that the most effective means of determining the truth is to place upon a skilled advocate for each side the responsibility for investigating and presenting the facts from a partisan perspective. Thus, the likelihood is maximized that all relevant facts will be ferreted out and placed before the ultimate fact finder in as persuasive a manner as possible."[39]

Essentially, this is the legal version of the "invisible hand" theory: Each party pursuing his or her own self-interest will adduce the most favorable evidence and generate the best arguments, yielding the fairest trial and the most just result. By the same token, statements of the opposition will be more vigorously monitored. Party prosecution assumes the testing of adverse testimony by rigorous adversary cross-examination.

Opinions on the utility of cross-examination are divided. In a famous quote, John Wigmore, the foremost authority on the law of evidence, called cross-examination "the greatest legal engine ever invented for the discovery of truth."[40] But cross-examination, even when used permissibly, can create critical distortion and profound misimpression.[41]

While a full discussion of the validity of the superior factfinding argument is reserved for a later chapter,[42] at first blush it seems plausible that partisan advocates would exercise more diligence and adduce more evidence than would a neutral investigator or judge in a nonadversary proceeding.[43] However, empirical research substantially qualifies this conclusion. A TW&A study found that the quantity of evidence produced in adversarial trials to be more *variable* than in nonadversary inquisitorial system trials. Adversary system attorneys in the study were more diligent in the search for evidence *only* when the facts given were *unfavorable* to the adversary attorney's client.[44]

The attorney's obligation of zealous advocacy on behalf of his client is an integral part of the system. But a vague behavioral standard coupled with attorney zeal can lead to untoward results. Attorneys often cross, or appear to cross, the ethical and/or legal bounds of propriety. Defenders of the system concede that tricks, distortions and other attorney malfeasance occur. Nevertheless, they say, the fault lies not with the system, but with the attorney who exceeds the proper limits of partisanship advocacy.[45]

Protection of Individual Rights

A recurring theme of the adversary system is the protection of individual rights. By "individual rights," system defenders such as Monroe Freedman mean certain cherished values, such as personal dignity and privacy.[46] To their vindication, says Freedman, even truth is subordinated.[47] Thus he argues that the value of the criminally accused's human dignity exceeds the search for truth.

[T]he Constitution has committed us to an adversary system for the administration of criminal justice. The essentially humanitarian reason for such a system is that it preserves the dignity of the individual, even though that may occasionally require significant frustration of the search for truth and the will of the state. An essential element of that system is the right to counsel.[48]

Adversarial emphasis lessens the risk that these cherished values will be disregarded for the sake of an unrestricted search for truth.[49] Freedman maintains that only through an attorney's zealous advocacy can one's rights be optimally defended. He concludes that the rights constitutionally guaranteed under Amendments Four (to freedom from unreasonable search and seizure), Five (to due process and the privilege against self-incrimination), and Six (to effective counsel and trial by jury) require zealous attorney representation for their preservation.

As suggested in Chapter 1, we put our ideology in proper perspective by contrasting it with the ideology of the inquisitorial system. That system *is* primarily devoted to the search for material truth. Hence Freedman's priorities would be anathema to inquisitorial theory. Other supporters of the adversary system believe that the inquisitorial process tends to depersonalize litigation by reducing the participation of the litigants. Consequently, they argue, the inquisitorial system is not as well suited to the protection of individual rights as its adversary counterpart.[50]

Not to be undervalued among the rights attorney advocacy is believed to help secure are property rights. The development of the adversary system in America during the eighteenth and nineteenth centuries coincides with the new wealth produced by dramatic industrialization. During this period, the number and types of disputes that were brought to the courts grew significantly. A legal mechanism was sought to protect freedom of contract and economic competition from government overreaching. Entrepreneurs wanted a legal system that could provide predictability and individual control (not judge control) of the proceedings. The adversary system nicely met this need. Therefore, due process, jury trial and other constitutional rights were motivated by the commercial interests of middle-class merchants.[51]

The attorney's role as protector of individual rights can be cast in different molds. Most commonly he is thought of as the professional agent, dispassionately performing his prescribed role. Harvard law professor and former U.S. Solicitor General Charles Fried portrays him differently. Fried analogizes the attorney to a friend, albeit for a special purpose: "When I say the lawyer is his client's legal friend, I mean the lawyer makes his client's interests his own insofar as this is necessary to preserve and foster the client's autonomy within the law."[52]

Fried might have added, "and insofar as those interests coincide with his own." As described in the next chapter, the incidence of attorney-client conflicts of interest are for more common than one might expect. Rather than trusting the attorney "friend" or "ally," the more practical course of action is for the client to actively monitor his or her attorney's behavior. This is hardly an appealing prospect. The stress impelling clients to seek legal counsel in the first place usually preoccupies them during the early stages of the lawsuit. When the attorney puts his own interests first to the detriment of the client, only two nostrums—both usually unavailing—remain. Conflict of interest claims filed against the attorney with the state bar are generally dismissed because the bar is self-policing. That leaves a malpractice action as the remaining remedy. This too has several shortcomings. Problems associated with the first lawsuit continue unresolved. Compounding this situation, the malpractice suit has its own needs and problems—in time and aggravation, new legal fees, and a new attorney-client relationship (the second attorney hired to sue the first attorney) with its own distinctive texture. As a remedy, therefore, the malpractice suit can be akin to the hair of the dog that bit you.

Identification With a Coalition

Similar to Fried's "lawyer as friend" concept is another psychologically satisfying benefit thought to accrue from zealous adversary representation: an alliance. Regardless of size, alliance members experience similar feelings: protection against common enemies, identification with a larger combined entity and an enhanced sensed of power. Clients commonly feel a sharing or apparent identity of interest with the attorney *qua* ally. This may imbue the client with a sense of belonging to a powerful coalition. Say Thibaut and Walker: "If parties perceive their attorneys as having interests convergent with their own, they may begin to experience the comforting strength of belonging to a coalition the total purpose of which is to gain a favorable verdict at the expense of the opposing party."[53]

Best Counteracts Decision Maker Bias

Proponents frequently allege the superiority of adversarial procedure at counteracting preexisting bias of the decision maker—whether judge or jury. To be sure, long-established, formal mechanisms already moderate this bias. All prospective jurors must survive the *voir dire* examination designed to ferret out potentially biased jurors.[54] For judges, tradition dictates that they cleave to the constraints of judicial neutrality and passivity. This is believed to immunize them from the tendency to become biased if they were to assume more responsibility for investigating the evidence. (See the related discussion in the section on "Judicial Impartiality.") Subtle yet effective aspects of adversary presentation mitigate the preexisting bias of any decision maker. As eloquently advanced by Harvard law professor Lon Fuller, this thesis has become philosophical dogma of the adversary trial:

What generally occurs in practice [as evidence is heard] is that at some early point a familiar pattern will seem to emerge from the evidence; an accustomed label is waiting for the case and, without waiting further proofs, this label is promptly assigned to it. It is a mistake to suppose that this premature cataloguing must necessarily result from impatience, prejudice or mental sloth. Often it proceeds from a very understandable desire to bring the hearing into some order and coherence, for without some tentative theory of the case there is no standard of relevance by which testimony may be measured. But what starts as a preliminary diagnosis designed to direct the inquiry tends, quickly and imperceptibly, to become a fixed conclusion, as all that confirms the diagnosis makes a strong imprint on the mind, while all that runs counter to it is received with diverted attention.

An adversary presentation seems the only effective means for combatting this natural tendency to judge too swiftly in terms of the familiar that which is not yet fully known.[55] (Emphasis supplied.)

Some of the earliest work of TW&A tested Fuller's contention. Their experiments indicated that, unlike the inquisitorial system, adversary presentation is much likelier to moderate preexisting bias.[56] Their conclusions were confirmed in a later study using subjects from France, an inquisitorial system country, suggesting that the bias-counteracting effect was not culturally based.[57]

How does adversary procedure counteract decision maker bias? Two theories attempt to explain the operative psychodynamics. The first lies in Brehm's theory of psychological reactance. When attempts were made to persuade subjects in his study to endorse views consistent with their own biases, they reacted by strongly resisting the influence. The implication is that the attempt to influence is construed as a threat to their freedom to entertain opposing views.[58]

Attribution theory offers an alternative explanation. Legal decision makers, it is suggested, are under role pressure to avoid the appearance of bias. Otherwise, their behavior may be attributed to improper motives. Consequently, they may feel constrained to exhibit a clear, distinctive resistance to information supporting their views.[59] Both theories share a commonality: The adversary mode forces decision makers to recognize their biases before rendering judgment.

JUDICIAL IMPARTIALITY AND PASSIVITY

The impartiality and passivity of the judge are corollaries of party control. Although the two terms are frequently used interchangeably in the literature on the role of the trial judge, they are distinct characterizations. Impartiality does not compel passivity. Adversary proceedings do. The inquisitorial system judge is expected to be impartial, but certainly not passive. Unlike her inquisitorial system counterpart, the adversary system judge does not control the proceedings and rarely calls her own witnesses. We are told this passivity best assures the judicial neutrality believed necessary for a fair decision. If the judge prosecuted the case and therefore conducted the inquiry, it is feared she would fall victim to the natural tendency to prejudge (as per Fuller's admonition). This is particularly important in nonjury cases where the judge is also the factfinder.

The potential pitfall of decision maker bias in judicial factfinding was carefully articulated in a joint conference report on professional responsibility by the American Bar Association and Association of American Law Schools.

The report predicts dire consequences from active judicial involvement in the trial. Role obfuscation, it suggests, threatens the integrity of the adjudicative process.

When he is developing for each side the most effective statement of its case, the arbiter must put aside his neutrality and permit himself to be moved by a sympathetic identification sufficiently intense to draw from his mind all that it is capable of giving,—in analysis, patience and creative power. When he resumes his neutral position, he must be able to view with distrust the fruits of this identification and be ready to reject the products of his own best mental efforts. The difficulties of this undertaking are obvious. If is true that a man in his time must play many parts, it is scarcely given to him to play them all at once.

It is small wonder, then, that failure generally attends the attempt to dispense with the distinct roles traditionally implied in adjudication.[60] (Emphasis supplied.)

Does the empirical data support this thesis? Research findings on judicial bias have been inconsistent. In general, they show that adversary procedures reduce some types of bias and enhance other types of bias.[61]

Other problems may arise from the judge's involvement in factfinding. The judge could become antagonistic toward evasive, disrespectful or hostile witnesses she is questioning; she may give undue weight to evidence she presents so that her intervention is seen to have served a useful purpose, thereby acquiring a commitment to her witness' credibility; she may acquire a pretrial bias by reviewing the evidence file presented to her (as is done in inquisitorial system proceedings); she may become so preoccupied with details that she fails to explore important points; she may weaken the motivation and diligence of the parties in calling all evidence favorable to their case; and most importantly, the jury—if there is one—may give the judge's witnesses undue credibility because of the judge's imprimatur.[62]

If the perceived fairness of the adversary system is promoted by party control, then so too must its corollaries, judicial impartiality and passivity. Proponents of the adversary system attach great import to the *appearance* of impartiality. Our iconography of Justice, the blindfolded goddess holding scales, bespeaks much of our cultural values regarding the judiciary. Blindfolded, the goddess is impartial towards the parties, shielded from biasing information. The scales reflect even-handedness.[63] If adjudication is to command the respect and allegiance of the affected parties, it is not enough that the decision be arrived at impartially; it must appear to be arrived at impartially as well. Judges often refer to Lord Hewart's famous dictum, "A long line of cases shows that it is not merely of some importance but is of fundamental importance that justice should not only be done, but should manifestly and undoubtedly be seen to be done."[64] The touchstone seems to be the separation of functions, imparting the adversary procedure with the appearance of objectivity.

The TW&A research suggests the importance of perceived judicial impartiality. Their findings on subjective perceptions of procedural models favor the adversary system. Subjects perceived adversary procedure and outcomes as fairer, more satisfactory and more acceptable.[65] What remains largely undetermined from the TW&A research are the *reasons* adversary procedure is so viewed. Specifically, is the appearance of impartiality a factor? If so, does the passivity of the judge contribute to this appearance? TW&A's major research review indicates affirmative answers to both questions: "The more responsible for the verdict the judge was perceived to be, the less he was trusted."[66]

Notwithstanding the traditional passivity of the judiciary, pressure for more expeditious case resolution has produced a trend toward greater judicial case management, particularly in the federal courts. Under the Federal Rules of Civil Procedure[67] and state codes, judges can and do exercise extensive influence during the pretrial conference and other judicially-supervised attempts at mediated settlement. To some, this threatens the extant adversary system and moves it dangerously toward the inquisitorial model. Enhanced judicial management may undermine the traditional constraints on the use of the judge's power. The concern is that the "hands-on" judicial approach will engender—albeit unwittingly—a stake in the outcome, exactly the kind of judicial bias adversary system proponents have long sought to eschew.[68]

JURY TRIAL[69]

In *The Federalist Papers*, Alexander Hamilton tells us that the Founding Fathers esteemed the virtues of the jury trial. The less enthusiastic of them considered it, at the least, "a valuable safeguard to liberty"; while others regarded it "as the very palladium of free government." All were "satisfied of the utility of the institution, and of its friendly aspect of liberty."[70] The jury has been called the conscience of the community, tempering the law's cold prescriptions with the common people's values of right and wrong.[71] Closely related is the contention that the jury system satisfies the demand of citizens for participation in government. This infusion of the common people's judgment, the argument goes, leads to decisions more acceptable to the public.[72]

After their distasteful experience with the English king's colonial judges, the framers of the Constitution sought to ensure judicial independence from the executive branch.[73] As further insurance, the framers placed limits on federal judges so as to vest substantial adjudicatory power in the people. Their instrumentality of court justice was to be the jury. Hence the jury's constitutional status in criminal[74] and civil[75] trials, and the corresponding limitation of appellate judicial review to law only, not facts.[76] Thomas Jefferson saw the jury as the public's defense against state oppression. For that reason, he once declared the right to jury trial even more important to a democracy than the right to vote.[77]

An important caveat distinguishes jury usage in criminal and civil cases. Most of the unrest surrounding the jury in the United States has been with regard to its use in civil cases. Hamilton, for example, held the criminal trial jury in "high estimation,"[78] but was unable to "readily discern the inseparable connection between the existence of liberty, and the trial by jury in civil cases."[79] Conversely, for Jefferson and others, the perceived need for the civil jury impelled amendment of the Constitution which, until then, contained no mention of a right to a jury in civil trials.

That debate survives today. The case for using juries in criminal trials is much stronger.[80] Criminal trials are especially necessitous of public acceptance for several reasons. In every criminal case, the people, represented by the state, are parties. Public funds finance the prosecution of the case—sometimes lasting years and often quite costly. And under the "government of laws" concept,[81] the precepts applying to one criminal defendant apply to all similarly-behaving members of the public. When the prosecutor "proves" the defendant's guilt to the jury, this helps the criminal justice system produce verdicts projecting behavioral norms that the public will readily accept.[82]

Another argument for using the jury in criminal cases is that it protects the criminal defendant against government abuse. Recall Jefferson's notion of the jury as a buffer against state oppression. Not that the law does not already provide the criminal defendant considerable procedural edges. Special rights and privileges—most prominently the presumption of innocence, the privilege against self-incrimination, and the prosecutor's unilateral obligation to reveal facts unfavorable to its case—afford the criminal defendant counterweights to offset the government's resources and other prosecutorial advantages. Even so, it is probably the constitutional right to jury trial that best ensures the criminal defendant a fair trial. Indeed, statistics show that juries are significantly more likely than judges (acting without a jury) to acquit, particularly when the defendant is accused of a felony.[83]

Proponents also claim juries to be better factfinders than judges. Explicating this view, renowned jurist Thomas McIntyre Cooley said: "The law has established this tribunal because it is believed that, from its numbers, the mode of their selection and the fact that jurors come from all classes of society, they are better calculated to judge the motives," and "weigh the possibilities . . . than a single man, however . . . wise . . . he may be."[84] But like so many other assumptions suffusing trial procedure, the claim of superior jury factfinding will remain untested, awaiting two prerequisites to a dispositive evaluation: first, a consensus as to what constitutes effective factfinding; second, using the standards so developed, credible studies comparing the performances of judges and juries.

In response to an extensive judicial survey conducted by the Association of Trial Lawyers of America, one judge wrote: "I think that twelve people can decide factual issues as well as any good judge, Ofttimes, they arrive at a more just result, unplagued by undue consideration of legal niceties we must consider."[85] One of the "niceties," however, is the applicable law. When rendering verdicts, juries have a special power to ignore the law, sometimes called "jury nullification" or, more disapprovingly, "jury lawlessness." If in the opinion of the jury the application of the law to the case at hand would be unjust, the jury can simply ignore the law. And because the commonly used general verdict imposes no obligation on the jury to explain its decision, the jury can do what a judge similarly disposed cannot. Explaining the rationale of this phenomenon, Wigmore wrote:

Law and justice are from time to time inevitably in conflict. . . . We want justice, and we think we are going to get it through 'the law,' and when we do not, we blame "the law." Now this is where the jury comes in. The jury, in the privacy of its retirement, adjusts the general rule of law to the justice of the particular case. Thus the odium of inflexible rules of law is avoided, and popular satisfaction is preserved. . . . That is what jury trial does. It supplies the flexibility of legal rules which is essential to justice and popular contentment. And that flexibility could never be given by a trial judge. The judge . . . must write out his opinion, declaring the law and the findings of fact. He cannot in this public record deviate one jot from those requirements. The jury, and the secrecy of the jury room, are the indispensable elements in popular justice.[86]

This license of juries, but not of judges, refers us to another claimed advantage of the jury system: The jury acts as a lightning rod, shielding judges from public outcry against unpopular decisions. In 1977, The Association of Trial Lawyers of America polled 6,544 judges across the United States. Of the 3,466 who responded, almost 90 percent favored retention of the jury system.[87] Given the political protection juries afford judges, this datum is unsurprising. Juries allow judges to pass the buck, as it were. The trial of John Hinckley, charged with the attempted assassination of former President Ronald Reagan, illustrates. After finding Hinckley not guilty by reason of insanity, the jury members were subjected to intense criticism. But they were quickly able to fade into anonymity, whereas a judge rendering the same ruling might well have been hounded from the bench.[88]

A NOTE ABOUT THE TW&A STUDIES

All theory awaits empirical validation. That is what the TW&A research seemed to do for much of the theory underpinning the adversary system. It thereafter had "scientific" cachet.

Or did it? Other studies had contrary findings. A University of Virginia study,[89] for example, found that traditional adversarial procedures received the highest rating when it produced a *favorable outcome* for the subjects, but the lowest rating when it yielded an unfavorable outcome. Therefore, perceived fairness was related to outcome—contrary to the 1975 TW&A study. The researcher's interpretation of the finding was that the subjects were *culturally predisposed* in favor of the traditional adversary procedure which increased their expectations of a successful outcome, but which correspondingly increased their frustration when an unsuccessful outcome occurred. This contradicts TW&A's argument that the preference for adversary procedure is related to the perceived *control* over the evidence by the parties. If the outcome is seen as unfair or otherwise displeasing, the procedural mode will be disfavored regardless of party control. Additional studies, including one by TW&A,[90] reported that procedural fairness and overall satisfaction were verdict-driven, that is, dependant upon outcome.

Findings by other researchers contradict the TW&A conclusion that adversary procedure is best at counteracting preexisting decision maker bias. Kaplan and Miller reported two studies indicating that adversary procedure *enhanced* preexisting biases—directly antithetical to the TW&A conclusions.[91] Furthermore, research showed that where observers see that several procedures could all be implemented in a reasonable way so that there is a fair opportunity to be heard, this neutralized the cultural preconception of adversarial dispute resolution superiority.[92]

TW&A claimed that by counteracting decision maker bias, the adversary system produced superior factfinding. Most damaging to that claim are research findings that the adversary process actually conduces biased testimony. An empirical study by Vidmar and Laird refutes (or at least contradicts) the TW&A conclusion that the adversary system is "superior in all dimensions" to a nonadversary system. Subjects viewing an event were called either for the plaintiff, defendant, or as a witness for the court. The testimony of the witnesses for either of the parties— but not for the court—was rated as biased and distorted both by judges and by objective raters.[93] This research suggests that at least some of the bias of adversary witnesses inheres in the demand of the role, irrespective of the further distorting and corrupting influence of contact with the attorney.[94] The bias effect was subtle—the evidence suggests the witnesses were probably unaware of it—yet powerful enough to influence the perceptions of the judges and raters of the testimony. Bias was seen in the *form* of the testimony: Although adversary (party) witnesses did not delete information, they described it with words and phrases that changed its meaning in a direction favorable to their assigned side. Bias was also exhibited by changes in inflection and choice of words.

Thus, the TW&A findings are clearly challengeable. But even more suspect was their *methodology*. Even if executed correctly, the TW&A experiments tell nothing about the relative merits of the adversary and inquisitorial systems because both are erroneously simulated in several respects. TW&A characterized the inquisitorial system decision maker as passive. But an essential feature of the inquisitorial system is the right of the investigating judge to seek out all the facts believed necessary to resolve the dispute. The TW&A simulation of the inquisitorial system consisted of having one person read all the facts of a hypothetical case to passive decision makers. The adversary system was simulated by having two people each read half the facts. "If anything at all was 'tested' in this experiment," observes TW&A critic Peter Brett, "it was . . . something about the different effects which appear when two people, rather than one, offer the same evidence. But that is all it could tell us."[95]

In fact it is the freedom of the inquisitorial system factfinder to follow all trails, rather than just two under the adversary system, which suggests the superiority of the inquisitorial method at truth-seeking. Compare the investigative techniques of scientists and historians. No competent practitioner in either discipline would knowingly limit themselves to considering only two conflicting sets of data offered by rival claimants.[96] "In short," reflects Brett, "the inquisitorial method is the one used by every genuine seeker of the truth in every walk of human life (not merely scientific and historical investigations) with only one exception that I know of—the trial system used in the common law [adversary system] world."[97]

The TW&A experimental design is also flawed in its characterization of the adversary system. In practice, adversarial trials frequently result in relevant facts not being presented. This happens if the facts are discovered only by the party disadvantaged by them, or if the facts could be potentially damaging to both sides. In either instance, the facts would be suppressed.[98] Vidmar's studies indicated that witness testimony is often distorted before the trial either intentionally (by the attorney) or unintentionally (by the nature of the adversary proceeding). Moreover, TW&A's paradigmatic basis for adversary system superiority—party control of the proceedings—is often belied or subverted by advocates with interests in conflict with their clients.[99] Any attempt to simulate the adversary trial without factoring in the effect of partisan attorneys on the evidence heard and the way it is presented is incomplete at best, misleading at worst.

Damaska faults the TW&A design method for yet another reason—it circumvents an integral aspect of the trial process. The decision makers were not presented evidence and then asked to ascertain the truth (as in a real trial); instead they were presented with *given* facts, and thus not really evaluating the evidence.[100] Evidence is not necessarily factual. In a trial, each side crafts their evidence so as to present a cohesive and credible story. Since the stories will conflict, very few cases find the parties in full accord on the factual inferences to be drawn from the evidence. If there were no conflict as to the facts, the judge would issue a directed verdict or summary judgment. The case would never progress to factfinding.

Damaska also suggests that TW&A were not asking the right questions, at least preliminarily. Before making any intersystem comparison of truth-finding proficiency or litigant satisfaction, it is imperative to understand the *values* which underlie the two trial systems,[101] a subject to which I recur in Chapter 5. Trial procedure, after all, is only a means of achieving certain broader *societal goals*. Once these goals are articulated, we may find substantially disparate notions of trial justice. Different goals require different means. Just as we would not compare deep sea fishing with the depth charge just because both ultimately seek to exterminate something living under the water, so we would not compare the trial systems of totalitarian and democratic societies just because they bear certain superficial similarities. Each system serves differing state goals. The same stricture holds true in comparing the adversarial and inquisitorial systems. Therefore, pronouncements of wholesale superiority of one system over another (as made by TW&A) betray an inattention to the possibility of dissimilar objectives.

NOTES

1. Robert Kutak, "The Adversary System and the Practice of Law." In David Luban, ed., *The Good Lawyer* (Totowa, N.J.: Rowman and Allanheld, 1983), p. 174.
2. Bernard Botein and Murray Gordon, *The Trial of the Future* (New York: Simon and Schuster, 1963), pp. 12-21.
3. Presumption of conflict and zero-sum remedies are not so considered. They are usually thought of merely as integral components which inform the system rather than features to be discretely justified.
4. Barry Boyer, "Alternatives to Administrative Trial-Type Hearings For Resolving Complex Scientific, Economic and Social Issues," 71 *Michigan Law Review* 111 at 148 (1972).
5. Charles Curtis, *It's Your Law* (Cambridge, Mass: Harvard University Press, 1954), p. 4.
6. James Marshall, "Trial Testimony and Truth," in S. S. Nagel, ed., *The Rights of the Accused* (Beverly Hills, Calif.: Sage Publications, 1972), pp. 237, 250.
7. H. W. Smith, "Components of Proof in Trial Proceedings," 51 *Yale Law Journal* 537 at 575 (1942).
8. Sir Frederick Pollock & Joseph Maitland, *The History of English Law*, vol. 2 (Cambridge: Cambridge University Press, 1895), pp. 632-34, and William Forsyth, *The History of Lawyers* (New York: J. Cockroft and Co., 1875), pp. 298-302. But see Stephen Landsman, "A Brief Survey of

the Development of the Adversary System," 44 *Ohio State Law Journal* 713 (1983), for a contrary view:

All the medieval methods of trial [including trial by battle] were premised upon divine intervention.... Accordingly, the system made very little use of evidence, the process was not orally contentious, and fact-finding was unnecessary because no facts were deduced from evidence. . . . It may safely be asserted that none of the medieval methods was even remotely adversarial. Further, . . . medieval practices did not serve as the intellectual or procedural basis upon which adversarial principles were eventually built. (p. 719)

But then the author appears to qualify this assertion with the following qualifications:

However, the medieval forms of procedure did contribute to the formulation of adversarial concepts in at least two ways. First, they helped to establish the principle that the parties to a dispute should play the preeminent part in the procedure leading to its resolution. This idea of active party participation is fundamental to the adversary system. . . . Second, medieval practice circumscribed the part to be played by judicial officials. (p. 719)

9.   Roscoe Pound, "The Causes of Popular Dissatisfaction with the Administration of Justice," 29 *American Bar Association Rep.* 395 at 404-5 (1906).
10.   E. Hoebel, *The Law of Primitive Man; A Study in Legal Dynamics* (Cambridge, Mass.: Harvard University Press, 1954).
11.   Id., p. 11.
12.   Id.
13.   When it came time for the retrial, Abramson's studied maternalism apparently faded. Depleted, the Menendez estate could not pay her fee for the retrial. Despite receiving $790,000 for the first trial (of which only $140,000 was for court costs), Abramson sought to be removed as Eric's defense counsel. Judge Cecil Mills ordered her to continue Eric's defense in fulfillment of her original contractual obligation. In high dudgeon, Abramson demanded to be paid $100 per hour out of public defender funds. Judge Mills again rejected her request. Abramson responded by publicly soliciting "at least one million dollars" from any and all friends of the Menendez brothers. Then, in an unusual turnabout, Judge Mills approved an agreement to pay Abramson from public defender funds at an annual fee of $125,000 for her legal services—and presumably renewed maternal instincts—in the retrial. See Alan Abrahamson, "Abramson to Defend Eric Menendez," *Los Angeles Times*, 4/6/94, pp. B1, B3.
14.   John Thibaut and Laurens Walker, *Procedural Justice: A Psychological Analysis* (Hillsdale, N.J.: Erlbaum Associates, 1975), p. 118.
15.   Id., p. 77.
16.   Id., pp. 94-5.
17.   The associates were Pauline Houlden, Stephen LaTour and E. Allen Lind.

18. The reaction of French subjects were reported in E. Allen Lind, John Thibaut and Laurens Walker, "A Cross-Cultural Comparison of the Effect of Adversary and Inquisitorial Processes on Bias in Legal Decisionmaking," 62 *Virginia Law Review* 271-283 (1976); those of German subjects were reported in Stephen LaTour *et al.*, "Procedure: Transnational Perspectives and Preferences," 86 *Yale Law Journal* 258 (1976).

19. Stephen LaTour, "Determinants of Participant and Observer Satisfaction with Adversary and Inquisitorial Modes of Adjudication," *Journal of Personality and Social Psychology*, *36(12)* (1978), pp. 1531-1545.

20. See the discussion on the ideal components of a justice system in Chapter 5.

21. George Adams, "The Small Claims Court and the Adversary Process: More Problems of Function and Form," 51 *Canadian Bar Review* 583, 592 (1973).

22. Of course, this theoretically presumes a range of remedies which courts have not or will not provide in practice. See the related discussions in Chapters 3 and 7.

23. Adams, *op. cit.*, p. 593.

24. Id., p. 598.

25. Id., p. 595.

26. Id., p. 598.

27. Elliot Cheatham, *Cases and Materials on the Legal Profession*, 2d ed. (Brooklyn, New York: Foundation Press, 1955), p. 18; Jerome Frank, *Courts On Trial: Myth and Reality in American Justice* (Princeton, N.J.: Princeton University Press, 1949), p. 92.

28. Mirjan Damaska, "Evidentiary Barriers to Conviction and Two Models of Criminal Procedure," 121 *University of Pennsylvania Law Review* 506 at 565 (1973).

29. Marian Neef and Stuart Nagel, "The Adversary Nature of the American Legal System From A Historical Perspective," 20 *New York Law Foundation* 123 at 162 (1974-5).

30. Edson Sunderland, "The Inefficiency of the American Jury," 13 *Michigan Law Review* 302 (1915).

31. Marian Neef and Stuart Nagel, "The Adversary Legal System in a Changing Society," *Et-al*, *3(3)* (1970), pp. 50 at 51.

32. Anatol Rapoport, "Theories of Conflict Resolution and the Law," in M. Friedland, ed., *Courts and Trials: A Multidisciplinary Approach* (Toronto: University of Toronto Press, 1975), pp. 22, 29.

33. John Noonan, "The Purpose of Advocacy and the Limits of Confidentiality," 64 *Michigan Law Review* 1485 at 1486 (1966).

34. Thibaut and Walker, *op. cit.*, p. 80.

35. E. Allen Lind, "The Psychology of Courtroom Procedure," in Norbert Kerr and Robert Bray, eds., *The Psychology of the Courtroom* (New York: Academic Press, 1982), p.19.

36. For a summary discussion of the research, see LaTour, *op. cit.*, pp. 1532, 1533, 1541. But cf. Laurens Walker, E. Allen Lind and John Thibaut, "The Relations Between Procedural and Distributive Justice," 65(8) *Virginia Law Review* 1401, 1416 (1979), finding that acceptability of outcome was *not* enhanced by perceived fairness of procedure for *observers*.

37. Walter Murphy and C. Herman Pritchett, *Courts, Judges and Politics: An Introduction to the Judicial Process* (New York: Random House, 1961), p. 317.

38. Gary Goodpaster, "On the Theory of American Adversary Criminal Trial," *The Journal of Criminal Law and Criminology*, *78(1)* (1987), pp. 141, 146.

39. Monroe Freedman, "Professional Responsibilities of the Civil Practitioner," in D. Weckstein, ed., *Education in the Professional Responsibilities of the Lawyer* (Charlottesville, Virg.: The University Press of Virginia, 1970), p. 152; See also Edward Barrett, "The Adversary System and the Ethics of Advocacy," 37(4) *Notre Dame Lawyer* 479 at 480-81 (1962); Frank, *op. cit.*, p. 80.

40. John Wigmore, *A Treatise on the Anglo-American System of Evidence in Trials at Common Law*, Vol. 1, 3d ed. (Boston: Little Brown, 1940), p. 3. For a brief discussion of the experience with cross-examination in civil law countries, see Mirjan Damaska, "Presentation of Evidence and Factfinding Precision," 123 *University of Pennsylvania Law Review* 1083, note 1 (1975).

41. For a fuller discussion of these dangers, see Chapter 5.

42. See Chapter 5. The experiments of TW&A provide empirical support for the factfinding justifications of the adversary system. See, generally, Thibaut and Walker, *op. cit.*, pp. 66, 118, wherein it is also noted that experiments showed that adversary presentation also better corrects potential judgment distortion stemming from the order of evidence presentation.

43. See Freedman, "Professional Responsibility of the Civil Practitioner," *op. cit.*, note 38.

44. E. Allen Lind, "The Exercise of Information Influence in Legal Advocacy," *Journal of Applied Social Psychology*, *5(2)* (1975), pp. 141-2.

45. The ethics and morality of attorney courtroom practices are covered in Chapter 5.

46. Some, such as *privacy*, have been adjudicated as within the "penumbra" of constitutional (First Amendment) rights; others, such as *dignity* or *autonomy*, have not been specifically adjudicated a right. They are

nonetheless worthy desiderata of the law, and will be subsumed within the term "individual rights."

47. Monroe Freedman, "Judge Frankel's Search For Truth," 123 *University of Pennsylvania Law Review* 1060, 1063 (1975).

48. Monroe Freedman, *Lawyers' Ethics in an Adversary System*, (New York: Bobbs Merrill, 1975), p. 8.

49. Id., p. 1060, 1065; see also D. Louisell and H. Williams, *The Parenchyma of Law* (1960), pp. 412-413; Botein and Gordon, *op. cit.*, pp. 46-7; John Kaplan, "Of Mabrus and Zorgs," 66 *California Law Review* 987, 990 (1978).

50. See, for example, Stephan Landsman, "The Decline of the Adversary System: How the Rhetoric of Swift and Certain Justice Has Affected Justice in American Courts," 29 *Buffalo Law Review* 487, 528 (1980).

51. Marian Neef and Stuart Nagel, "The Adversary Nature of the American Legal System from a Historical Perspective," 20 *New York Law Forum* 123 (1974).

52. Charles Fried, "The Lawyer as Friend," 85 *Yale Law Journal* 1060 at 1073 (1976).

53. Thibaut and Walker, *op. cit.*, p. 83.

54. This will be discussed in Chapter 4.

55. Lon Fuller, "The Adversary System," in *Talks on American Law*, Harold Berman, ed. (New York: Random House, 1961), pp. 43-4.

56. John Thibaut, Laurens Walker and E. Allen Lind, "Adversary Presentation and Bias in Legal Decisionmaking," 86 *Harvard Law Review* 386, 397 (1972). (Subjects had been prebiased with certain information relevant to the experiment.)

57. Lind, Thibaut and Walker, *op. cit.*, note 8, p. 282.

58. R. Jones and J. Brehm, "Persuasiveness of one- and two-sided communications as a function of awareness there are two sides," *Journal of Experimental Social Psychology* (1970), pp. 47-56.

59. E. Jones and K. Davis, "From act to dispositions: The attribution process in personal perception," in L. Berkowitz, ed., *Advances in Experimental Social Psychology*, Vol. 2 (New York: Academic Press, 1965); H. Kelley, "Attribution theory in special psychology," in D. Levine, ed., *Nebraska Symposium on Motivation* (Lincoln, Neb.: University of Nebraska Press, 1967).

60. Lon Fuller and John Randall, "Professional Responsibility: Report of the Joint Conference," 44 *ABA Journal* 1160 (1958).

61. Lind, "The Psychology of Courtroom Procedure," *op. cit.*, p. 22.

62. Neil Brooks, "The Judge and the Adversary System," presented at the *Conference on the Canadian Judiciary*, (Toronto, Canada: Osgood Hall Law School of York University, 1976), pp. 89, 115-17.

63. Judith Resnik, "Managerial Judges," 96 *Harvard Law Review* 376 at 383
     (1982). Practice has followed ideology—the Supreme Court has
     consistently required an impartial judge. See, for example, *Ward v. Village
     of Monroeville*, 409 *U.S.* 57 (1972); *Goldberg v. Kelly*, 397 *U.S.* 254, 271
     (1970); *In re Murchison*, 349 *U.S.* 133 (1955).

64. *R. v. Sussex Justices, Ex parte McCarthy*, (1924), in K.B. 256 at 259. See
     Hugh Silverman, "The Trial Judge: Pilot, Participant or Umpire?" 1977
     Alberta Law Review, 40, 43 (1973); Paul Weiler, "Two Models of Judicial
     Decision-Making," 46 *Canadian Bar Review* 406, 413 (Summer 1968).

65. Lind, "The Psychology of Courtroom Procedure," *op. cit.*, p. 19.

66. Thibaut and Walker, *op. cit.*, p. 100.

67. Rule 16. Pretrial Conferences; Scheduling; Management.

68. Resnik, *op. cit.*, pp. 380, 424-30; Stephen Landsman, "The Decline of the
     Adversary System," *op. cit.*, pp. 495-501, 525-526; Stephen Landsman,
     The Adversary System: A Description and Defense (Washington, D.C.:
     American Enterprise Institute, 1984), p. 30.

69. For a full discussion of juries as they relate to the adversary system, see
     Chapter 4.

70. *The Federalist*, No. 83, Alexander Hamilton (Washington, D.C.: National
     Home Library Foundation, 1937), pp. 542-43.

71. William Luneberg and Mark Nordenberg, "Specially Qualified Juries and
     Expert Nonjury Tribunals," 67 *Virginia Law Review* 887, 888 (1981),
     quoting Charles Joiner, *Civil Justice and the Jury* (Englewood Cliffs, N.J.:
     Prentice-Hall, 1962); Larry Pressler, "Right to Jury Trial," *Trial
     Magazine*, *19(9)* (1983); Wallace Loh, *Social Research in the Judicial
     Process* (New York: Russell Sage Foundation, 1984), p. 42.

72. Loh, *op. cit.*, p. 427; Harry Kalven and Hans Zeisel, *The American Jury*
     (Chicago: University of Chicago Press, 1971), p. 7.

73. See Chapter 4 for a synopsis of the jury's roots in the United States.

74. *U.S. Constitution*, art.III, sec.2, cl.3 and Amend. VI.

75. Id., Amend. VII.

76. Id., art.III, sec.2, cl.2.

77. John Guinther, *The Jury in America* (New York: Facts on File, 1988), p.
     xiii.

78. Alexander Hamilton, *loc. cit.*

79. Id.

80. Kalven and Zeisel, *op. cit.*, p. 9; *Duncan v. Louisiana*, 391 *U.S.* 145,
     156-57 (1968).

81. Ours is said to be a "government of laws, not of men." This means that
     legal decisions are determined by the rule of law, not by individuals, who
     can be inconsistent or prejudiced or both.

82. Goodpaster, *op. cit.*, p. 146.

83. Guinther, *op. cit.*, p. 40.

84. Quoted in Frank, *op. cit.*, p. 126.
85. *American Jury System* (Washington, D.C.: Roscoe Pound Foundation, 1977), p. 97, quoting Judge Albert Stiftel of Delaware.
86. Quoted in Frank, *op. cit.*, pp. 127-8. On jury nullification, see, generally, Mortimer Kadish and Sanford Kadish, *Discretion to Disobey: A Study of Lawful Departures from Legal Rules* (Stanford, Calif.: Stanford University Press, 1973).
87. *American Jury System, op. cit.*, p. 97.
88. Guinther, *op. cit.*, p. 44.
89. William Austin *et al.*, "Effect of Mode of Adjudication, Presence of Defense Counsel, and Favorability of Verdict on Observers' Evaluation of a Criminal Trial," *Journal of Applied Social Psychology, 11(4)* (1981), pp. 281, 285, 296-97.
90. La Tour, *op. cit.*
91. Martin Kaplan and Lynn Miller, "Reducing the Effects of Juror Bias," *Journal of Personality and Social Psychology, 36(12)* (1978), pp. 1443-55.
92. Austin *et al.*, *op. cit.*, p. 285.
93. Neil Vidmar and Nancy Laird, "Adversary Social Roles: Their Effect on Witnesses' Communication of Evidence and the Assessments of Adjudicators," *Journal of Personality and Social Psychology, 44(5)* (1983), pp. 888, 893-94.
94. Id., pp. 889, 890, 895.
95. Peter Brett, "Legal Decisionmaking and Bias: A Critique Of An Experiment," 45 *University of Colorado Law Review* 1, 20 (1973).
96. Id., p. 23.
97. Id.
98. Robert Hayden and Jill Anderson, "On the Evaluation Of Procedural Systems in Laboratory Experiments: A Critique of Thibaut and Walker," *Law and Human Behavior, 3(1/2)* (1979), p. 27.
99. See the related discussion in Chapter 3.
100. Mirjan Damaska, "Presentation of Evidence and Fact Finding Precision," 123 *University of Pennsylvania Law Review* 1083, 1098-99 (1975).
101. Id., pp. 1104-5.

CHAPTER 3

HOW MUCH JUSTICE
CAN YOU AFFORD?

[T]he adversary trial seems from outside like back-handedness or trickery which approaches a travesty on justice; a dragging, awkward, unreliable machinery at best; at worst, one which is manipulated. In consequence . . . there is not one sole excrescence of trial machinery that will find one sole jot of support from any person in the court except the lawyer.

—Karl Llewellyn[1]

No litigator worked the delay tactic better than the late Bruce Bromley. His defenses in antitrust cases are monuments to forensic game-playing. One of his clients, Paramount Pictures, had been accused of the antimonopoly practice of block-booking in sixty-two cities. Bromley prevailed in his insistence that the court sit, and the government separately prove its case, in each of those cities. This helped prolong the suit for fourteen years, fulfilling Bromley's vow to make a "stupendous production" out of the case.[2]

But Bromley's crowning achievement surpassed even that. Defending the American gypsum industry against price-fixing charges, Bromley managed to drag the case out for *eighteen years*. During the latter part of this saga, he admitted, "I stirred up a fight among the co-defendants just to keep the case going a little longer."[3] In both cases, Bromley conceded that had he been asked by the judge to admit the acts complained of, he would have done so. Without such judicial intervention, however, all was fair in Bromley's game.

And how was Bromley regarded by his bar brethren for these spectacular feats of delayed justice? With due scorn and righteous indignation? Guess again. In 1963, the New York City Bar Association feted him, dedicating its annual Twelfth Night Party to "Bruce Bromley, Esquire, Michigan's Gift to the New York Trial Bar." The Bar heralded the event with a poster depicting Bromley as a barefooted country bumpkin, under a scroll bearing this doggerel:

BUST IF YOU MUST
THIS GIANT TRUST,
BUT LETS TAKE
DEPOSITIONS[4] FUST.[5]

As the Bromley strategm illustrated, the adversary system of trial procedure is very much a game. In trial, the rules of the game become more important than the outcome. Often, the casualties are truth, justice and the intent of substantive law.

Our trial model pits professionally trained advocates against each other to vie for a prize. Prescribed rules of procedure govern the contest. An objective third party, the judge, acts as referee. The likeness of such an exercise to an athletic contest did not escape Roscoe Pound. In a famous 1906 address to the American Bar Association—which Chief Justice Warren Burger later hailed as "the first truly comprehensive, critical analysis of American justice,"[6]—Pound declaimed the adversary system to be "the sporting theory of justice." What he meant by this disparaging appellation was that the "exaggerated contentious procedure" of the adversary system distorted litigation into a game, similar to a sporting contest.[7]

The historic trial by battle has always been the seminal analogy to our adversary system. But Pound's critique presaged and perhaps evoked much of the subsequent criticisms. The dean of evidence law, John Wigmore, observed that the common law originated in a community of sports and games, which he compared to "legalized gambling."[8] Legal scholar and psychologist James Marshall saw the trial as an occasion for the parties to engage in a "sporting duel."[9] Experienced litigator Irving Younger repeatedly analogized it to a game of chess.[10]

Critics charge that the game aspect of the adversary system corrupts the trial's search for truth and results in unjust decisions. Working within the system, attorneys manipulate trial procedure and exploit procedural errors. Burger noted the unfortunate effect on public attitude. "The willingness of some [trial attorneys] to elevate procedural maneuvering above the search for truth," he said, is "a large factor in the American cynicism about the law and the urge to want to 'beat the law.'"[11] Burger's indictment is only one of many. Numerous other criticisms discussed in this chapter reveal an ancient system which today serves justice poorly—if at all. Indeed, those engulfed in the system's clutches often find their problems exacerbated.

TRUTH-FINDING DEFECTS[12]

Arguably, the most compelling claim supporting the adversary system is that it is the best-known judicial system for truth-finding. In the context of a trial, truth is found by presenting relevant facts and uncovering the spurious claims of the opposition. The U.S. Supreme Court has stated, "The basic purpose of the trial is the determination of the truth."[13] Given the importance of adequate and reliable factual evidence to a just decision, the validity of the truth claim is essential to the defense of the adversary system.

A common explanation of the basis for the truth claim is that truth emerges from the clash of opposing arguments. "When two men argue, as unfairly as possible, it is certain that no important consideration will altogether escape notice."[14] Jerome Frank, legal scholar, federal judge, one-time chairman of the SEC and the most oft-quoted critic of the adversary system, called this the "Fight Theory" of trial procedure, derived from the trial as a substitute for battle. This is the premise of the adversarial trial method. In his eloquent critique, *Courts On Trial*, Frank contrasts the Fight Theory with the "Truth Theory," a trial system designed to yield the truth about the facts of a suit. He challenges those who would equate the two. His premise is simple: "[T]he partisanship of the opposing lawyers blocks the uncovering of vital evidence or leads to a presentation of vital testimony in a way that distorts it."[15] After cataloguing several of the truth-seeking flaws of the adversary proceeding, such as witness-coaching and the impact of opposing litigants with disparate resources, Frank concludes: "To treat a lawsuit as, above all, a fight, surely cannot be the best way to discover facts. Improvement in factfinding will necessitate some considerable diminution of the martial spirit in litigation."[16]

Other critics disparage the high level of endorsement the Fight theory has achieved. Judge Marvin Frankel, a leader in the movement to give truth a greater value in trials, concedes that "[d]ecisions of the Supreme Court give repeated voice to this concept . . . that 'partisan advocacy on both sides,' according to rules often countenancing partial truths and concealment, will best assure the discovery of truth in the end."[17] But like Frank before him, Frankel was shocked by this wanton leap of logic.

We are not so much as slightly rocked in this assumption by the fact that other seekers after truth have not emulated us. . . . [W]e . . . would fear for our lives if physicians, disagreeing about the cause of our chest pains, sought to resolve the issue by our forms of interrogation, badgering, and other forensics. But for the defendant whose life is at stake—and for the public concerned the defendant is a homicidal menace—this is thought to be the perfect form of inquiry. We live, at any rate, as if we believe this.[18]

Commenting on the implausibility of the truth-from-fight assumption, Thurman Arnold writes in *The Symbols of Government*:

Bitter partisanship in opposite directions is supposed to bring out the truth. Of course no rational human being would apply such a theory to his own affairs . . . [M]utual exaggeration of opposing claims violate(s) the whole theory of rational, scientific investigation. Yet in spite of this most obvious fact, the ordinary teacher of law will insist (1) that combat makes for clarity, (2) that heated arguments bring out the truth, and (3) that anyone who doesn't believe this is a loose thinker.[19]

Opposition to the Fight Theory is grounded on two unalloyed verities: First, party control dictates that the sole source of the truth comes from evidence offered by the partisan parties through their attorneys[20]; second, under the mandate of zealous advocacy, the attorney's professional goal, his legal obligation and his financial interest lie with the realization of his client's success. If the truth is incompatible with this objective, then the attorney must do all he can to hide or distort the truth. In *Partisan Justice*, Frankel decries the essential incongruity between the adversary trial and the discovery of truth. "The contest by its very nature is not one in which the objective of either side, or of both together, is to expose 'the truth, the whole truth, and nothing but the truth.'"[21] Nevertheless, attorney control over the quantity and quality of evidence is the signature of the adversarial trial.

The belief that truth is the product of conflicting views may have its roots in the classic dialectic. Plato's dialogues and the scholastic *disputation* are thought to be historical analogues of the adversary system. Plato believed truth emerges only in dialogue: "By conversing many times and by long, familiar intercourse for the matter's sake, a light is kindled in a flash, as by a flying spark."[22] The similarity of scholastic *disputation* rules to the rules of trial procedure is apparent: "To every *disputation legitinia* there belongs question, answer, thesis, agreement, negation, argument, proof and concluding formulation of the result."[23]

Closer scrutiny reveals the superficiality of the trial-dialectic analogy. In a dialectic, the presumed objective of both sides is truth through logical argumentation. Conversely, the objective in an adversary trial is victory. "In short," says Frank, "the lawyer aims at victory, at winning the fight, not at aiding the court to discover facts."[24] Whatever the philosophical roots of the adversary system in Platonic and scholastic dialogue, the nexus is severed by common courtroom practices. When two biased accounts of the facts are presented, will they cancel out, leaving the truth (as assumed in dialectic theory), or will they pile up in confusion? The latter scenario seems more likely.[25] Moreover, dialogue cannot yield truth when the participants lie or engage in the equivalent of lying, for this is antithetical to the truth-seeking purpose of dialogue. That trial lawyers lie and otherwise distort the truth has been a rallying point for adversary system critics. Typical is Frank's assessment that cases are decided more on the "preponderance of the perjury" than the preponderance of the evidence.[26]

A second theory underlying the truth claim involves motivation. Adversary system defenders contend that partisan advocates will be more diligent and thus more productive at seeking and producing favorable evidence than their neutral inquisitorial system counterparts.[27] But in empirical studies, those acting as adversary system attorneys generally did not differ in their diligence from those acting as inquisitorial system attorneys except when the original distribution of facts was unfavorable to one party. Further, the claim that the adversary system results in more facts being presented to the factfinder was also not substantiated.[28] The scientific evidence suggests that the usual process of direct examination, hostile cross-examination, then redirect and recross examination is not apt to produce more information or more reliable information[29] than obtainable by other less adversarial means of eliciting a narrative.[30]

Beyond the theoretical weakness of the truth claim, both quantitative and qualitative truth-finding defects of the adversary system are apparent in everyday trial practice. The first type of defect consists of those factors that narrow the scope of evidentiary information introduced at trial. They would include all rules that allow for the exclusion of relevant evidence, such as the hearsay exclusion, the privilege against self-incrimination (in criminal cases), and all information exchanged between attorney and client inadmissible in court due to the attorney-client privilege.

Major truth-seeking pitfalls attend party control, that is, allowing adversaries control over the development of trial evidence. Relevant evidence may intentionally be kept from the decision maker by one or both parties. In certain cases, the parties may agree not to submit certain facts, albeit relevant, to the decision maker. Other relevant evidence may be kept from the decision maker due to a reluctance of the parties to exchange information, or because of the information-limiting nature of "yes" or "no" witness responses when there is no opportunity for the passive factfinder to ask clarifying questions. As a result, the factual basis for the decision may be incomplete.

The second (qualitative) defect arises because zealous advocacy informs evidence presentation. Evidence admitted in the adversarial trial is not perforce pristine. Attorneys constantly strive to influence how evidence is processed by the factfinder. In a sense, all evidence introduced in a party-controlled adversarial proceeding must, to some extent, be suspect. The attorney presents his evidence as part of an overall packaged story containing various degrees and shades of truth. There was no illusion in Frankel's mind about the attorney's commitment to full disclosure. "It is the rare case," he said, "in which either side yearns to have the witnesses, or anyone, give *the whole truth*."[31]

Factfinders have many problems evaluating the reliability of witness testimony. The importance of this cannot be understated. Witness testimony is the single most fertile source of evidence to the factfinder. But witnesses are commonly "coached." In coaching sessions, witnesses tend to adopt the attitudes and meet the expectations of the attorney interviewing them. Consequently, gaps in the witness' memory tend to be filled with images favorable to the interviewing attorney's thesis.

Another difficulty arises in connection with cross-examination. In the hands of a skilled attorney, reliable testimony may easily be made to look debatable, and clear information may become obfuscated.[32] Pound used manipulation of testimony to illustrate how attorneys distort litigation. The adversary system, Pound observed, turns witnesses into partisans, prevents the court from restraining witness-bullying, and generally impairs the functioning of a witness.[33] Hence the relevant evidence which is not excluded is often presented to the factfinder in incomplete form. And whether by statute, court practice or sheer ignorance, the factfinder is usually prevented from asking questions to fill in the gaps.

Attorneys rarely present evidence in a dispassionate manner. Factfinders process not only what is said, but also *how* it is said—with trappings, paraphernalia, bells and whistles. As human beings, they have no alternative. In a skilled presentation, context can belie content; emotion can cloud reason. Attorneys know this. They will use the license the adversary system gives them to wrap whatever informational content their evidence and argumentation contains with emotional appeals to favorably rouse, confuse or otherwise bias the factfinder.

In any adversarial proceeding, the attorney is part thespian, part psychologist and part orator. During the 1989 congressional Iran-contra hearings, Senate majority counsel Arthur Liman chided his witness, Oliver North, for repeatedly conferring with his (North's) counsel, Brendan Sullivan, before answering Liman's questions. In what became a celebrated reproach of Liman, Sullivan sharply retorted, "I am not a potted plant here." Indeed not. More than any other characteristic, the attorney's zealous advocacy of his client's interest in any adversary proceeding defines his role and performance. Zealous advocacy translates to aggressive trial tactics. Be they base and pandering appeals to the emotions of the factfinder(s), repeated diversionary objections, or attacks on the testimony of a hostile witness known (by the attacking attorney) to be telling the truth, trial tactics are geared to victory, not to the discovery of truth. British political leader Lord Brougham's frequently quoted words in the trial of Queen Caroline are often cited as the essential encapsulation of the advocate's role:

An advocate, in this discharge of his duty, knows but one person in all the world, and that person is his client. To save that client by all means and expedients, and at all hazards and costs to other persons, and, amongst them to himself, is his first and only duty; and in performing this duty he must not regard the alarm, the torments, the destruction which he may bring upon others. Separating the duty of a patriot from that of an advocate, he must go on reckless of the consequences, though it should be his unhappy fate to involve his country in confusion.[34]

Further investigation of the circumstances surrounding Brougham's statement gives us pause to reconsider the applications of zealous advocacy. The statement was made in Brougham's 1820 defense of Queen Caroline against King George IV's charge of adultery. Years later, Brougham revealed that he used the statement as a tacit threat to reveal the king's secret marriage to a Catholic. If made public knowledge, this information would have cost the king his crown.[35]

Difficulties in the search for truth are not confined to the factfinder. During his pretrial investigation, the attorney is entitled to request relevant information from the other party which that party knows or to which that party has access. The procedure is known as discovery. According to the U.S. Supreme Court, discovery is designed to serve as the principle mechanism by which "[m]utual knowledge of all the relevant facts" will be achieved.[36] But the attorney is often denied full disclosure of his opponent's case. These practices contravene the intent of pretrial discovery, and with it, the ability of counsel to provide optimal or, in some cases, even effective representation.

In criminal cases, the Sixth Amendment of the U.S. Constitution requires that the defendant "be informed of the nature and cause of the accusation" against him. Although all jurisdictions permit the defendant some pretrial discovery, the scope of that discovery varies widely. As currently interpreted, the Constitution grants the states considerable flexibility in determining the appropriate scope of pretrial discovery.[37]

Pretrial discovery problems in criminal cases can pale by comparison with those in civil suits. Some critics charge that zealous advocacy is responsible for nothing less than the corruption of the principle purpose of civil discovery.[38] To gain victory for their clients, attorneys regularly manipulate people and the flow of information. The specific means of discovery abuse are many and varied.[39] One of the most common smothers an adversary with extensive discovery demands, such as lengthy sets of "canned," multipurpose interrogatories and excessive requests for documents. All too often, the purpose behind the request is psychological and economic harassment, not the production of relevant evidentiary data. In short, minimal reflection reveals a *fundamental antagonism* between the goal of truth through discovery disclosure and zealous advocacy, resulting in frustration of the purpose of discovery.[40]

Truth is not the only casualty of discovery abuse. Other goals of the civil justice system suffer. As discussed later in this chapter, the time and cost of excessive discovery place the civil suit beyond the reach of many individuals as a means to redeem their legal rights.

It is simply too facile to blame the deficiencies of courtroom truth-finding on overzealous or unethical attorneys. Criticism of the system is more appropriate. Charles Curtis, although an outspoken defender of the adversary system, conceded, "The administration of justice is no more designed to elicit the truth than the scientific approach is designed to extract justice from the atom."[41]

JURY INCOMPETENCE[42]

Jury trials are under siege. Detractors claim that in our increasingly complicated society, the lay jury is an outmoded vehicle for realizing trial justice. Jury incompetence, they say, leads to unjust results, leaving suspect the legitimacy of trial by jury. Hence some critics advocate outright abolition of the jury in certain cases.[43]

The putative drawbacks of juries are so commonly heard they have collectively come to be referred to under the rubric of "jury incompetence." As so used, "incompetence" does not refer to the inability of any individuals or groups of individuals to act as jurors. Rather, it denotes the observed failure of lay juries to perform according to the paradigm of jury functioning.[44]

Two kinds of limitations cause juror incompetence: intrinsic and imposed. The first kind, intrinsic, refers to the natural limitations of all individuals who lack legal training. The second kind acknowledges the additional burdens imposed on jurors by the rules of trial procedure.

Intrinsic Limitations

Perhaps the most commonly stated intrinsic limitation of jurors is their inability to comprehend the facts of the case before them. A large part of the comprehension problem lies in an infelicity. As our society and lifestyles have become more complicated, the facts to be found in trials have become commensurately more complex. But the jury's factfinding role has not changed; the trial proceeds much as it would have 100 years ago.

As noted in Chapter 1, the original jurors were those who knew something of the dispute being tried. They were required to have an acquaintance with the litigants and with the germane facts. Today, such specific knowledge disqualifies a prospective juror on grounds of pre-existing bias. "Abysmal ignorance constitutes a condition precedent in the qualification of jurors" writes one jury commentator.[45]

Modern trials can present any or all of three cognitive problems for jurors: too long, too complex or too technical. A jury may be able to recall all of the witnesses in a burglary case, but surely cannot be expected to resolve the conflicts in the testimony of 100 witnesses in an antitrust case. A recent murder trial in California amply demonstrates the plight of jurors. After twenty-two days of deliberation, the jurors appeared deadlocked. They passed a note to the judge stating their inability to arrive at a unanimous decision. Seeking to avoid a mistrial, the judge offered to have any or all of the testimony read back to the jurors. The jurors agreed to listen to a complete reading of the testimony of two key witnesses, which took about seven days—over 1,000 pages in all![46]

Complex cases test the compartmentalization and logical-ordering skills of most jurors beyond their capacities. Jurors tend to confuse evidence in trials involving multiple parties, causes of action, or offenses. As a result, they use evidence admitted on one issue to resolve other issues.[47]

But the type of trial most beyond the comprehension of the average juror is one containing scientific or other technically-specific issues. For example, cases in which the issues relate to statutory securities law, patent infringement or medical malpractice often implicate matters that only lawyers, scientists or medical doctors, respectively, could satisfactorily appreciate. And how well could inexperienced jurors sitting in a complicated shareholder derivative action determine whether a challenged business practice is improper on the basis of conflicting expert testimony?

Another frequent charge levied against untrained jurors is their inability to understand the judge's legal instructions. Under the trial paradigm, jurors apply the law per the judge's instructions to the facts as found. Yet credibility is surely strained to casually assume that lay jurors understand and correctly apply instructions sometimes mind-numbingly complicated and lengthy, often replete with esoteric legal concepts and jargon. For example, jurors are instructed in negligence cases to apply the legal standard of "ordinary care." Marcus Gleisser, author of *Juries and Justice,* provides a typical jury instruction on the meaning of this term:

"Ordinary Care" means that degree of care which persons of ordinary care and prudence are accustomed to use and employ, under the same or similar circumstances, in order to conduct the enterprise engaged in to a safe and successful termination, having due regard to the rights of others and the object to be accomplished. . . . By the term "Ordinary Care," as used here, is meant such care as ordinarily prudent persons ordinarily exercise, under the same or similar circumstances, in conducting and carrying on the same or similar business, and this applies to the defendant so far as the negligence complained of is concerned, as well as to the plaintiff in regard to contributory negligence on his part.[48]

This would confound most jurors. But even if the jurors assimilate this instruction in one reading, further difficulties await them. The explanation of one term can introduce another term with special legal significance. In the instruction just quoted, for example, the term "ordinarily prudent person" also has special meaning requiring additional instructions.

The length of many instructions often compounds their complexity. In order to avoid a mistrial in the recent California murder trial just mentioned, the judge also offered to read back to the jurors any or all of the instructions. They were over 100 pages long and, in parts, difficult to the point that "people schooled in the law would find complicated."[49]

One might ask, Why not simplify the instructions? The answer lies in this conundrum:

a. the law seeks the benefit of the common person's judgment by asking him or her to apply legal rules often beyond the comprehension of one not trained in the law, but

b. the simpler and more intelligible the instructions, the more likely they will miss or inadequately state a relevant point of law, thereby creating grounds for appellate reversal.

Juries are put to tasks they cannot perform due to *inconsistent assumptions* in the law. Courts treat the jury as if it were an idiot savant. On the one hand, the jury is presumed able to perform feats of great mental prowess. Our paradigm of jury performance has twelve lay jurors understanding and applying legal instructions—no matter how lengthy and complicated—to often lengthy and complex evidence presumed accurately remembered.

Paradoxically, these same jurors are repeatedly presumed incapable of correctly weighing some of the most simple evidence. Courts simply withhold this evidence from the jury. For instance, the judge can exclude any evidence, even evidence which could affect the outcome of the case, if she feels its impact on the jurors would be too emotionally prejudicial. As illustration, recall the notorious "Twilight Zone" case. While filming this movie, director John Landis was charged with allowing explosions too close to a helicopter flying overhead as part of the scene. Claiming prejudiciality, the defense attorney deftly prevented the jury from seeing a reenactment of the movie set conditions which resulted in gruesome fatalities when the helicopter crashed. The emotional impact, if not the instructive content, of this evidence could have decisively damaged defendant Landis. When courts make this kind of determination, a great deal of relevant evidence is excluded from the jury's scrutiny.

The cause of this schizoid treatment of jurors is clear. "Part of the great disparity between the jury and the law as vehicles of that elusive goal 'justice,'" says James Marshall, "is that the *laws that govern jury trials do not take cognizance of what we know about many aspects of human behavior.*"[50] (Emphasis supplied.) Consider, for instance, the questionable presumption that jurors can impeccably follow the judge's instructions to "disregard" remarks just heard. The remarks are deemed eradicated not only from consciousness, but from memory as well—much like one would delete text from a computer word processor. But as every trial attorney knows, you can't "unring the bell."

Even more implausibly, jurors are sometimes asked to consider evidence for one purpose, but to ignore it for another. This happens, for example, when a prosecutor discloses a defendant's past crimes (if the defendant has testified in his own behalf). The jury is instructed to consider the past crimes to determine the defendant's credibility, but to ignore it in determining his culpability, that is, whether the defendant committed the alleged crime. With patent inconsistency, the court assumes that the jury which has insufficient capacity to make the necessary discrimination of ignoring the past crimes evidence on culpability has the ability to perform the psychological feat of confining its use to credibility. Studies consistently indicate jurors do not (or cannot) comply with this instruction.[51] Instead, they unconsciously integrate the forbidden or restricted-use information to make sense of proceeding events, a psychological phenomenon known as "hindsight bias."[52] Complicating the picture further is the fact that courts make ostensibly contradictory assumptions concerning when instructions to disregard evidence will be followed.[53]

Axiomatic to jury functioning is that the jury must be indifferent and base its verdict only on evidence presented at the trial.[54] Yet this ostensibly simple charge has proven to be highly problematic. The University of Chicago Jury Project was the most extensive jury research study ever conducted. It suggested that juries routinely consider many of the factors legally prohibited them by the judge's charge. For instance, in jurisdictions allowing a contributory negligence defense to a claim of negligence, the jury defies the law if it awards the plaintiff *anything* after finding the plaintiff contributorily negligent, even minimally. Inquiry into the degree of negligence is prohibited. Nevertheless, juries tend to vary the damage award by the degree of plaintiff's negligence found—in direct contravention of the articulated rule which provides a complete defense if *any* of the plaintiff's negligence contributed to the injury. And where the extent of liability and damages are unclear, juries improperly tend to vary damage awards with the number of dependents looking to the plaintiff for support.[55] The Project's studies also indicate that juries consider taxability of the award, attorneys' fees, interest and insurance—all in contravention of the judge's instructions.

Legal theory is not mythology. Lawmakers should confront the invalid supposition that juries do exactly as told by the judge. The unequivocal inference from the available evidence is that jurors do incorporate these "extra-legal" or "nonevidentiary" factors into their decision making. Some researchers suggest that extralegal bias may affect the verdict in half the cases where the evidence is less than unequivocal.[56] Whether jurors wittingly evaluate nonevidentiary factors begs the point.

Nowhere is intentional jury abandonment of adherence to the evidence more controversial than in instances of "jury nullification," where juries deliver verdicts clearly at odds with the law. Nor is this a practice which can easily be remedied by extant trial procedure. Under the prevalent general verdict, juries are not required to explain their findings of fact or verdicts in any way. Their deliberations and decisions are as secret as the infamous star chambers. In a society which takes pride in its checks and balances on the arbitrary exercise of governmental authority, the power to decide someone's fate without any corresponding accountability is decidedly anomalous. And if, in its cloistered redoubt, the jury decides in contravention of the law, does it not stand the democratic ideal of a "government of laws, not men" on its head?

Another intrinsic limitation of jurors is their susceptibility to attorney suasion. Attorney behavior itself is an extralegal factor. The manner of attorney speech, dress and gesture are not evidence, nor are attorney opinions or the clear implications of attorney questions. Nevertheless, attorney courtroom performance is designed to and often does influence the jury. Trial strategy commonly includes appeals to the emotions and prejudices of the jurors. Dale Broeder, a key researcher in the Chicago Jury Project, described the juror's environment this way: "The typical trial is surcharged with emotion. The calm essential for dispassionate deliberation . . . is almost entirely absent."[57] That is why a current topic of heated discussion is whether attorneys subvert justice by using empirically based psychological persuasion techniques to gain advantage over their opponents.[58]

The attorney's attempts to sway the juror are especially noticeable during the one phase of the trial which allows two-way communication between attorney and juror: *voir dire* (jury selection). Critics say *voir dire* consumes too much time and is frequently used to abuse the system. Attorneys tend to indoctrinate jurors instead of simply probing for bias. In response to these criticisms, some states have recently adopted judge-controlled *voir dire*.[59] Other states with strong practitioner lobbies have moved toward greater attorney control.

Imposed Limitations

Adding to the problems created by their own limitations, jurors must cope with limitations *imposed* upon them by court procedure. A daunting array of restrictions profoundly impede juror factfinding. To wit, many courts impose some or all of the following strictures:

1. Jurors cannot take notes.

2. Jurors cannot ask questions.

3. Jurors cannot hear evidence in a logical, sequential order.

4. Jurors cannot get a transcript of the testimony.

The rule on juror note-taking is particularly fatuous. Lawyers and judges can take unlimited notes. Jurors cannot. The major rationale: a fear that the best note-takers will be overly influential with the other jurors.[60] The illogical solution is an attempt to secure equally handicapped jurors.

Others justify the restriction by claiming that note-taking can distract the other jurors; moreover, they might abuse the privilege and "doodle."[61] This is another illustration of the law's schizophrenic attitude toward jurors. We entrust jurors with a duty of profound gravity and consequence while confounding their ability to execute the duty with parental-type, officious restrictions. In any event, why would note-taking be undesirable for trial factfinding when it is permitted and even encouraged in all comparable activities, such as attending lectures and seminars?

Even more restricting is the jurors' inability to ask questions. (What could be a more basic tool for a factfinder?) Experiments suggest this one-way communication creates several potential problems:[62] Jurors can distort all but the simplest information; omissions of relevant evidence cannot be remedied; and the inability to ask questions encourages jurors to engage in inappropriate speculation. Conversely, two-way communications would allow feedback from the jury. The sender (usually the attorneys) could rectify unclear transmissions and supply missing data without which a message may be incomplete or confusing. Trials lose the value of such two-way communication. Justice suffers accordingly.

Other features of trial procedure further reduce the jury's factfinding efficiency. The presentation of evidence is disorderly, with interruptions more the rule than the exception. Evidence is segmented and scattered. If the trial were a true scientific inquiry, evidence would be presented in a manner that maximized jury comprehension: All the evidence bearing on a particular issue would be presented at once. Instead, evidence on the same issue is presented at multiple and possibly far removed points of the trial.

Furnishing jurors a transcript of the testimony would seem a reasonable amenity and aid to their job. But for various ill-considered reasons, courts treat the request for all or part of the transcript as problematic. In the King II case, for instance, the judge not only denied a jury request to review the testimony of a key witness, but also forewarned the jury that he would deny all such similar requests. His reason: He did not want the jurors to place more importance on the testimony of one witness than on that of any other witness. Yet there were *sixty-one* witnesses in this case. By imposing this kind of restriction, judges—however well-intended—inhibit the use of juror analysis and reasoning in favor of the jurors' "overall impression" of the case, as if this were preferable. Actually, the latter is more a function of the story each attorney tries to "sell" the jury. As a result, jury factfinding is subordinated to attorney story-telling.

Lawyers also use[63] myriad *exclusionary rules* to keep relevant evidence from the jury by.[64] Many of these rules are based on an antediluvian distrust of jurors, another manifestation of the law's ambivalence toward jurors. Assessing the various sources of the exclusionary rules, the eminent evidence scholar Edmund Morgan concluded: "The adversary theory of litigation is directly responsible for many of them; and judicial distrust of the jury for not a few."[65]

In contrast, exclusionary rules are virtually absent in continental European trials, where the inquisitorial system prevails. Without a jury, they are unnecessary. Former German judge and law professor Karl Kunert describes the differences as follows:

The typical feature of the Anglo-American evidence law that distinguishes it from the Continental system is the existence of exclusionary rules of probative policy. These rules stem from the use of the jury trial and reflect varying and conflicting notions of the jury's mental capacities. . . .

On the other hand, the typical feature of . . . [inquisitorial] evidence law is the strong and active position of the judge, reflecting an enormous confidence in his ability to be both active and impartial and to give every item of relevant evidence the weight that it deserves.[66]

More than case-specific evidence is withheld from the jury. Courts frequently refuse to allow the jury to be instructed (by the judge) or informed (by the attorneys) of highly instructive psychological findings regarding the reliability of certain evidence they hear.[67] Eyewitness testimony, for instance, is the evidence most heavily relied upon by jurors. What jurors do not know—and are forbade from being told—is that eyewitness testimony is notoriously untrustworthy.[68] Enlightening juries to such social science findings might radically effect jury decision making. Ignorance often leads jurors to draw improper inferences from witness demeanor. An example can be found in the typical juror reaction to witnesses who change their recollection of observed events. Contrary to popular (and therefore juror) belief, studies show that witnesses who change their initial recollection are generally *more* accurate than those who do not.[69]

Of this information blackout and its likely underlying cause, James Marshall writes:

In a civilization so largely founded on scientific method, and in which daily living is so dependent upon the application of scientific findings, the theory and practice of law remain largely immune to this prevailing cultural pattern. Though science appears in the courtroom at times in the form of evidence, . . . those findings of the psychological sciences which apply directly to and challenge the precepts and practices of our courts are largely ignored. It is as though lawyers and judges indulged in the psychological process of denial. . . . The conservatism of lawyers is supported by their intellectual and economic vested interest in traditional concepts and behavior which . . . are threatened by change. The common attitude of the bar . . . is that knowing these defects in our trial system . . . [i]t does not help to make an issue of the assumptions on which our laws of evidence are based.[70]

Relations between the law and social science were not always so inhospitable. The Supreme Court's psychological and sociological analysis that attended the *Brown* desegregation case seemed, at the time, the precursor of a new era of social science jurisprudence. But, alas, anyone still clinging to that hope need only refer to *Lockhart v. McCree,*[71] where the Court expressed "serious doubts about the value" of the social science research to predict actual behavior in the legal system,[72] notwithstanding virtual consensus among the social science community regarding the issue of concern—the biasing impact of death qualification for jurors. (Death qualification is the determination during jury selection in a capital punishment case of those prospective jurors who could not under any circumstance vote to impose the death penalty.) Such high court pronouncements engender predictable attitudes among the lower courts. "Judicial hostility, much more than corporate tax credits, has a way of trickling down, especially when it emanates from the Supreme Court."[73]

Imposed limitations hinder jury understanding of the law as well as of the facts. It was previously noted how the *wording* of the judge's instructions is often incomprehensible to many jurors. *Timing* and *form* strictures further aggravate the jurors' problems with instructions. Courts withhold instructions from the jurors until *after* all the evidence is heard. Then they usually must apply the instructions, no matter how lengthy and complex, without benefit of written copies.

A final criticism of the jury system is directed to the selection process: Many of the best potential jurors never serve. Liberal exemption rules account for some of this. Numerous white-collar professionals and other well-educated individuals are exempted if they claim that their jury service would create a work hardship. Their absence does more than detract from the quality of juries. Professionals often mold community opinion, the very element the law seeks in jury deliberations.

Attorney challenges during *voir dire* eliminate other potential jurors who have knowledge relevant to the particular case at trial on grounds that their knowledge biases them. And if the challenge for cause is successfully resisted, the attorney can simply use one of his allotted peremptory challenges. Simply put, attorneys often select jurors for incompetence.[74] In both instances—work-related exemptions and *voir dire* challenges—the loss of such individuals is peculiarly inconsonant with the often sophisticated requirements of jury functioning.

Given this state of affairs, another criticism of the jury follows: The ideal of jury representativeness—jurors are supposed to represent a cross-section of the community—is honored only in the breach. It is more myth than reality. Therefore, the average jury is arguably not only less competent than the average judge, but also less competent than a random sample of twelve citizens from the community.[75]

INAPPROPRIATE FOR MANY DISPUTES

One of the obligations of the law and the legal profession, writes Warren Burger, is "to serve as healers of human conflicts." He prescribes,

To fulfill our traditional obligation means that we should provide mechanisms that can produce an acceptable result in the shortest possible time, and with a minimum of stress on the participants. That is what justice is all about.[76]

Burger and others, including his successor, U.S. Chief Justice William Rehnquist, contend that as a means for realization of this ambitious goal, the adversary system is often lacking. At times it is clearly dysfunctional. Alternative methods are more appropriate for an increasing variety of cases. Most notably, the adversary system ill serves all parties who desire or need *continuing postlitigation relations*. This category includes all disputes involving family relations (divorce, child custody and adoption), landlord-tenant relations, partnerships and employee grievances.

The unsuitability of the adversary process to the resolution of a family dispute was readily apparent to one young attorney. For Mahatma Ghandi, it was a formative revelation:

I saw that the litigation, if it were persisted in, would ruin the plaintiff and defendant, who were relatives and both belonged to the same city. . . . [I]t might go on indefinitely and to no advantage of either party. . . . In the meantime, mutual ill-will was steadily increasing. I became disgusted with the profession.[77]

Adversary proceedings polarize the parties and exacerbate any existing hostility between them. The prospect of resuming working relations is inhibited or destroyed. A study of a Small Claims Court in New York is instructive. The court allowed litigants to choose between the usual adjudication and an informal arbitration process. Adjudication was disdained by most persons who had previously tried to reconcile their differences, indicating the existence of an ongoing relationship. Of those who chose adjudication, more subsequently experienced a termination or worsening of their relationships than did those opting for arbitration.[78]

The adversary system is also counterproductive in cases where the time and expense of conventional litigation renders such actions impracticable. Most small claims can't be litigated because the cost to bring suit is greater than the complainant could settle for, or conceivably win, in damages.[79] A more widespread problem is the time it takes most filed suits to come to trial. Adversarial trials are slow. As more claims are brought to trial, court calendars become seriously backlogged. It takes years for filed actions to be tried in the major urban centers. The resulting delay deprives our legal system of the capability to meet its obligations as articulated by Burger. Justice delayed is indeed justice denied.

The principal cause of the litigation logjam may not be, as many believe, excessive American litigiousness.[80] Legislation and case law have authorized adjudication of many problems which historically were private matters. Beginning in the 1960s, new civil rights and liberties proliferated. Legislation repeatedly upheld—and frequently enhanced—by the courts brought expanded civil rights in employment, housing, health, and racial and sexual equality. A corollary explosion of regulatory agencies followed to protect the identified public constituencies. By 1983, approximately two-thirds of all federal agencies were less than twenty years old.[81] Environmental protection, consumer protection, safer working conditions and fair employment practices became part of a general new social order. The court system became at once the instrument for achieving these desiderata and for defining their often-vague parameters. Our courts have become overburdened, says Burger, because "[r]emedies for personal wrongs that once were considered the responsibility of institutions other than the courts are now boldly asserted as 'legal entitlements.' The courts have been expected to fill the void created by the decline of church, family and neighborhood unity."[82] Predictably, court cases grew at record rates. Federal cases doubled between 1960 and 1980; some state court systems experienced even greater increases.[83] Protracted cases also mushroomed. Between 1960 and 1981, the number of federal trials longer than one month quintupled.[84]

Because of their frequency and length of time to trial, certain disputes would benefit from cheaper and quicker alternative resolution. Prime candidates are cases involving auto insurance, most other personal injury suits and landlord-tenant disputes. An administrative mechanism which eliminated the factfinding inquiry would clearly save time. An example of this approach is no-fault insurance. In *The Litigious Society*, author Jethro Lieberman estimates that up to one-third of all civil suits would be removed from the civil courts by perfection of the no-fault alternative.[85]

Cases addressing complex public policy or program issues also make for suboptimal adjudication under the adversary system. Traditional adversarial technique works best if well-defined, isolated circumstances lead to a dispute where picking a single winner and awarding damages satisfactorily resolves the issue(s). Conversely, courts do not perform well where complex public policy is at issue, the dispute is multidimensional, there are numerous parties and the need is for flexible and sometimes unprecedented solutions. Rarely, for example, is an environmental dispute litigated on the real issues.[86] In the public policy arena, the adversary trial is inapt, says Lieberman, because "[l]itigation is not a panacea; social policies are not necessarily carried out because there is an avenue open to some. Suing is an inefficient means of securing systematic compliance with a general policy."[87]

To illustrate the unsuitability of adversarial dispute resolution in public programs, take public university personnel management—disputes among students, administration and faculty. The individualistic, competitive nature of the adversary system, being grounded in the political and economic values of the private sector, is foreign to the public classroom. As U.S. Supreme Court Justice Lewis Powell stated in *Goss v. Lopez*,[88] the interests of the schools and the pupils are not bipolar. The precepts of the adversarial model would be incongruous with the values of community sought to be developed within the public school environment. Adversary procedure is inspired by private property and free enterprise. This theoretical anchoring is incompatible with administering public resources according to the goals of substantive and distributive justice implicit in the Keynesian managed economy model.[89]

Equally inappropriate to adversarial jurisdiction are matters where there is little or no actual underlying dispute. Common examples are uncontested divorces and most probates. No sound reason exists to insert the state as an adverse party. These matters should be diverted from the courts for administrative processing.

Using a neoUtilitarian approach, Chief Justice Rehnquist[90] justified the virtual elimination of adversarial litigation from another group of cases. Common to all cases in the group is his judgment that adversarial adjudication of the individual claim would be unacceptably inimical to a valued societal institution. Rehnquist cited four types of cases in this category: (1) review of the decision of an ecclesiastical court, (2) review of a collective bargaining agreement, (3) review of parents' decisions regarding their minor children, and (4) entertainment of "heart balm" suits—breach of promise to marry, seduction and alienation of affections. In the first, the courts did not want government to interfere with the free exercise of religion. In the second, the courts deferred to the arbitration provisions typically contained in collective bargaining agreements. In the third, the courts sought to avoid the strain on family relations attending an adversary hearing pitting child against parent. And in the last example, most legislatures abolished these suits because of their susceptibility to blackmail and abuse of court process. In each, the potential danger to a private institution—church, collective bargaining and family unity—were believed to outweigh the virtue of an adversary proceeding. "There are times," writes Rehnquist, "when the claim of the individual should be subordinated to those of the . . . private institution which serves a useful purpose."[91]

INADEQUATE REMEDIES

More than the combative nature of the trial is inappropriate for certain disputes. Traditional court remedies too can be inadequate for meaningful resolution of underlying problems. In fact, the court's cure sometimes worsens the ailment.

Most court remedies[92] are of the winner-take-all (WTA), zero-sum kind. (Zero-sum means that one party's gain is only at the expense of an equal loss to the other party.) This erroneously implies that one side is always completely right and the other completely wrong, that is, an angel-devil dichotomy. (Even if this is so in a particular case, the wrong side may nonetheless win.) As extensions of legal thinking, court remedies operate within inflexible, polar concepts—right/wrong, win/lose, rights/duties.[93] Solutions tailored to the specific individual circumstances are extremely rare.

Two correlative beliefs form the premise of court remedies. The first is that the disputants must be truly competitive adversaries. This implies that they vie for the same things. If the dispute could be settled to the satisfaction of both with each receiving something different, then their adversarial status is at least partially illusory. Thus the first belief posits the classic zero-sum situation. But this is a shaky premise if applied to all disputes that are litigated. Disputes come in multifarious forms. They are not necessarily over conflicting claims to the same thing. The many that are may nevertheless be resolved so that each disputant comes away with something.[94] Marshall points out areas which, although initially adversarial, hold no advantage to "win" over the other party to the transaction or dispute. On the contrary, the win-win, positive-sum outcome is far more desirable. One example is the corporate merger: Both corporations and their shareholders want as much ownership and control over the merged corporation as possible, but both must perceive some gain, that is, mutual "winning." Another illustration lies in collective bargaining: Labor's extreme position may force the employer out of business; management's one-sided victory may engender the lasting hostility of the employees.[95]

A corollary of the first belief (competitive adversaries) is that the medium of the court remedy will be mutually acceptable to both parties. This holds true if they are vying for the same thing. Court remedies are almost always material, typically money damages. Nonmaterial needs, such as services in lieu of payment or emotional satisfaction (an apology, for example), are typically disregarded. To assume that nonmaterial needs will never be equally desirable to at least one of the parties clearly is a myopic perspective of the human condition. Whenever there are multiple issues, there is the potential for a variable-sum remedy. Trade-offs between issues become possible. This is seen most commonly in collective bargaining where a wage stalemate is broken by management's offer of more fringe benefits, more days off or flex-time in exchange for a reduced wage demand.

Society pays a heavy price for its embrace of adversarial trial remedies to the exclusion of others. Trials may have little concrete value in actually bringing the operative problem under control. Indeed, trials further alienate the parties. The underlying battle premise of the trial becomes a self-fulfilling prophesy, fomenting hostility and polarization between the parties and, most damagingly, frustrating reconciliation.

Reconciliation is important in criminal as well as civil disputes. Most crimes occur within continuing relationships, which are complex and where neither the complainant nor the defendant are entirely blameless. Lon Fuller labeled these polycentric problems. Such disputes do not meet one of Fuller's prerequisites for adjudicable disputes: The problem must be isolated as a single issue capable of a zero-sum outcome.[96]

Trials can be particularly punitive to crime victims. Some, such as rape victims, are so embarrassed and intimidated by the media attention, confrontation with the offender and subjection to grueling cross-examination that they decline to press charges. Other victims risk job insecurity and financial loss due to attendance at the trial. Meanwhile, imprisoning the offender virtually guarantees that restitution will not be made. From a psychological perspective, perhaps the most damaging feature of the criminal process is the victim's lack of any meaningful participation in the process, particularly in the more than ninety percent of cases which are plea bargained (plead guilty to a lesser offense in exchange for the prosecutor's agreement to drop the more serious charge). Although the state is the nominal injured party in a criminal case, the victim is verily the injured party and certainly the only one directly affected. Yet the criminal process denies victims any real payback—either in the opportunity to reconcile difference with the offender, or in meaningful participation in the prosecution of the case.

WTA is another feature of adversarial trial remedies carrying weighty opportunity costs. It undermines reconciliation between the parties and precludes individualized solutions. Given these sacrifices, we must ask why WTA remains the preeminent mode of remedy in the adversary trial. Obversely, what is repellant about alternatives to WTA, such as court-imposed compromise? Hoary and passe notions of trial justice shed some light. Adversary trials may have a symbolic value to the public: the highly ritualized, dramatic struggle between good and evil, resulting in a cathartic sense of justice being served. If not symbolism, perhaps the attraction of WTA, however inelegant and imprecise, is simplicity: one winner. Truth is more soothing if one-sided.

As we dig deeper into our legal credo, other explanations for WTA's appeal surface. Remedies other than WTA may be perceived as an erosion of the law's function as a *standard of morality*. At the core of our preference for WTA may be the need for certainty in the law. Northwestern University law professor John Coons wrote:

[W]e tend to expect the law to enunciate a standard of conduct having relevance to all men. However shabby the syllogisms that support the final judgment, men can cling to it as a plank in a shipwreck. It may seem all that separates them from the descent into the Maelstrom of uncertainty. For the law to callously recognize its own bafflement in a compromise judgment would appear a form of treason to its constituents.[97]

Court-imposed compromise can be narrowly circumscribed and predictable.[98] But it contravenes the traditional American fear of enhanced judicial discretion. A corollary of the faith reposed in the adversary process is judicial distrust. WTA is most compatible with the egocentric dialectic of the adversary system: either-or and absolute, not allowing of shades of gray between the black and white. "The combative aspects of the search for reality in our courts," notes Coons, "obviously puts a premium upon the assertion of polarized persuasions."[99]

Compromise may be seen as tantamount to a moral indeterminacy inconsistent with the tenets of natural law. A compromise remedy smacks of uncertainty and fallibility. On the other hand, natural law is certain and infallible. Briefly, natural law is "true" or divine law, which is believed by its followers to be "discovered" by the rational exercise of human intellect. As pointed out in Chapter 1, trial history was informed by the notion of God as the actual decision maker. Few modern legal philosophers are exponents of natural law. Nevertheless, natural law suffuses much of modern law. Its moral dimension—the fundamental imperative to seek the higher law—perseveres. An example would be the American penchant for making human rights a criterion for judging all nations. Roscoe Pound commented, "The American lawyer, as a rule, still believes that the principles of law are absolute, eternal, and of universal validity."[100]

Portraying legal rights and principles as absolutes is obviously appealing. But that inevitably and unduly beggars creative and thoughtful discourse of complex issues. It has been said that for every problem there is an answer which is simple, obvious and wrong. To that adjectival condemnation we can add "confining and corruptive." Casting involute moral and social questions in the language of absolute rights limits our understanding of those questions and our ability to formulate enduring solutions. Absolute rights are troublesome. When they conflict, impasses arise. No way is left to evaluate and resolve competing claims. As our society waxes turgid with new rights, the rigidity of legal language impoverishes our wherewithal to cope with major social dilemmas. Instead, absolutism polarizes individuals and groups, truncating constructive debate in the process.

Take, as illustration, the abortion controversy. In *Abortion and Divorce in Western Law*,[101] Mary Ann Glendon points out how rights language stunts the American abortion debate. Among twenty Western democracies, the United States stands alone in its way of framing the issue—the right of the fetus versus the right of the woman to control her body. If a majority of the Supreme Court ever decides that a fetus is a person with an absolute right to life, then abortion may be banned and even criminalized just as readily as the right to abortion was established under *Roe v. Wade*. In contrast, writes Glendon, European countries acknowledge the fetus as a life deserving protection, but do not confer upon it the absolute right to be born. Instead, government takes a gestalt approach by weighing the attendant policies and social consequences. What are the dangers of unwanted and abused children? What institutional protections—financial aid, family planning—are available to the mother? Respect is given the woman's right to choose, but she may be required to substantiate her decision or participate in counseling.[102] In short, the decisional calculus is one recognizing a variety of circumstances and policies bearing upon the ultimate determination.[103]

The second belief underpinning court remedies goes to the philosophical core of adjudication: All disputes can be adequately resolved through application of a general rule of law by a third party.[104] Acceptance of this premise precludes all case-specific remedies based on the uniqueness of the particular circumstances of the dispute. There is an incontrovertible irony to this. The vaunted litigant satisfaction said to follow from adversarial proceedings is putatively derived from the control and prerogatives of the parties. Yet the same system withholds the fruits of this advantage by denying the parties freedom to formulate individualized, mutually agreeable remedies. The wonderful promise of the adversary system's flexibility is served up in Procrustean form.[105]

Trial strictures preclude negotiating creative and unique approaches to problem solving. For example, the court would not rule in a typical landlord-tenant eviction suit that the landlord should assist the tenant in locating alternative housing in exchange for the tenant's commitment to vacate the landlord's premises by a certain date. Yet that could be the most satisfactory arrangement for both parties. The tenant's concern would be met. And in the long-run, this could be cheaper, faster and less risky for the landlord than an eviction action.[106]

Courts are supposed to serve justice. When they respond to the multiplicity of human needs with just a few standardized remedies, the quality of justice is correspondingly diminished. Surprisingly, American judges have considerable discretionary power in granting remedies, especially in civil proceedings. They may grant whatever relief is "appropriate,"[107] even relief not explicitly requested. For example, they may award damages in excess of the amount requested. But most judges do not *use* their power. With the exception of lawsuits that affect transcending interests (public interest litigation), judges rarely venture beyond the stated prayer for relief.[108]

Sometimes judges circumvent the traditional remedy limitations of the court. They do so when they aggressively urge settlement at pretrial settlement conferences,[109] or when they suggest out-of-court arrangements that exceed their authority to order, but which they can informally approve. However, potential pitfalls attend this kind of judicial activism. The low visibility of these informal arrangements means they are usually unreviewable. And that is exactly what the disputants may need when the informality of the settlement procedure deprives them of traditional procedural safeguards against abuse of the court's authority.[110] On the other hand, if this problem solving flexibility was formally incorporated into the normal scope of the trial, these pitfalls could be avoided.

The system's inadequacy of remedies can also be seen as an outgrowth of the mind-set fostered by the adversarial trial. Better remedies aren't devised because once in trial litigants ignore the real issues of their conflict. Adversary advocacy stifles what could be creative engagement. Its formalism is a constrained mold which causes the litigant to see his or her opponent only in a hostile context. Simply stated, the system discourages litigants from considering their own true ends or confronting those of their opponents.[111]

INCOMPATIBLE ATTORNEY-CLIENT GOALS

The most impotent player in the trial is the one with the most at stake—the litigant. As noted earlier, clients imagine their attorneys' interests converging with their own, thus experiencing the comfort and strength of belonging to a coalition. Further, they tend to think that their own participation would not be productive. Consequently, they usually cede virtually all power in handling their cases to their attorneys.[112]

Great potential for disservice exists here because the interests of the attorney and client frequently conflict. Both desire the same general ends, but each has his or her own agenda. The attorney's "win" and his client's needs may not be synonymous; in fact, they may be antithetical. A curious juxtaposition of perspectives exists with regard to the attorney-client relationship. The individual client may experience a sense of converging interests with his or her attorney. But when those interests diverge, a well-grounded public distrust issues from the fear that the attorney will pursue his own interests at his client's expense.[113] The adversarial ideal that parties control their advocates[114] is often belied and subverted by advocates whose interests conflict with their clients.[115]

Various incentives impel attorneys to pursue tactics and ends contradictory to the client's expressed wishes. The client wants to cut litigation costs and so tells the attorney. Nevertheless, the attorney may believe that adversarial maneuvering which increases the opponent's costs will improve the likelihood of victory. Costly discovery demands, for example, are commonly used to bully opponents into submission. Being paid by the hour lures the attorney to prolong discovery. Thus attorneys are prone to choose tactics costly to both sides which promise the greatest probability of victory and the largest fee.[116]

In *Lawyer and Client: Who's In Charge*, Douglas Rosenthal describes another fundamental conflict of interest between the negligence attorney and his client. Assume you hire counsel to bring a personal injury suit, a type of action in which the attorney's fee is contingent upon eventual recovery. You may want what you feel is your due, and no less. If you are able to do so, waiting out the defendant's insurer is in your financial interest. In contrast, the attorney's interests are typically better served by seeking a quick out-of-court settlement for a lesser amount. Fast, easy settlement money is more attractive to the attorney than the uncertainty of prolonged litigation for the larger amount the client wants.[117] Therefore, the lawyer may spend as much time trying to convince you to accept a settlement offer than on preparing the case. Attorneys are quite successful in these endeavors: Estimates are that over ninety percent of all civil litigants settle without trial.[118]

Conversely, if his fee is based on work performed, the attorney may eschew a settlement offer, albeit in his client's best interest, in order to pad his fee by increasing billable hours. This is often done by resort to sharp tactics, such as repeated motions and extended depositions. Such acquisitiveness was parodied in the anecdote about an English barrister whose clients were heirs to a large fortune. Upon hearing that the heirs might settle their protracted and bitter suit, the barrister protested, "What? And allow that magnificent estate to be frittered away among the beneficiaries?"[119] Racking up at least 2,000 billable hours per year is a common prerequisite for advancement of new law firm associates. Practices like this hold the profession up to public derision. When, in 1992, the California State Bar came out against sex between attorneys and their clients, some suggested it was because the bar did not want the clients to be billed twice for the same service.

But sometimes the client refuses to settle a civil case or plea bargain a criminal case. Instead the client staunchly insists on "having his day in court." The client naively perceives this possible by telling his or her story personally to the judge or jury—just like in the civics texts. The attorney has other ideas. His game plan is to win, not provide a therapeutic forum for the client's ventilation. Hence, criminal defense attorneys frequently persuade their clients that the best strategy is not to testify at all. In a civil case, if the client chooses to testify, he or she can expect a thorough advance rehearsal by the attorney. Should the client defer to the attorney's judgment, the client's resulting testimony may be unrecognizably different from what was originally intended.[120] Again, the client's wishes are thwarted.

Attorney-client goal differences may be endemic to the adversary process. As he becomes immersed in the lawsuit, the attorney's single-minded pursuit of victory can deter him from his client's objectives. Winning, as Vince Lombardi observed, becomes not the most important thing, but the only thing. This monomania impairs the attorney's ability to provide his client detached advice about the prospect of victory and the advisability of compromise settlement. A litigation attorney warns businesses:

There is an inherent conflict of interest between prospective business litigation clients and their litigation counsel. . . . In seeking advice as to whether to proceed with litigation (and, of course, later in seeking advice as to whether to propose or accept settlement), they are simultaneously asking such counsel whether it wishes to accept or decline a substantial flow of fees. Such "conflict" is inevitable. But fine businesses—prudent in so

many other aspects of their business—frequently underestimate or ignore this conflict.
. . . Cases are illogically commenced and then prolonged while litigation counsel and
their clients pursue victories rather than reason.[121]

Even with the most conscientiously loyal attorney, the strictures of the
adversarial process can make some measure of attorney-client goal dissonance
practically unavoidable. The *design* of adversary advocacy creates a proceeding
whereby "[t]he client's own ends are reduced to crude pretexts for the standard
partisan approach the lawyer takes on behalf of all his clients."[122]
Notwithstanding his best intentions to effectuate the client's stated objectives, the
attorney can only operate within certain narrow parameters. The process itself
has a corrupting influence on client goals.

EFFECT OF MISMATCHED ATTORNEY SKILLS AND RESOURCES

Trial attorney skills are manifested through the tactics and strategies
employed during pretrial and trial proceedings. They are an integral part of the
attorney's performance and largely determinative of his success. Under the
adversary system, judges give attorneys broad latitude in the courtroom. When
the evidentiary facts or apposite law of a case are adverse to his client's
interests, the attorney's courtroom dexterity in swaying the judge or jury come
to the fore. He may distort or dissemble the facts. He may use highly charged
argumentation, even histrionics, to appeal to the jurors' emotions. He may
distract the jury during his opponent's questioning of witnesses. He may even
ferociously attack the credibility of a hostile witness he knows to be telling the
truth.

Crafty attorneys undoubtedly win jury cases that they shouldn't. When the
facts and law are unavailing, they succeed by manipulating witnesses and juror
passions. Indeed, evidentiary facts, selectively chosen, are often no more than
entree to the attorney's performance. A skilled trial attorney is part thespian,
part chess master. His questions, tone and volume of voice, facial expressions
and body language are all geared to influencing, not informing the jury.
Predictable results follow. Superior advocacy strategy and tactics frequently
overcome unfavorable facts. Commenting on the juror's receptivity to attorney
suasion, Marcus Gleisser observed:

So it is that the experienced lawyer, knowing well this weakness, passes lightly over facts
he would have stressed before a judge alone, and instead puts his emphasis on the
dramatic aspects of his case. Here is where the orator takes over and leaves the lawyer
behind: he knows that each juror is influenced by his own background, training and
heredity; that the listener, as in all audiences, can be led about by his emotions and
prejudices. So the lawyer hits these hard. He puts aside his professional desire for
objectivity in justice and instead attempts to capitalize upon the whimsical excesses that

juries are known for. . . . These very emotions which a lawyer tries to grasp firmly are a major obstacle in the way of a jury sincerely seeking to find the facts about a case before it.[123]

We would expect the range of impacts that attorney performances have on juries to be as broad as the range of skills among trial attorneys. Yet this fairly safe assumption is curiously inconsistent with fundamental adversary theory. Underlying the theorized fairness of the adversary system is a surprisingly implausible presumption: Opposing attorneys will have *roughly equal competence.*[124] Critics refer to this dubious supposition as "the adversary myth." As the gap between the equality ideal and reality widens, the alleged benefits of the system correspondingly diminish. Yet the gap is undeniable. In many, if not most cases, both the skills of the opposing attorneys and the resources of the litigating parties are palpably mismatched.

Theory notwithstanding, the actual incidence of decisively mismatched attorneys may seem infrequent. After all, every attorney must attend law school and pass a bar exam. And once in practice, any attorney can avail himself of a plethora of trial tactics. Given these equalizing factors, isn't the quality of advocacy important only in cases where the weight of evidence is about equal? Put differently, aren't cases overwhelmingly decided on their merits? No one can say for sure. However, two considerations suggest schooling and equal availability of trial tactics have a minimal "smoothing" effect upon the levels of attorney performances.

First, performance on law school or bar exams is an unreliable indicator of prospective courtroom competence. For the most part, bar exams only measure a particular type of cognitive ability: legal analysis. Albeit useful in general practice, this is essentially unrelated to effective courtroom advocacy. Furthermore, the quality of law school education varies enormously. Many states have law schools unaccredited by either the ABA or the state bar. Students of these schools—some of whom do not have a baccalaureate degree—can qualify to take the state bar merely by first passing an abbreviated "baby" bar after the first year of school.

Second, the availability of trial tactics is one thing; skill in their use is another. Trial attorney skills vary widely. Some attorneys are barely competent.[125] According to a 1989 study by the ABA, underpaid court-appointed attorneys were so often wildly incompetent that the federal courts find constitutional errors in about 40 percent of the capital habeus corpus cases they reviewed.[126] At the other end of the scale, many trial attorneys use their repertoire of trial tactics and stratagems to command six- or seven-figure fees. In a market economy, the price a professional can demand and a client will pay for services is a traditional barometer of the worth of the services. Legal services are no exception; in fact, legal fees are a particularly reliable indicator of relative skills, especially in civil cases where what is at stake for the client is typically measurable in money or money's worth. Unlike the artist the value of whose work is very much a matter of personal taste, the attorney must usually justify his fee in stark, unadorned pecuniary terms.

If fees are insufficient evidence of the great inequality in skills among trial attorneys, then track record certainly is. Every generation has its legendary courtroom figures who almost never lose a case. In legal circles, their names are mentioned in hushed tones. These luminaries are not clairvoyants. They win cases through superior skill, not by divining what a judge or jury will think, nor by consistently choosing the "right" client. The question is not whether a broad disparity of skills prevails among trial attorneys. It does. Rather, the issue is the effect on the many trials where the opposing attorneys *are* significantly mismatched. The attorney-jury chemistry then assumes great importance. A disparity in the skills of the opposing attorneys certainly may affect or determine a jury's decision. The determinative difference may come about simply by one attorney ingratiating himself with the jury more than his opponent does—the so-called "likability factor."[127] Or the advantage may be gained by decisive superiority of forensic skills. This happens whenever an attorney whose proficiency of style and technique succeeds where an attorney with skills approximating the opponent's would have failed. When this state of affairs obtains, the jury functions according to novelist Honore de Balzac's definition: "twelve men chosen to decide who has the best attorney." Put differently, juries sometimes try the attorneys, not the case. If so, trial justice is denied or, at best, serendipitous.

The controversial Charlie Chaplin paternity suit in 1945 illustrates the persuasive power of attorney guile. Conclusive scientific evidence—a blood test—refuted Joan Barry's claim that Chaplin had fathered her child. Even so, she prevailed due to a masterful appeal to the emotions of the jurors by her attorney, the rancorous, seventy-seven-year-old Joseph Scott. He portrayed Chaplin as the wealthy villain, callously indifferent to the consequences of his alleged indiscretions. Among other flamboyancies, he characterized Chaplin as "a master mechanic in the art of seduction" and accused him of "lying like a cheap Cockney cad." Scott also brought attention to Chaplin's refusal to apply for American citizenship, a fact of undeniable impact during World War II.[128] Scott's presentation featured a dramatic juxtaposition of the infant's face next to Chaplin's so that the jury could "see" the physical similarities. Later, he climactically shed tears over the plight of his destitute client and her child. A professional courtroom actor thus bested one of the foremost film actors of all time. We can only speculate whether the irony was lost on Chaplin.

How often are jury verdicts affected when there is a mismatch of skills between the opposing attorneys? Empirical studies of actual cases are decidedly scant. However, a large-scale jury opinion survey I conducted in 1988[129] of over 3,800 Los Angeles jurors (hereafter, the Los Angeles survey) explored the effect of mismatched attorney skills on case outcomes. The survey found mismatching had a profound impact on jurors. A majority of the survey respondents left the jury experience believing that mismatched attorney skills can affect the outcome of a case.[130] And *in the actual case they served on*, over one-third both saw a difference in attorney courtroom skills and felt it "probably affected the verdict."[131] Many jurors found mismatched attorney skills a justice-corrupting influence. About two-fifths thought that the difference in attorney skills was anywhere from "partly" to "completely" responsible for a *wrong* decision by the jury they sat on regarding "the verdict, size of the award or length of sentence."[132]

These findings suggest a disturbing hypothesis: The adversary system's theoretical cornerstone—roughly equal competence of the opposing attorneys—may be its fundamental weakness. If either litigant lacks competent counsel, then even the staunchest defenders of the adversary system would concede a resulting problem: Relevant facts, law and persuasive arguments may never be heard by the jury; false claims of the opposition may remain unchallenged. As the disparity in opposing attorney skills in a given trial widens, the more likely that the merits of the case will not determine the outcome. The problem goes beyond trials pitting a competent advocate against an incompetent one. Competence is relative. A trial matching a highly skilled attorney against a moderately skilled one may still betoken a verdict determined by forensic talent instead of the merits of the case.

The survey just discussed measured the effects of attorney influence of which jurors were aware. Left unassessed is the effect of *subconscious* forensic persuasion. Many of the modern psychological techniques being used in trial advocacy are designed to subconsciously induce jury decisions on legally improper bases—extralegal factors and hidden biases. This "covert advocacy" threatens both the jury and adversary systems because it cannot be identified by the jurors nor countered by opposing counsel or the judge.[133] "[T]he goal of covert advocacy," says Loyola law professor Victor Gold, "is to induce a jury to employ bias while concealing from the jury their reliance on bias."[134]

Use of the new techniques gives *wealthy* clients a double advantage. First, linguistic patterns of the wealthy tend to have more credibility with jurors (although there is no scientific basis to believe wealthy witnesses more than nonwealthy witnesses). Forensic psychologists say that "powerless" speech—hedging language, meek delivery—tends to be used by poor, unemployed and uneducated witnesses.[135] Such testimony has far less credibility than the antithetical powerful speech used predominantly by the rich. Experiments show that jurors consistently assign more credibility to powerful speakers and give larger damage awards to plaintiffs whose witnesses use powerful speech.[136]

A second advantage devolves to the rich because their wealth can buy the benefits of the new advocacy technology. Only the wealthy can afford the expense of hiring a psychologist who can provide a variety of litigation support services. Witnesses, for example, can be taught to adopt a powerful speech style. The psychologist may reveal insights to verbal and nonverbal juror behavior both during *voir dire* and during the trial. The psychologist may also help the attorney assess juror reactions to particular questions, arguments and overall strategy. To this end, some wealthy clients have even hired "shadow juries" as sounding boards. A shadow jury is a group composed of members of the community whose demographic traits (such as age, sex, education, occupation), are the same as the actual jury.[137]

Along similar lines, only the rich can assume the cost of another burgeoning pretrial technique: conducting a survey of the community from which the jury panel will be drawn. The purpose is to ascertain the values and biases of prospective jurors—a decidedly gainful datum during jury selection.[138] From this, they can determine what demographic traits are typical of those whose attitudes are most favorable (or unfavorable) to the client's case. In sum, the ideal of a fight between equals grows further and further remote. Instead of a conventional battle of adversaries relying on their legal intuition, we now have the well-heeled litigant arming his or her advocate with an arsenal of professional psychological assistance and case-specific scientific data.

Hiring one or more expert witnesses is another means for the wealthy litigant to gain the whip hand. Expert testimony is now commonplace in high-stakes civil suits and many major criminal cases (the King trials, for example). Because their testimony can be highly persuasive with juries, experts routinely command fees in the thousands of dollars for a single appearance. This prices their services out of the market for most. When costs dictate that only one side has the benefit of expert testimony, that side has a decided and perhaps decisive edge.

For litigants who can afford them, new communications technologies provide almost limitless advantages. Two recent trends demonstrate the competitive edge communications technology offers. Attorneys increasingly use computer-generated animation to illustrate eyewitness testimony or the testimony of forensic experts attempting to recreate a crime scene. Jurors are immeasurably influenced by such animations. But the high cost of their production—$10,000 and up—supplies another opportunity for exploitation of the great disparity of resources so common between opposing litigants.

Attorneys employ other cutting-edge technologies during trials to advance the interests of their wealthier clients. One such technology is a laser disc retrieval system. Consider the adversarial advantages of being able to project information stored on compact discs—videotaped depositions, photos, documents and other exhibits—onto large screen TV monitors in the courtroom at the touch of a finger. Witnesses may even be confronted with images of themselves giving earlier, contradictory testimony. (This occurred in the King II trial.) The cost of this system, however, can be yet more expensive than computer animations, creating one more instance where superior resources can and do bias trial outcomes.

Shouldn't this give us pause to reflect on the kind of justice served by our adversarial jury trial? Notwithstanding that we live in a country upon whose Supreme Court pediment are engraved the words, "Equal Justice Under Law," trial court justice is anything but equal. In *Unequal Justice*, Jerold Auerbach decries the distribution of legal talent in the United States. It is clearly not random. The bar elite overwhelmingly chooses to serve the most privileged social stratum—distinguished by ethnicity, class lines and, most importantly, wealth.[139] The partiality of the bar for wealthy clientele was captured in a *New Yorker* cartoon showing an attorney talking to a prospective client. The caption reads, "You have a pretty good case, Mr. Pitkin. How much justice can you afford?"[140] Echoing this sentiment, Frankel said, "we staff a system in which justice is to a large degree for sale."[141]

This brings distributive justice into issue. What kind of justice is that which essentially can be purchased? The adversary system fosters a legal environment in which the side with superior resources thereby obtains superior representation. Nevertheless, absent socialization of legal services (and the radical disempowerment of ensconced and vested interests that would entail), we can expect perduration of the status quo as regards for whom and how attorneys perform in the courtroom. As one observer of the jury system noted, "The lawyers who have piled up a long string of lucrative victories resulting on the . . . weaknesses of the juries will do all in their power to keep the situation as it is now."[142]

When guileful trial attorneys prevail in contravention of the true merits of a case, the fault lies not with the individual attorneys who employ morally or ethically questionable practices. Instead, we should look to the system which permits, and the profession which encourages, their use. The lawyer's duty to exploit the jurors' emotions is urged in countless professional publications.[143] And both trial and appellate courts overlook all but the most inflammatory practices. For example, courts have not only held that the shedding of attorney tears is permissible, but have even suggested it was the attorney's duty to do so under proper circumstances.[144] Use of these techniques by attorneys to undermine the rational judgment of juries exacerbates the declining public respect for the legal profession, the courts and the rule of law.[145]

The influence of a trial attorney's personality and theatrical performance on the outcome of a trial, especially a jury trial, cannot be overstated. Consider the following two items. The first is an ad in a legal newspaper announcing a seminar entitled, "Acting For Attorneys," offering to teach attorneys how to act in the courtroom. (The accompanying illustration shows the classic tragedy and comedy masks flanking each side of the Scales of Justice.) The ad informs us that the California State Bar has approved the course and will offer attendees six credits toward the continuing education required of all practitioners.

The second item comes from an article describing another trial advocacy seminar, this one sponsored by the Orange County (California) Bar Association.

The seminar was called "All the Court's a Stage." It featured Keith Evans, a member of the English and California bars, who teaches advocacy as theater. "The court of law is a theater," proclaims Evans. "It is your job to make it professional theater." How does one do this? "To be a good trial lawyer," he says, "you've got to be an actor, and you've got to be a good one." In order to be entertaining and capture jurors' attention, Evans advocates starting by telling them a story. Because people have enjoyed stories from their childhood, Evans advises trial attorneys to turn witness examinations into stories. His other advice includes tips on dressing and voice training, including pacing your speech, varying your tone and using pauses for emphasis. He even suggests attorneys choreograph their movements during trial. "You wouldn't have come to the trial bar unless there was a bit of an actor in you," he asserts.[146]

So there you have it. The profession which spawned and nurtured Lincoln, Holmes and Cardozo now gives its imprimatur to courses instructing on the ways of the thespian and the snake oil salesman. What a bathetic turnabout. If oleaginous sideshow smarm has become a prescription for trial justice, then something is grievously awry with the process. The "Acting for Attorneys" course is a metaphor for much of what is wrong with the adversary system: It focuses too much attention on the attorney to the exclusion of a rational, purposeful search for truth and, ultimately, justice.

Adversarial trials are staged like theatrical performances. The judge sits much higher than all others, in the front and center of the courtroom, covered in black robes. She is aloof and reserved. Yet she is the supreme authority in the room, a god-like presence that may intervene but usually remains passive. The judge is the legal counterpart of the *deus-ex-machina* of Greek drama. Jury members are even more passive than the judge. They are the audience. Unable to ask questions or participate in any meaningful way, they sit together against the wall facing the "show." The show is the action taking place in the arena, bounded on the jury's right by the witness stand and judge's bench, and on the left by the attorneys' tables. Indisputably, the attorneys are the performers. Only they walk freely in the arena, to and from the witness stand, the bench and the jury box. They gesture, flail and point. But mostly they talk: They bluster, blather, harangue, sermonize and beguile. They laugh, cry and bristle; they make the jurors laugh, cry and bristle. It is the greatest show in town because it involves real people with real problems and high stakes: prison or freedom; child custody or childlessness; recompense for serious bodily injury or destitution and welfare. Should matters of such consequence be resolved by a process which elevates showmanship over dispassionate and rational inquiry?

An inevitable concomitant of a party control system is the concern that attorney advocacy may destroy the delicate balance of courtroom power, and with it the intended objectives of trial justice. Victor Gold warns:

The diffusion of power in the courtroom among the judge, jury and advocates has been motivated by a desire to avoid an excess concentration in the hands of the judge. However, little attention has been paid to the possibility that power could become too concentrated in the hands of the advocates. The great danger of the adversary process always has been that advocates might become too good at what they do. . . . As a result, the advocates may supplant the judiciary as the greatest courtroom threat to truth and democratic ideals.[147]

Despite the potential injustice produced by mismatched attorneys, courts have done little to identify disparities great enough to be considered rectifiable. Individual judges may exercise their discretion about when to intervene but, as the next section describes, not without risk. Supreme Court standards have been established in only one area: effective criminal defense representation. Defense counsel may be deemed so inept as to constitute a violation of the Sixth Amendment right to counsel. In *U.S. v. Cronic*, the Court observed that under the constitutional right to counsel, assuring fairness in the adversarial process necessitates that accused have a counsel who subjects the prosecution's case to the "crucible of meaningful adversary testing." Accordingly, "when a true adversarial criminal trial has been conducted—even if defense counsel may have made demonstrable errors—the kind of testing envisioned by the Sixth Amendment has occurred." Conversely, the Sixth Amendment right is violated when defective representation causes "the process [to] lose . . . its character as a confrontation between adversaries."[148]

A companion case established two prerequisites to prove constitutionally ineffective representation. Both incompetence and prejudice must be demonstrated. That is, the incompetence must be of such a magnitude that "there is a reasonable probability that, but for counsel's unprofessional errors, the results of the proceeding would have been different."[149] But the Court's majority specifically rejected any empirical or preexisting (e.g., ABA) standards. Instead, courts were to apply a more subjective, case-by-case evaluation. Anything less than the most egregious incompetence would still ensure "the proper functioning of the adversarial process." The Court noted: "Because of the differences inherent in making the evaluation, the court must indulge a *strong presumption that counsel's conduct falls within the wide range of professional assistance.*"[150] (Emphasis supplied.)

Three years later the Court illustrated its lax application of the incompetence standard. Defense counsel had failed to present substantial mitigating evidence relating to the defendant's background in a capital sentencing (death penalty) hearing. Notwithstanding the life-or-death role such information can play in a capital sentencing hearing, the Court found that this omission did not fall outside "the wide range of professionally competent assistance."[151] Given this minimal safety net, the vast majority of decisive mismatching remains tolerable under the adversary system.

JUDICIAL PASSIVITY

Judicial impartiality does not bar the judge's prerogative to intervene in the case before her. What remains at issue is the appropriate occasion for her intervention. Legislation and court rules mandate judges to accelerate the pace of litigation.[152] Clogged court dockets mother this necessity. Consequently, judges now play a more active role in encouraging and facilitating out-of-court settlements.[153]

Addressed here, however, is injustice, not expeditiousness. Judges generally hew to the passive line when it comes to mitigating the effect of mismatched advocates. And rarely do they intervene to curb adversarial excess. Several reasons temper any such inclinations. Ordinarily, the *contemporaneous objection rule* limits the judge's prerogatives. It provides that a party typically must request relief before a judge will intervene.[154] The rule is a clear corollary of the party control concept, based on the notion that a trial is essentially a private quarrel. If an attorney does object to an opponent's impermissible tactic, the usual judicial directive to the jury is a *curative instruction*, advising jurors to disregard what was seen and/or heard. This is usually ineffective. Moreover, it is time-consuming and cumbersome.

The judge has another tool: holding the mischievous attorney in contempt. But judges generally eschew contempt citations. They have potential for arbitrariness, and tend to be overkill.[155] Further, ruling on any motion for sanctions requires an expenditure of time that most judges are loathe to make.

Another constraint on judicial intervention is the lack of prescribed positive obligations of the judge. The ABA Code of Judicial Conduct fails to impose any affirmative duty on the judge to seek justice. Her main adjudicative constraint is to perform her duties impartially.[156] During the trial, impartiality is manifested as passivity, which can make the judge an unwilling abettor of intolerable injustice.

Even when explicitly authorized to intervene, judges are reticent to do so. Take, as example, the judge's power to summarize and comment upon the evidence for the jury. The federal courts and a few state courts follow the English model in allowing it. When doing so, the judge can suggest the proper weight to be given the credibility of the witnesses. A slightly larger number of states allow the judge only a summary, while many others forbid any kind of evidence review by the judge.[157] Those American judges that have either power rarely exercise them. In only three of the seventeen states that allow judicial summary only does the judge summarize the evidence in a majority of the trials.[158] Moreover, data from the *American Jury* reveal that judges are not more likely to use their controls of summary and commentary when there is a disparity in the quality of the opposing attorneys.[159]

Only in the adversary system is the judge's passivity assumed necessary to maintain her impartiality. Outside of the United States, most of the Western world's courts use the inquisitorial system, wherein the judge controls the investigation. Unlike her American counterpart, the inquisitorial judge is obliged to actively pursue all the evidence she feels is necessary to a just decision.

Even within the United States, the trial judge's passivity is unique among those serving in formal dispute resolution roles. In administrative hearings, (including those referred from the courts), arbitrators play an active role without the loss of their impartiality. In collective bargaining, federal mediators rescue legions of sessions from stalemate. And at the local and private sector levels, conciliators of all kind successfully function as neutral but active third-party facilitators in quasi-judicial roles. Clearly, impartiality and passivity are not necessarily corollaries.

Why do we prefer our judges passive? Speculation is plentiful. Some cite our historic distrust of government and concentrated power. A psychological slant credits our need to preserve the image of the judge as a beneficent, distant idol above the human struggle of the courtroom. But this image is purchased at a dear cost. As Alfred Ehrenzweig explains in *Psychoanalytic Jurisprudence*, "[T]he Anglo-American judge's image and functions as those of a mere moderator of a contest . . . have left his seemingly powerful figure (and with him the parties) at the mercy of professional combatants.[160]

Yet quite a few career-minded judges prefer the passive role. Fostering the notion that the judge is "above the fray," exercising her authority solely in accord with her conscience and interpretation of the law, is more appealing to the judge if she must stand for election to retain her seat. Election creates a potential conflict of interest: Political considerations may influence the judge's actions. Passivity serves to buffer elective judges against public recriminations from unpopular decisions, particularly in no-jury cases.

The judge runs another career risk should she feel compelled to shed her passivity in the name of justice. Every trial has a subtle, secondary battle. Litigation attorneys are vigilant for any intervention by the judge that can be used for appealing an unfavorable decision. Trial judges dread appellate court reversals. They perceive them as public pronouncements of their errors by a higher authority. Furthermore, a significant number of appellate reversals virtually eliminates any aspirations the oft-reversed judge may have had for appointment to an appeals court.

ROLE-BASED IMMORALITY

Few subjects evoke greater passion—and sometimes sardonic laughter—than attorney ethics.[161] How do we judge a trial attorney's otherwise immoral or amoral conduct if it is performed within the loose constraints of the adversary system? Put differently, is the attorney's professional role behavior exempt from moral judgment? This issue is often raised when the attorney represents a client whose claim or actions the attorney believes is immoral. It is commonly felt that the adversary system allows an attorney to disclaim moral as well as legal responsibility in representing these clients. The MRPC (Model Rules of Professional Conduct) states that there is no need for the attorney to share his client's values.[162]

The most prominent spokesperson for this view is Monroe Freedman, dean and professor of law at Hofstra University. His book, *Lawyers' Ethics In An Adversary System*, has become the standard articulation of the "minimalist" position on attorney ethical responsibilities. His views are widely quoted by others. One writer, for example, reports that Freedman hails "taking every advantage available within the bounds of the law. . . . The idea of some old-boy obligation to forgo tactics that are both legal and ethical and in the interests of the client is a highly offensive notion."[163]

If these views sound extreme, note that Freedman is not some loose cannon operating at the fringe of the profession: He has chaired several legal ethics and professional responsibility commissions, and he is known as a "lawyer's lawyer," having successfully represented about a dozen attorneys in matters involving questions of professional responsibility. Coincidentally, Freedman's position on legal ethics parallels the position on business ethics of an even more illustrious professor with a similar name: Nobel economist Milton Friedman. Freedman's view is to attorney professional responsibilities what Milton Friedman's view is to corporate social responsibility. The latter contends that the corporation's sole obligation is to obey the bare minimum standards of the law. Any additional company resources expended purely for corporate social responsibility constitutes a breach of the corporation's fiduciary duty to the shareholders. By the same token, Monroe Freedman maintains that any concession by the attorney—in the name of ethics or professional responsibility—to his opponent beyond that legally required is a breach of the attorney's fiduciary duty to his client.

Many disagree with Freedman. They would hold the attorney morally accountable if he helped his client achieve an immoral outcome. Virtually all of the dissenters, however, recognize one exception: representation of the criminal defendant. Once again, preferential rules apply to criminal defense. In particular, a continuing debate rages as to whether defense counsel must abide by the general rule requiring disclosure of the client's perjurious testimony to the court or other party.[164]

In discussing the ethicality and morality of the attorney's role behavior under the adversary system, one is inevitably drawn to the MRPC. It purports to define the ethical parameters of legal practice. Some of its rules are obligatory and subject to disciplinary action for violation. Others are descriptive of the lawyer's role but need not be followed.[165] The MRPC prescribes several obligatory rules regarding candor toward the court and fairness to the opposition. Typical restrictions imposed by the rules are contained in the explanatory comment to Rule 3.4 which says, in part: "Fair competition in the adversary system is secured by prohibitions against destruction or concealment of evidence, improperly influenced witnesses, obstructive tactics in discovery procedure, and the like."

Designed to address public criticism of sharp attorney tactics as well as provide an ethical polestar to attorneys, much of the MRPC is nonetheless little more than a sop. Ethical rules of conduct have become the bar's toothless answer for its failure to instill and enforce personal and professional responsibility among its members. As Grant Gilmore said in *The Ages of American Law*: "The better the society, the less law there will be. In Heaven there will be no law, and the lion will lie down with the lamb. . . . The worse the society, the more law there will be. In Hell there will be nothing but law, and due process will be meticulously observed."[166]

Attorneys commonly do precisely what the MRPC says they shouldn't.[167] Trial advocates practice more as suggested in advocacy publications and seminars. That is because neither the bar nor the bench make a serious, substantive effort to enforce the MRPC. When advocacy infractions occur, they are routinely winked at by judges and bar association ethics committees. As a result, the trial lawyer ostensibly enjoys a special privilege in plying his trade: He is largely unanswerable to society for behavior that would be morally questionable in other contexts. This led the venerable jurist Felix Cohen to lament: "How the edifice of justice can be supported by the efforts of liars at the bar and ex-liars on the bench is one of the paradoxes of legal logic which the man on the street has never solved."

Given then that attorneys *qua* attorneys routinely commit acts otherwise immoral, can this be justified by their role within the adversary system? Perhaps, if the adversary system—as practiced, not as prescribed—produces a countervailing higher good. Does it? Adversary system proponents would make two arguments for an affirmative answer. The first is institutional: The attorney's immoral role-differentiated behavior is justified if his actions are dictated by and in the service of an *accepted societal institution*—the adversary system. The response to this is that there is nothing *inherently* good or virtuous about the adversary system. It must have some external validation. But public confidence in the legal system is decidedly shaky. UCLA professor of law and professor of philosophy Richard Wasserstrom says,

[W]e are . . . certainly entitled to be quite skeptical both of the fairness and of the capacity for self-correction of . . . the legal system. To the degree to which the institutional rules and practices are unjust, unwise or desirable, to that same degree is the case for the role-differentiated behavior of the lawyer weakened if not destroyed.[168]

The second argument seeking to justify role-differentiated attorney behavior refers to the various benefits claimed for the adversary system in Chapter 2. This view holds that these benefits collectively justify attorney role behavior which is otherwise immoral. However seductive in the abstract, this contention falls short on empirical grounds. Analysis and testing render many of the alleged benefits doubtful. Several of the claims are spurious and the associated benefits illusory.[169]

TIME-CONSUMING AND EXPENSIVE

[T]he adversary system . . . is not without a deleterious side. . . . [I]ts relentless formalities and ceaseless opportunities for splitting hairs are time consuming and expensive. It is not available therefore to everyone, and if it is the only system for obtaining redress then justice cannot be done. For that reason, it may mislead us as a society into supposing that its availability is a guarantee of safety.[170]

With this assessment, Jethro Lieberman synopsized the most widespread criticisms of the adversary system. Waits of four years or more just to get a trial date for a filed suit are commonplace. For many, costs of suit are prohibitive.

Time and cost are not independent problems. Jobian patience may be a virtue, but it can be an expensive one when it comes to litigation. The longer the period from filing the suit to its ultimate resolution, the more the costs to the parties. That which lengthens the suit tends to be expensive; pretrial discovery and motions are prime examples. In addition to costs, trial delay has other untoward consequences, including:

1. increased pressure for plea bargaining in criminal cases

2. reduced concentration and recollection of events by witnesses and jurors

3. inability or unwillingness by many citizens to serve as jurors.

Although there are few detailed, reliable studies of trial lengths in the United States, the available data indicates a significant increase in trial times. For example, a 1953-'54 Los Angeles survey found that felony trials heard by a jury averaged three days.[171] A 1971 report estimated the average Los Angeles felony trial heard by a jury to last almost five days.[172] The most recent data on trial length comes from a study by the National Center for State Courts (NCSC). Using cities in California, Colorado and New Jersey, the NCSC looked at average times of jury trials. Average time of felony trials heard by a jury varied from one and a half to two days in New Jersey to one and a half weeks in California.[173]

Our trials are much longer than their inquisitorial counterparts.[174] In Germany, for example, the average trial time for a serious criminal offense was from three quarters of a day to slightly less than one and a half days. (Trials of less serious offenses required an average of about two hours.)[175] For the litigant, a more relevant measure of the time invested in a lawsuit begins with the time of filing. Here again inquisitorial litigation is notably faster. In Germany, for instance, over 80 percent of the 1984 municipal court cases were disposed of within six months of filing.[176]

This is not to suggest that any adversarial trial is innately inefficient. A study comparing New York and New Jersey trials showed a significant difference in trial times (New Jersey's were much shorter) *due largely to the degree of contentiousness.*[177] Observes Hastings law professor Gordon Van Kessel, "Though the adversary process results in some delay when compared to the nonadversary approach, the primary source of our current intractable delay can be traced to our adversary excesses, including extreme lawyer dominance and aggressiveness and exceedingly complex rules of evidence and procedure."[178]

Delay is a potent weapon in the trial attorney's arsenal. Defense attorneys use it as a trial tactic. Incentives abound. Incriminating witnesses may die or disappear. Criminal defendants accused of nonviolent acts can usually remain free upon posting bail. Civil defendants use delay to defer the payment of damages.

Juries substantially prolong trial delay. John Langbein, a foreign law scholar at the University of Chicago, observed that "the Anglo-American jury system has grown ever more cumbersome, while the continental mixed court injects lay participation in a fashion that greatly accelerates trial procedure by dispensing with the trappings of jury control."[179] Both the NCSC study and the Annual Report of the Administrative Office of the U.S. Courts found nonjury trials to be very short. Over 80 percent were completed in one day, and over 93 percent in two days.[180] Hans Zeisel, coauthor of the seminal work on jury research, *The American Jury*, estimates that bench trials (judge sitting without a jury) would be 40 percent faster than jury trials.[181] The posturing and polemics attorneys employ solely for the benefit of prospective jurors during jury selection consumes much if not most of the time of the jury trial. Use of lay juries in civil cases outside of the United States is extremely rare; nowhere are they used as extensively.

Much of the blame for the length and expense of adversarial trials can be assigned to attorney abuse of the discovery process. Few limits exist as to the number of discovery requests a party can make, as long as the requests are at least tenuously related to the action. In a nationwide Harris survey of 1,000 federal and state trial judges, (hereafter, the Harris survey), abuse of the discovery process was the most frequently cited cause of runaway litigation costs. A large majority said that attorneys' use of discovery "as an adversarial tool to intimidate or raise the stakes for their opponents" was a major cause of excessive litigation costs.[182] According to former President George Bush's Council on Competitiveness, more than 80 percent of the time and cost of the typical civil suit is attributable to discovery.[183]

Excessive discovery and other forms of pretrial "hardball" tactics raise attorneys' fees, accounting for a hefty portion of all recoveries. Conversely, claimant recoveries are surprisingly small by comparison. Plaintiff recoveries are actually less than transaction costs, the most significant component of which is attorney fees. In 1985, for example, a study by the Rand Corporation's Institute for Civil Justice reported that the legal system incurred $16-19 billion in transaction costs to deliver another $14-16 billion in compensation to plaintiffs.[184]

Attorneys' fees for civil litigation in the United States are the highest in the world—in absolute terms and as a percentage of total expenditures of the liability system.[185] Plaintiffs' attorney fees are high because of the contingent fee arrangement virtually unique to the United States.[186] Under this arrangement, the attorney takes as his sole compensation a percentage of the amount awarded to his client. This percentage varies, depending upon how far the case progressed and the work invested by the attorney before disposition. Few attorneys will take a case for less than one third of the total recovery. But how high can the attorney's percentage go? Consider this anecdote published in the old *New York Morning Journal*:

A New Yorker asked William Maxwell Evarts what he would charge for managing a certain case. "Well," said Evarts, "I will take your case on a contingent fee."

"And what is a contingent fee?"

"My dear sir," said Mr. Evarts, "I will tell you what a contingent fee to a lawyer means. If I don't win your suit I get nothing. If I do win it you get nothing. See?"[187]

Since our jury awards tend to be very high by international standards, contingency fees are commensurately high. In other countries, contingency fees are either prohibited or considered a violation of the rules of professional conduct.[188] Defense attorney fees are also high in comparison with those of other countries. The main reason is that American defense attorneys bill by the hour, whereas defense attorneys in most other countries bill for specific services. Because American trials are the most complex and lengthy, defense attorney fees as a percentage of total expenditures of the liability system are also substantially greater in the United States than elsewhere.[189] Other countries generally regulate attorney fees. They are set by the court or by fee tables compiled by professional organizations. Only a minority of American states, including Florida and California, set a maximum percentage of recoveries that plaintiff's attorneys can charge, and then do so for just certain types of services.[190]

Attorneys' fees are only one major component of increased litigation costs. Another is the growth in the size and frequency of damage awards against U.S. businesses. Our civil justice system has come under increasing public attack in recent years. The primary focus of the attack is the tort liability system. Critics charge that unrestrained tort litigation puts a drag on the economy by raising production costs, which are passed on to consumers in the form of higher prices. Consequently, many U.S. goods and services are withdrawn from the marketplace, to the detriment of our productivity and competitiveness in the global market. Stories of the adverse effects of unconstrained litigation are legion. A recent survey by the Conference Board, a group of 3,600 organizations in over 50 nations, reports that due to potential liability concerns:

- 47 percent of U.S. manufacturers have withdrawn products from the market.

- 25 percent of U.S. manufacturers have discontinued some form of production research.

- 15 percent of U.S. companies have laid off workers as a direct result of product liability experience.[191]

What is it about the U.S. system that creates this competitive disadvantage? Several factors peculiar to our system are responsible, but none more so than the jury. Its influence on civil litigation will be discussed in the next chapter.

The cost and time of traditional litigation have been the greatest impetuses spurring alternative dispute resolution (ADR).[192] Voluntary and court-ordered arbitration, mediation and other ADR mechanisms wax in response to growing disaffection with the time and expense of lawsuits. It is a measure of the time and cost problem that the ADR movement has extensively altered the terrain of dispute resolution in America.

COURTROOM INJUSTICE

Among the oldest of debates is whether morality is absolute or relative. A similar dichotomy carries over to the concept of courtroom justice. In the United States, it has a narrowly drawn, idiosyncratic meaning. The disparity between courtroom justice and more common notions of justice is the subject of this critique.

As applied to a trial, the common notion of justice would indicate an outcome based on the factual and legal merits of the case (assuming that the law as applied in the individual case was fair). Granted, these are not always easily determinable. But conceptually, this model is clearly distinct from one which prescribes that the trial is akin to a game to be won by the better player. All trials, and especially jury trials, are games. They have rules (court procedure), players (litigants, jurors and attorneys), scoring devices (witness testimony and other evidence, argumentation), a referee (the judge) and a goal (winning the verdict).

Courtroom justice is an idiomatic term, referring merely to adherence to the procedural rules of the trial. Hence courtroom justice is also known as procedural justice. (Substantive justice is the province of legislatures, whose laws must be more responsive to and thus presumably reflect popular views of right and wrong.) The principal focus of courtroom justice is the process. In any given case, actual *outcome* has significance only to the specific parties affected by the decision, whereas compliance with the procedural rules of the process is the primary concern of the court system. The "how" is more important than the "who" or the "what." That is the symbolism of the blindfold on the Statue of Justice. To be sure, justice as popularly conceived does not ignore procedure;[193] it just makes it ancillary to outcome. If a procedure produced verdicts which were unfair or immoral by popular standards, it would matter little that the procedure was thought technically or mechanically impeccable.

All this directly relates to the adversary system. For it is the particular type of procedure we employ, the warp and woof of the trial. Trials cannot be just if the adversary system is unjust. Ideally, a just trial court decision process would possess the following qualities:

Informed. The U.S. Supreme Court has frequently emphasized that the basic purpose of a trial is the determination of truth.[194] Thus the decision maker should have as many facts germane to the dispute as possible. Without truth the trial process reaches just decisions more by serendipity than design.

Rational. Morgan characterized the traditional or "Blackstonian" concept of the judicial process this way: "The system is designed to produce . . . a rational investigation and rational adjustment of disputes."[195] And according to researchers Miller and Boster, one of the popular images of the trial is that of a rational event.[196] Therefore, the means of the trial process should be rational and logical in light of its goals; functionalism should obtain.

Fair. Most importantly, the process should be designed so that the parties get what they deserve. Civil case decisions should be consonant with the respective degrees of right and wrong behavior of the parties. Criminal punishment should be condign.

Let us now superimpose this paradigm of a just trial onto the adversary system and test for correspondence. First, is the factfinder adequately informed? We see that their predetermined roles leave each significant participant either without the power or without the responsibility to seek truth and justice. Under party control theory, the informing function falls to the advocate, not the factfinder. The latter is only a passive recipient of information. Given the partisan nature of the process, the advocate's overriding goal of victory, the abundance of exclusionary rules to hide evidence, and the minimal checks and balances on the advocate's use of truth-distorting tactics, there is a substantial gap between theory and practice. The advocate's aim is to influence, not inform in a dispassionate, instructive manner. Thus the means of attaining the truth goal (informing) are demonstrably questionable.

In theory as well as in practice, the quantity and quality of the information reaching the court appear wanting. The factfinder hears only *two* versions of the facts, both unreservedly partisan. In contrast, the inquisitorial system permits, indeed requires, a neutral investigator to pursue *all* facts necessary to a just resolution of the dispute.

In factfinding, the jury has notable shortcomings.[197] "[O]f all the possible ways to get at the falsity or truth of testimony," observed Frank, "none could be conceived that would be more ineffective than trial by jury."[198] Discarding of judicial passivity could help. In jury trials, judicial activism—calling and questioning witnesses, including court-appointed experts—could counteract the predicament of a jury hamstrung by procedural limitations on truth-seeking. Of course, by so doing, the American judge risks influencing the jury, as well as calling her own impartiality into question. The issue is whether jury questioning, appellate review and other safeguards render this an acceptable risk in light of the problem.

Moving to rationality, the adversary process is questionable in several respects. Consider the attorney's paradoxical role. Only the attorney informs the decision maker as to the evidentiary facts, yet the attorney will present only as much of the truth as benefits his case, hiding or distorting the rest. The opposing counsel may fill in some of the gaps, but just as likely may be engaged in his own dissembling.

Rationality is also lacking in the unsuitability of the adversary process to certain types of disputes, the limitations on the types of court remedies and the dysfunctional nature of much of the process. Lawyer-infused hostility, for example, often magnifies underlying problems. Several premises of the jury system are counterintuitive; some are irreconcilable. Jurors with no legal experience or training are asked to apply abstruse legal rules to often complex facts. No other factfinding process uses adversariality as its exclusive investigatory vehicle, nor total neophytes as the factfinders. Then there is the schizophrenia of the exclusionary rules. They are based on distrust of the jury's ability to properly consider the excluded evidence, even though the same jurors are presumed capable of understanding and applying complex legal rules the first time they hear them. This prompted Charles Boston, a leader of the American Bar during the early twentieth century, to remark, "We . . . regard [the jury] as wholly incompetent for the purpose for which we established it."[199]

Other ostensible irrationalities lie in the use of the jury as the medium through which the law is effectuated. Procedural justice is cold and objective, devoid of any moral precepts beyond evenhandedness. Presumably, we implement our sense of right and wrong through the substantive law contained in the judge's charge (instructions) to the jury. Not true. Empirical studies indicate that juries frequently do not understand much of the instructions. Even when they do, they can ignore the law with impunity, unencumbered by the duty to explain the basis of their decisions. Adding to the confusion, juries are not informed they have this power. To the contrary, the judge solemnly admonishes them to cleave to the law contained in her instructions. Consequently, only *some* juries so disposed actually ignore the law. Surely this cannot be Morgan's "rational adjustment of disputes."

Least of all is the adversarial trial fair. Unfairness resonates from the huge gap between the myth and reality of adversary advocacy. No reason exists to assume that opposing counsel are roughly equally matched any more than there is to assume that the litigants' resources are equal. The merits of a case often pale before the impact of superior advocacy skills, frequently resulting in an inequitable verdict.

Finally, the limits of court remedies can unfairly skew distributive justice. Zero-sum remedies impoverish our creativity, while WTA outcomes distribute the contested property rights as if the parties were either entirely right or entirely wrong. When that is not the case, all-or-nothing consequences are unjust and smack of gamesmanship mentality. Just as the all-or-nothing consequences of the contributory negligence rule were unfair (and led to the widespread adoption of comparative negligence), so too the WTA aspect of the adversary system is unfair in the many cases where the winner is not an angel nor the loser a devil.

NOTES

1. Karl Llewellyn, *Jurisprudence: Realism of Theory and Practice* (Chicago: University of Chicago Press, 1962), pp. 446-47.
2. Philip Stern, *Lawyers On Trial* (New York: New York Times Books, 1980), p. 152.
3. Id., p. 153.
4. A deposition is a pretrial interrogation of a witness taken out of court but under oath. Attorneys often stretch the questioning out for days.
5. Stern, *op. cit.*, p. 153.
6. Warren Burger, "Agenda for 2000 A.D.—A Need For Systematic Anticipation," 70 *F.R.D.* 83 at 83 (1976).
7. Roscoe Pound, "The Causes of Popular Dissatisfaction with the Administration of Justice," orig. 29 *ABA Reports* 395 (1906), reported in 35 *Federal Rules Decisions* 241 at 281-82 (1964).

8.   John Wigmore, *A Treatise on the Anglo-American System of Evidence in Trials at Common Law*, 3d ed., Vol. 1 (Boston: Little Brown, 1940), sec. 1845 at pp. 374-75.

9.   James Marshall, *Law and Psychology* (Indianapolis: Bobbs-Merrill, 1966), p. 106.

10.   Irving Younger, Remarks at Discovery Seminar in Phoenix, Arizona, February 6, 1987.

11.   Burger, *op. cit.*, p. 91.

12.   For a fuller discussion of the arguments supporting and challenging the claimed truth-finding superiority of the adversary system, see Chapter 5.

13.   *Tehan v. U.S. ex rel Shott*, 382 *U.S.* 406, 416 (1966).

14.   Jerome Frank, quoting the nineteenth century English historian and essayist Lord Thomas Babington Macauley, in *Courts on Trial: Myth and reality in American Justice* (Princeton, N.J.: Princeton University Press, 1949), p. 80.

15.   Id., p. 81.

16.   Id., p. 102.

17.   Marvin Frankel, *Partisan Justice* (New York: Hill and Wang, 1978), p. 12. Frankel cited *Herring v. New York*, 422 *U.S.* 853, 862 (1975), as authority.

18.   Id.

19.   Thurman Arnold, *The Symbols Of Government*, (New York: Harcourt, Brace & Co., 1962), pp. 183-85.

20.   Judges rarely exercise their authority to question witnesses or call their own witnesses.

21.   Frankel, *op. cit.*, p. 14.

22.   Plato, Seventh letter, 341 c, quoted in J. Pieper, *Guide to Thomas Aquinas* (New York: Pantheon Books, 1962), p. 74.

23.   M. Grabmann, *Scholastiche Methode,* Vol. 2, p. 20, quoting Magister Radulfus. This theory is very similar to that of Sir Karl Popper's theory of scientific rationality, whereby truth is arrived at through a wholehearted dialectic of conjecture and refutation. See Karl Popper, *Conjectures and Refutations: The Growth of Scientific Knowledge,* Vol. 4 (London: Routledge and Kegan Paul, 1963), pp. 33-65, 114-19, 353, 355-63.

24.   Jerome Frank, *Courts On Trial, op. cit.*, p. 85.

25.   David Luban, "Calming the Hearse Horse: A Philosophical Research Program for Legal Ethics," 40 *Maryland Law Review* 451, 469 (1981).

26.   Jerome Frank, *op. cit.*, p. 85. The practice is hardly new. In *Attic Nights* (I,6,4), Second century A.D. Latin author Aulus Gellius quotes Titus Castricius: "It is the rhetor's [trial lawyer's] privilege to make statements that are untrue, daring, crafty, deceptive, and sophistical, provided they have some semblance of truth and can by any artifice be made to insinuate themselves into the minds of the persons who are to be influenced."

The specific means of trial attorney lying and distortion are covered more extensively in Chapter 5. For a descriptive taxonomy of trial lawyer duplicity, see Richard Underwood, "Adversary Ethics: More Dirty Tricks," 6 *American Journal of Trial Advocacy* 265 (1982).

Besides hindering the factfinder's role, attorney truth-corruption raises another issue: Can such behavior be ethically justified? Is the attorney exempt from moral judgment when he acts pursuant to the special professional ethics of the bar? This issue is discussed in Chapter 5.

27. Finman, T., *Civil litigation and professional responsibility* (Chicago: American Bar Center, 1969), p. 152.

28. E. Allen Lind, "The Exercise of Information Influence in Legal Advocacy," *Journal of Applied Social Psychology, 5(2)* (1975), pp. 127-43; John Thibaut and Laurens Walker, *Procedural Justice: A Psychological Analysis* (Hillsdale, N.J.: Erlbaum Associates, 1975), Chapter 5.

29. See R. Buckhout, "Eyewitness Testimony," *Scientific American, 231(6)* (December 1974), p. 23.

30. Philip Shuchman, "The Question of Lawyers' Deceit," 53 *Connecticut Bar Journal* 101, 102 (1979).

31. Marvin Frankel, "The Search for Truth: An Umpireal View," 123(5) *University of Pennsylvania Law Review* 1031, 1038, (1975).

32. Id., p. 1094.

33. Roscoe Pound, "The Causes of Popular Dissatisfaction With the Administration of Justice" 29 *American Bar Association Report* pp. 281-82 (1906).

34. J. Nightingale, ed., *Trial of Queen Caroline*, 3 vols., Vol.2 (London: J. Robins & Co., Albion Press, 1820-21), p. 8.

35. David Melinkoff, *The Conscience of a Lawyer* (St. Paul, Minn.: West Publishing, 1973), p. 188.

36. *Hickman v. Taylor*, 329 *U.S.* 495, 501, (1947).

37. See, e.g., *Brady v. Maryland*, 373 *U.S.* 83 (1963); *Clewis v. Texas*, 386 *U.S.* 707 (1967); *U.S. v. Gleason*, 265 *F. Supp.* 880 (S.D.N.Y., 1967), but cf. *U.S. v. Campagnuolo*, 592 *F.2d* 852 (5th Cir., 1979); and *U.S. v. Agurs*, 427 *U.S.* 97 (1976).

38. See, e.g., Wayne Brazil, "The Adversary Character of Civil Discovery," 31 *Vanderbilt Law Review* 1296-1361 (1978).

39. See Chapter 5 for illustrations.

40. Brazil, *op. cit.*, p. 1291.

41. Charles Curtis, "The Ethics of Advocacy," 4 *Stanford Law Review* 3 at p. 12 (1951).

42. For a more extensive and referenced assessment of the theoretical and empirical-based criticisms of the jury system, see Chapter 4.

43. See, e.g., Milton Green, "Juries and Justice—The Jury's Role in Personal Injury Cases," *University of Illinois Law Forum* (Summer 1962), pp. 152-171; Bruce Rashkow, "Abolition of the Civil Jury: Proposed Alternatives," 15 *DePaul Law Review* 419-21, 435 (1966); Gordon Bermant et al., *Protracted Civil Trials* (Washington, D.C.: Federal Judiciary Center, 1981), p. 1.

44. There has been little attempt to define competent jury decision making. One way is to break down the jury's task into components and see how it deals with each. For a useful list, see Nancy Pennington and Reid Hastie, "Juror Decision Making Models: The Generalization Gap," *Psychological Bulletin, 89* (1981), pp. 246, 249-55.

45. Rashkow, *op. cit.*, p. 419.

46. G.M. Bush, "Maniscalco Jurors Seek 2d Reading Of Key Testimony, " *Los Angeles Daily Journal,* 10/30/90, p. 2.

47. J.Alexander Tanford and Sarah Tanford, "Better Trials Through Science: A Defense Of Psychologist-Lawyer Collaboration," 66 *North Carolina Law Review* 741, 750 (1988).

48. Marcus Gleisser, *Juries and Justice* (New York: Barnes and Co., 1968), p. 229.

49. Bush, *op. cit.*

50. James Marshall, *Law and Psychology in Conflict*, 2d ed. (New York: Bobbs Merrill, 1980), p. 140.

51. For a report on a recent representative study, see Michael Allen, "When Jurors Are Ordered to Ignore Testimony, They Ignore the Order," *Wall Street Journal*, 1/25/88, p. 33.

52. Lisa Eichhorn identifies six factors which can impair a juror's ability to follow instructions to disregard evidence or use it for a limited purpose:
    1. Repetition of the inadmissible evidence at trial.
    2. Perceived salience of the evidence.
    3. Style and level of insistence of the judge in delivering the instruction to disregard.
    4. Jurors' perceptions of an invasion by the judge of their role on the decision process.
    5. Jurors' understanding of and agreement with policies underlying exclusionary rules.
    6. Jurors' comprehension of language used in instructions.
    Lisa Eichhorn, "Social Science Findings and the Jury's Ability to Disregard Evidence Under the Federal Rules of Evidence," *Law and Contemporary Problems 52(4)* (Autumn 1989), pp. 341 at 349.

53. Compare two Third Circuit cases: In *U.S. v. Gray*, 468 *F2d*. 257, 259-60 (1972), the prosecution asked the defendant, "You say your wife was killed. You killed her, didn't you?" In *U.S. v. Heckman*, 479 *F.2d* 726, 730-31 (1973), the jury heard testimony that the defendant was told "you

did a fine job of fire bombing the . . . [b]uilding." The court reached opposite conclusions in the two cases as to whether the statement in question "irretrievably seared itself into the conscious and subconscious minds of the jury."

54. See, e.g., *Irvin v. Dowd*, 366 *U.S.* 717, 722 (1961).

55. A complete exposition of this project is by Professor Harry Kalven, Jr., "Report on the Jury Project," from *Conference on Aims and Methods of Legal Research* (Ann Arbor, Mich.: University of Michigan Law School, 1955).

56. See Hans and Vidmar, *op. cit.*, p. 74; Hans Zeisel and Shari Diamond, "The Effect of Peremptory Challenges on Jury and Verdict: An Experiment in a Federal District Court," 30 *Stanford Law Review* 491, 525-30 (1978).

57. Dale Broeder, "The Functions of the Jury: Facts or Fiction," 21 *University of Chicago Law Review* 386, 393 (1954).

58. Victor Gold, "Covert Advocacy: Reflections on the Use of Psychological Persuasion Techniques in the Courtroom," 65 *North Carolina Law Review* 481 (1987); Cf. Tanford and Tanford, *op. cit.*

59. See John Riley, "Voir Dire Debate Escalates Over Lawyers' Participation," *The National Law Journal,* December 24, 1984, pp. 1, 24; Valerie Hans, "The Conduct of Voir Dire: A Psychological Analysis," *The Justice System Journal, 11(1)* (1986), pp. 40, 47.

60. The probable origin of the rule stems to the time when illiteracy was common. See Victor Flango, "Would Jurors Do A Better Job If They Could Take Notes?" *Judicature, 63(9)* (April 1980), pp. 436, 437. Yet despite current levels of literacy, the rule perseveres.

61. See, e.g., Ralph Slovenko, Commentary on "Rethinking the Adversarial Trial," *American Journal of Forensic Psychiatry, 14(3)* (1993), p. 48.

62. Bertram Edises, "One-Way Communication: Achilles' Heel of the Jury System," 13 *Judges Journal* 78-80 (1974).

63. To be precise, the attorney can only request the exclusion. The judge has the discretion to grant or deny the request. See, e.g., Federal Rules of Evidence 403: "Although relevant, evidence may be excluded if its probative value is substantially outweighed by the danger of unfair prejudice, confusion of the issues, or misleading the jury, or by considerations of undue delay, waste of time, or needless presentation of cumulative evidence." *Federal Rules of Evidence for United States Courts and Magistrates* (St. Paul, Minn.: West Publishing, 1975).

64. Among the more common evidence-excluding rules are the hearsay rule, the Fourth Amendment exclusionary rule, the Fifth Amendment right to refuse to testify, the prejudicial evidence rule (e.g., prior crimes), all privileged communications, the opinion rule and the best evidence rule.

65. Edmund Morgan, "The Jury and the Exclusionary Rules of Evidence," 4 *University of Chicago Law Review* 247, 249, (1936). As a means of attaining these non-truth values the adversary system thus arguably acquires an independent justification notwithstanding its role in detracting from the jury's search for truth.

66. Karl Kunert, "Some Observations on the Origin and Structure of Evidence Rules Under the Common Law System and the Civil Law System of 'Free Proof' in the German Code of Civil Procedure," 16 *Buffalo Law Review* 122, 163 (1967).

67. Nancy Pennington and Reid Hastie, "Practical Implications of Psychological Research on Juror and Jury Decision Making," *Personality and Social Psychology Bulletin, 16(1)* (March 1990), pp. 90, 91.

68. See, generally, Buckhout, *op. cit.*, pp. 23-31; Elizabeth Loftus, *Eyewitness Testimony* (Cambridge, Mass.: Harvard University Press, 1979).

69. James Marshall, Kent Marquis and Stuart Oskamp, "Effects of Kind of Question and Atmosphere of Interrogation on Accuracy and Completeness of Testimony," 84(7) *Harvard Law Review* 1620, 1637 (1971).

70. James Marshall, *op. cit.*, pp. 157.

71. 476 *U.S.* 162 (1986).

72. Id., p. 171.

73. Craig Haney, "Psychology and Legal Change: The Impact of a Decade," *Law and Human Behavior, 17(4)* (1986), pp. 371 at 378.

74. See J. Van Dyke, *Jury Selection Procedures*, (Cambridge, Mass.: Ballinger Publishing, 1977); Valerie Hans and Neil Vidmar, *Judging The Jury* (New York: Plenum Press, 1986), pp. 63-78.

75. Phoebe Ellsworth, "Are Twelve Heads Better Than One?" *Law and Contemporary Problems*, *52(4)* (Autumn 1989), pp. 205, 207.

76. Warren Burger, "Isn't There A Better Way," 68 *American Bar Association Journal* 274 (March 1982).

77. M. Katish, quoting Mahatma Ghandi's autobiography in *Taking Sides: Clashing Views On Legal Issues*, 2d ed. (Guilford, Conn.: Dushkin Publishing Group, 1986), p. 14.

78. Austin Sarat, "Alternatives in Dispute Processing: Litigation in Small Claims Court," *Law and Society Review, 10* (1976), pp. 339-375.

79. A small claims court would be a practical alternative, but this has certain drawbacks. See Chapter 6.

80. See Marc Galanter, "Reading the Landscape of Disputes: What We Know and Don't Know (And Think We Know) About Our Allegedly Contentious and Litigious Society," 31 *UCLA Law Review* 4 (1983).

81. Sanford Jaffe, "The Adversary System: Is There A Better Way?" *New Jersey Law Journal*, 5/26/83, pp. 1, 9.

82. Burger, "Isn't There A Better Way?" *op. cit.*, p. 275.

83. Id.

84. Id., p. 276
85. Jethro Lieberman, *The Litigious Society* (New York: Basic Books, 1981), p. 173.
86. Jaffe, *op. cit.*, p. 9.
87. Lieberman, *op. cit.*, p. 171.
88. 419 *U.S.* 565 at 591 (1975).
89. Paul Verkuil, "The Ombudsman and the Limits of the Adversary System," 75 *Columbia Law Review* 845, 853 (1975).
90. William Rehnquist, "The Adversary Society: Keynote Address of the Third Annual Baron de Hirsch Meyer Lecture Series," 33 *University of Miami Law Review* 1 (1978).
91. Rehnquist, *op. cit.*, p. 18.
92. In civil cases, the typical remedies are money damages, rescission or some injunction to do or not do something. Courts ordinarily would not allow such remedies as barter of services, exchange of properties, apology or other form of retribution. As an example of the latter, some altruistic plaintiffs injured in products liability cases requested that the defendants rewrite their products' warnings to prevent similar injuries to others. Carrie Menkel-Meadow, "Toward Another View of Legal Negotiation: The Structure of Problem Solving," 31(4) *UCLA Law Review* 754 at 789, 805 (April 1984).
93. See Stuart Scheingold, *The Politics of Rights* (New Haven, Conn.: Yale University Press, 1974), p. 159.
94. See, generally, R. Fisher and W. Ury, *Getting To Yes: Negotiating Agreement Without Giving In* (New York: Penguin Books, 1981).
95. James Marshall, "Lawyers, Truth and the Zero-Sum Game," 47 *Notre Dame Lawyer* 919, 923 (1972).
96. Lon Fuller, "The Forms and Limits of Adjudication," (unpublished paper, 1958), p. 36.
97. John Coons, "Approaches to Court-Imposed Compromise—The Use of Doubt and Reason," 58 *Northwestern University Law Review* 750 at 771 (1964).
98. See the discussion of court imposed compromise in Chapter 7.
99. Coons, *op. cit.*, p. 788.
100. Roscoe Pound, quoted in Jerome Frank, *Law and the Modern Mind* (Garden City, N.Y.: Doubleday, 1930), p. 60.
101. Mary Ann Glendon, *Abortion and Divorce in Western Law* (Cambridge, Mass.: Harvard University Press, 1987).
102. I disagree with these specific requirements. They are mentioned only as part of an overall problem solving approach which, in many instances, may be preferable to our characteristic all-or-nothing rights approach.
103. Larry Letich, "Abortion: Bad Choices," *Tikkun*, *4* (July-August 1989), pp. 22-26.

104. Scheingold, *op. cit.*, pp. 151-2. See generally, J. Shklar, *Legalism* (Cambridge, Mass.: Harvard University Press, 1964).

105. Of course, deviation from the rule-solubility of disputes concept implies a measure of divergence from our near-exclusive reliance on precedent. Advocating the circumstances and mechanics of such a departure is beyond the scope of this book. It is intended here only to suggest that rigid adherence to pre-existing rules of law renders us the servants of the law, a state of affairs deserving re-evaluation.

106. David Ebel, "Bar Programs—Other Ways To Resolve Disputes," 6 *Litigation* 25, 52 (1980).

107. FRCP 54(c), 15(b). The federal courts and the many states adopting the federal rules have the most liberal pleading system.

108. See Mirjan Damaska, *The Faces of Justice and State Authority* (New Haven, Conn.: Yale University Press, 1986), pp. 118-19.

109. See, e.g., FRCP 16(b).

110. Resnik, *op. cit.*, p. 380. Other problems arise in connection with the enhanced role of the judge in pretrial management. In urging parties to settle, she must avoid coercion. Further, immersion in the details of the case may impair her impartiality at trial (see the discussion *infra*); but this objection can be met by assigning a different judge to the trial.

111. William Simon, "The Ideology of Advocacy: Procedural Justice and Professional Ethics," 1978 *Wisconsin Law Review* 29 at 125 (1978).

112. Douglas Rosenthal, *Lawyer and Client: Who's In Charge?* (New York: Russell Sage Foundation, 1974), p. 175.

113. Jerold Auerbach, *Unequal Justice: Lawyers And Social Change In Modern America* (New York: Oxford University Press, 1976); Jerome Carlin and Jan Howard, "Legal Representation and Class Justice," 12 *UCLA Law Review* 381 (1965); Austin Sarat, "Studying American Legal Culture: An Assessment of Survey Evidence," 11 *Law and Society Review* 427 at 435-38, 464-65 (1977).

114. John Thibaut and Laurens Walker, *Procedural Justice: A Psychological Analysis* (Hillsdale, N.J.: Erlbaum Associates, 1975), pp. 117ff; Stephen LaTour *et al.*, "Some Determinants of Preference for Modes of Conflict Resolution," *Journal of Conflict Resolution*, *20* (1976), pp. 1531-45.

115. Robert Hayden and Jill Anderson, "On the Evaluation of Procedural Systems in Laboratory Experiments: A Critique of Thibaut and Walker," *Law and Human Behavior*, *3(1/2)* (1979), p. 32.

116. Brazil, *op. cit.*, pp. 1314-15.

117. Rosenthal, *op. cit.*, pp. 96, 144.

118. See Alvin Rubin, "A Causerie on Lawyers' Ethics in Negotiation," 35 *Louisiana Law Review* 577 (1975). See also Marc Galanter, *op. cit.*; Rosenthal, *op. cit.*; L. Ross, *Settled Out Of Court: The Social Process Of Insurance Claims Adjustment*, 2d ed. (1980).

119. Geoffrey Hazard, *Ethics In The Practice Of Law* (New Haven, Conn.: Yale University Press, 1978), p. 133.
120. This is not to intimate that attorneys routinely suborn perjury. Clients are certainly coached, however, on the style of their prospective testimony and what not to volunteer.
121. Mack Borgen, "Structural Inadequacies and True Costs Lurk," *Los Angeles Daily Journal*, 10/16/91, p. 7.
122. Simon, *op. cit.*, p. 125.
123. Gleisser, *op. cit.*, pp. 253-254.
124. See, e.g., Edmund Morgan, *Some Problems of Proof Under the Anglo-American System of Litigation* (New York: Columbia University Press, 1956), p. 34; Martin Golding, "On the Adversary System and Justice," in Richard Bronaugh, ed., *Philosophical Law* (Westport, Conn.: Greenwood Press, 1978), p. 115.
125. In a famous critique, former Chief Justice Warren Burger decried the lack of skills among trial advocates. Among other inadequacies, he scored the lack of skill in direct and cross-examination, and the time wasted in developing irrelevant facts. Warren Burger, "The special skills of advocacy: Are special training and certification of advocates essential to our system of justice?" 1973 *Fordham Law Review* 42, 227 (1973).
126. See "Habeus Corpse," *The New Republic*, July 15 and 22, 1991.
127. See Frank, *Courts On Trial*, *op. cit.*, p. 121.
128. See Peter Cotes and Thelma Nicklaus, *The Little Fellow: The Life and Work of Charles Spencer Chaplin* (London: Bodley Head, 1951), p. 77; and Charles Maland, *Chaplin and the American Culture* (Princeton, N.J.: Princeton University Press, 1980), pp. 201-206.
129. Franklin Strier, "Through The Jurors' Eyes'," *The ABA Journal*, 74 (October 1988), pp. 78-81.
130. Id., p. 80.
131. Id.
132. Id.
133. Gold, *op. cit.*, pp. 498, 501-504, 511.
134. Id., p. 494.
135. William O'Barr, *Language, Power and Strategy in the Courtroom* (New York: Academic Press, 1982), p. 69.
136. Id., pp. 71-75.
137. James Gobert, "Can Psychologists Tip The Scales Of Justice?" *Psychology Today* (February 1984), pp. 38-39.
138. Gold, *op. cit.*, pp. 492-93, 496.
139. Auerbach, *op. cit.*, p. 5.
140. *The New Yorker*, 12/24/73, p. 52.
141. Marvin Frankel, "An Immodest Proposal," *The New York Times Magazine*, 12/4/77, p. 92.

142. Gleisser, *op. cit.*, p. 326.
143. See, e.g., O'Barr, *op. cit.*, on the Duke University Law and Language Project studies of courtroom strategies. See, also, the studies conducted under the aegis of the National Institute for Trial Advocacy using computer technology to evaluate the effect of advocacy tactics on jury thinking, reported in "Judge and Jury Wired in Nita City," *The Docket* (Winter 1986), at 1.
144. *Ferguson v. Moore*, 98 *Tenn.* 342, 351 (1897).
145. See Warren Burger, "The State of Justice," *A.B.A. Journal* (April 1984), at 62 (citing the steep decline of public confidence in attorneys).
146. William Vogeler, "All the Court's a Stage," *Los Angeles Daily Journal*, 4/18/93, section II, pp. 1, 18.
147. Gold, *op. cit.*, p. 502.
148. 466 *U.S.* 648 (1984).
149. *Strickland v. Washington*, 466 *U.S.* 668 (1984).
150. Id.
151. *Burger v. Kemp*, 107 *Supreme Court Reporter* 3114 (1987).
152. Typical are the delay-reduction standards adopted by the Los Angeles Municipal Courts for civil cases, beginning in 1991. The rules establish as court policy strict judicial management for case disposition: 90 percent of all civil cases must be completed within one year of filing; 30 days for unlawful detainer and small claims court actions. The rules complement similar standards adopted earlier for criminal cases. See Jean Guccione, "Delay-Reduction Standards Adopted," *Los Angeles Daily Journal*, 12/12/90, p. 3.
153. See Resnik, *op. cit.*
154. An exception applies to criminal cases in federal and most state courts. Under the "plain error rule," an appellate court may reverse a court decision in the event an attorney fails to make a timely objection to improper conduct by the opposing attorney, if the action of the opposing attorney constituted "plain error." See Federal Rules of Evidence 103(d). However, "invocation of the plain error doctrine is often urged, but appellate courts seldom oblige." Graham Lilly, *An Introduction to the Law of Evidence* (St. Paul, Minn.: West Publishing, 1979), p. 381.
155. Charles Wolfram, *Modern Legal Ethics* (St. Paul, Minn.: West Publishing, 1986), pp. 620-22.
156. ABA, *ABA Code of Judicial Conduct* (Chicago: Author, 1989), Canon 3.
157. Lilly, *op. cit.*, p. 14.
158. Harry Kalven and Hans Zeisel, *The American Jury* (Chicago: University of Chicago Press, 1971), pp. 418-421.
159. Id., p. 425.
160. Albert Ehrenzweig, *Psychoanalytic Jurisprudence* (Dobbs Ferry, N.Y.: Oceana Publications, 1971), p. 265.

161. This subject is discussed in greater detail in Chapter 5.
162. See MRPC 1.2(b): "A lawyer's representation of a client, including representation by appointment, does not constitute an endorsement of the client's political, economic, social or moral views or activities."
163. Quoted in Frey, "Nice Guys Don't Have to Finish Last," *Manhattan Law*, 8/9/88, p. 9.
164. See Comments to MRPC 3.3.
165. MRPC, p. 7.
166. Grant Gilmore, *The Ages Of American Law* (New Haven, Conn.: Yale University Press, 1977), p. 111.
167. See, e.g., Wolfram, *op. cit.*, pp. 622-25, 645-54; Underwood, *op. cit.*
168. Richard Wasserstrom, "Lawyers as Professionals: Some Moral Issues," 5 *Human Rights* 1 at 13 (1975).
169. See, generally, this chapter, *supra*; Wolfram, *op. cit.*, pp. 566-68.
170. Lieberman, *op. cit.*, p. 171.
171. James Holbrook, *A Survey of Metropolitan Trial Courts, Los Angeles Area* (Los Angeles: University of Southern California Press, 1956), pp. 12-122.
172. Ralph Anderson and Associates, Judicial Council of California, *Guidelines for Determining the Impact of Legislation on the Courts* (San Francisco: Judicial Council, State of California, 1974), p. D-4.
173. National Center for State Courts, *On Trial: The Length of Civil and Criminal Cases* (Williamsburg, Virg.: Author, 1988), p. 3.
174. Id.
175. Gerhard Casper and Hans Zeisel, "Lay Judges in German Criminal Courts," 1 *Journal of Legal Studies* 135 at 149-51 (1972).
176. Werner Pfennigstorf and Donald Gifford, *A Comparative Study of Liability Law and Compensation Schemes in Ten Countries and the United States* (Oak Brook, Ill.: Insurance Research Council, 1991), p. 95.
177. Hans Zeisel *et al.*, *Delay In The Court*, 2d ed. (Westport, Conn.: Greenwood Press, 1978), pp. 181-86.
178. G. Van Kessel, "Adversary Excesses in the American Criminal Trial," 67 *Notre Dame Law Review* 405 at 475-76, (1992).
179. John Langbein, "Mixed Court and Jury Court: Could the Continental Alternative Fill the American Need?" 1981 *American Bar Foundation Research Journal* 195 at 196 (1981).
180. U.S. Department of Justice, *Sourcebook of Criminal Justice Statistics* (Washington, D.C.: Author, 1988), 539, tbls. 5, 12.
181. Zeisel *et al.*, *op. cit.* (1959), p. 88.
182. Louis Harris and Associates, *Judges Opinions On Procedural Issues* (April 1988), p. 91.
183. *Agenda for Civil Justice Reform*, A Report of the President's Council on Competitiveness (Washington, D.C.: Author, 1991), p. 3.
184. Id., p. 4.

185. Pfennigstorf and Gifford, *op. cit.*, p. 157.
186. To a much smaller extent, Japan has some contingent fee arrangements.
187. Eli Perkins, ed., *Wit and Humor of the Age* (Albany, N.Y.: Ross Publishing House, 1889), p. 387.
188. Pfennigstorf and Gifford, *op. cit.*, p. 78.
189. Id., p. 157.
190. E.g., *Florida Stat.* sec. 768.595 (1987); *California Bus. and Prof. Code*, sec. 6146 (West Supp. 1988).
191. E. P. McGuire, *The Impact of Product Liability* (New York: The Conference Board, 1988), pp. 8, 20.
192. See, e.g., Charles Rosenberg, "Alternatives to Litigation: Long-Term Solutions or Short-Term Fad?" *Management* (Fall 1983), p. 7.
193. The central thrust of the Thibaut and Walker findings is that procedure is a significant variable in the perception of trial justice.
194. *Estes v. Texas*, 381 *U.S.* 532, 540 (1965); *Tehan v. United States ex rel Shott*, 382 *U.S.* 404, 416 (1966); *United States v. Wade*, 388 *U.S.* 218, 256 (1967).
195. Edmund Morgan, "Judicial Notice," 57 *Harvard Law Review* 269 (1944).
196. Gerald Miller and F. Joseph Bolster, "Three Images of the Trial: Their Implications for Psychological Research," in Bruce Sales, ed., *Psychology in the Legal Process* (New York: Spectrum Books, 1977), pp. 23-28.
197. See the discussion of jury incompetence, this chapter, *supra,* and Chapter 4.
198. Frank, *Courts On Trial, op. cit.*, p. 20.
199. Charles Boston, "Some Practical Remedies for Existing Deficiencies in the Administration of Justice," 61 *University of Pennsylvania Law Review* 1 (1912).

CHAPTER 4

THE VERDICT ON JURIES

The jury trial is at best the apotheosis of the amateur. Why should anyone think that 12 persons brought in from the street, selected in various ways for their lack of general ability, should have any special capacity for deciding controversies between persons?

—Erwin Griswold[1]

Early 1993 began a year of infamy for jury trials. Fueled by omnipresent media reports, four sensational criminal trials captured the public's attention. Each involved a serious charge: murder, attempted murder or mayhem. Each defense attorney argued to the jury that the defendant was really a victim. Each defense worked.

Damion Williams was videotaped braining truckdriver Reginald Denny with a brick amidst the riotous maelstrom following the King I verdict. Defense counsel Edi Faal claimed that Williams, an African American, succumbed to a form of group or mob insanity resulting from the verdict. Therefore, Faal concluded, the jury should temper its verdict with an empathetic understanding of Williams' outrage. The jury complied. Williams was acquitted of the most serious charges.

A second case involved Lorena Bobbitt, who cut off her husband's penis while he slept and tossed it out the window. Lorena's butchery was in retaliation for alleged prior physical and emotional abuse she suffered at the hands of her husband John. The jury acquitting her of mayhem believed that she too was a victim.

The dual trials of the Menendez brothers, (discussed in Chapter 2), were the third and fourth cases. Lyle and Eric Menendez emptied their rifles into their parents (who at the time were watching TV and partaking of strawberries and cream), then went outside, reloaded, returned and finished the job. They were acting in self-defense according to their attorneys. The boys claimed to have been physically and sexually abused by the father, and allegedly feared for their lives. As previously noted, both juries hung (deadlocked). One juror actually voted for *involuntary* manslaughter.

However controversial, the Williams, Bobbitt and Menendez cases were not isolated aberrations from otherwise sound jury decisions. Around the same time these cases were being tried, other juries were delivering comparable verdicts. Some illustrations:

- In the same courthouse where juries deadlocked over the guilt of the Menendez brothers, a jury deliberated the fate of Moosa Hanoukai. He had bludgeoned his unarmed wife to death with a wrench. The defense attorney claimed Hanoukai was the victim of years of his wife's psychological abuse that included her insistence that he sleep on the floor. The jury sympathized, rejecting a murder conviction in favor of manslaughter. According to Hanoukai's attorney, some of the jurors came to the sentencing hearing to request probation.[2]

- In Fort Worth, Texas, a man was tried for fatally shooting two unarmed men. No problem: The defense attorney argued that the shooting was induced by "urban survival syndrome," a consequence of the tribulations of life in a slum. The jury hung.[3]

- A California case eerily similar to those of the Menendez brothers involved a young man charged with the murder of his father by rifle shooting. Years of physical and sexual abuse by the father were alleged. The defendant lay in wait after a family party before shooting a bullet into the victim's brain. When the defendant saw the victim was still breathing, he shot him twice more. The jury reduced the murder charge to manslaughter.[4]

Common to all these defenses—and perhaps a new Zeitgeist of jury trials—was a questionable thesis: Perpetrators of violent crimes are less culpable because they themselves were victims of some earlier abuse. The excusing abuse need not have come from the defendant's victim or even from any individual; general social or political conditions may be the source. There is another abuse here. Juries are abusing the judicial process and their role in it by swallowing wholesale the abuse excuse.

Few subjects evoke more spirited discussion and debate than juries. They are at once the object of public ridicule and acclaim. Some say the jury is largely obsolete, creating unnecessary delay and, as the above discussed trials illustrate, total unpredictability. Others praise it as a unique opportunity for the common citizen to participate in the administration of justice.

Juries are expected to ascertain the facts of the case from the evidence presented. Then they are assumed able to understand and correctly apply the law in arriving at their verdict. In both roles, the law presumes that jurors can suspend prejudices or biases formed outside of the courtroom.

The relationship between the jury and the adversary system is rarely discussed. Is it a benign interaction, or one which facilitates adversarial excesses? Anne Strick, author of *Injustice For All*, notes how the jury has been variously portrayed as both a convenient scapegoat and a panacea for our major complaints about the adversary trial.

[I]s the law too unjust? The fault lies not with adversary procedure, but with the often ignorant and prejudiced occupants of the jury box. Are our courts clogged, justice too slow? The drawn-out empaneling and deliberation of juries is responsible. Is the outcome of trial too unpredictable? The fault is not with the premise of legal certainty, but with the untutored laymen who apply law to facts. . . . Is the application of law, on the other hand, too mechanical? The jurors' human touch will ameliorate. Contrariwise, are judges too softhearted? The jury's down-to-earth hardheads will compensate. Is the Bench too calloused? The jurors bring a fresh, alert [approach to] each and every case. . . . Do the self-interested litigants present too narrow a picture? The jurors' composite acumen [and] competence will see beyond the partisans' bias. Is adversary procedure too brutal? The presence of those "emotionally susceptible" jurors (not the adversary ethic) encourages excess. Are the jurors biased? Jury *voir dire* is at fault. Does adversary procedure ignore context? *Voir dire* will inject it. Are the Court's instructions bypassed? The jury has capriciously nullified them. Does adversary procedure offer only bipolar solution? That same "jury nullification" is an escape hatch. Clearly, if juries did not exist, adversary procedure would invent them.[5]

Adversarial trials would be dramatically different without juries. Appearing before nonjury tribunals (trials without a jury, appellate courts and administrative hearings) attorneys are notoriously less histrionic and more straightforward in their presentations. Courtroom forensics, indeed the whole texture of the trial, radically change when there is no jury. Whether or not this is a consummation to be desired is discussed below. But first, a brief summary of the jury's development provides historical context.

Trial by jury is said to represent the rational mode of adjudication. That is because juries competed with and eventually replaced trials whose objective was not rational, but instead the ascertainment of divine will: Trial by oath, ordeal and battle.[6] In contrast, jury functioning involves use of reason rather than faith.

The first jurors were probably the Athenians, circa 400 B.C. Disputants argued their cases before large numbers of their peers—501 to 1,501 in criminal cases, 201 in civil cases. (Odd numbers were used to break ties.) Unlike our modern jurors, the Athenian jurors were constantly in court, and thus well acquainted with the legal rules. Yet as Aristotle's writings show, these juries prioritized general equitable considerations over strict application of legal principles. Individual treatment was preferred to precedent. The results, according to many, were excellent.[7]

To ensure the independence of their juries, known as *dikasteries*, the Athenians went to great lengths. When a prospective juror, or *dikast*, was selected for service, he was immediately segregated from all outside contact. Assignment to a case came only after such isolation. But the large size of the *dikasteries*—to prevent random contamination of *dikasts* with a particular bias—was also its principal weakness. Panels of this size prevented meaningful discussion, the essence of jury functioning. Instead, the dikasts merely voted, with the majority prevailing.[8]

More directly antecedent to the Anglo-American jury was the *jurare*. Developed in the Carolingian period by Charlemagne and his successors,[9] a *jurare* was a group (usually 12) of well-born neighborhood citizens appointed by the king to inform him or his representative of any crimes or land disputes. (Common litigants were the king, local lords or the church.) *Jurares* performed by swearing to the truth of their reportage—*jurare* means "to swear."

William the Conqueror brought this "royal tool for investigating into the affairs of common people"[10] to England following the Norman Conquest. To consolidate his power, he appointed royal factfinders known as "recognitors," who reported on tax and land disputes. As opposed to modern jurors, both the *jurare* and the recognitors functioned as witnesses. A prerequisite to their selection was personal knowledge of the facts and/or parties of the dispute.

A contrast of the early Greek and English juries reflects their respective cultures. "Congenial the jury may have been to the democratic soul of Athens," writes John Guinther, author of *The Jury In America*, "but hardly to a world in which the nobility and the priesthood were the self-announced, exclusive vessels for carrying out the will of God."[11] Recognitors were instruments of royal design, not of justice. They served at the pleasure and for the benefit of the king.

Jury use greatly expanded in England under Henry II. He plied it deftly in his power struggle against the church and feudal lords. The key to Henry's success was the notion of jury justice. Henry's courts provided a better and fairer quality of justice than the competing manorial courts of the barons and other feudal lords. By accurately divining the appeal of "judgment by neighbors," his courts approached hegemony, first in tax and land disputes, and later in other civil disputes and criminal cases. Only in the king's courts did poorer plaintiffs have a chance of prevailing over wealthy defendants. Royal court rulings were also more likely to be enforced. Modern common law has its roots in the rulings of Henry's courts because their judgments became accepted as common to all of England. Integral to the popularity of Henry's courts was the independent factfinding powers of the jury in civil cases. This not only allowed individuals to settle their own affairs, but also to successfully contest the church in the land disputes which frequently occurred. Thus evolved the first jury system since Athens by which individuals could seek resolution of their cases from their peers.[12]

Henry's battle with the barons led to one of history's most ironic twists. His courts' use of the jury weakened the barons' courts. In 1215 they retaliated by forcing Henry's son, John, to accept the reforms of the Magna Carta. One of its provisions profoundly entrenched the jury system: No "freeman" could be criminally penalized without a trial by his "peers." Of course, what the barons intended was that they would be judged only by other barons and feudal lords. Not for a moment did they envision the scope "freeman" would assume. Hence the elite group weakened by the jury became the instrumentality of its establishment as a pillar of Anglo-American trial justice for the masses.[13]

Gradually, the jury underwent changes. As lawyers increasingly brought their own eyewitnesses to confirm their clients' claims, juror-witnesses became subordinated to party-witnesses. The jury slowly transformed into its modern role of hearing witnesses, rather than acting as witnesses; from fact-reporting to factfinding.

Another transformation of the jury's role occurred during the Tudor-Stuart reigns (1485-1649). Rather than a "royal tool," the jury was increasingly seen as protection *against* the crown, whose judges and juryless Star Chamber courts were perceived as unscrupulous agents of royal will. Initiated in 1487, the Court of the Star Chamber became the scourge of those accused of political crimes. Jury verdicts against the crown were not without peril because the Star Chamber commonly used tactics borrowed from the Spanish Inquisition. Jurors deciding for the Crown's opponent often found themselves called before the Star Chamber, then imprisoned, fined and even starved to induce a reversal. Not until what came to be known as Bushel's Case in 1670 were jurors immunized from punishment for acquitting a defendant.[14] So juries came to be popularly regarded as a check on royal judges doing the Crown's bidding.

In the American colonies, juries often stood up to the hostile, British-controlled judges. The most chronicled instance was the sedition trial of publisher John Peter Zenger in 1734.[15] Zenger's paper, the *New York Weekly Journal*, had published articles highly critical of New York's unpopular new royal governour, William Cosby. Under the law, this was seditious libel. Cosby had Zenger arrested. When Zenger could not pay the prohibitively high bail, he was jailed. Zenger had no legal defense under the prevailing law—not even the truth of the published accusations. But the jurors responded to the emotional appeal of Zenger's attorney. He exhorted them to challenge Britain's tyranny over American freemen. In one of the early instances of jury nullification (discussed later in this chapter), the jury acquitted Zenger. Thus arose the jury's widespread reputation in America as a bulwark against oppressive government.

Still another fundamental change in the American jury occurred in the nineteenth century. Until then, juries generally had the right to decide issues of law as well as questions of fact. The Federalists, representing merchants, industrialists and creditors, sought a more predictable trial system, and one more sympathetic to their interests. Judicial control over the legal issues met this need. Nevertheless, following the Bushel case it was still generally conceded that jurors could determine law as well as facts in England and her American colonies. This juries did with regularity. A prominent example was the refusal of northern juries to convict those who aided fugitive slaves in violation of the Fugitive Slave Act. Not until late in the nineteenth century was the primacy of judges over questions of law clearly established. Since then, when juries ignore the judge's instructions in their decision making, they do so in spite of the law, not in pursuance of it.

Two forces impelled the spread of the lay jury beyond England and America. An expanding British Empire exported it to Asia and Africa (as well as America), while the French Revolution triggered the growth of the lay jury (as a populist check on government) to most of the other nations of continental Europe. Jury use in most of these countries, however, was limited to trials of major crimes. Eventually, the lay jury failed in all but the United States and British Commonwealth countries.[16] Even England has virtually eliminated it in civil cases. But other forms of lay participation in the judicial process persist, most notably the mixed lay-professional "juries" of France and Germany. These trials use a combination of lay and professional members.[17]

The United States thus remains the last bastion of extensive lay jury use in criminal and civil cases. Yet there are major exceptions in American courts. Jury trial is generally unavailable as a matter of right to criminal defendants if the maximum sentence they can receive cannot exceed six months. Larger exceptions apply to civil cases. Only cases at common law (essentially those demanding money damages) are triable by jury as a matter of right. Inherited from England is the exclusion of juries in all equity cases. Also generally exempt are rights arising solely out of statutory law. Moreover, a waxing cry for elimination of the jury trial in cases involving complex legal and factual issues (discussed later in this chapter) may presage further constriction of jury use.

Given its unique position in American history and lore, the jury has been the subject of myriad writers without as well as within the legal profession. Because popular opinion is greatly informed by major American fiction writers, University of Illinois English professor Emily Watts evaluated their depictions of juries. Watts' investigation revealed decidedly unflattering portrayals. She concludes that the typical jury is characterized as incompetent and ill-motivated.

Its deliberations often revealed ignorance, personal prejudice, and lack of concern. The juror's presumed impartiality is often shown to have been compromised by local, family, racial and/or political prejudice. It is also characterized as an institution in which its members are easily corruptible by money, fear, the enticement of a better job or a gain in status and power, and *manipulation by skillful attorneys*. . . . [T]he jury is more often depicted negatively and cynically than it is in positive and admiring tones. The jury is more often described as representing the lowest common denominator of the people rather than as the common man personified by dignity, independence and morality. The jury as an institution in American literature is generally tainted by prejudice, ignorance, and lack of will.[18] (Emphasis added.)

Are these disparagements generally accurate? Or are they hoary literary canards? The remainder of this chapter undertakes a response to this critical question.

Both intrinsic and imposed limitations can cause jury dysfunction, commonly referred to as jury "incompetence." Intrinsic limitations result from using lay jurors to perform roles which, for them, are novel and often difficult. Court-imposed limitations, in the form of procedural rules, often exacerbate the innate difficulties facing the jurors. Finding the facts and applying the law to them are the jury's basic functions. The following describes how intrinsic juror limitations plus those imposed by court procedure bear adversely upon jury performance.

FACTFINDING

The jury is the "finder of fact." More descriptively, it chooses from competing versions of the facts presented by the opposing attorneys. Unlike other factfinders, it does not independently develop the facts. Essentially, it is the passive recipient of information. At various points of the trial the judge instructs the jury as to the admissibility of the evidence, the specific purpose for which it is to be used, and (sometimes) the weight to be given it.

Intrinsic Limitations

The belief grows that a lay body is inadequate to the factfinding role of the jury. Typical is the criticism of historian Carl Becker: "Trial by jury, as a method of determining facts, is antiquated and inherently absurd—so much so that no lawyer, judge, scholar, prescription-clerk, cook, or mechanic in a garage would ever think for a moment of employing that method for determining the facts in any situation that concerned him."[19]

Much research supports this charge, indicating that jurors lack adequate memories for recalling trial testimony and have difficulty making decisions based on statistical or probabilistic information.[20] Most of the criticism focuses on civil cases, especially complex litigation. For it is here that jurors most commonly confront the lengthy, complicated and highly technical fact situations. In their book on jury performance, Selvin and Picus explain some of the reasons why jury performance in these cases is suspect.

Psychological theory indicates that when presented with complex information on a great number of facts, individuals generally perceive one or a few generalizations that summarize and provide meaning for the information rather than the specific details. As a result, memory is "reconstructive"; people recall the general impression of an event or the information presented along with some of the details.[21]

The authors go on to note that the jury's *collective* understanding and memory may be better than most individual jurors, especially when enhanced by jury room discussion. "However," they add, "some researchers have recently demonstrated that in terms of understanding, juries rarely perform up to the ability of their best member."[22]

An especially perplexing task for lay jurors is to assimilate and select in some rational manner from the competing testimonies of *expert witnesses*. This "battle of the experts" tends to confound factfinders, especially juries. Studies show juries attach great weight to expert testimony.[23] Because of the jury's ignorance and naivete, this creates obvious potential for corruption of jury decision making. An advantage lies with the party whose expert has the most persuasive forensic skills rather than the most authoritative and meritorious testimony.

This problem is avoidable. Courts could make greater use of neutral, court-appointed experts. A continuing curiosity is why they do not. We can speculate generally that this reluctance is in part due to the judiciary's traditional concern for retaining the appearance of impartiality and the cognate fear of unduly influencing the jury.

Another concern is that court-appointed experts would be too influential. That is, jurors may give more weight to the testimony of a court-appointed expert than an expert hired by one of the parties (a partisan expert) by dint of the fact that the former is chosen by the court. If so, there may be a corollary lowering of juror motivation to analyze and question the content of the nonadversarial expert's testimony. Yet none of these concerns were confirmed in a recent study.[24]

A basic assumption of the law has been that the jury can understand the case presented to it. In a case involving complex application of the antitrust law, the Third Circuit Court of Appeals said, "The law presumes that a jury will find facts and reach a verdict by rational means. It does not contemplate scientific precision but does contemplate a resolution of each issue on the basis of a fair and reasonable assessment of the evidence."[25] When the subject matter of litigation is perceptibly beyond the ken of the jury, some litigants have sought to circumvent a jury trial (in favor of a bench trial) in order to attain the "fair and reasonable assessment of the evidence" presumed by the law. But these litigants faced a constitutional impediment. The Seventh Amendment provides the right of jury trial in all suits at common law where the amount in controversy exceeds twenty dollars. Hence any attempt to avoid a jury trial must support a constitutional gloss which permits a *complexity exception* to the Seventh Amendment. Some federal courts have so interpreted the Constitution.[26] Each relied on a footnote to a 1970 U.S. Supreme Court decision, *Ross v. Bernhard*.[27] In *Ross*, the court said: "[T]he legal nature of an issue is determined" in part, "...by *the practical abilities and limitations of juries,...*" (Emphasis added.)[28]

In order to understand the constitutional significance of this language, one must appreciate the historical context of the law/equity distinction. At the time of the writing of the Seventh Amendment in 1791, cases in equity and cases in law were tried in separate courts. (Subsequently, they were merged so that the same court could hear and resolve both equitable and legal issues in one disposition.) The Seventh Amendment only grants the right of jury trial to cases at common law, that is, non-equity suits. Courts have generally interpreted this using an historical approach: A right of jury trial exists only when the suit involves a legal issue or remedy, most commonly the basic money damages suits. The *Ross* footnote suggests an inherent complexity exception when cases are too complicated to be heard in a suit at common law. Put differently, when a case is too complex to be amenable to jury resolution, there is no remedy "at common law." Therefore, the only trial remedy is in equity, where there is no jury. Language from Alexander Hamilton in the *Federalist Papers* buttresses this interpretation.

[T]he circumstances that constitute cases proper for courts of equity are in many instances so . . . intricate that they are incompatible with the genius of trials by jury. They require often such long, deliberate, and critical investigation as would be impracticable to men called from their occupations, and obliged to decide before they were permitted to return to them. The simplicity and expedition which form the distinguishing character of [the jury] mode of trial require that the matter to be decided should be reduced to some single and obvious point; while the litigations usual in chancery [equity] frequently comprehend a long train of minute and independent particulars. . . . [T]he attempt to extend the jurisdiction of the courts of law to matters of equity will . . . tend gradually to change the nature of the courts of law and to undermine the trial by jury, by introducing questions too complicated for a decision in that mode.[29]

The Third Circuit Court of Appeals took another tack in granting a motion to strike a demand for jury trial.[30] Rather than looking to the Seventh Amendment, this approach instead relies upon the Due Process clause of the Fifth Amendment, guaranteeing the right to a fair trial. This right is violated, said the court, when the complexity of the case exceeds the jurors' powers of comprehension. "We conclude that due process precludes trial by jury when a jury is unable to perform this task with a reasonable understanding of the evidence and the legal rules."[31] Where they ostensibly clash, the court found "the most reasonable accommodation between the requirements of the Fifth and Seventh amendments to be a denial of jury trial."[32] Thus this argument circumvents the need to find a complexity exception inherent in the Seventh Amendment.

The cases recognizing a complexity exception to the Seventh Amendment involved complex issues: accounting, securities, antitrust and patent infringement. But the complexity of litigation reflects that of modernity. As we progress scientifically and technologically, more and more litigated issues will be of far greater complexity than that contemplated by the drafters of the Constitution in 1791.

The model of jury factfinding embodied in the Constitution[33] holds that jurors are impartial. Controverting that model is the argument that jurors are naturally biased, and thus incompetent. For example, the juror's national or ethnic origin may influence his or her decision.[34] Ethnic origin and juror bias can be a particularly troublesome mix in civil rights cases.[35] Other examples of natural juror bias abound. Anthropologist William O'Barr has extensively studied the impact of witness speech patterns and appearance on jurors. O'Barr and his colleagues found that jurors tend to make decisions about witness credibility based on their style of speech, clothing, occupation and social status—notwithstanding the lack of any actual correlation.[36] For criminal cases, jurors tend to assume the defendant's guilt if he or she has a criminal record or has been charged with multiple offenses.[37]

Beliefs traditionally affecting jury decisions and decision making are frequently based on erroneous and archaic assumptions. For instance, jurors place more weight on eyewitness testimony than perhaps any other form of evidence. Yet a century of research shows that eyewitness accounts are notoriously unreliable.[38] Another misimpression relates to the weight given confident testimony: The more confidence displayed by the witness, the more accurate jurors treat his or her testimony, even though there is virtually no relationship between confidence and accuracy.[39]

Juror impartiality is but one facet of the adversary myth. Another is the presumed superiority of jury factfinding. Reason suggests otherwise. On the modern jury, "Abysmal ignorance constitutes a condition precedent in the qualification of jurors."[40] A writer who advocates abolition of the jury in civil cases observes of trial procedure:

[It] not only permits, but encourages the exclusion of jurors possessing the slightest knowledge of the facts he is supposedly summoned to determine. Thus, that which specifically qualified one to act as a juror at the inception of the system now specifically disqualifies him. This evolution has been termed progress.[41]

One undesirable consequence of the jury's ignorance, bias and susceptibility to influence by expert witnesses and attorneys is the unpredictability of *civil damage awards*. The secrecy and nonaccountability permitted by the jury's general verdict wreaks havoc with the predictability of the law. Frank lamented:

The general-verdict jury-trial, in practice, negates that which the dogma of precise legal predictability maintains to be the nature of the law. A better instrument could scarcely be imagined for achieving uncertainty, capriciousness, lack of uniformity, disregard of former decisions—utter unpredictability.[42]

Unpredictability of jury trial outcomes inestimably impairs the ability of business to furnish needed goods and services at affordable prices.[43] Voluminous pretrial discovery requests and drawn-out litigation deter managers from productive work. And, as noted in Chapter 3, the threat of potential liability leads substantial numbers of U.S. manufacturers to withdraw products from the market, discontinue product research and lay off workers. For those opting to stay and compete, available liability insurance dwindles. Predictability, on the other hand, facilitates settlement by decreasing the disparity between the expectations of the parties—as to their respective probabilities of prevailing at trial and the likely size of the award—and the actual outcome. A more stable economic environment liberates business to take the risks essential to a growth economy.

Several factors specifically contribute to erratic and capricious jury awards. First, a different jury hears every case, lessening the possibility of consistent awards applied to similar cases. Second, the courts use randomly selected laypersons, rather than professionals or a career judiciary. Third, the decision of twelve people is more unpredictable than that of one. Fourth, the general verdict shields juries from accountability or any obligation to explain the rationale of their awards. Last and most importantly, judges do not provide meaningful standards for damages. In fact, the instructions tell jurors that no guidelines exist.[44] Jurors receive only an instruction that the tort plaintiff is entitled to "fair, just and reasonable compensation" for his pain, suffering and disability now and into the future.[45] An obvious guideline would be what each party would have settled for. But jurors are never informed of the parties' pretrial settlement offers. The result, says Connecticut Superior Court Judge Robert Satter, is that juries "are forced to act blindly, without the most obvious guidelines."[46]

The lack of damage award guidelines for juries has fostered extremely high awards. In England, juries were abolished in personal injury cases partly because it was felt the damages awarded were unreasonably large.[47] In the United States, juries putatively award higher amounts if the defendant is perceived as having "deep pockets," that is, wealthy—typically corporations and governments. This view was confirmed by a series of studies conducted by the Rand Corporation's Institute of Civil Justice[48] and mock jury studies.[49]   A finding of the Harris survey judges also indicates the excessiveness of jury awards. About three-fourths of the federal judges and 45 percent of the state judges reported having reduced a jury damages award.[50]

U.S. jury damages awards grew markedly in recent decades, far exceeding those prevalent in their foreign counterparts. The most current data comes from one of the Rand studies in 1987. It compared jury verdicts in Cook County (Illinois) and San Francisco County from the early 1960s to the early 1980s. During that twenty year period, the average size of a plaintiff's verdict rose 217 percent in Cook County and 358 percent in San Francisco County. Almost all of the growth occurred between 1975 and 1984.[51]

Without guidelines, other factors influence American juries. For instance, although the existence and amount of a plaintiff's insurance coverage is inadmissible, jurors recognize that insurance companies—perceived as both demon and deep-pocket by many jurors—usually pay damage awards, and act accordingly. Moreover, plaintiffs' attorneys and the expert witnesses they increasingly retain have become far more proficient in eliciting large damage awards from juries. This is reflected in the Rand study data. Personal injury plaintiffs were 30 percent more likely to prevail in Cook County in the 1980s than in the 1960s; and 20 percent more likely in San Francisco County.[52]

A recent illustration of the waste jury unpredictability can cause occurred in a New York federal court. Author and psychoanalyst Jeffrey Masson sued *The New Yorker* magazine and writer Janet Malcolm for libel. Malcolm had interviewed Masson in 1983 and wrote two derivative articles for the magazine. Masson claimed Malcolm intentionally misquoted him regarding his iconoclastic views and sexual obsessions. This, he said, rendered him unemployable and a laughing stock in academic circles. The case went on for nine years, through appeals and rulings—including a 1991 ruling by the U.S. Supreme Court which established a new standard in libel cases—eventuating in an odd decision by the jury which left the case in limbo. The jury concluded that Malcolm had indeed libeled Masson under the new Supreme Court standard, but it was hopelessly deadlocked on monetary damages. The jury's inability to agree on damages wasted nine years of court time and considerable public and private resources.[53]

Why does this happen? The reason is clear: Jurors are not given damages guidelines. Juries certainly should be allowed the flexibility to exercise some judgment, but completely unguided discretion can lead to untoward results. The jury may give wild and erroneous awards. Or, as the Masson case demonstrated, the absence of guidelines can hamstring the lay jury just as surely as an inflexible formula.

A current trend indicates further unpredictability. Recently, smaller juries (less than twelve, typically eight or six) were instituted to realize administrative savings. Such benefits, however, may have dissipated. Smaller juries are now widely thought to increase the likelihood of bias and other sources of irrationality, resulting in more unpredictable and varying verdicts.[54] Evidence exists too that a smaller size impairs the jury's collective memory.[55] Another disadvantage of the move to smaller juries is that it reduces their (community) representativeness. The irony here is that the movement to smaller juries coincides with recent developments—statutes requiring more broadly based jury panels and increasing judicial control over *voir dire*—designed to increase jury representativeness.

Imposed Limitations

Compounding intrinsic factfinding limitations are numerous strictures *imposed* by traditional court procedure. Some of the strictures are imposed directly on juries, such as the widespread prohibition of juror note-taking and question-asking. Others impact jurors more indirectly but with as much consequence. Jurors can hardly be blamed for their factfinding incompetence. The trial process is more culpable: Attorneys offer evidence in no apparent logical order; exhibits are introduced without reference to their relevance; evidentiary items are left in abeyance, with nexuses furnished days later, if at all; witnesses rarely have the opportunity to offer straightforward narratives before disrupting objections by opposing counsel (after some objections, the jury must leave the courtroom while the evidential issue is argued before the judge). Absent the ability to ask clarifying questions, this procedural morass presents sizable cognitive impediments to jury factfinding.

As applied to a jury trial, the term "factfinding" is frequently a misnomer. When there are no eyewitnesses or dispositive physical evidence, the final decision devolves to juror determination of which side's testimony is more credible. In this exercise, jurors confront Procrustean limitations, not only by the ban on questions, but also by the truth-seeking guidelines prescribed or suggested by the judge. For instance, in determining the veracity of a witness, judges commonly urge jurors to observe additional things about the witnesses beyond the abstract content of their testimonies. These supplemental factors include the characters and motivations of the witnesses, the plausibility and internal consistency of their stories and, most importantly, the *demeanor* accompanying their testimonies. From these perceptions, it is believed, the falsity of the liar's testimony and the truth of the honest witness' story will be revealed.

But such judicial guidelines are hardly foolproof and, in some instances, outright unreliable. Illustrative is the consistency criterion just mentioned. "Unfortunately," comments lawyer and clinical psychologist Rex Beaber, "the data clearly indicates that honest people are often inconsistent, often telling varying versions of their truthful story, and commonly remember slightly different details depending on the circumstances. Indeed, honest people often make verifiable mistakes about unimportant details."[56]

Furthermore, without more specific guidance, these behavioral indices are useless in the hands of untrained observers. Some behaviors are more telling than others. Notwithstanding the old adage, "The eyes are the window to the soul," vocal stress and lower body language reveal more. In this regard, an interesting irony attends the factfinding environment presented the juries. As previously noted, judges often suggest to the juries that they take note of the witness' demeanor for insight into the veracity of the concomitant testimony. Yet the most revealing nonverbal behavior, lower body language, is usually hidden from the jury's view by the witness box.[57]

Asking Questions

Nothing inhibits factfinding more than an inability to independently investigate. In a trial, the primary means of investigating—witness interrogation—is typically denied the jury. One might be led to believe, therefore, that the occasional allowance of juror questions is a new trend. Yet Blackstone tells us that juror interrogation was permitted in English courts in the eighteenth century.[58] American trial records show juror questions were allowed by a few courts in the nineteenth century, with the practice becoming formalized in the United States in the 1970s. To date, no court has ruled juror interrogation unconstitutional.[59] Nevertheless, jurors rarely get to question a witness. Hardly any courts will affirmatively offer this prerogative to the jury, and the judiciary still generally rejects the occasional request by a jury seeking this power on its own initiative.

Why not allow juror questions? After all, "while justice is blind, jurors need not also be."[60] From the juror's perspective, the potential truth-seeking advantages of juror interrogation are obvious: Responses to juror questions can increase the information upon which the jury decides by fleshing out neglected evidence, clarifying the evidence and law, and identifying areas of misunderstanding.[61] Furthermore, by involving them more in the trial process, questions by jurors probably increase their attention and interest in the case.[62] Attorneys can benefit by restructuring their evidence presentation to improve juror understanding. Additionally, juror questions may flag juror biases to the judge and attorneys. This allows for correction before jury deliberation, when it is too late.

On the rare occasions when juror questions are permitted, a proposed question must first be approved by the judge and the attorneys. Tactically, this can pose a Hobson's choice to the attorney who objects to a juror's question: Either risk offending the juror or allow the introduction of incompetent but damaging evidence in response to the question. In the latter event, the only protection is the vigilance of the judge, who cannot be presumed to catch all inappropriate questions before they are answered nor all inadmissible testimony given in response to an improper juror question.[63] Indeed, the potential for profoundly upsetting courtroom protocol inheres in juror questions: They may result in surprises and destroy the attorney's strategy; they might become a nuisance to the judge; and the jury might draw wrong inferences if any attorney successfully objects to a juror's question. Another key concern over jury interrogation is that it can undermine juror impartiality: In questioning, the juror may become an advocate. Interrogating jurors may develop biases which threaten the integrity of the system.[64] Nonetheless, studies have not confirmed any of these concerns.[65] Moreover, any of them can be remedied on appeal.[66]

Taking Notes

Another substantial limitation imposed on juror factfinding is the inability to take notes. Curiously, neither the judge nor attorneys are expected to recall the proceedings without benefit of notes. Not so the untrained lay juror. No federal policy or law address note-taking specifically; the issue is entirely within the discretion of the trial judge. But a source in the Administrative Office of the Courts estimates that 90 percent of the federal judges do *not* allow it.[67] State court practice varies widely. Some states specifically disallow note-taking, usually by case law.[68] Others permit it by statute, although not all of these states permit the jurors to take their notes into the jury room. None allow jurors to take their notes home to study.[69] Most states leave it to the discretion of the trial judge, where the privilege has effectively been denied simply by not informing the jury of this option. Jurors are usually unaware of the possibility, or afraid to ask.

Given the prevalence of note-taking in the classroom, on the job and elsewhere, the resistance to note-taking is anomalous. The probable origin of the opposition stems from the time when illiteracy was common. Courts then may have feared the few literate jurors would exert disproportionate influence on the others.[70] Despite today's widespread literacy in America, a similar concern perversely endures. Opponents feel that while most jurors can take notes, few do, and those who do will emerge as leaders imposing their will on the others. The more skilled the notetaker, the argument goes, the more power wielded during deliberations.

A second objection voiced about note-taking is that it distracts jurors. Jurors may devote too much attention to their notes, especially trivial points, and miss important points or fail to notice witness demeanor. Alternatively, note-taking by some jurors may distract other jurors or the attorneys as they present their cases and interview witnesses. A third concern is that juror notes will be inaccurate or biased. Once in the jury room, both note-taking and nonnote-taking jurors may rely too heavily on the notes taken to the exclusion and detriment of their recall, producing a distorted view of the case.

None of the research to date has borne out any of these hypothesized disadvantages. Instead, experiments indicate that note-taking engages jurors, allowing them to feel more involved with the trial and therefore more satisfied with trial procedure.[71] Most importantly, note-taking aided juror recall.[72] Further, attorneys and judges responded positively to it.[73]

The same empirical findings did not support the concern that note-takers will exert undue influence. But even if they did, it is unclear why this is an inferior or undesirable means of the inevitable emergence of leaders within the group. Put differently, why is jury domination by forceful speakers better than domination by good note-takers?

Whether it be by express prohibition or the failure of the court to advise jurors of their note-taking privilege, the nonuse of note-taking precludes a potentially inestimable advantage to the trial process: substantially improved factfinding. Research indicates that note-taking improves recall and the overall performance of the note-taker.[74] The note-taking restriction is an unreasonable and needless impediment to the jury's search for truth.

Seeing a Transcript or Videotape of the Testimony

The note-taking restriction forces jurors to rely unnecessarily on their recall. Courts constrain the same reliance by denying jurors the opportunity to see a transcript of the testimony. Although the jury may request the opportunity to review specific testimony, most courts will respond simply by having the court clerk *reread* the requested testimony rather than providing a written transcript. As the California murder trial mentioned in Chapter 3 amply demonstrated, the testimony in lengthy trials can easily exceed the ineluctable limits of human recall.[75] Further demonstrated was the inefficacy of merely rereading voluminous amounts of testimony. Courts could permit jurors to review the evidence in a comprehensible manner by providing access to a transcript of the testimony plus copies of all other evidence of record.[76] Included would be charts, exhibits, summaries, depositions and other documents. The court could facilitate their retrieval by establishing a filing and indexing system.[77]

With the advent of videotaped testimony, a superior tool for jury factfinding and deliberation becomes available. California is presently experimenting with videotape as a substitute record of the trial, replacing stenographer notes. However, review of the videotape is apparently reserved for the attorneys and judge; jurors cannot avail themselves of it.[78] Tape has the advantage of replaying the demeanor which accompanies witness testimony. It remains to be seen whether courts will continue to prohibit juror viewing of requested testimony from videotaped trials, simply rereading the testimony instead. To do so would make little economic sense. Rereading would require a transcript from the tape, which presumably would defeat the cost savings of the videotape. But customs, especially legal customs, obdurately resist change. If the past is indicative, neither the transcribed nor videotaped trial will be available to the jury *in toto*.

Separating and Sequencing Issues

The continuous, unitary trial is also a major imposed obstacle to effective jury factfinding. We litigate everything at once. All the evidence on all the potential issues—no matter how lengthy, complicated, technical or scientific—is heard in one nonsegmented continuous trial. Adversary presentation does not lend itself to understanding of evidence. Partisan evidence presented by one side, often in disjointed segments, is separated by long delays from testimony on the same subject from opposing counsel. The resulting hodgepodge confounds the logical ordering of evidence necessary to systematic consideration of findings on specific issues.

A more juror-friendly approach would be to sever the trial issues. Potentially dispositive issues would be presented first, hearing evidence from both sides, and then would be resolved by the jury. In this way, the scope of subsequent issues could be narrowed or obviated. Occasionally, for instance, the issues of liability and damages in a civil case are severed and considered separately. A finding of no liability obviates the need for the jury to hear any evidence related to damages. Experiments also suggest that after a finding of liability the parties will settle.[79]

This seriatim examination of issues should markedly enhance jury factfinding by enabling the jury to focus on one issue at a time. Evidence thereby becomes more orderly and understandable to the jurors. Even if all the issues must eventually be considered, mitigating the confusion which attends processing evidence on multiple issues greatly simplifies the jurors' cognitive task. The longer and more complex the trial, the greater the potential benefits of issue separation. From 1968 to 1988, the percentage of civil trials in federal court which took no more than one day halved, while the number of trials lasting ten or more days almost quintupled.[80] As longer trials become more commonplace, the need for such severed-issue trials grows.

Despite the potential advantages and availability[81] of issue severance, it is rarely used. A 1989 Harris poll indicated strong judicial support for the practice.[82] Opposition to it more likely originates from the bar than the bench. A 1988 study found that issue severance may decrease the likelihood of a plaintiff verdict.[83]

Discontinuing Evidence Exclusions

Jury factfinding under the adversary system is as much the product of evidence *not* heard as by evidence which is. Myriad exclusionary rules can keep highly probative evidence from the jurors. Much of the bases for exclusion again trace to distrust of juror judgment—concern over possible misunderstanding or misuse of certain evidence. Morgan thought the exclusionary rules presume a jury composed of "a group of low-grade morons."[84] The exclusionary rules, writes Frank, can "limit, absurdly, the courtroom quest for the truth. The result, often, is a gravely false picture of the actual fact."[85]

John Maguire, one of the foremost scholars of American evidence law, cautions us against the false assumption that all evidence in a trial which is relevant and probative will be admitted for consideration.

[T]he real truth is that courts and legislatures, most particularly in these United States, have over the years made up many rules for excluding from trials a great deal of relevant evidence. Operating these rules has kept judges and lawyers and law professors so fully occupied that they have not yet satisfactorily explored the important questions of evidential cogency. They have been too busy deciding what should be kept out to make, much less teach, systematic appraisal of what they let in. So . . . evidence has to do with exclusion rather than evaluation.[86]

Yet it is Wigmore, the dean of evidence scholars, who sounds perhaps the harshest criticism of the exclusionary rules. Analogous to Pound's disparaging characterization of the adversary system as "the sporting theory of justice," Wigmore says of the exclusionary rules: "They serve, not as needful tools for helping the truth at trials, but as game-rules, afterwards, for setting aside the verdict."[87]

Exclusionary rules blindfold jurors to relevant evidence. But the blindfolding is often based on erroneous assumptions about how such information would influence juror behavior. For example, jurors may not be told that a civil defendant carries liability insurance[88] out of concern that the presumed deep pockets of the insurance company will lead jurors to inflate damage awards. If, however, the defendant is *not* insured, but—as is often the case—it is the jurors' *expectation* that he is insured, the defendant will have to pay an excessive amount.[89]

Distortions produced by the combination of blindfolding the jury and erroneous assumptions can also arise in criminal cases. Illustrative is the situation in state capital punishment cases where the jury is not informed of available alternative sentences if the capital defendant (the convicted murderer) is not sentenced to death, specifically life imprisonment without chance of parole. Exclusion of this information assumes the jury will be uninfluenced by the issue of whether and when the defendant will be released if not executed. In fact, ample evidence exists that jurors do consider the safety of the community in this circumstance.[90] Ignored (by the assumption) is the real possibility that jurors may be biased to opt for the death penalty when unaware of the community protection afforded by the alternative sentence.

In these and other situations, benighted assumptions about the salutary effect of exclusionary rules on jury behavior may unfairly bias litigants. One alternative would be to admit heretofore excluded evidence but with an instruction to the jury to disregard it or use it for a limited purpose. However, studies show such an instruction is usually ignored.[91] A more promising alternative is for the judge to *suggest* to jurors that they ignore the evidence, coupled with an explanation for the rationale for the suggestion.[92] This has a twofold advantage: It precludes the exclusion of evidence from corrupting jury decision making; and it treats the jury with respect for its judgment, a respect consonant with the paradigm of rational jury decision making. Conversely, indiscriminate perpetuation of the present exclusionary evidence rules risks grave pitfalls. Excluding relevant evidence forces the jury to operate in an information vacuum, within which untested, erroneous assumptions can wreak havoc with the right to a fair jury trial.

Just as long-held behavioral assumptions behind exclusionary rules can be flawed, so too can exceptions to those rules. The most common exclusionary rule, hearsay, has numerous exceptions. Nonetheless, little research has been done to test their validity. For instance, one of the hearsay exceptions applies to statements made during emotional arousal, the "spontaneous exclamation" rule. A statement made under this condition is admissible even though the person being quoted is not in court to be cross-examined by counsel and viewed by the jury, which is the rationale for excluding hearsay. The assumption is that people tell the truth under emotional stress. Little psychological evidence supports this. Moreover, the spontaneous exclamation rule ignores evidence that emotional stress tends to impair the accuracy of perception and recall.[93]

This is not to suggest that the law alacritously adopt all new empirical social science findings on jury behavior and change trial procedure accordingly. There is a constant tug and pull between the social sciences and the law. On the one hand, an economic vested interest in the *status quo* induces the conservatism of lawyers. On the other, social scientists urge the courts to modify established trial procedure to comport with the ever-expanding body of behavioral research. Typical is this admonition: "[D]ecisions about blindfolding would be better informed by systematic empirical evidence than by the untested behavioral assumptions that have traditionally undergirded decisions about whether to deny jurors information."[94] Clearly, the need for consistency and predictability in trial procedure militates against quick change, however cogent the appeal. By the same token, some responsiveness is necessary when unequivocal and consistent findings of jury behavior patterns contradict the assumptions behind trial procedure. In their book, *Inside The Jury*, Hastie, Penrod and Pennington weigh the opposing arguments regarding the historical resistance of procedural law toward change. They recommend a balanced view: Relax the barriers, but with due caution.

Legal institutions are conservative. They exhibit great resistance to new findings and new procedures. Resistance is greatest when new concepts challenge traditional assumptions or methods. Modern behavioral science creates many such threats to fundamental assumptions. New conceptions of motivation and preference replace the concept of free will; new empirical methods for determining truth challenge traditional rational analysis and trial procedures; and new trial tactics extend the adversarial competition to jury selection and beyond. However, the conservatism of legal institutions is sensible. . . . Uncritical acceptance of social science findings and theories is a mistake. . . .

In many instances the adversarial system shields the legal process of determining truth from the influence of equivocal or weak scientific procedures, such as clinical analysis of insanity or polygraphic lie detection. However, the acceptance of unequivocal, valid scientific results is also frustratingly slow. . . . [L]egal scholars, practitioners, and policy makers should be more open to the findings of behavioral science. Just as with the laws of society, those who ignore the laws of science will be controlled by those who understand them.[95]

ADMINISTERING THE LAW

Understanding the Judge's Instructions

After factfinding, the second component of the jury's role is administering the law to the facts as found. This, in turn, involves two discrete cognitive functions: understanding the law as given in the judge's instructions and correctly applying it to the facts. If juries do not understand the instructions, even the most astute and accurate factfinding may result in an incorrect verdict.

Wording of Instructions

Understanding the law is often the most difficult task for the juror; legal instructions can be extraordinarily complex and/or long.[96] Nonetheless, this task constitutes a critical interface between community standards—as represented by the jury—and the accumulated law, with all its nuances, subtleties and idiomatic jargon. The very legitimacy of the jury system is inextricably tied to a successful devolution of the law's administration from the bench to the jury. Albeit taking a relatively small part of the jury's time of service, the significance of this process cannot be underemphasized. All the received wisdom of the ages contained in the law is to no avail if the jury cannot understand the judge's instructions.

How well do jurors comprehend the instructions? To answer this question, we must put current practice into historical perspective. Prior to an 1895 U.S. Supreme Court decision, *Sparf and Hansen v. U.S.*,[97] juries decided issues of law as well as fact. *Sparf* created the obligation of judges to communicate, and juries to follow, the law via instructions to the jury. The resulting legal chaos was predictable. Each set of instructions bore the vagaries and often unintelligible idiosyncrasies of the instructing judge. Frank decried the situation:

What a crop of subsidiary semi-myths and mythical practices the jury system yields! Time and money and lives are consumed in debating the precise words the judge may address to the jury, although everyone who stops to see and think knows that these words might as well be spoken in a foreign language—that, indeed, for all the jury's understanding of them, they are spoken in a foreign language. Yet, every day, cases which have taken weeks to try are reversed by upper courts because a phrase or sentence, meaningless to the jury, has been included in, or omitted from the judge's charge [instructions].[98]

As more and more verdicts were reversed on appeal due to faulty instructions, the solution to the problem was the adoption of standardized "pattern" instructions. In 1938, a committee of California judges and lawyers published the *Book of Approved Jury Instructions*. By 1980, thirty-nine states had adopted some such version of pattern instructions.[99] Impelled by the desire to avoid appellate reversal, pattern instructions nonetheless sacrificed clarity, simplicity and, most importantly, comprehensibility.

A highly regarded series of studies by Elwork, Sales and Alfini tested the comprehensibility of pattern instructions. The subjects were divided into three groups: The first group received the standard Michigan pattern instructions on negligence; the second group received a version rewritten to improve comprehensibility; and a third group received no instructions at all. The results confirmed the fears of critics. Pattern jury instructions were about as effective in helping jurors understand the law as no instructions at all. Moreover, the group receiving pattern instructions made far more clear mistakes of law directly impairing the accuracy of their verdicts. That part of the negligence instructions relating to plaintiff's contributory negligence was ignored, rendering their findings incompatible with a verdict for the plaintiff. Pattern-instructed jurors were also more prone to discuss legally inadmissible evidence, such as whether the defendant or the insurance company would pay the award. Conversely, performance significantly improved in the group receiving the rewritten instructions.[100] Other studies confirm the appallingly low levels at which jurors comprehend instructions: Studies in six states place the level of comprehension at below 50 percent.[101]

Inaccurate verdicts due to incomprehensible instructions translate to gross miscarriages of justice. An example occurred in Washington, D.C., where a jury misunderstood the judge's instructions and found a defendant guilty when it really meant to free him. A *Newsweek* article recounts the story.

The case turned on the fate of Andre Sellars, charged with the murder of an acquaintance, one Epluribus Thomas, during a fight in a grocery-store parking lot. Sellars pleaded self-defense. The jury listened carefully to evidence that Epluribus and his brother Clyde had threatened Sellar's life through a whole weekend of arguments. When testimony ended, the jury heard a whole half-hour's worth of [judicial] instructions couched in classic legalese. . . . After deliberating overnight, the nine women and three men announced that they had found Sellars guilty—not of second degree murder as he was charged, but of manslaughter.

Later, chatting in the jury lounge, several of the jurors discovered that they had really meant to find Sellars innocent, but had misunderstood the judge's instructions. They knew that Sellars had killed Thomas, and thought that if they accepted Sellar's self-defense plea, manslaughter was the appropriate verdict.[102]

(The rule against double jeopardy barred another murder trial for Sellars. But the jury's error left open the possibility of a retrial for manslaughter.)

Pattern instructions create four problems for jurors. To begin with, instructions are usually replete with legal jargon and esoteric words. Second, the language tends to be abstract instead of concrete. Third, sentences are often lengthy, complex and grammatically constructed in the most confounding way, rife with subordinate clauses and double negatives. Fourth, the instructions are not presented in an organized way.

On the other hand, rewritten instructions using "hierarchical" or "algorithmic" organizational structures are easier to comprehend and memorize. A hierarchical structure parses high-level concepts into their lower-level components and then integrates them. Using an algorithmic structure, each idea presented is necessary to understand succeeding ones.[103]

One would think that given our knowledge of what causes confusion and misunderstanding of jury instructions: (a) the wording of instructions would be made more understandable, (b) attendant procedures would be adjusted accordingly (for example, providing written copies of the instructions), and (c) judges would take pains to assist jurors with supplemental explanations and clarifying illustrations. Nothing of the sort has happened. Ameliorative changes in procedure and wording are still just experimental in most states.

The absence of reform in this area of trial procedure may be more a function of politics than law or social science. That is, the tacit objective in retaining clearly deficient jury instructions and the restrictions on jurors seeking clarification may be to keep the instructions obfuscatory. Says Wallace Loh, an expert on the psychology and politics of trial procedure:

[W]riting (or rewriting) of instructions is not simply a technical task. It is also a political process that implicates (unarticulated) normative choices under the guise of correctly stating the law. It is not by chance that committees responsible for drafting pattern instructions are composed of members who represent a spectrum of views. *If improved clarity reduces conviction rates, the interests served are those of criminal defendants, not those of law enforcement and society in general. Assuming that the clarity can be calibrated, the determination of the degree of comprehensibility with which an instruction is drafted is an issue of policy rather than science.* Indeed, if clarity were the preeminent value, jurors could be informed by means of comprehensive lectures by judges (before and/or after the presentation of the evidence, together with an opportunity to ask questions) in lieu of brief instructions. The present system of instructions can be seen as the product of a series of practical, Solomonic accommodations between clarity and ambiguity, judicial authority versus jury discretion, and uniform rules versus individualized justice. Rendering the instructions more understandable would upset the equilibrium.[104] (Emphasis supplied.)

Timing and Form of Instructions

As if the wording of instructions were insufficiently troublesome to jurors, trial practice compounds the problem with timing and form strictures. Jurors reach a verdict by applying the dispositive law to the facts as they believe them to be. The law is withheld from them, however, until *after* they hear all the evidence. The objective is to keep them open to all information. Instead, this imposed ignorance denies them the capacity to discriminate the key factual issues from the mass of information they receive. They must interpret the evidence before they know what their decisional choices are. Essentially, the rules of the game are unknown to them until the game is over. Envision attempting to be the scorekeeper of an athletic contest without knowing what acts receive points or penalties until after the conclusion of the game. An already difficult task thus becomes harder.

Once the evidence is heard, other trial court practices compound the jurors' difficulties. Jurors are usually not given written copies of the instructions to take into the jury room or informed they can ask for help with the instructions. Those who do request help simply get the instructions reread to them, often to no avail. In a study of 405 jury trials, researchers Severance and Loftus found that, almost without exception, judges responded to juror requests for clarification of the instructions by refusing to paraphrase or in any way explain the confounding instructions.[105] Although research indicates distinct advantages to using written instructions, many judges oppose them. Their reasons include more work, delay, and concerns that only portions of the instructions will be read, and that blind or illiterate jurors will be at a disadvantage. All of these concerns are either groundless or easily remedied.[106]

Arguably, the practice of merely rereading unclear instructions violates the law in many states and certainly does nothing to further the interests of a just trial. The issue has gone before several state supreme courts.[107] In general, these decisions confirmed the judge's responsibility to ensure that the jury understand the law. Typical is this language from *Commonwealth v. Smith*:

[W]hen the trial judge has not succeeded in delivering instructions on the law in such a way that they will be understood by the jury, his charge is inadequate and justly open to objection by the defendant. As the very object of the instructions is to inform the jury as to the law applicable to facts of the case, the charge fails of its purpose when the jury is ignorant of the law applicable to any material question in the case.[108]

One jury's experience exemplifies the travails of jurors who seek clarification of unclear language from the court. Following King I and II, Rodney King sued the city of Los Angeles, the responsible police officers and their superiors in federal civil court seeking compensatory and punitive damages for his injuries. During deliberations over punitive damages, one of the jurors brought in a dictionary for a definition of "reprehensible," a word used in the judge's instructions. Judge John Davies promptly censured the juror, had the dictionary removed and admonished the jurors to consult only him for definitions. But when, a few days later, the jury requested the definitions of "combative resistance, aggressive resistance and active resistance"—terms which had been used repeatedly by use-of-force witnesses—Judge Davies told the jurors those terms were "not subject to legal interpretation. Give them whatever definition you think is appropriate."[109]

Applying the Law to the Facts

The preceding discussion dealt with the jury's ability to understand the instructions. Comprehension, however, is no guarantee that the jury will apply the law per the instructions in arriving at its verdict. The fact that the jury can understand the applicable law does not necessarily bespeak a willingness to apply it.

Jury Nullification

Most commonly, jury disregard of the law in criminal cases is in favor of leniency. Some judges and other procedural policymakers fear that clarifying jury instructions may broaden the jurors' perceived scope of discretion, leading to a form of jury lawlessness known as jury nullification: the intentional disregard of the law by the jury to avoid an unjust result. A paradox of the jury's role is that jurors are sworn to uphold the law (as instructed by the judge), yet can disregard it with impunity.

History is flush with examples of nullification.[110] Originating in the 1670 *Bushel* case in England, the first instance of nullification in America was the aforementioned *Zenger* trial in 1734. Juries commonly disregarded the fugitive slave laws in the nineteenth century and the prohibition laws in the 1920s. As might be expected in an area with no external control over or guidance to the jury, nullification cases lead to inconsistencies in the law. Two euthanasia cases illustrate. In the first, a New Jersey court heard the case of young Lester Zygmanik, accused of murdering his older brother, George. A serious motorcycle accident had left George paralyzed from the neck down. George pleaded to be put out of his misery. Lester complied in what he described as an act of love. Despite the judge's ruling that the term "mercy killing" could not be used, the jury acquitted Lester.[111]

In contrast, consider the case of Roswell and Emily Gilbert, an elderly Florida couple. Emily suffered intractable pain from osteoporosis and Alzheimer's Disease, both incurable. She too pleaded for an end to her misery. When the aggrieved Roswell responded to her importunings, the jury convicted him of first degree murder.[112]

Nullification has also been used by juries to reverse the effect of criminal laws fair on their face but unjust when applied in particular situations. Such was the case in *Wisconsin v. Leroy Reed*, notable as the first instance when TV cameras were allowed to videotape a jury's deliberations. The defendant, a dull-witted ex-con, was accused of breaking his parole by illegal possession of a firearm which he purchased for security of his new business. When he learned that possession of the firearm violated his parole, he informed his parole officer, who referred the case to the district attorney. In an obvious abuse of prosecutorial discretion, the district attorney opted to bring charges. The comments of the jurors show they unequivocally knew that Reed had broken the law. Also clear was that the jurors were unaware of their nullification power (the judge had declined the defense counsel's request for a nullification instruction). But the perceived overreaching and pettiness of the prosecutor in bringing the case to trial appalled the jurors. They sent a message of disapproval with their verdict of not guilty.[113]

Although defenders of jury nullification usually point to the jury's historical moorings as a defender against arbitrary and abusive criminal charges, jury nullification is also quite common in civil cases. In the absence of accountability, jurors have the power to ignore willy-nilly the law of *any* case. The contributory negligence defense is instructive. The all-or-nothing nature of this defense—any negligence by the plaintiff, no matter how inconsequential, fully defeats the plaintiff's case—frequently meets with juror disapproval. So they ignore it. Generally, the more complex the applicable law, the more likely jurors will be guided by their own experiences, their own sense of fair play and their own preexisting biases rather than the instructed law.

Jury nullification defies normal legal classifications. Is it a "right" or a "power"? The latter is the ability to effect a specific legal outcome, such as termination of an employment contract. A right, on the other hand, is the rightful use of a power whose exercise cannot be legally penalized. Thus one may have the power to fire an employee or end a partnership, but if the right to do so did not exist, liability for breach of contract would attach.

Courts steadfastly decline attorney requests to inform jurors of their nullification ability.[114]Indeed, the vast majority of courts enjoin the jurors to hew to the law as instructed.[115] Yet numerous instances of nullification persist. U.S. Supreme Court rulings on nullification are unclear at best, inconsistent at worst. In the 1895 *Sparf* case, the Court apparently reversed the age-old practice of permitting the jurors to decide the law as well as the facts, declaring that jurors "cannot be allowed to increase the penalties or create laws of their own" and "cannot be allowed to reduce such penalties or nullify the law."[116] Since then, however, the Court has consistently affirmed lower court rulings reaffirming the jurors' innate power of nullification, even though the exercise of that power is a violation of their explicit oath. In *Duncan v. Louisiana*, for example, the Court recognized the jury's power to displace unjust law or unjust application of the law by appeal to conscience as "fundamental to our system of justice."[117]

How then is this nullification power to be classified? If it is also a right, then trial judges would not specifically admonish jurors not to exercise it. If it is a power without an accompanying right, then its exercise would subject the user to penalty. But the nonaccountability of jurors precludes any such eventuality. Clearly, the ambiguity stems from the distinct historical experience of the jury in America. Apparently, the nullification power is unique, a right which exists despite jurors being told it does not.

The jury nullification debate will undoubtedly persevere. Proponents say nullification tempers the law with justice; it brings the "common sense" of the average citizen and the "conscience of the community" to bear on individual cases, supplying needed flexibility and equity to the law. Perhaps, but before waxing lyrical over the emotive pull of these words, we should heed Guinther's eloquent admonition:

All these phrases have a nice ring to them, but by their subjective nature, each is undefinable and not necessarily benign. What, for example, do we say of the "common sense" in the south that blacks were inferior to whites, and which saw to it that only the white "conscience of the community" was present on its juries? Towards what equities were Hitler and the compliant masses moving when millions of Jews were slaughtered? What, after all, is oppression but the justice of those who have power to impose it?

From the lessons of history, we thus have cause to worry about the conscience of any community and reason to be cynical about the likelihood of it displaying common sense, or invariably sensing where equities are.

Based on this reasoning, our conundrum is apparently of no mean proportions. For if a law is unjust or will create injustice when applied to a particular case, then the jury's right to reach a conscience verdict can protect us from it. But if we permit that right, and even encourage its expression by explaining it to a jury, we may be allowing into our courts forces that can be as dark with the danger of a lynch mob as those bright with justice.[118]

One of the "forces" of which Guinther warns is the displacement of the rule of law—ours is a "government of laws, not men"—with anarchy. In *U.S. v. Dougherty*,[119] Justice Leventhal specifically addressed the danger of informing jurors of their nullification power. He felt that would foster courtroom anarchy. (The *Dougherty* case was undoubtedly influenced by the inflammatory Vietnam War trials of the late 1960s and early 1970s, such as the trial of the "Chicago

Seven." *Dougherty* was similar, involving the "D.C. Nine," who ransacked Dow Chemical offices in protest of the company's manufacture of napalm.) Dissenting Justice Bazelon disagreed. To him, candor was the optimal approach. Candor impels a movement to mandate that judges inform all jurors of their inherent power of nullification. Supporters of the movement advocate adding to the constitution of every state a Fully Informed Jury Amendment. Only through its passage, they contend, can we rescue from judicial usurpation the true intent behind the constitutional right to jury trial.[120]

Jury nullification would be impossible without secret jury deliberations. Given the importance the law places on both the jury trial and the secrecy of jury deliberations, it would seem axiomatic that some paradigm of jury deliberations would be suggested to the jurors. None are. Only the jurors know how they deliberated. Anecdotes tell of jury decisions based on grossly flawed reasoning or recall, physical and emotional intimidation by other jurors or sheer exhaustion. Any of these may lead to quotient balloting (arriving at a monetary award by averaging the twelve juror-estimates), coin flipping or other forms of inappropriate decision making.

In some instances, hopefully rare, the jury simply finds its duties inconvenient. Recently, five jurors in Portland, Oregon, requested a new trial for a man convicted of conspiring to murder a sheriff and an IRS agent. According to the jury foreman, he and four other jurors changed their votes to "guilty" in the 1991 trial of George O. Jones "to reach a verdict in time to attend to personal business." They had deliberated a grand total of eight hours.[121]

Given the shoddy quality of much jury decision making, many conclude that verdicts survive appeal only because the commonly used general verdict enables the jury to shroud its decision making process. Judge Curtis Bok said, "If we required a reasoned argument in support [of the jury's decision], the jury system would blow up in a week, and hence wisely we do not require it."[122] We commonly perceive the jury as a popular symbol of democracy. In another sense, however, it is the antithesis of democracy: The jury is not accountable to anyone; its members are anonymous. After delivering the verdict, jurors disappear, leaving no one to blame. Conversely, the judge, being subject in most states to re-election, must be prepared with rational and legitimate explanations for her decisions.

The general verdict intensely frustrates jury critics. They cannot document their criticisms of the system with accurate statistical data because jury deliberations are inviolably secret. Conclusive empirical proof of another claimed jury system deficiency also eludes critics. They feel that many attorneys corrupt the selection of the jury, a process known as *voir dire*.

VOIR DIRE (JURY SELECTION)

Voir dire is a fertile area for trial attorneys to ply their trade.[123] During the *voir dire* examination, attorneys may dismiss prospective jurors by *challenges*. Those whose responses to the *voir dire* questions indicate probable bias are challenged for *cause*. Attorneys may perceive other prospective jurors who would not view their client's case favorably, but whom the judge may not agree are sufficiently biased to challenge for cause. Such individuals can be challenged by *peremptory* challenges. Unlike challenges for cause, peremptory challenges require no stated reason by the requesting attorney; however, they are limited in number. A common number is six for each side, but in cases of serious crimes, the number may be twelve or more. Because of their limited availability, a premium is put on the attorney's skill in using peremptory challenges.

Statute and case law require the panel from which the jury is selected be drawn from a representative cross-section of the community in which the case is filed. To this end, courts use voter lists as the primary source for jury panel members. Theoretically, the varying views within the community, if represented on the jury, would make for vigorous and salutary debate. The hope is that conflicting prejudices will cancel each other out.[124]

Representation of community values is only one desideratum of jury selection. The overarching goal is an impartial jury. Extensive pretrial publicity of a case presents the most difficult problem in finding unbiased jurors from the local community. When a case has received a lot of press, and at least one party seeks jurors unbiased by the press reports, the *voir dire* may be conducted individually, out of the presence of other prospective jurors, so those who have not heard the press reports will not hear the responses of those who have.[125] When the court feels media coverage has been so pervasive that a fair trial cannot be held in the community in which the alleged offense occurred (where it is filed), the judge will grant a change in venue. As the King and McDuffie cases painfully demonstrated, this can have calamitous consequences. If the values of the community to which the trial is moved are decisively different from those where the alleged crime took place, widespread dissonance, sometimes lethal, may ensue.

A continuing debate regarding *voir dire* has special significance for the adversary system: Who should conduct the *voir dire* examination—judge, attorneys or both? The greater the control of the attorneys, the greater the likelihood that the jury will be skewed in favor of the attorney with superior jury selection skills. In the federal courts, the judge does the questioning. She has sole discretion whether to ask or not ask any or all additional questions submitted by the attorneys prior to the examination. In the state courts, both attorney and judge commonly do the questioning. Often, the rules of the particular judge or court determine the allowable scope of attorney questions.

At the center of the debate is a bench-bar conflict of views. Each side has a substantively different perspective of *voir dire* practice. Much of the judiciary objects to attorney abuse of the *voir dire* process. Theoretically, its sole purpose is probative: ascertaining bias. Instead, the judges complain, lawyers use the examination to gain adversarial advantage. New York Judge Whitman Knapp voices a typical bench attitude: "The vice [of attorney participation] is that *voir dire* is used to condition jurors, not to select jurors."[126]

By strategic use of peremptory challenges, the attorney tries to assemble a jury most receptive to his case. As candid practitioners readily admit, lawyers conduct *voir dire* not to get unbiased jurors, but to get jurors favorably biased. In writing their book, *Judging the Jury*, jury mavens Valerie Hans and Neil Vidmar interviewed many attorneys. Their confessions reveal a troubling commentary on adversarial corruption of the *voir dire* process.

Attorney Herald Price Fahringer admits that jury selection involves some deception. Lawyers begin the selection process by claiming to the jury panel that their only wish is for fair and impartial jurors. Yet they do not desire impartiality but rather favorability. . . . In jury selection, he claims, "we lie to them and they in turn lie to us."[127]

Attorneys do more than merely try to ferret out prospective jurors with biases potentially hostile to their clients. Attorneys also seek competitive advantage by attempting to influence prospective jurors while interviewing them. The assumption that well-matched attorneys result in the selection of only neutral jurors presumes no other motives than discovering and eliminating apparently prejudiced prospective jurors. Yet Ann Ginger's popular book, *Jury Selection in Criminal Trials*,[128] lists eight other purposes for *voir dire* not traditionally recognized as legitimate:

1. To move the jury as a group

2. To discover "friendly" jurors

3. To teach jurors important facts in the case

4. To expose jurors to damaging facts in the case

5. To teach jurors the law in the case

6. To develop personal relationships between lawyer and juror

7. To expose opposing counsel

8. To prepare for summation

Most of this is designed to *create* bias in prospective jurors—via indoctrination, education and socialization—rather than detect it. The Trial advocacy tracts (some even appearing in law school textbooks) are replete with advice on how to gain adversarial advantage during *voir dire*. Several studies support the conclusion that the vast majority of the attorney's efforts in time[129] and questions[130] are concerned with using *voir dire* for achieving an illegitimate goal: gaining adversarial advantage rather than screening for bias. The findings of the earlier studies were confirmed by the Los Angeles survey. More than one-third agreed that "one or both attorneys were trying to persuade me in addition to probing for bias."[131] This suggests numerous attorneys are using *voir dire* for inappropriate didactic purposes.

Such misuse does not occur for lack of written standards. Federal and state rules prohibit attorney abuse of *voir dire*. Procedural rules ban attorney attempts at extensive indoctrination, ingratiation and other diversionary tactics.[132] Rules, however, are ineffective without enforcement. Two substantial preconditions limit the enforcement of these rules: First, they can only be implemented upon the objection of opposing counsel; and second, the judge must be willing to sustain the objection if she agrees that the alleged abuse is extensive. The nature of the adversary system makes satisfaction of either condition problematic. Attorney skills vary widely. Less alert or aggressive or competent attorneys may not object to any but egregious abuses. Even if objection is made, the prescribed role neutrality of the judge (not to mention fear of appellate reversal) constrains her to intervene only in unequivocally extreme situations.

Another judicial concern about attorney *voir dire* is the additional time most attorneys take to conduct the examination, and the associated costs. Long *voir dire* examinations exacerbate case backlogs. The pragmatic desire to curtail lengthy *voir dire* provides the impetus for many states to adopt the federal judge-control model.

Attorneys vigorously expostulate to any such restrictions. They maintain that judge-conducted *voir dire* has its own drawbacks. Judges don't know the issues as well as do the attorneys, they claim. This leads to superficial questioning. As a result, judge questioning is often less effective at rooting out bias.[133] Moreover, attorneys claim that prospective jurors are less likely to admit biases to the judge. Why? Contemplate the setting in which judge and prospective juror meet. The judge's arrival is heralded by the bailiff's call, "All rise." No one can sit until the judge does. Clad in robe and seated on elevated platform in the center of the room, the judge projects a physical and symbolic eminence which intimidates many prospective jurors. Conversely, the ingratiating, folksy approach of most good trial attorneys has the opposite effect.

Attorneys have other arguments against judge-conducted *voir dire*. As nonadvocates, judges do not have the financial and professional motivation to question prospective jurors as thoroughly as attorneys. Nor, say the attorneys, are judges sufficiently skilled in the art of asking questions to probe effectively for bias.

The arguments on both sides of the judge-versus-attorney *voir dire* debate are compelling, resulting in a patchwork of practices at the state level. Generally, judges give attorneys more flexibility during criminal trials, prioritizing clients' rights over time and cost concerns. Buffeted by arguments from both sides, the experience in California is enlightening testament to the bumpy road *voir dire* rules can take. In 1981, the California Supreme Court held that trial counsel must be allowed to ask questions "reasonably designed" to help them exercise peremptory challenges—irrespective of whether the answers reveal grounds to challenge for cause.[134] Subsequent (1987) legislation gave trial judges authority to bar questions that "indoctrinate" or "prejudice" prospective jurors. Most recently, the Code of Civil Procedure was amended to ensure that judges cannot exclude trial attorneys from the jury selection process.[135] After initial oral examination by the judge, each attorney can ask additional questions via questionnaires whose contents are to be determined by the court "in its sound discretion." The court may also allow follow-up oral examination by the attorneys. The judge sets limits on the scope of the attorneys' *voir dire*. But those limits must not be unreasonable; specific time limits that are unreasonable are statutorily prohibited.[136] On the criminal side, legislative inertia in ameliorating case backlog led to the passage of a ballot initiative placing *voir dire* completely within the judge's domain.[137]

The extension of adversary theory to the *voir dire* examination is premised on these consecutive assumptions: (a) well-matched attorneys will challenge prospective jurors who seem most favorably disposed to the opposition, thereby canceling each other out; and (b) the resultant jury will be composed of impartial jurors, or at least of a jury whose biases are equally balanced. The assumption of a jury entirely composed of impartial jurors has minimal plausibility. According to the U.S. Supreme Court, requiring that jurors lack any preconceived notions about the trial is an "impossible standard."[138] No one who has not had a recent lobotomy can be totally impartial about matters jurors must decide. As long as we use people and not computers as jurors, biases formed by prior beliefs and experiences will always significantly affect our deliberations and judgments. Even a *voir dire* which eliminates the most obviously biased individuals will not produce a literally unbiased panel—there is no such thing.

That leaves the assumption of a jury with equally balanced biases to salvage the ideal of a fair trial through impartial jurors. And indeed that is what the law hopes to approximate by seeking a broad cross-section of community attitudes on juries. In some Supreme Court decisions, the ideal jury is one characterized by "diffused impartiality." This is just an aspirational fiction. Achieving "equally balanced biases" among jury panel members on a regular basis is one of the law's convenient but illusory chimeras. No magical procedure or formula exists for converting a group of individuals into an impartial jury or even an equally balanced one.

An inexorable reality of the trial is that who decides the case is just as important to the outcome as what is to be decided. That is why so many trial attorneys believe the case is won or lost during jury selection, before the trial has begun. And to the extent attorneys continue to play a role in selecting the jury, the better *voir dire* attorney has a decided edge. Both common sense and the empirical studies so indicate. Most notably, Zeisel and Diamond conducted a widely cited study to test the boasts of trial lawyers that they occasionally "win" their cases during *voir dire* by the shrewd use of peremptory challenges.[139] Prospective jurors who had been peremptorily excused were asked to remain as "shadow jurors"[140] and reveal how they would have voted. Their responses were then compared with those of the actual jurors. If the outcome would have been different, the winning attorney was credited. The study found considerable variability in performance among different attorneys. It reports:

The first conclusion emerging from this study is that there are cases in which the jury verdict is seriously effected, if not determined by *voir dire*. At times, one attorney will significantly outperform the opposing attorney in challenging hostile jurors.[141]

Zeisel and Diamond concede they have no firm basis for estimating how often this occurs, but nonetheless conclude from their data: "We are . . . tentatively persuaded that cases in which peremptory challenges have an important effect on the verdict occur with some frequency."[142] As to the consequences of adversarial mismatch, the authors say: "Occasionally, one side performed well in a case in which the other side performed poorly, *thereby frustrating the law's expectation that the adversary allocation of challenges will benefit both sides equally.*"[143] (Emphasis supplied.)

In accord is the survey of 420 federal judges by psychologist Gordon Bermant. Eighty percent agreed that "There are great differences among lawyers in this skill. Some are very talented in the selection of jurors, and some are not."[144] This led Bermant to dismiss the assumption of well-matched attorneys leading to an impartial jury as an "adversarial myth."[145]

Anecdotes of winning jury selection strategies are legion. The obvious scheme is to challenge prospective jurors who seem the most biased against your client or opposed to what you hope to establish. But some successful tactics involve choices based on projections comparable to those of a chess master. In some criminal trials, for example, defense attorneys with weak cases choose a combination of jurors whose interpersonal chemistries create a "poison pill." They pick jurors they predict will dislike each other—intensely. That way, deliberations may grind to a halt without the verdict being reached. No verdict, no conviction. A Florida defense attorney describes the ploy.

Sometimes, I would intentionally set out to polarize the jury. For instance, I would purposely pick a militant African-American who was once a card-carrying Black Panther to sit on the same jury as a lily-white, redneck-ish farmer from the South. In some cases that did in fact prove to be successful. We'd get a hung jury. The more conflict I create, the greater the chance there won't be a conviction.[146]

Jury consultant Amy Singer employed the same strategy to elicit a mistrial in the infamous Miami River Cops case in 1987. She deliberately picked jurors "who would explode, would hate each other. That's what you want to do in a criminal case when it is obvious that people are guilty. You go for personalities." Then, "you hope the personalities will combust."[147]

Mismatched attorneys present a dual threat to the empaneling of an impartial jury. The more skilled attorney may be able to select a favorably prejudiced jury by adroit use of peremptory challenges. However, the same ends may be achieved through the bias created during *voir dire* examination.

The most recent *voir dire* controversy surrounds the use of so-called "scientific" or "systematic" jury selection. Systematic jury selection began in 1971 with the successful defense of the "Harrisburg Seven," a group of Vietnam War protesters accused of, among other things, conspiring to destroy selective service records and kidnap Henry Kissinger. Federal prosecutors selected Harrisburg, Pennsylvania, as the trial site because it was a politically conservative area. The defense counsel recruited social scientists who surveyed over 1,000 Harrisburg residents, then made follow-up interviews. Based on the results and aided by computer technology, the defense fashioned demographic profiles of individuals most likely to be sympathetic or unsympathetic to the defendants. Armed with this data, the defense selected its jury. Despite the investment of considerable time and money by the prosecution commensurate with the attention given the trial by the media—the government spent about two million dollars on the case[148]—it ended with a hung jury. Thereafter, systematic jury selection mushroomed into a multimillion dollar industry.

Jury selection experts, typically forensic psychologists, use an array of techniques which include mock juries, pretrial focus groups, community attitude surveys and background checks on prospective jurors. Of these, mock jury studies and community surveys have problems of external validity, that is, the empirical conditions do not adequately simulate the real trial. Their use as a basis for trial strategy is accordingly problematic. Another jury selection aid, however, goes a long way toward solving the external validity problem: the so-called "shadow jury." A shadow jury is a group selected by a trial consultant to mirror the demographic mix and individual views of the real jury. Shadow jurors observe the actual trial in anonymity and without knowledge of which side hired them. They can then provide trial lawyers immediate feedback not available from other methods.[149]

One of the most elaborate and comprehensive uses of systematic jury selection was that employed by MCI in its antitrust suit against AT&T in 1980.

MCI's jury researchers first conducted an extensive poll of local residents to ascertain the demographic characteristics of individuals likely to side with or against MCI. Then, mock juries composed of individuals with varying sympathies toward MCI listened to abbreviated presentations of both sides by MCI's attorneys. During the mock jury deliberations, MCI's attorneys and researchers watched and listened from behind one-way mirrors. From their observations, the MCI attorneys learned what jurors to challenge during *voir dire*. They also gained strategic insights into the types of arguments to employ with different types of people. Their efforts were amply rewarded. The jury awarded MCI $600 million. After tripling these damages per antitrust law, the total judgment was a hefty $1.8 billion, the largest antitrust judgment of all time.[150]

Notwithstanding the ostensible successes of systematic jury selection, we cannot categorically assume its efficacy; it is nearly impossible to test with certainty. But theory and research strongly suggest its superiority over traditional jury selection methodology. Intuition and stereotypical attitudes dominate the latter. The received wisdom on jury selection covers presumptions regarding every imaginable demographic trait, including gender, profession, nationality, race, religion, physical features, economic strata, and even gait. Typical are Clarence Darrow's recommendations for jury shopping:

Never take a wealthy man on a jury. He will convict unless the defendant is accused of violating the anti-trust law, selling worthless stocks or bonds or something of that kind. . . . An Irishman is emotional, kindly and sympathetic. . . . Keep Unitarians, Universalists, Congregationalists, Jews and other agnostics.[151]

On the other hand, the social science approach has clear advantages. First, it is more case-specific; demographic research is conducted in the specific community from which the jury is to be selected. Second, social science uses multiple rating factors, all of which must agree before inferences are drawn. And third, the systematic approach constitutes a team effort, with the correlated benefits of consultation and feedback.

Apart from effectiveness, systematic jury selection raises issues of ethics and fairness. Background checks on prospective jurors are clear invasions of privacy. Fairness is an even greater concern. Specialized jury research tailored to the litigant's case is an advantage affordable only by the wealthy. When only one party can afford jury selection experts, it puts into relief the imbalances created by a mismatch of client resources. Does not giving large corporations and wealthy individuals such an advantage over their opponents undermine the very foundation of a fair trial? Might not the resulting competitive disadvantages of poorer litigants have a chilling effect on the exercise of their constitutional rights?

Hans and Vidmar project this line of thought further. They refer to critics who believe the potential imbalance created by systematic jury selection threatens the institutional justifiability of the jury and adversary system.

Within the adversarial context, it is presumed each side will eliminate those prospective jurors most favorable to the other side and that the end result will be an impartial jury. Yet *this assumes equal resources and skills for the two sides. The viability of the adversary system to ensure a fair and impartial jury and trial, in jury selection as well as in other stages of the trial, is sorely tested when the adversaries possess unequal resources.* In this light, the major ethical problem with social science in the courtroom is not the techniques themselves but rather *the fact that in our society the condition for equality of resources is most often not met.* Jury experts may exacerbate the impact of such disparities. There are no easy answers in this ethical quagmire, since the issues extend beyond the techniques themselves to the nature and functioning of the adversary system itself. But the ethical issues must constantly be confronted by those who conduct and those who benefit from the new developments in jury selection.[152] (Emphasis supplied.)

An ethical issue for social scientists retained by trial counsel persists. Social scientists who participate in the adversarial attempt to obtain favorable jurors tarnish the image of their profession.[153] Serving in this capacity, the paid expert should have no false illusions; no one wants to hire an "ivory tower" consultant to assist in selecting a "fair and impartial" jury.[154] Jury selection is every bit as adversarial as the rest of the trial. The goal is to maximize the number of favorably biased jurors. Consultants who facilitate this must appreciate that their efforts contribute to an end of questionable propriety.

CONCLUSION

Criticism of the jury trial does not denote criticism of jurors and juries. For example, psychology professors Saul Kassin and Lawrence Wrightsman staunchly defend juries. But in the concluding remarks of their fine book, *The American Jury On Trial*, they concede that the jury trial *process* is problematic.

Trials are very well orchestrated events structured according to a complex network of rules, constraints, and rituals. And what are these rituals based on? They are based on assumptions—often misassumptions—about human behavior. In the end, it is the American jury *trial*, not the jury *per se*, that should be tried.[155]

In retrospect, both the jury and the adversary system were intended as tools to diffuse the power of government (in the form of the judge). The jury was the vehicle for decentralizing power and imbuing the decision making process with community values. The adversary system also diffuses courtroom power, transferring control of the scope and conduct of the trial inquiry to the parties and their advocates. Yet one cannot help but be struck by the dysfunctionalism resulting from the melding of the jury and adversary systems. Due process, which is the standard by which the fairness of our trials are gauged, presumes a jury capable of understanding the facts and applying the law.[156] At the same time, the adversary system enables the attorney to exploit the weaknesses in jurors which would generally be unavailing against the judge, who is usually better educated, more sophisticated and less susceptible to attorney suasion. Attorneys commonly select ignorant and malleable jurors, obfuscate their factfinding, and befuddle with emotional appeals their ability to apply the law correctly. As a result, the legitimacy of the jury trial is often jeopardized when lawyers merely do what they are supposed to do.

NOTES

1. Erwin Griswold, Harvard Law School Dean's Report, 1962-63,pp. 5-6.
2. Gail Cox, "Abuse Excess: Success Grows," *National Law Journal*, 5/9/94, p. 1.
3. Id.
4. Id.
5. Anne Strick, *Injustice for All* (New York: Penguin Books, 1977), p. 194.
6. See the discussion in Chapter 1.
7. See, e.g., Paul Vinagradoff, *Historical Jurisprudence*, Vol. 2 (1922), pp. 7-11, 78-79,; Calhoun, "The Greek Legal City," 24 *Columbia Law Review* 154 (1924); George Calhoun, *Introduction to Greek Legal Science* (Oxford: Clarendon Press, 1944).
8. Godfrey Lehman, "A Short History of Judicial Abuse," *Los Angeles Daily Journal*, 5/3/91, p. 6.
9. Frank suggests this may have been borrowed from fifth century Roman procedure. Jerome Frank, *Courts On Trial: Myth and Reality in American Justice* (Princeton, N.J.: Princeton University Press, 1949), p. 108.
10. Marcus Gleisser, *Juries and Justice* (New York: Barnes and Company, 1968), p. 35.
11. John Guinther, *The Jury in America* (New York: Facts on File, 1988), p. 8.
12. Id., p. 12.
13. Sir Frederick Pollock and Frederic Maitland, *The History of English Law*, Vol. 2 (Cambridge: Cambridge University Press, 1895), p. 173; Charles Rembar, *Law of the Land* (New York: Simon and Shuster, 1980), p. 168.
14. Bushel's Case, 124 *Eng. Rep.* 1006, (1670). Edward Bushel was a juror in the sedition trial of William Penn and William Mead. Bushel was the alleged leader of the group of jurors who refused to find the defendants

guilty even after the judge fined and imprisoned them for their failure to do so.

15. For the events leading to the trial and Zenger's own transcript of the trial, see Livingston Rutherford, *John Peter Zenger* (New York: Peter Smith, 1941).

16. The other holdouts are Australia, Belgium, Norway, Denmark, Greece, parts of Switzerland and some Latin American countries. Harry Kalven and Hans Zeisel, *The American Jury* (Chicago: University of Chicago Press, 1986), p. 13, n13.

17. A comparison of the performance of lay versus mixed juries holds promise for improvement—before abandonment—of juries in cases where their continued use is an issue.

18. Quoted in Rita Simon, *The Jury: Its Role in American Society* (Lexington, Mass.: Lexington Books, 1980), pp. 11, 12, 14.

19. Quoted in Frank, *Courts On Trial, op. cit.*, p. 124.

20. E.g., see Judith Pendell, "Enhancing Juror Effectiveness: An Insurer's Perspective," *Law and Contemporary Problems*, *52(4)* (Autumn 1989), 311 at 314.

21. M. Selvin and L. Picus, *The Debate Over Jury Performance: Observations from a Recent Asbestos Case* (Santa Monica, Calif.: Rand Corporation, Institute of Civil Justice, 1987), p. 45.

22. Id.

23. A. Raitz *et al.*, "Determining Damages: The Influence of Expert Testimony on Jurors' Decision Making," *Law and Human Behavior*, *14(4)* (August 1990), pp. 385, 393.

24. N. Brekke *et al.*, "Of Juries and Court-Appointed Experts: The Impact of Nonadversarial versus Adversarial Expert Testimony," *Law and Human Behavior*, *15(5)* (October 1991), p. 451 at 468-469.

25. *In re Japanese Electronic Products Antitrust Litigation*, 631 *F.2d* 1069, 1073 (1980).

26. See, e.g., *In re Boise Cascade Securities Litigation*, 420 *F.Supp.* 99 (W.D. Wash. 1976); *In re United States Financial Securities Litigation*, 75 *F.R.D.* 702 (S.D. Cal., 1977); and *Bernstein v. Universal Pictures, Inc.*, 79 *F.R.D.* 59 (S.D.N.Y., 1978).

27. 396 *U.S.* 531.

28. Id., at 538.

29. Alexander Hamilton, *The Federalist*, No. 83 (Washington, D.C.: National Home Library Foundation, 1937).

30. *In re Japanese Electronics Products Antitrust Litigation, op. cit.*, p. 1080.

31. Id., at 1084.

32. Id., at 1086.

33. Amendment VI.

34. The University of Chicago Jury Project found such bias in criminal cases: "Persons with German and British backgrounds were more likely to favor the government whereas Negroes and persons of Slavic and Italian descent were more likely to favor acquittal." D. Broeder, "The University of Chicago Jury Project," 38 *Nebraska Law Review* 744, 748 (1959).

35. Consider the court's observation in *Lawton v. Nightingale*: "If a jury could be resorted to in actions under [42 U.S.C. Sec. 1983], the very evil the statute is designed to prevent would be attained. The person seeking to vindicate an unpopular right could never succeed before a jury drawn from a populace opposed to his views." 345 *F.Supp.* 683 at 684 (1972).

36. William O'Barr, *Linguistic Evidence*, (New York: Academic Press, 1982); Albert Mehrabian and Martin Williams, "Nonverbal Concomitants of Perceived and Intended Persuasiveness," *Journal of Personality and Social Psychology, 13* (1969), pp. 37-38; Norman Miller *et al.*, "Speed of Speech and Persuasion," *Journal of Personality and Social Psychology, 34* (1976), pp. 615-17; John Conley, William O'Barr and E. Allan Lind, "The Power of Language: Presentational Style in the Courtroom," 1978 *Duke Law Journal* 1375 (1978).

37. Sarah Tanford and Steven Penrod, "Biases in Trials Involving Defendants Charged with Multiple Offenses," *Journal of Applied Social Psychology, 12* (1982), pp. 453, 475-78; Doob and Kirschenbaum, "Some Empirical Evidence on the Effect of Section 12 of the Canada Evidence Act Upon an Accused," 15 *Criminal Law Quarterly* 88, 93-96 (1973); Roselle Wissler and Michael Saks, "On the Inefficiency of Limiting Instructions: When Jurors Use Credibility Evidence to Decide Guilt," *Law and Human Behavior, 9* (1985), pp. 37, 43-47.

38. See the related discussion in Chapter 3.

39. See Gary Wells and Elizabeth Murray, "Eyewitness Confidence," in G. Wells and E. Loftus, eds., *Eyewitness Testimony: Psychological Perspectives* (Cambridge: Cambridge University Press, 1984), pp. 155, 159-65; Kenneth Deffenbacher, "Eyewitness Accuracy and Confidence: Can We Infer Anything From Their Relationship?" *Law and Human Behavior, 4* (1980), pp. 243, 257-58.

40. Bruce Rashkow, "Abolition of the Civil Jury: Proposed Alternatives," 15 *De Paul Law Review* 418, 419 (1966).

41. Id., p. 418.

42. Frank, *Law and the Modern Mind* (Garden City, New York: Doubleday, 1930), p. 172.

43. See generally, Committee for Economic Development, *Who Should Be Liable?* (New York: Author, 1989); P. Huber, *Liability: The Legal Revolution and Its Consequences* (New York: Basic Books, 1988).

44. H. Kalven, "The Jury, the Law, and the Personal Injury Award," 19 *Ohio State Law Journal*, 158-79 (1958).

45. Robert Satter, "Why Civil Juries Don't Work," *Connecticut Law Tribune*, *15(47)*, 11/27/89, pp. 1, 11.
46. Id., p. 11.
47. Michael Zander, "The Jury in England," *American Jury System* (Washington, D.C.: Roscoe Pound Foundation, 1977), pp. 33-34.
48. M. A. Peterson and G. C. Priest, *The Civil Jury: Trends in Trials and Verdicts, Cook County, Ill., 1960-1979* (1982); M. A. Peterson, *Compensation of injuries: Civil Jury Verdicts in Cook County*, (1984); A. Chin and M. A. Peterson, *Deep pockets; empty pockets: Who Wins in Cook County Jury Trials* (1985). All published in Santa Monica, CA: The Rand Corporation.
49. See, e.g., Valerie Hans, *Perceptions of corporate versus individual responsibility for wrongdoing*, paper presented at the annual meeting of the American Psychological Association, New York (August 1987).
50. Louis Harris and Associates, *Judges' Opinions on Procedural Issues* (April 1988), p. 86.
51. M. Peterson, *Civil Juries in the 1980s: Trends in Jury Trials and Verdicts in California and Cook County, Illinois* (Santa Monica, CA: Rand Corp., 1987), pp. 13, 21, 22, 27, 33, 35, 36.
52. M. Peterson, *op. cit.*
53. Jennifer Warren, "Mistrial Ends New Yorker Libel Case," *Los Angeles Times*, 6/4/93, pp. A3, A28.
54. G. Thomas Munsterman and Janice Munsterman, *A Comparison of the Performances of Eight and Twelve Person Juries* (Alexandria, Virg.: National Center for State Courts, April 1990).
55. Daniel Goldman, "Juries Hear Evidence And Turn It Into Stories," *New York Times*, 5/12/92, C1.
56. Rex Beaber, "Truth Duels Rarely Have Clear Winners, " *Los Angeles Daily Journal*, 10/18/91, p. 6.
57. See P. Elkman and W. Frieden, "Nonverbal leakage and clues to deception," *Psychiatry*, *32* (1969), pp. 88-106. For a review of studies confirming the findings of Elkman and Friesen, see M. Zuckerman, B. M. Depaulo and B. M. DePaulo, "Verbal and nonverbal communication of deception," a chapter appearing in L. Berkowitz ed., *Advances in Experimental Social Psychology*, *14* (New York: Academic Press, 1981).
58. 3 W. Blackstone, *Commentaries on the Laws of England* (1978; reprint of 1783 ed.), p. 373; for a detailed history of jury questions, see Comment, "The Questioning of Witnesses by Jurors," 27 *American University Law Review* 127 (1977).
59. Michael Wolff, "Juror Questions: A Survey of Theory and Use," 55 *Missouri Law Review* 817 (Summer 1990).

60. M. McLaughlin, "Questions to witnesses and notetaking by the jury as aids in understanding complex litigation," 18 *New England Law Review* 687 at 697-98 (1982).

61. Larry Heuer and Steven Penrod, "Juror Notetaking and Question Asking During Trials: A National Field Experiment," *Law and Human Behavior, 18(2)*, 1994, pp. 121, 142.

62. Michael Wolff, "Juror Questions," *op. cit.*, pp. 821-825.

63. Id., pp. 826-828.

64. Id., pp. 829-30.

65. L. Heuer and S. Penrod, "Increasing Jurors' Participation In Trials: A Field Experiment with Jury Notetaking and Question Asking," *Law and Human Behavior, 12(3)* (1988), pp. 231-261; Heuer and Penrod, "Juror Notetaking and Question Asking During Trials," *op. cit.*, pp. 121-150.

66. Michael Wolff, "Juror Questions," *op. cit.*, p. 839.

67. National Center for State Courts, *Center for Jury Studies Newsletter*, May 1979, p. 4.

68. National Center for State Courts, *op. cit.*

69. S. Kassin and L. Wrightsman, *The American Jury on Trial: Psychological Perspectives* (New York: Hemisphere Publishing, 1988), p. 128.

70. Victor Flango, "Would Jurors Do a Better Job If They Could Take Notes?" *Judicature, 63(9)* (April 1980), p. 436.

71. David Rosenhan, Sara Eisner and Robert Robinson, "Notetaking Can Aid Juror Recall," *Law and Human Behavior, 18(1)* (1994), pp. 53-61; Heuer and Penrod, "Increasing Jurors' Participation in Trials," *op. cit.*, p. 246; Cf. Heuer and Penrod, "Juror Notetaking and Question Asking During Trials," *op. cit.*, pp. 121-150.

72. Rosenhan, Eisner and Robinson, *op. cit.*

73. Heuer and Penrod, "Increasing Jurors' Participation in Trials," *op. cit.*, pp. 248-49.

74. See K. A. Kiewra, "Notetaking and Review: The Research and Its Implications," *Instructional Science, 16* (1987), pp. 233-249.

75. The length of the *Maniscalco* case pales in comparison to those of some of the civil megatrials. See, e.g., *In re U.S. Financial Securities Litigation*, 609 *F.2d* 411 (1979).

76. This was allowed in *SCM Corp. v. Xerox Corp.*, 77 *F.R.D.* 10, 15 (D. Conn. 1977) (pretrial ruling). See also Rule 53(d) of the *Uniform Rules of Criminal Procedure*.

77. J. Withrow and D. Suggs, "Procedures for improving jury trials of complex litigation," *The Antitrust Bulletin* (Fall 1980), pp. 493 at 509, 510.

78. William Vogeler, "The Court of the Unblinking Eye," *Los Angeles Daily Journal*, 7/11/91, sec. 2, p. 1.

79. Address by Clyde Adkins, Senior Judges' Committee of the American Bar Association, entitled "Litigation on the Fast Track/ Clearing the Path to Settlement: A View from the Bench," August 5, 1988.

80. Stephen Adler, "Can Juries Do Justice to Complex Suits?" *Wall Street Journal*, 12/21/89, at B1, Col.4.

81. The federal courts and most state courts allow issue severance. Research by Aetna Insurance's legal department discloses that only Connecticut, Hawaii, Illinois, Louisiana, Nebraska, New Hampshire and Texas do not allow it in personal injury cases.

82. Louis Harris & Associates, *op. cit.*

83. Boyle Curry and Rosemary Snider, "Bifurcated Trials: How to Avoid Them—How to Win Them," *Trial* (March 1988), pp. 47-52.

84. Edmund Morgan, *Some Problems of Proof Under the Anglo-American System of Litigation* (New York: Columbia University Press, 1956), p. 105.

85. Frank, *Courts on Trial*, *op. cit.*, p. 123.

86. Quoted in Kunert, "Some Observations on the Origin and Structure of Evidence Rules Under the Common Law System and the Civil Law System of 'Free Proof' in the German Code of Civil Procedure," 16 *Buffalo Law Review* 122, 127 (1967).

87. Wigmore *Evidence*, Vol. 1, *op. cit.*, Sec.8c.

88. Federal Rules of Evidence 411.

89. In a survey conducted for the Roscoe Pound American Trial Lawyers Foundation, Guinther reported that over half of the surveyed 286 jurors in civil trials thought the defendant carried insurance. Guinther, *op. cit.*, p. 98.

90. S. Diamond, J. Casper and L. Ostergren, "Blindfolding the Jury," *Law and Contemporary Problems*, *52(4)* (Autumn 1989), p. 247 at 255.

91. See Lisa Eichhorn, "Social Science Findings and the Jury's Ability to Disregard Evidence Under the Federal Rules of Evidence," *Law and Contemporary Problems, 52(4)* (Autumn 1989), pp. 341.

92. Diamond, Casper and Ostergren, *op. cit.*, p. 259.

93. E. Elwork, B. Sales and D. Suggs, "The Trial: A Research Review," in B. Sales, ed., *The Trial Process* (New York: Plenum Press, 1981), p. 42.

94. Diamond, Casper and Ostergren, *op. cit.*, p. 249.

95. R. Hastie, S.Penrod and N. Pennington, *Inside The Jury* (Cambridge, Mass.: Harvard University Press, 1983), pp. 239, 240.

96. See the related discussion in Chapter 3.

97. *Sparf and Hansen v. U.S.* 156 *U.S.* 52 (1995).

98. Jerome Frank, *Law and the Modern Mind*, *op. cit.*, at 181.

99. A. Elwork *et. al.*, "Toward Understandable Jury Instructions," *Judicature, 65(8-9)* (1982), p. 433.

100. A. Elwork, B. Sales and J. Alfini, "Juridic Decisions: In Ignorance of the Law or in Light of It?," *Law and Human Behavior*, *1(2)* (1977), pp. 163-189.

101. A. Elwork and B. Sales, "Jury Instructions," Chapter 11 of Saul Kassin and Lawrence, Wrightsman, eds., *Psychology of Evidence and Courtroom Procedure* (Beverly Hills, Calif.: Sage, 1984), pp. 280 at 283.

102. "Guilty, I Mean Innocent," *Newsweek*, 10/20/75, at p. 64.

103. Elwork, Sales and Alfini, *op. cit.*, pp. 165-169. For the most complete analysis of psycholinguistic problems with jury instructions, see R. Charrow and V. Charrow, "Making legal language understandable: A psycholinguistic study of jury instructions," 79 *Columbia Law Review* 1306-74 (1979), and B. Sales, A. Elwork and J. Alfini, "Improving Comprehension For Jury Instructions," in B. Sales, ed., *Perspectives in Law and Psychology: The Criminal Justice System*, Vol. 1 (New York: Plenum Press, 1978), pp. 23-90.

104. Wallace Loh, "The Evidence and Trial Procedure: The Law, Social Policy, and Psychological Research," in S. Kassin and L. Wrightsman eds., *The Psychology of Evidence and Trial Procedure* (Beverly Hills, Calif.: Sage Publications, 1985), pp. 13 at 30-31.

105. L. Severance and E. Loftus, "Improving the ability of jurors to comprehend and apply criminal jury instructions," *Law and Society Review, 17* (1982), pp. 153-197.

106. Robert Forston, "Sense and Non-Sense: Jury Trial Communication," 1975 *Brigham Young University Law Review* 601, 620 (1975).

107. See, e.g., *People v. Miller*, 6 *N.Y.2d* 152 (1959); *People v. Gonzalez*, 292 *N.Y.* 259 (1944); *Commonwealth v. Smith*, 221 *Pa.* 552 (1908).

108. *Commonwealth v. Smith, op. cit.*, p. 533.

109. "King Jury Asks Judge's Help in Defining Terms," *Los Angeles Times*, 5/24/94, p. B2.

110. For a splendid history of jury nullification, see A. Scheflin and J. Van Dyke, "Jury nullification: The contours of a controversy," *Law and Contemporary Problems*, *4* (1980), pp. 52-115.

111. For a full description of the trial, see Paige Mitchell's book, *Act of Love: The Killing of George Zygmanik* (New York: Knopf, 1976).

112. Associated Press, "Man, 75, gets life for wife's death," *Kansas City Times*, 5/10/85, p. A-4.

113. The full trial is available in PBS' *Frontline* show, "Inside the Jury Room" (1986), produced by Al Levine and Stan Hertzberg.

114. There are rare exceptions. During the Vietnam War, for instance, a defendant war protester's attorney convinced the federal trial judge to advise the jury of its jury nullification power.

115. The constitutions of Maryland and Indiana allow the jury in criminal cases to be judges of the facts *and* the law, but the courts of neither state appear to take the rule literally. Kalven and Zeisel, *op. cit.*, Chapter 33, note 4.

116. *Sparf and Hansen v. U.S.*, *op. cit.*

117. *Duncan v. Louisiana*, 391 *U.S.* 145 (1968).

118. Guinther, *op. cit.*, p. 224.

119. 473 *F.2d* 1113. (1972).

120. See Godfrey Lehman, "Saving the Jury From Oblivion," *Los Angeles Daily Journal*, 12/14/90, p. 6.

121. "Jurors Seek New Trial on Murder Plan," *Los Angeles Daily Journal*, 5/13/93, p. 3.

122. Curtis Bok, "The Jury System in America," 287 *Annals of the American Academy of Political and Social Science* (1953), pp. 92, 94.

123. Although *voir dire* roughly translates from the French as "see them talk" or "say," *voir* is actually a corruption of the Latin *verus*, meaning "true" or "truthful." Thus *voir dire* refers to speaking the truth, which is what the examiner is seeking from the responses of prospective jurors.

124. Note the similarity of this presumption with the belief, discussed in Chapter 3, that the battle of conflicting views by the opposing attorneys will yield the truth.

125. *Report of the Committee on Juries of the Judicial Council of the Second Circuit* (New York: Author, 1984), p. 33.

126. Quoted in Franklin Strier, "Through The Jurors' Eyes," *The ABA Journal, 74* (October 1988), p. 80.

127. Valerie Hans and Neil Vidmar, *Judging the Jury* (New York: Plenum Press, 1986), p. 74.

128. Tiburon, Calif.: LawPress, 1977.

129. Dale Broeder, "Voir dire examinations: An empirical study," 38 *Southern California Law Review* 503-528 (1965).

130. R. Balch *et al.*, "The socialization of jurors: The voir dire as a rite of passage," *Journal of Criminal Justice, 4* (1976), pp. 271-283.

131. *Juror Perceptions of the Trial Process: A Survey*, (Carson, Calif.: Bureau of Business Research Services, 1988), p. 7.

132. See J. Alexander Tanford and Sarah Tanford, "Better Trials Through Science: A Defense of Psychologist-Lawyer Collaboration," 66 *North Carolina Law Review* 767-71 (1988).

133. Elwork, Sales and Suggs, *op. cit.*, p. 18; Donald Lay, "Can Our Jury System Survive?" *Trial Magazine, 19(9)* (1983), pp. 53-54.

134. *People v. Williams*, 29 *Cal 3d* 392.

135. *California Code of Civil Procedure*, Section 222.5, effective January 1, 1991.

136. Carol Angel, "Some Don't Know of the New Voir Dire Law," *Los Angeles Daily Journal*, 5/17/91.

137. The law was known popularly as The Speedy Trial Initiative of 1990.

138. *Irvin v. Dowd*, 366 *U.S.* 723 (1961).

139. Hans Zeisel and Shari Diamond, "The Effect of Peremptory Challenges on Jury and Verdict: An Experiment in a Federal District Court," 30 *Stanford Law Review* 491 (1978).

140. See the discussion of shadow juries, *infra*.

141. Id., p. 519.

142. Id.

143. Id., p. 529.

144. Gordon Bermant, *Conduct of the voir dire examination: Practices and opinions of federal district judges* (Washington, D.C.: Federal Judiciary Center, 1977).

145. Id.

146. Quoted in Christine Evans and Don Van Natta, Jr., "The Verdict on Juries: Only Human," *The Miami Herald*, 5/2/93, 1A at 24A.

147. Id.

148. Kassin and Wrightsman, *op. cit.*, p. 57.

149. Reese Ehrlich, "Shadow of a Verdict," *California Lawyer* (August 1991), pp. 36 at 87.

150. Hans and Vidmar, *op. cit.*, pp. 79-80.

151. *Criminal Law Bulletin, Recent Decisions*, *1(1)* (February 1965), p. 18.

152. Hans and Vidmar, *op. cit.*, pp. 93-94.

153. Id.

154. Ralph Gallagher, "The Use of a Consultant in Voir Dire," *Trial Diplomacy Journal, 7* (Winter 1984), at 24, 25.

155. Kassin and Wrightsman, *op. cit.*, pp. 215-216.

156. See *In re Japanese Electronic Products*, *op. cit.*, at 1084.

CHAPTER 5

CAN LAWYERS LIE?
TRUTH, JUSTICE, AND
ADVOCACY ETHICS

Justice is truth in action.
—Benjamin Disraeli[1]

In July 1973, two girls in Lake Pleasant, New York, disappeared. Alicia was sixteen, Susan twenty-one. Thinking her a runaway, Alicia's parents began advertising in a newspaper, pleading for her to return. In the meantime, a man was arrested and charged with the murder of an eighteen-year-old boy in the same mountainous area. Hearing this, Susan's father rushed to talk with the accused's attorneys, beseeching them for information about his missing daughter. Despite his persistent, poignant entreaties, the attorneys steadfastly maintained their silence, thereby denying him even the right to grieve—what he suspected but could not confirm to be—his loss. In fact, they knew of Susan's whereabouts because their client had confessed to them of murdering Susan and Alicia. Moreover, the attorneys had gone to where the mutilated bodies were hidden, having been directed there by their client. They photographed the bodies where they lay, one in a well bottom, the other in the thick brush of a cemetery. Not only did they deny this information to the girls' parents, they also withheld it from the police. Only after the client confessed to the crimes six months later did the attorneys reveal the location of the bodies. Despite their stonewalling, the attorneys were held innocent of any crime or breach of professional ethics.[2] To have done otherwise would have violated the confidentiality of client statements under the attorney-client privilege.

The Lake Pleasant story illustrates more than the adversary zeal for which criminal defense attorneys are notorious. It shows how the attorney-client privilege can be used to contravene common notions of decency in pursuit of victory—all within the bounds of the attorney's professional ethics. Frequently, however, zealous advocacy exceeds even the minimal constraints of the adversary system. And adversary excess is not confined to the defense bar. Prosecutors also push the envelope. Some examples:

- In Orange County, California, two 1991 murder convictions were reversed because the prosecutor had withheld witness statements that tended to exonerate the accused. Tactics by the same prosecutor led to reversal of another conviction. During the trial of the surgeon who attacked John Wayne's daughter, this prosecutor suggested to the jury that the defense had fed them a pack of lies.[3]

- The child molestation convictions of five defendants in Bakersfield, California, were thrown out in 1990 because the prosecution had made personal attacks on the defense, improperly questioned witnesses and tried to get inadmissible evidence before the jury.[4]

- In 1990, a Los Angeles County Grand Jury found that for years the District Attorney's office tolerated suspected perjury by jailhouse informants in order to win cases. The testimony was usually obtained in deals with the informants which were concealed from judges and juries.[5]

- Israeli authorities found evidence that U.S. Justice Department lawyers concealed evidence that eventually exonerated John Demjanjuk, accused of being the infamous Nazi concentration camp guard "Ivan the Terrible."[6]

- A former San Diego prosecutor received a two year suspension for altering taxi records to show that the accused had been in the area where two murders occurred. Fearing reprisals, the prosecutor attempted to cover-up his malfeasance by offering the defendant a lower sentence in return for dropping his appeal.[7]

Many other complaints cite growing misconduct by rogue government attorneys who break the rules to win convictions. The Demjanjuk case was but one of many involving misconduct by federal prosecutors, prompting U.S. Attorney General Janet Reno to review Justice Department procedures for handling complaints about its lawyers. University of San Diego law professor Robert Fellmeth led the effort in California to reform attorney discipline. He lamented, "I would like a system where if attorneys lied, something would happen to them."[8]

Adversarial corruption abounds in civil cases too. In a developing case with potentially devastating consequences for the tobacco industry, recent information implicates attorneys for the industry in gross abuse of the attorney-client privilege. Leaked documents showed the attorneys had advised cigarette manufacturers in the 1960s to fund scientific research projects on smoking and health. According to Yale Law School ethics expert Geoffrey Hazard, these projects apparently were to be overseen by the attorneys so that the attorney-client privilege would shield the likely damaging findings from public view. "There is no possible reason for a law firm to be doing this except to gain the protection of the privilege," Hazard said.[9]

TRUTH

The frequency of such occurrences suggests that our trial procedure and its governing ethos need to be critically reevaluated. Too often lost in the quotidian hubbub of trials are the overarching goals of our court system: truth and justice. Without truth, trial justice is serendipitous. The U.S. Supreme Court has frequently emphasized that the central purpose of the trial is the determination of truth.[10] Authorities as diverse as Jeremy Bentham and professors Wigmore and McCormick have concurred. Indeed, Wigmore's observation that adversary cross-examination is "the greatest legal engine ever invented for the discovery of truth" is probably the most quoted line in adversary system literature.[11]

Trial justice, to be sure, requires more than determining the truth. The court is not merely a laboratory. Rules of law—sometimes based on vague ethical and moral standards—must be applied in reaching a decision. But the most Solomonic decision maker applying the soundest legal principles is only as good as his or her tribunal's truth-seeking efficiency. That is why the claimed superior factfinding of the adversary system ranks as one of its major justifications.

Truth is a necessary but not sufficient condition for trial justice. As with morality and ethics, justice is a value-laden concept. A society's notions of justice reflect its dominant cultures and mores. Justice has different meanings in different contexts. It can obviously vary among different countries, and can even refer to different concepts within the same legal system. Our law is bifurcated: procedural and substantive. The justice of substantive law relates to its allocation of rights and duties, whereas the justice of procedural law refers to whether our trials (and other government procedures) follow prescribed rules designed to be fair. Depending upon your perspective, it is either the great strength or the great failing of the American trial system that it frames trial justice solely in terms of procedure. For attorneys and judges will concede that the fairness of trial procedure is no guarantee of the truth-finding capacity of trials.

Oliver Wendell Holmes once said that the law had nothing to do with justice. Notwithstanding Holmes' observation, people expect the law, and particularly trial law, to be just. The machinery of trial justice is the adversary system. That is why its full descriptive title is "the adversary system of justice." Literature on the trial system frequently raises issues of justice: Is justice a function of the system? A purposive (and primary) end-product of the system? A mere byproduct of a system whose main objective is dispute resolution? Or, at worst, the serendipitous result of a flawed process?

This chapter investigates the trial goals of truth and justice through the lens of the adversary system. In so doing, key questions surface. How well does the system work to achieve either goal? What is the relationship between the two goals? To what extent does the "truth" and "justice" of adversarial trial procedure conform to common notions of truth and justice? Lastly, what are the ethics of trial advocacy, and do they promote or frustrate the realization of truth and justice?

Trial Truth is Unknowable

Some commentators despair of finding truth through trial procedure. Professor Hazard believes truth, in the scientific sense of pure factfinding, is unattainable in a trial. Once in trial, the parties have already conceded that which can be proven objectively. What remains, he concludes, is hopelessly ambiguous, corrupted by decision maker bias and attorney distortion.[12] Hazard's point is well taken. "Facts" in legal jargon are different than facts in other disciplines. In law, findings of fact are usually not empirically verifiable, nor do they correspond to something real; they are either the judge's findings, or assumed from the jury's general verdict.[13]

Evidentiary presumptions are assumed facts in a trial. But there is *little or no empirical basis* for most of these substitutes for proof. For instance, few of the behavioral assumptions behind our exclusionary rules have been empirically tested. Moreover, experiments have indicated that adversary trial procedures in general, and hostile cross-examination in particular, are not conducive to the most accurate testimony.[14] James Marshall writes:

[T]estimony is constantly dissected and contradicted and reshaped toward partisan ends. That is the essence of a trial; it is not a scientific or philosophical quest for some absolute truth, but a bitter proceeding in which evidence is cut into small pieces, distorted, analyzed, challenged by the opposition, and reconstructed imperfectly in summation.[15]

Substantial difficulties inhere in ascertaining the truth in an adversarial trial. Indeed, they led philosopher Max Radin to conclude that the accurate determination of facts is a permanent, insoluble problem of the law. For "events are unique, and no imagined or imitative reconstruction will precisely reproduce them."[16] Proponents claim that the adversary system is the best method to find the truth.[17] Yet it is surely a suboptimal means because the individuals controlling trial procedure, the attorneys, subordinate truth-seeking to winning.

So much of what is referred to as "factfinding" is not really a determination of facts, but rather evaluative judgments. Even if the facts are known with certainty, what constitutes "negligence" or "criminal intent" is ultimately a subjective determination. So much of what we call factfinding is essentially subjective that it is misleading to think of the trial as a pristine search for truth. Though that may be the goal of the system as articulated in the purple prose of the appellate courts, it is not the goal of the litigants. Truth is incidental to their prepotent objective—victory, to which their zealous advocates strive.

Truth and Nontruth Values

Will technological advances improve trial truth-seeking? Even with the advent of more accurate factfinding techniques, such as DNA testing, the adversarial process will continue to subvert the truth by subordinating it to competing values. Peter Sperlich, who writes on the use of scientific evidence, says:

The adversary system maximizes the opportunities to obscure the facts, coopt the experts, and propagandize the judge. . . . The greatest single obstacle to complete and accurate scientific information . . . is the adversary system.[18]

The ostensible purpose of our trials is more the peaceful resolution of a dispute than the acquisition of information. Truth competes with considerations which resist measurement by any single ideal. The obfuscation of pattern jury instructions, for instance, may be by design, that is, a policy decision. Studies show that more comprehensible revised instructions (a) leads to fewer guilty convictions, and (b) may broaden the jury's awareness of their discretion to disobey the law.[19] If clarity were the preeminent value of the instructions, judges would give lectures on the apt law before and/or after the instructions, with question and answer opportunities, instead of all the legal instructions at the end of the trial, with no opportunity for juror questions.

Among the values that institutions of justice are meant to serve, truth is too often sacrificed at the altar of legal victory. For example, litigant satisfaction is an operative goal of the American trial. To achieve this end, we have party—rather than court—control of the trial.[20] But by the same token, party control permits a host of attorney devices to distort and dissemble the truth.

Judge Frankel decried the low value truth is accorded under the adversary system. To the practicing trial attorney, says Frankel, it is but a nominal goal:

Employed by interested parties, the process often achieves truth only as a convenience, a byproduct, or an accidental approximation. The business of the advocate, simply stated, is to win if possible without violating the law. . . . His is not the search for truth as such. . . . [T]he truth and victory are mutually incompatible for some considerable percentage of the attorneys trying cases at any given time.[21]

Thus the preeminent goal of victory profoundly corrupts the reliability of the adversary system as a vehicle for truth. Frankel challenges the legal profession: Hold the adversary process up to the light of reality; as a search for truth, how does it measure up against the procedures in other fields and in other countries?

Despite our untested statements of self-congratulations, we know that others searching after facts—in history, geography, medicine, whatever—do not emulate our adversary system. We know that most countries of the world seek justice by different routes. What is more to the point, we know that many of the rules and devices of adversary litigation as we conduct it are not geared for, but are often aptly suited to *defeat*, the development of the truth.[22] (Emphasis added.)

Other values incompatible with truth-seeking nevertheless obtain in the adversarial trial: individual dignity, privacy, freedom from unreasonable state regulation and the presumption of innocence in criminal cases. In criminal cases, the Constitution erects specific impasses to the search for truth. Hence the Fourth Amendment right of freedom from unreasonable government search excludes much relevant evidence at trial. And the Fifth Amendment privilege against self-incrimination cuts off the most fruitful source of evidence in a criminal case. In this light, the criminal trial is not a true search for truth, but a test of the prosecutor's proof. Striving for internal consistency, legal scholars have sought either to reconcile the incompatible goals of adversary procedure, or to establish their priorities. In response to Frankel's charge that truth is accorded too low a priority in the system, Monroe Freedman counters that the trial is not an abstract search for the truth. He points to the Fourth, Fifth and Sixth Amendments, plus language from U.S. Supreme Court decisions to support his contention that truth often must be *subordinated* to more "fundamental ideals."[23] Frankel's proposal to establish truth as the overriding goal of the adversary system, says Freedman, would violate these constitutional limitations. Freedman then accuses Frankel of engaging in the very kind of tactics Frankel decries:

One suspects that in minimizing his advertence to that critical [constitutional] aspect of the problem, the umpireal judge was backsliding into a bit of lawyerly adversariness. For if we ask . . . just how strongly arguable is the case for the "more fundamental ideals," we will find either that we are being asked to sacrifice those ideals in some substantial measure . . . or that Judge Frankel's measure is wholly impractical, because regard for those ideals precludes a single-minded search for truth.[24]

But Frankel is not proposing the abrogation of constitutional rights if their exercise may result in hiding the truth. Rather, he suggests we reevaluate the priorities given to truth and nontruth values in trial in order to produce a more just result. It is noteworthy that Freedman only refers to constitutional language and Supreme Court dicta suggesting the permissible sacrifice of truth in criminal cases. In so doing, he elides the multifarious ways in which the adversary system facilitates the frustration of truth in *civil* cases. Yet criminal and civil cases are the two faces of the same adversary system. Freedman applies his touchstone to only one, but generalizes to all trials. Perhaps it is he who is doing the backsliding.

Discovery Problems

One of the most significant trial mechanisms for ascertaining the truth was developed during the New Deal. Under a procedure called discovery, a litigant may request of the opposing party any relevant information (not protected by privilege) which that party has or to which that party has access. One objective was to do away with the element of surprise in a trial; another was to encourage out-of-court settlement, a solution presumed more likely once both sides were fully apprised of the facts. The major discovery device is the deposition, an interrogation under oath. It preserves the testimony of someone who will not or may not be available at trial. It may also be used to contradict a witness who later offers conflicting testimony at trial. Depositions are conducted orally, but the questions may also be written in advance—"depositions upon written questions." Another discovery tool is the interrogatory, a set of written questions to which written answers are prepared and signed under oath. (The difference between interrogatories and depositions upon written questions is that the former can only be directed to litigants.) Discovery can also be used to obtain documents, admissions, physical and mental examinations and other potential evidence within the respondent's control, such as photos.

Initially, discovery was hailed as a boon to truth-seeking, fairness and expedited case disposition. No longer. Discovery abuses now constitute the single greatest source of dispute, delay, cost and trickery in the adversary system. University of Missouri law professor Wayne Brazil catalogued the specific discovery tactics attorneys for both sides commonly use, either to bully the opposition into submission or to limit and distort the flow of information. Either result defeats the principle purposes for which discovery was designed. Some of the most prevalent abuses by attorneys making discovery demands are as follows:

- trying to smother a relatively impecunious adversary with extensive discovery demands and resultant costs;
- using written interrogatories as weapons for purely tactical purposes if doing so might promote their client's interests and generate fees for themselves;
- "fishing expeditions" which include serving numerous and far-reaching questions, not to obtain information about disputed matters, but to search for evidence that might support new claims, uncover competitor's business secrets, or harass an opponent into a favorable settlement;
- charging many different clients the full cost of drafting the original set of questions.

Responding attorneys employ an equally mischievous array of tactics, including:

- creating false, diversionary leads and generating obfuscating clouds of irrelevant information;
- providing as little information as possible, and making the acquiring of that information as difficult and expensive as possible;
- refusing to respond to written requests that are not free of virtually all ambiguity, imprecision, overbreadth, irrelevance, or other technical deficiencies;
- burying significant documents in mounds of irrelevant or innocuous materials; and
- aggressively interposing disruptive objections to the form or relevance of questions.[25]

Depositions provide the "hardball" litigator with an especially effective adversarial weapon. As Brazil explains, "Because depositions can be used to require the presence of the deponent for lengthy periods of time, they also have great adversarial potential for harassing and embarrassing adverse parties or witnesses and for disrupting their lives and businesses."[26] A survey of Chicago litigators found a similar widespread use of discovery as an aggressive tactical weapon. The idea, said one survey respondent, is to "see if you can get them mad," to put them "through the wringer, through the mud," so that "they are frightened to be a witness and . . . are a much worse witness."[27]

Unfortunately, civil discovery abuse is widespread; it epitomizes the system of which it is a part. Zealous advocacy, a shibboleth of the adversary system, and the ascertainment of truth are ineluctably incompatible. Brazil writes,

My point here is not simply that such obstructionist devices are available and employed, but that the intense competitive pressures of the adversary system make resort to them a constant temptation. Indeed, some lawyers might argue that a thoroughgoing adversarial professionalism commands the use of such obstructive devices whenever they appear to promise significant advantages for a client.[28]

Not all discovery abuse issues from unethical or illegitimate motives. Fear of malpractice liability contributes to discovery overuse. As with their medical counterparts who essay to leave no diagnostic tool unused, not because it is good medicine, but out of fear of malpractice lawsuits, so too attorneys take depositions that are either too long or unnecessary, make document requests that are too voluminous, and inflict word processor-generated interrogatories which have little relevance to the issues in the case.[29] This "overlawyering" breeds a conflict of interest between attorney and client. Consequently, overdiscovery prices many would-be civil litigants out of the market. William Schwarzer, a federal judge and director of the Federal Judicial Center, estimates that discovery has made litigating a case for less than $200,000 "rarely economically feasible."[30] He concludes: "In short, the transaction costs of dispute resolution have reached unaffordable levels."[31]

EXCLUSIONARY RULES

At the beginning of the Watergate trial, Judge John Sirica reportedly announced his intent to relax the rules of evidence "in the interest of finding the truth."[32] Sirica's candor indicated an ongoing problem. Several procedural rules inhibit truth-seeking in the adversary system trial. Collectively they are known as exclusionary rules because their implementation excludes relevant evidence from consideration by the factfinder. Already mentioned were the expansive exclusions under the Fourth and Fifth Amendments (in criminal cases), and the attorney-client privilege.

Large amounts of relevant evidence are also excluded under the hearsay rule. Hearsay—statements allegedly made out of court—is inadmissible because there is no opportunity to subject the statement-maker to adversarial cross-examination. Consequently, hearsay statements are generally deemed unreliable. But their total exclusion is a draconian measure. Decisive information may be withheld, vitiating the search for truth and any semblance of an informed verdict.

Another reason may explain perpetuation of the hearsay exclusion. The primary impetus for the hearsay rule today could be judicial distrust of juror capabilities. Judges remain skeptical of lay juror ability to assign the proper weight to hearsay testimony—even with cautionary instructions from the judge. When, during the sixteenth century, witness testimony supplanted personal knowledge as the basis for jury decisions, the inherent dangers of hearsay became clear. In 1603, the treason trial of Sir Walter Raleigh reified this concern. Two damaging pieces of hearsay evidence were introduced by the prosecutors. Raleigh strenuously objected: "[I]f witnesses are to speak by relation to one another, by this means you may have any man's life in a week, and I may be massacred by mere hearsay."[33] Raleigh was correct. He was convicted and executed on the disputed hearsay. Thereafter, "upper class English judges" were ever-weary of the incompetence of "lower class . . . jurors" to properly distinguish direct and hearsay evidence.[34]

In his five volume *Rationale of Judicial Evidence*, Jeremy Bentham deprecated the implied assumption that jurors were incapable of properly weighing hearsay evidence. He wrote:

[T]he system of exclusion is . . . precipitate and indefensible. You conclude they will be deceived by it: why so hasty in your conclusions? To know whether they have or have not been deceived by it, depends altogether upon yourself. What? Can you not so much as stay to hear their verdict? . . . Apply, where as yet there is no disease, a remedy, and a remedy worse than the disease?[35]

The presumption of juror incompetence undergirding the hearsay exclusion is anachronistic. It persists without reference to the fact that present-day jurors are far more educated and sophisticated than their predecessors. In the mid-nineteenth century, when the rules of evidence solidified in the United States, the number of students graduating from high school was less than 2 percent. A century later, that number increased fortyfold.[36] This should give pause to perpetuating the hearsay rule. Attorneys and judges have long tended to resist changes in procedural rules. But the societal pressure to keep improving substantive law (which defines rights and duties) is absent with procedural law (regulating the courts and other government bodies in enforcing substantive law). As Professor Morgan pointed out, "our adversary system makes entirely impracticable the process of competent procedural reform by judicial decision in contested cases."[37]

The presumed juror incompetence regarding hearsay defies empirical verification. Bentham called on judicial rulemakers to test whether hearsay actually deceived jurors. Until recently, no researchers embraced his challenge. But new research findings raise doubts about the validity of the presumption. Research subjects properly discounted hearsay testimony.[38] These results strongly militate in favor of eliminating or modifying the hearsay exclusion. An alternative approach involves cautionary instructions to jurors from the bench. This tack elicits objections from adversary system stalwarts. They say unbridled judicial discretion in selecting which hearsay to allow, allow with instructions, or eliminate "could threaten the adversarial balance which cedes control and proof-adducing process to lawyers rather than judges."[39] Still, is this sufficient reason to preclude further inquiry into the feasibility of a potential salutary change, one that would markedly enhance the scope of relevant information admitted into evidence?

Priority of Truth in the Inquisitorial System

As opposed to the adversary system, the inquisitorial system trial is remarkably unencumbered in its search for truth. To begin with, there is no hearsay exclusion because there is no reliance on a lay jury for factfinding. (Peculiarly, hearsay exclusions in the adversary system also apply when the judge hears the case without a jury.) Furthermore, the inquisitorial system trial does not suffer the same degree of incompatible purposes as its adversarial counterpart. State inquiry into the relevant facts is the dominant characteristic of the inquisitorial system proceeding. In contrast, nontruth values (individual dignity, and so forth) are greater in adversary system trials because of the distrust of the state.

Under the adversary system, state resources give the prosecution a decided advantage in criminal trials. To counteract this, the system erects special evidentiary barriers which impede the truth and protect criminal defendants. Because of this disparity of underlying systemic values, Mirjan Damaska[40] concludes that the two trial processes cannot be compared accurately.

Thibaut and Walker nevertheless made extensive comparisons of the two systems. They concluded that an autocratic procedure which delegates both process and decision control to a disinterested third party, that is, a model mirrored in the inquisitorial system, is optimal for the determination of the truth. Discovered evidence is presented more accurately than that presented by adversarial processes.[41] Such a process "increases the likelihood of obtaining the relevant information, reduces the strain of assimilating and tracking information, and minimizes the risk of failing to reach the correct solution."[42]

Privileged communications are also excludable in the adversarial trial. These are statements made between parties in certain specially protected confidential relationships, such as communications between attorney and client. This "confidentiality" rule prohibits the admission of evidence which was the subject of attorney-client communication. Without this protection, clients would be reticent to make full disclosure to their attorneys. Full disclosure enables the attorney to apprise the client of his or her rights, potential claims and defenses, and to make the most effective presentation of those claims and defenses. Accordingly, the attorney-client privilege endures despite its adverse effect on the pursuit of truth.[43]

However compelling in the abstract, the rationale for each exclusionary rule must still be vetted individually. Prominent federal judge Jack Weinstein admonished:

The incremental erosion of the truth-finding capability of triers in general is, to be sure, relatively small as each such rule of exclusion is created. But the truth-finding criterion for rules of evidence is so important that even minor mandatory distortions need to be viewed very critically. It is necessary to constantly bear in mind Wigmore's warning that only the clearest and most over-riding necessity warrants interfering with the fact-finding ability of the courts because of extrinsic social policy.[44]

No Responsibility of the Attorney for the Truth

Some believe the Platonic dialectic to be the prototype for the adversary system's approach to truth-finding.[45] This analogue would be more credible if the sole or major responsibility of trial counsel were to seek the truth objectively, as did the participants of the dialectic. No such duty burdens the attorney. In fact, attorney trial tactics are the single greatest source of truth distortion and dissimulation in the adversary system. Bentham undoubtedly had this in mind when he penned the following:

Were we to go over the history of tribunals, and select all the rules of practice which have been established to the prejudice of truth, to the ruin of innocence and honest right, the picture would be a most melancholy one. . . . [L]awyers, . . . contemplating every judicial operation as a source of gain, have labored to multiply unjust suits, unjust defenses, delays, incidents, expenses. . . . [L]egal fictions, nullities, superfluous forms, privileged lies have covered the field of law. . . . Lawyers have put themselves beyond the reach of attack, by wrapping themselves up in mystery, and have even tried to extract a title to glory from this very obscurity, which, like the shade of a machineel tree, diffuses poison all around.[46]

The attorney's overriding allegiance is to his client, not to the truth. In pursuing his role of zealous advocate, it remains unclear to what lengths the attorney may go in distorting or hiding the truth. This is not to suggest there are no formal limitations on attorney behavior under the adversary system. There are.[47] The problem is that they are generally vague and/or rarely enforced. Hence the scope of attorney tricks are really limited more by the abundant fecundity of attorney imagination than by clear and enforced restrictions. A complete taxonomy of attorney trial duplicity would daunt the most ambitious writer. But some of the common attorney artifices bear mention.

Many trial counsel submit briefs or memoranda containing distorted facts or law.[48] Notwithstanding a relatively unambiguous prohibition of this in the MRPC (Model Rules of Professional Responsibility),[49] appellate decisions report gross violations. They include statements of purported fact unsupported or contradicted by the record,[50] distorted quotations,[51] or deliberate omissions of controlling authority.[52]

A standard practice in the United States is for attorneys to interview their witnesses in preparation for testimony.[53] The practice is known by a variety of sobriquets—rehearsing, horseshedding, prepping and sandpapering—but the most common is coaching. Both the MRPC[54] and its predecessor, the Code of Professional Responsibility[55] proscribe any attorney inducement of false testimony. Yet courts casually accept, and even condone coaching, as language from this North Carolina case attests.

It is not improper for an attorney to prepare his witness for trial . . . and to go over before trial the attorney's questions and the witness' answers so that the witness will be ready for his appearance in court, will be more at ease because he knows what to expect, and will give his testimony in the most effective manner that he can. Such preparation is the mark of a good trial lawyer . . . and is to be commended because it provides a more efficient administration of justice and saves court time.[56]

The dangers of coaching are substantial: An attorney who knows the testimony of all friendly witnesses can orchestrate a common story that can better "avoid the pitfalls of contradiction and refutation by judicious fabrication."[57] In the course of coaching their witnesses, attorneys suggest "better" answers which, if not in clear contravention of the witness' original intended answer, subtly but effectively shade, dissemble or distort the truth. Despite the prevalence of coaching, an objecting opposing attorney can expect little, if any, help from the trial judge. Says Wigmore:

[The right to prepare witnesses] may be abused, and often is, but to prevent abuse by any definite rule seems impracticable. It would seem, therefore, that nothing short of an actual fraudulent conference could properly be taken notice of; there is no specific rule of behavior capable of being substituted for the proof of such facts.[58]

Attorney coaching is not confined to pretrial preparation. By asking leading questions on direct examination (of a friendly witness) experienced trial attorneys easily circumvent bars on otherwise inadmissible evidence because this practice is essentially coaching a witness while on the stand. And it will be ruled inadmissible if objected to by opposing counsel. Attorneys know this. Yet knowing objection to it will be sustained, they still deliberately ask leading questions because the desired answer is then known to the witness. After the objection, the witness can then answer a non-leading question with the desired answer. Consider this exchange from a reported case during direct examination of a witness:

Question: Directing your attention back to July, 1966, did you buy some virgin metal, virgin nickel from anyone in July 1966?

Answer: Yes sir, I did.

Question: Did you buy approximately eleven hundred ninety-nine pounds of metal back at that time?

Answer: I did.

[Defense Counsel]:   I object to leading. He should know how much he bought.

[The Court]:   I sustain the objection.

[Defense Counsel]:   I ask that the jury be instructed.

[The Court]:   The jury is instructed they are not to consider the question for any purpose. I sustained the objection.

Question: Do you recall how much of this virgin nickel you bought back in July of 1966?

Answer: I bought eleven hundred ninety-nine pounds.

[Defense Counsel]:   I objected after the leading question was asked of him and he turned around and asked how much. As important as that is to this case, I object to that being bought into evidence. He put words in his mouth and then asked him again.

[The Court]:   That's overruled.[59]

Additional strategic reasons militate in favor of asking impermissible leading questions. Repeated objections to them by opposing counsel may incur the jury's resentment and leave the impression that the objecting attorney is trying to hide the truth. Even when the objection is sustained, cautionary instructions from the judge to the jury are often ineffective, and sometimes counterproductive.[60]

Many trial attorneys use cross-examination to distort the truth. Although they employ tactics of questionable morality in any other context, the adversary system allows them to destroy hostile witnesses with impunity. System defenders fondly quote Wigmore's comment that cross-examination is the "greatest legal engine ever invented for the discovery of truth."[61] But they neglect to mention that Wigmore also referred to the witness stand as "the slaughterhouse of reputations."[62] During cross-examination, attorneys employ a plethora of nasty and dirty tricks. Interrogated witnesses are to be pitied, for cross-examination questions "are loaded with unsupported insinuations of improper motives, negligence, incompetence, perjury or, worse, suspicion of guilt of the crime for which the defendant is on trial."[63]

Crafty cross-examiners use more than the content of their questions to impeach a witness' credibility. Also influential with jurors is the behavior accompanying the question or its answer. Arched eyebrows and dropped jaw, for example, evince disbelief and disdain for the testimony of the hostile witness. The cross-examiner "wants to know if you have ever been in state prison, and takes your denial with the air of a man who thinks you ought to have been there."[64]

Cross-examiners commonly introduce improper matters to the attention of the factfinder through innuendo. For example, attorneys circumvent the rules by inserting their personal opinions in their questions. How? A California appellate court describes one popular method: "These 'did you know that' questions designed not to obtain information or test adverse testimony but to afford cross-examining counsel a device by which his own unsupported statements can reach the ears of the jury and be accepted by them as proof have been repeatedly condemned."[65]

Another rank artifice exploits the myth of perfect witness recall. While questioning witnesses, attorneys commonly engage in this kind of repartee: "When did this happen? Oh, you *think* it was February. You're saying you're unsure? So your testimony then is that you don't recall?" The clear purpose is to make the incriminating witness say, "I don't remember" as many times as possible. In *How to Cross-Examine Witnesses Successfully*, Lewis Lake urges: "No matter how clear, how logical, how concise, or how honest a witness may be or make his testimony appear, there is always some way, if you are ingenious enough, *to cast suspicion on it*, to weaken its effect."[66]

One of the more insidious tools in the cross-examiner's arsenal is the presumptuous cross-examination question. This question implies a serious charge against the witness for which the attorney has little or no proof. Some examples: "Isn't it true that you have accused men of rape before?," "What do you do to liven things up at a party?" (implying extrovertedness). Although the implication is unsubstantiated, these innuendos are particularly effective against expert witnesses. A recent mock jury study found that merely posing these questions severely diminished the expert's credibility, *even when the witness denied the allegation and his attorney's objection to the charge was sustained.*[67] This study clearly indicates that the presumptuous cross-examination question is a dirty trick which can sway jurors' evaluations of a witness' credibility.

Explanations for the effectiveness of this tactic vary. Communications research suggests people believe that when a speaker offers a premise, he or she has an evidentiary basis for it.[68] With their pristine mind sets, lay jurors conceivably assume that the derogatory premise of an attorney's question is supported by information. Another explanation lies in the possible confusion of jurors as to the sources of their information. The longer the trial, the less likely jurors will be able to distinguish information suggested by the attorney's presumptuous question from that imparted by the witness' answer.

And what of the ethical rules governing this tactic? The MRPC specifically forbids allusion to "any matter that the lawyer does not reasonably believe is relevant or that will not be supported by admissible evidence."[69] Although we expect attorneys to adhere to the rules of evidence and confine their strategies to the ethical boundaries of the rules, they often bend the rules and stretch the strategies.[70] Further, practice indicates that judges do not enforce the MRPC's standards. Instead, their lax demand is merely that attorneys have a "good faith belief" in the veracity of the assertions contained within their cross-examination questions.[71]

No other part of the adversarial trial spotlights the attorney's persuasive skills more than the closing argument, or "summation". In summation, attorneys must base their arguments only on matters already in evidence or fairly inferable from facts in evidence. Not unexpectedly, attorneys view their summation prerogatives broadly. Traditionally, attorneys have a certain rhetorical license in "summing up." Just as certainly, they repeatedly abuse it. A long-time mischievous practice of attorneys is to insert inadmissible comments during closing arguments. Injecting irrelevant and inflammatory matter, arguing based on facts not in the record, asserting personal opinions or beliefs, and vilifying opposing counsel or witnesses are the common tools. The following appellate court opinion is illustrative.

In his closing argument, defense counsel characterized plaintiffs' attorney as a "slick attorney from Chicago." . . . Defense counsel claimed that plaintiffs' counsel "manufactured" evidence, had a "wild imagination," and was not worthy of the jury's trust. He further stated that plaintiffs' counsel was the "captain of (the) ship" who was "piloting" the testimony of plaintiffs' expert witness. In addition, defense counsel compared the relationship between plaintiffs' counsel and his expert witness to that existing between the "Cisco Kid and Poncho" and "Matt Dillon and Chester."[72]

A distinct type of attorney deception is disruptive advocacy. Sometimes referred to as "dumb shows," this category consists of indecorous behavior intended to distract or mislead the jury. Some of the tactics include:

Deliberately raising an objection simply to interfere with his adversary's flow in opening or summation or to interrupt the witness solely for the sake of interruption. . . . Dropping books and paraphernalia on the floor to distract the jury during opposing counsel's summation, influencing jurors with unsubtle remarks or gestures in the hallway during recess, positioning exhibits not in evidence so jurors will see them.[73]

A novel subterfuge was attributed to the legendary Clarence Darrow: "A nearly invisible wire is inserted into a cigar so that when the cigar is smoked everyone's attention will be focused on the ash, which magically does not fall."[74] An even more distracting dumb show sure to elicit jury sympathy is having the defendant's small child crawl to the attorney during his closing argument. A trial attorney describes the ploy this way:

If the kid's a crawler, the best time to let him loose is during final argument. Imagine that little tyke crawling right up to you (make sure he comes to you and not the DA or, worse yet, the judge; a smear of Gerber's peaches worked for me) while you're saying: "Don't strike down this good man, father to little Jimmy. Why Jimmy!" Pick the child up and give him to Daddy. If the DA objects and gets them separated, so much the better. Moses himself couldn't part a father and son without earning disfavor in the eyes of the jury. Babies are true miracles of life; they've saved many a father years of long-distance parenting. If your client's childless, rent a kid for trial.[75]

Do dirty tricks pay? Owing to a lack of meaningful regulation and sanctions, they often do. The MRPC specifically outlaws only some. Others are only actionable under general prohibitions against disruptive conduct or against disregarding court rules or orders.[76] Based on law school curricula[77] and other indicia of their welcome status within the profession, dirty tricks are still viable options for many trial attorneys.

Yet dirty tricks pale in comparison with a more profound truth-corrupting attorney behavior. In measuring the reliability of the adversary system as a truth-seeking process, the foremost inquiries are whether attorneys (a) can and (b) do lie (or otherwise affirmatively suppress the truth). Answering the latter and easier query first, attorneys unquestionably lie and affirmatively suppress the truth. Indeed we have come to accept, and even expect, a certain amount of attorney lying and deception.[78] This is especially so if we include nondisclosure of a relevant fact and building upon the perjurious testimony of a client or friendly witness as more circuitous forms of lying and deception.

The literature is rife with jeremiads of attorney lying and deception. "For years, we have 'winked, blinked and nodded' at blatant, if not outrageous, lying and deception in pleading, negotiating, investigating, testifying, and bargaining," complains one law professor.[79] Samuel Thurman, another long-time "toiler in this vineyard" complains, "For too long, deception has been rationalized as a necessary adjunct to the adversary system."[80] Echoing Pound's "sporting theory of justice" theme, a trial judge offers his impressions of how attorneys' stories change as the trial progresses:

The sporting lawyer's concern is whether the story is convincing, whether it adequately meets the opposing story, not whether it is true or false. Thus it is not at all unusual to hear a courtroom story unfold like a novel, changing as the trial proceeds. Sometimes the story becomes clearer, sometimes fuzzier, sometimes contradicted as it is orchestrated by the lawyer-maestros. As one side crafts a story, the other side expresses outrage at the opponent's fiction and responds by fictionalizing its own story. The story is not as dismaying as the attorney's acquiescence in it. In this sort of liar's paradise, truth ceases to be a Heidegerrian revelation; instead, trial evidence becomes a progressive sedimentation, with new layers of lies overlaying the original ones.[81]

In her popular book, *Lying*, Sissela Bok limns the ambivalence within the legal profession regarding attorney lying. Contrasting common beliefs with those held within the profession, she writes:

[I]t is easy to tell a lie, but hard to tell only one. . . . [A]fter the first lies, moreover, others come easily. . . . Can it be argued that such lies are so common by now that they form an accepted practice that everyone knows about—much like a game of bargaining in a bazaar? . . . The fact is that, even though lawyers may know about such a practice, it is not publicly known, especially to jurors, much less consented to.[82]

Unresolved and more troublesome to the profession than whether lawyers *do* lie is whether, in pursuance of their duties, lawyers *can permissibly* lie, suborn perjury or build upon their clients' perjurious testimony. A criminal defense attorney can try to impeach the credibility of the state's witness, even if the attorney knows the witness to be telling the truth. Can he further obscure the truth? In one of the earlier articles on advocacy ethics (1951), Charles Curtis says the attorney's duty to client extends to lying and presenting arguments the attorney doesn't personally believe.[83] Monroe Freedman asserts that occasions arise when the criminal defense attorney may properly present perjured testimony.[84] Opponents, led by Frankel, disagree. They say that not only shouldn't the attorney ever lie, but that the attorney has an obligation to come forward with facts or law adverse to his client's case.

None of this is to suggest that attorney lying and deceit are not condemned by the rules of the profession. Rule 8.4 of the MRPC would appear to prohibit—by act, omission or acquiescence—lying or deception by providing:

It is professional misconduct for a lawyer to . . .
    (c) engage in conduct involving dishonesty, fraud, deceit or misrepresentation;
    (d) engage in conduct that is prejudicial to the administration of justice.

More specifically, attorneys cannot offer evidence known to be false[85] nor knowingly make false statements of material fact or law to the tribunal.[86] The MRPC also forbids the advocacy equivalent of passive fraud: Counsel must come forward and disclose material adverse facts or legal authority.[87] Judges occasionally sanction attorneys under the Federal Rules of Civil Procedure for not disclosing adverse authority.[88] Even if the attorney innocently presents false evidence, later discovery of its falsity requires "reasonable remedial measures," including the attorney's withdrawal from the case or, if necessary, disclosure to the court.[89]

Thus the MRPC appears to establish rigorous standards. In at least one instance, however, it significantly qualifies the attorney's duty to the truth. Assume the criminal defendant refuses to be dissuaded from perjurious testimony. The MRPC is ambivalent as to the attorney's proper response, as seen from the Comments to Rule 3.3:

If withdrawal [of the perjurer's attorney] will not remedy the situation or is impossible, the advocate should make disclosure to the court. . . . However, the definition of the lawyer's ethical duty may be qualified by constitutional provisions for due process and the right to counsel in criminal cases. In some jurisdictions these provisions have been construed to require that counsel present an accused as a witness if the accused wishes to testify, *even if the counsel knows the testimony will be false*. The obligation of the advocate under these Rules is subordinate to such a constitutional requirement. (Emphasis supplied.)

The murkiness of the MRPC's ethical waters extend beyond the attorney's role. Assume, as the MRPC dictates, the criminal defense attorney enlightens the court as to his client's intended perjury. According to the MRPC's Comments, the court's discretion is to inform the jury, order a mistrial, or do nothing.[90] What is remarkable is that the latter option *involves the court in perjury*.

Even the U.S. Supreme Court is ambivalent on the issue. In *Nix v. Whiteside*,[91] the Court divided sharply on the attorney's proper role in the face of criminal client perjury. Although the majority favored attorney disclosure to the court, the dissenters strong disapproval moved them to proclaim their disfavor to judges, attorneys and students. Not even the concurring justices viewed the case appropriate for resolving the "thorny problem" of client perjury.[92] Justice William Brennan, for example, in his concurring opinion, warned:

[L]et there be no mistake. The Court's essay regarding what constitutes the correct response to a criminal client's suggestion that he will perjure himself is pure discourse without force of law. . . . Lawyers, judges, bar associations, students and others should understand that the problem has not been "decided."[93]

Similar MRPC equivocation regarding the attorney's obligation of disclosure is found in the section on "Transactions With Persons Other Than Clients". The Rules seem to impose disclosure requirements comparable to those owed to the court, but then appear to rescind it all with the proviso, "unless disclosure is prohibited by Rule 1.6."[94] Rule 1.6 outlines the attorney's rather broad confidentiality obligations to the client, and thus to nondisclosure.

An anecdote of the famed evidence expert Samuel Williston epitomizes the profession's attitude toward the attorney's duty of candor to the court. Recounting an experience representing a client, he recalls:

In the course of his remarks the Chief Justice stated as one reason for his decision a supposed fact which I knew to be unfounded. I had in front of me a letter that showed his error. Though I have no doubt of the propriety of my behavior in keeping silent, I was somewhat uncomfortable at the time.[95]

Curtis supported Williston's behavior because "[a] lawyer is required to be disingenuous. He is required to make statements as well as arguments which he does not believe in."[96] Others in the profession have more ambivalence but come to the same conclusion. If an attorney knows the judge or opposing counsel is laboring under a misimpression not of the attorney's doing, the conventional wisdom is that silence is permissible, subject to the constraint against assisting another in committing a crime or fraud, and subject to MRPC Rule 3.3(a)(4) on the use of evidence later discovered to be false.[97]

Little controversy attends other instances where attorneys routinely distort and dissemble the truth. General agreement exists, for instance, that a criminal defense attorney may cross-examine a hostile witness known to be telling the truth in order to attack the witness' credibility.[98] Former U.S. Supreme Court Justice Byron White's defense of the practice has often been quoted:

If [defense counsel] can confuse a witness, even a truthful one, or make him appear at a disadvantage, unsure or indecisive, that will be his normal course. . . . [M]ore often than not, defense counsel will impeach [the prosecution's witness] if he can, even if he thinks the witness is telling the truth, just as he will attempt to destroy a witness he thinks is lying.[99]

Many counsel in civil cases undoubtedly take the same liberties. Conversely, the prosecutor's duty to "confess error" has yet to be imposed in civil litigation. That duty, which has a constitutional dimension, follows from an intentional pro-defense skewing inapplicable to civil cases.

Two conclusions arise in view of the mixed signals from the Supreme Court, the MRPC and prominent legal scholars. First, the assertions of Freedman and others that attorneys can occasionally present perjured testimony and otherwise dissimulate the truth remain unrepudiated. Second, we cannot expect meaningful movement toward trial practices dedicated to the search for truth.[100]

Given all the exclusionary exceptions and conflicting values moderating the trial as a truth-seeking exercise, defining its function defies facility. Theorists posit different models or images of the trial. One is that of a rational, rule-governed event involving the parties in a collective search for the truth. Exponents of this image claim the primary function of the trial is to ascertain truth via a *dialectic*. But, as noted earlier, adversary advocacy departs from the classical view of the dialectic because the latter is an *objective* exercise into what happened. Biased presentation of evidence renders the dialectic ideal elusive, if not impossible to achieve. Further, this image incorrectly assumes that witnesses accurately and objectively recount events. Studies belie both assumptions.[101] Therefore, this image of the trial does not mirror reality.

From the problem of biased presentation of evidence emerges a second image of the trial. It is compatible with the first in its reliance on the assumption that the primary function of the trial is to seek the truth. Acknowledging biased presentation of evidence, it casts the trial as a test of credibility. However, there are no universally agreed-upon means of credibility testing. Those commonly employed—the physical appearance and behaviors of witnesses—have been shown unreliable. This renders doubtful the validity of both the first and second images of the trial.[102]

A third and more realistic image of the trial is that of a conflict-resolving ritual. This view's proponents say trial outcome is less important than the *shared perception* that the legal system provides efficient conflict resolution. Critics of this view do not gainsay its validity. They just resent it. In their view, operation of the courts pursuant to this image legitimizes and perpetuates the present power structure to the detriment of just conflict resolution.[103]

Expert Witness Problems

Additional factfinding flaws inhere in the trial process. A spirited debate surrounds the use—and misuse—of expert evidence. Untoward results follow when expert evidence in complex cases is presented in adversarial fashion. Expert witnesses are manipulated for partisan purposes. Some relevant scientific findings are never introduced, while unwarranted conclusions are not distinguished from valid research.

The adversary system is the source of most grievances about the law from forensic scientists. They say it isn't a dependable method of arriving at factual truth in litigation. The more complex and technical the subject matter, the less well suited the system is to full and accurate communication of findings. Evidence is presented in fragments, separated by substantial intervals. No logical or sequential order of presentation is followed. Incomprehensible bench instructions frequently fail to remedy the confusion. Consequently, adversarial trials rarely resolve contradictions.

But the most basic problem is that the proceedings assign sole responsibility for conducting the inquiry to the functionaries who may be least interested in exposition of relevant scientific evidence. The attorney will want to omit and distort any evidence not presenting his client in the best possible light. When expert witnesses are pushed into advocacy roles, attorneys and the system corrupt the value of their expertise. Attention is too often focused on the personal characteristics of expert witnesses instead of the quality of their evidence.

Scientists incorrectly assume the law values truth as highly as does science. The primary objective of the trial is to resolve disputes in a just and fair way. In doing so, nontruth goals may be valued more highly. The reason: Trials are policy-driven as well as evidence-driven; the secondary status of truth can't be understood without recognition of the political nature of trial procedure.[104]

In a 1987 book compiling papers and comments presented at a conference on social research and the courts, the participants reached consensus on these points:

- Law and social science serve disparate ends. Case disposition, not truth-seeking, is the primary function of the courts.[105]

- Scientists serving as expert witnesses must expect to be used (and misused) for partisan purposes.[106]

- The adversary system is not a reliable means of bringing all the relevant scientific data to the adjudicator's attention, or for separating valid research from unwarranted conclusions.[107]

Similar problems occur in all learned disciplines—not only scientific—whose members are approached to offer expert testimony. Factfinders, especially juries, place great significance on expert testimony. Yet critical cognate issues remain unresolved. For instance, courts have not definitively explained what constitutes "expertise." Nor have they promulgated any clear, uniform standards on what is valid, reliable expert opinion. Some standards have been articulated. In the landmark 1923 case of *Frye v. U.S.*,[108] the appellate court established the rule to be applied in the federal courts: Only expert testimony which was "generally accepted" as valid among other experts in the field would be admitted. But when the more liberal Federal Rules of Evidence were codified in 1975, they made no mention of *Frye*.[109] In a 1993 case involving birth defects alleged to have been caused by use of the prenatal drug Bendectin, the U.S. Supreme Court resolved the apparent inconsistency of standards. The Court held that the flexible rules of evidence superseded the *Frye* standard, thus giving judges wider latitude to admit expert testimony.[110] As a result, almost any practitioner's view, no matter how iconoclastic, may be welcome.

Litigation involving the misuse and nonuse of science and scientific theories is legion. The granddaddy of nonuse was probably the Charlie Chaplin paternity suit, which began in 1943. The court ignored what should have been conclusive scientific evidence that Chaplin (Blood Group O) and the plaintiff, Joan Barry (Blood Group A), could not have spawned Barry's daughter, Carol Ann (Blood Group B). In his book, *Galileo's Revenge: Junk Science in the Courtroom*, Peter Huber recounts numerous legal victories attesting to the astounding weakness of scientific truth in the courtroom. Some illustrations:

- Three-month-old Michelle Graham suffered severe brain damage shortly after receiving a whooping cough vaccine produced by Wyeth laboratories. The plaintiff's scientific "expert" presented data that overstated the toxoid levels of the vaccine by between five and fifty times. More importantly, the judge barred critical testimony from Michelle's pediatric ophthalmologist, who found evidence of the brain damage *prior* to the vaccination. Although a later CT scan strongly supported the preexisting condition, the judge felt this inadmissible. She reasoned that the vaccine, not the stroke, was on trial. The jury awarded Michelle 15 million dollars.[111]

- Electronic fetal monitoring (EFM) began in 1972. Its popularity generated a spate of lawsuits against doctors, nurses and hospitals failing to use it. Specifically, juries became increasingly persuaded by hired experts that cerebral palsy could be averted with proper use and understanding of the EFM trace. Multimillion dollar verdicts or settlements became commonplace as a result of alleged failure to interpret fetal monitor readings showing the fetus in distress. Yet the overwhelming weight of scientific research and authority indicates that EFM does *not* prevent cerebral palsy. In 1990, for example, the largest (six year) study of EFM by American and Canadian researchers found that not only didn't EFM improve infant neurological development, but in most comparisons it was inferior to using stethoscope monitoring.[112]

- Many of those exposed to chemical pollution have reaped an economic bonanza thanks to self-acclaimed experts in "clinical ecology." Their successful argument: Workers and residents who become ill after exposure have contracted "chemically induced AIDS." Despite the absence of classic signs of immune system failure and a lack of solid scientific evidence establishing a link between chemical pollution and the ills complained of, juries and appellate courts have accepted the rationale that because chemicals can cause harm they *do* cause harm. That is what happened in the case of thirty-two residents of the town of Sedalia, Missouri. They sued the neighboring Alcolac Corporation, whose plant manufactured soap and cosmetic chemicals. Highly questionable tests "proved" that every one of the plaintiffs had suffered an impaired or potentially impaired immune system due to pollution from the plant. The jury agreed. It awarded an additional 43 million dollars in punitive damages to 6.2 million dollars in compensatory damages.[113]

Two factors undoubtedly contribute to this state of affairs: Social scientists generally shirk the responsibility to expose the limits of their own expertise; and overzealous attorneys knowingly recruit and often induce dubious and unsubstantiated views from "expert" witnesses. "Indeed," writes psychology professor Stephen Golding, "one is sometimes (cynically) led to believe that better expertise (which, by definition, is more neutral and therefore may not advance a proponent's view of the facts) may be at the bottom of the adversarial agenda."[114]

Venal expert witnesses must share the blame. They create a market at which civil litigators shop. By advertising their availability and pliability in legal journals, experts put their testimony up for sale and become the whores of their profession. Nowhere is this more prevalent than in psychiatry and psychology. Mercenary forensic psychiatrists have become professional testifiers. Their corrupt symbiosis with trial attorneys brings disrepute to themselves and the many honorable members of their profession.

Let us recapitulate. Truth-finding is one of the most popular justifications of the adversary system. Yet the notion that trial by combat, whether by weapons or words, will reliably yield the truth is both counterintuitive[115] and empirically contradicted.[116] Attorneys acting well within their legal and ethical bounds can block or distort the presentation of truthful evidence and otherwise corrupt the trial process. In return, they are rewarded and admired by members of the bench and bar alike. Chapter 3 noted the accolades the New York Bar bestowed upon Bruce Bromley, who made an art of litigation delay. The wildly successful Gerry Spence is another hero of the litigation bar. In his lectures and articles, Spence advocates putting as much improper evidence as possible before the jury by asking improper questions. He reasons that this will sufficiently prejudice the jury to decide favorably despite the facts and law.[117]

Further confounding the search for truth under the adversary system is the demonstrably false assumption—upon which the system is based—of equally competent opposing attorneys. A disenchanted former prosecutor puts the lie to this assumption:

[T]his [equality] is frequently not the case. Particularly in criminal cases, the ability of the adversarial system to produce a just result is dubious where defense counsel lacks comparable skill and dedication to that of the prosecution. . . . Unfortunately, the extent of inadequate criminal defense is not insignificant. . . . In fact, prosecutors sometimes take advantage of inferior adversaries to accomplish results not otherwise attainable. And, under an adversary model, there is no incentive for prosecutors to rescue defendants from the inadequacies of defense counsel.[118]

Recognizing the potential weakness of adversarial truth-seeking, defenders of the system are wont to revert to alternative or, at least, nuanced versions of the truth justification. One is that most trial truth is ultimately unknowable. Therefore characterizing the trial as a search for truth is misleading. Whatever the merits of this argument, it cannot cogently justify all the truth obfuscation committed under the adversary system. To the extent truth can be objectively found in the courtroom, attorneys do as much to impede its discovery as facilitate it.

A dichotomy of goals separates the system and the litigants. The goal of the system may be a search for truth, but the goal of the litigants is winning, irrespective of the truth. Hence the system employs rules and mechanisms to ensure that attorney behavior does not detract from the decision maker's ability to find the facts and apply substantive legal principles properly. These rules prohibit perjury and bribes, require the sharing of evidence, and so on.

This perspective has surface credibility. But it does not correspond to practice. Current safeguards—as actually employed by judges, if not as written—are patently inadequate to the tricks plied by attorneys bent on concealing or distorting the truth.

Adversary system defenders acknowledge the truth-seeking flaws of the adversary system, but maintain with a symbolic shrug the lack of a better alternative. Even critics of the adversary system have taken this position. This is inexplicable. Chapter 6 discusses myriad current nonadversarial ADR mechanisms with effective factfinding. Foreign models reveal how this can work in an adjudicative process, so that the unique benefits of adjudication—constitutional protections, development of the law—can be preserved.

Even if extant models did not exist, an alternative to the ills of adversarial truth-seeking would seem deducible on an *a priori* basis: Change the role or identity of the person(s) developing the evidence. The factfinder in the adversarial trial—be it judge or jury—is misnamed. "Fact receiver" is more apt, given the factfinder's passive role. With virtually no involvement in investigating, developing or clarifying the evidence, the adversarial factfinder is little more than audience. Nowhere but the adversarial trial does this curious and ungainly role anomaly obtain.

JUSTICE

Some adversary system proponents may concede the lowered priority of truth in adversarial trials without admitting that this detracts from the fairness of the system. After all, it is the "adversary system of justice," not the "adversary system of truth." Let us consider the validity of that position.

Truth is but one value subsumed within the concept of trial justice. Although truth may be universal, justice is the most relative of concepts. Trial procedures in different countries reflect different notions of justice. Incorporated into each are the underlying values of the host society.

In countries using inquisitorial system trials, truth is the dominant value; the trial is an inquiry into the truth for the purpose of implementing social policy. For other societies and countries, including the United States, other values compete with truth. Social harmony, for instance, may be thought more important. An example is the Eskimo song duel, mentioned in Chapter 2. In this procedure, the truth (of the allegations) and fault (of the parties) are irrelevant. Our social harmony counterpart would be the increasingly popular no-fault schemes. In addition to no-fault auto insurance and no-fault divorce, workers compensation and strict tort liability utilize the no-fault approach. Removing the assignment of fault eliminates the hostility of the adversarial process. Instead, no-fault redresses injury and restores harmony.

In totalitarian societies, another value inexorably competes with the truth during trials: The government must validate its beliefs. Retaining power, the foremost objective, often necessitates the brutal suppression of dissidence. Therefore, along with objective inquiries into the truth, totalitarian society courts commonly use forced confessions and other truth-suppressing tactics.

In the United States, adversarial truth corruption is the single most corrosive influence on trials. But other aspects of the adversary system bear adversely upon the quality of trial justice. They are advocacy ethics, the maldistribution of legal services, and judicial passivity.

Advocacy Ethics

Critics charge attorneys with amoral (and sometimes immoral) behavior in the pursuit of their clients' interests. Behavior dictated by the attorney's role often conflicts with ordinary concepts of morality, as illustrated by the various trial attorney tricks and stratagems. Are litigators just "amoral technicians committed to winning the adversary battle"?[119] Those who say "Yes" point to the attorneys who zealously represent anyone regardless of the morality of the person's acts or goals. Some attorneys represent those they know or believe to be greedy civil litigants or even persons guilty of vicious crimes. Defenders of advocacy ethics maintain that the uniqueness of the attorney's role justifies application of distinct ethical and moral standards.

Case law and ethical codes impose few limits on a lawyer's zealous advocacy, even under the more "enlightened" MRPC. Lawyers' acts in the courtroom—improper or immoral as they may seem in other contexts—are justified as allowable mechanisms for attorneys to assert and defend their client's rights. To the legal profession, the lawyer's acts are thought to be morality-neutral role behavior. Legal ethicist Charles Wolfram concludes that this is "institutionally schizophrenic . . . a lawyer's objective within the system is to achieve a result favorable to the lawyer's client, possibly despite justice, the law and the facts."[120] Hereupon, some of the rationales for separate ethical standards for trial advocates, and their counterarguments.

One common justification concedes that lawyers engage in "role-differentiated behavior" which sometimes is amoral or immoral. Defenders say this behavior is nonetheless legitimate in that it is dictated by, and in the service of, an *accepted societal institution*—the adversary system of justice.[121] This roughly approximates a "means justifying an ends" rationale. But what about this end? Role-differentiated lawyer amorality is justifiable on institutional grounds only to the extent of our trust and confidence in the institution—in this case the adversary system. Behavior which is otherwise morally indefensible cannot be sanitized by service to a system whose rules are unjust. The adversary system is not an end in itself, but a means to the objectives of our justice system. Conduct justified in terms of the importance of the adversary system must be subordinated to consideration of its impact on the broader goals of the justice system. If adversarial procedure frustrates these goals in practice, then it cannot be justified by arguing that it furthers the adversary system.[122]

Another attempted exculpation of role-based attorney conduct looks to common expectations about attorney statements in court. Because truth-telling and truth-seeking are not the paramount goals of the trial or the lawyer, this argument goes, lawyers do not deceive in their professional roles. Deceit requires (a) that the deceiver represents himself or herself as believing the truth of his or her statements, and (b) an intent that the listener or reader rely on the truth of the representations. The lawyer's audience knows he does not represent a belief in the truth of his statements, but rather intends only to persuade. Therefore no reliance or deceit occurs. "The lawyer realizes that his audience is justified in not taking him seriously as regards the truth of his statements."[123]

This, too, strains credibility. No empirical datum confirms the contention that factfinders think attorneys may not believe their own trial statements. The lawyer may only be playing a part, but factfinders do not perceive the trial court as a theater. Irrespective of contradictory personal beliefs, lawyers strive mightily to persuade others of the truth of their arguments.[124]

William Simon, who has written extensively on the ethics of trial advocacy, expounds on four ideological rationalizations used by the legal profession to justify the apparent aberrance of advocacy ethics.

(1) *Neutrality*: *The lawyer keeps to himself his personal view of the justness of his client's claim;*[125] *he does not sit in judgment of the client's cause.* Hence neutrality is used by the attorney to disclaim responsibility for his partisan actions and their consequences.[126] The decision as to what is just is made by the court and jury. Stalwart trial advocates fondly refer their wavering colleagues to the words of the famous Dr. Samuel Johnson who, when asked his personal view of his client's case, reportedly said:

Sir, you do not know it to be good or bad till the judge determines it. . . . An argument which does not convince yourself, may convince the judge, to whom you urge it; and if it does not convince him, why, then, Sir, you are wrong and he is right.[127]

(2) *Partisanship*: *The attorney uses all legal means to advance his client's ends, even those improper in a nonprofessional context.* In practice, this often translates to deception, delay and even lying.[128] Just as attorneys use Neutrality to disclaim responsibility for their clients' morality, clients use Partisanship to disclaim responsibility for the lawyer's actions.[129] Partisanship is the rationale for the attorney's ethical duty of zealous advocacy, the polestar of the adversary system. Lord Brougham's injunction that attorneys should pursue their clients' objectives single-mindedly, without regard to the interests of others,[130] remains the quintessential description of the attorney's role within

the adversary system. Simply stated, once an attorney takes a client, the adversary system model dictates zealous representation, regardless of whether this furthers or defeats the interests of justice, however defined. All of the ethical codes adopted for the legal profession in the twentieth century incorporate this model in some form.[131]

This is not to deny the existence of countervailing attorney obligations. The MRPC[132] prescribe a limited number of duties to the court and third parties. Of these, the better-defined duties are to the former, as an "officer of the court."[133] Despite these requirements, few doubt that the MRPC contemplates anything but the predominant model of the attorney who does everything to win for his client. Stephen Gillers, a renowned expert in legal ethics, observed: "The lawyers who approved the Rules looked after their own. They have given us an astonishingly parochial, self-aggrandizing document, which favors lawyers over clients, other persons, and the administration of justice in almost every line, paragraph, and provision that permits significant choice."[134]

(3) *Procedural Justice: There is an inherent legitimacy to the judicial proceeding which justifies actions by the lawyer regardless of the consequences.*[135] But this legitimacy is based on the adversary myth: Each side in a lawsuit has roughly equal representation and resources. Despite the unproven and often erroneous nature of this assumption, the myth persists. Unquestioning faith in the Procedural Justice rationale causes litigants to ignore the real issues of their conflict; norms are seen as strategic props in a contest defined by procedure. Adversary advocacy stifles and sublimates what could be creative conflict. Moreover, the rigid formalism of the adversary trial is a Procrustean mold. It causes the litigant to see his or her opponent only in a hostile context, without regard for his or her own true ends or without confronting those of the other party.

(4) *Professionalism: It is up to lawyers collectively as a profession to be the sole determiners of the ethics of the profession.*[136] One problem with this rationalization is that advocacy ethics focus on the duty to the *client*. The attorney's duties are external to his own values. Legal education and ethical codes inculcate the lawyer's duties to others—primarily the client, but also the court, the legal profession, perhaps even society—yet do not advocate adherence to a duty to self. Take, as illustration, the National Institute of Trial Advocacy simulation model. It reports that lawyer skills courses make these assumptions:

• Lawyers have no obligation to seek the truth, only to obtain victory, even by use of manipulative techniques.[137]

• Law practice is a game; its only meaning comes from playing the game well.[138]

- The fictitious client's ends are always imputed to be win at any cost by any lawful means.[139]

Without obligation to one's own values, any actions for the benefit of the client's case falling within the minimum behavioral standards are permissible, even though those actions could transgress duties to self and, consequently, to widely held moral values. This emphasis on the lawyer's duty to others to the exclusion of the duty to self leads to the attorney as "hired gun" perspective. Carried to the extreme, this could aptly be characterized as the "Nuhrenberg Defense" model of legal ethics: Any action on behalf of the client is justified.[140]

The legal profession is hardly united in support of such an expansive ethical standard. Many legal theorists reject it. But even those clamoring for ethical reform generally feel that the attorney's role-differentiated behavior is morally justifiable in representing the criminal defendant. The basis for the criminal defense exception is that the consequences of conviction can be so grave. Deprivation of life or liberty are the most serious penalties society can exact.

Another reason suggests the criminal/civil distinction. Basic tenets of the adversary system simply do not apply in criminal litigation. Effective implementation of the adversary system requires that the advocates be roughly equal in adversariness, resources and competence. In reality, none of these strictures consistently obtain in criminal cases. Prosecutors are not supposed to effect equal adversariness; indeed they must affirmatively disclose evidence favorable to the accused. Conversely, the policy of protecting the criminal defendant from wrongful conviction allows defense counsel almost any adversarial tack. Further, the prosecution must turn over to the defense virtually all relevant evidence. No comparable disclosure duty obligates the defense to ensure that the guilty do not go free. Thus the rules allow the defense counsel to be more adversarial than the prosecution. As to the other presumed equalities, government resources devoted to prosecuting any given case are rarely matched by the defendant—particularly not by defendants with appointed counsel. And equality in attorney competence occurs only by happenstance.

In other instances, however, attorney role-differentiated behavior "is almost certainly excessive and at times inappropriate."[141] An attorney who assists a client to achieve an immoral outcome in a civil trial is to be as morally accountable for it as when functioning as an attorney outside of the court. Such accountability is already recognized in the expressed rules of professional behavior.[142] What is more, attorneys usually have far more discretion to accept or reject civil clients and causes.

Litigator behavior which is otherwise amoral or immoral deserves condemnation. The adversary system encourages the lawyer *qua* lawyer to be competitive rather than cooperative, aggressive rather than accommodating, ruthless rather than compassionate, and pragmatic rather than principled.

Unfortunately, it is highly unlikely that these traits will easily be changed because they are the same traits valued by one of the dominant ideals of our culture—the capitalist, laissez-faire ethic.[143] Nevertheless, change is in order. However valuable in their natural environs—economic markets, sports contests, and so forth—competitive drives are not felicitous to the sensitivities and subtleties of just dispute resolution. Whether or not to reform this state of affairs is not the issue. How to is.

Maldistribution of Legal Services

Another justice-related issue of the adversary system concerns the availability and quality of legal representation. The adversary system contributes to the maldistribution of legal services in the United States because it is a modern version of the battle of champions. To a great degree, a litigant's resources determine his or her fate in court. Ordinarily, the best champion, i.e., the best legal expertise, is available only to the wealthy. In the social history of the bar, the promise of equal justice under the law has been subverted by the bar itself.[144] Empirical studies confirm the common belief of laymen: Only a small minority of people—overwhelmingly composed of the wealthy and powerful—have ever been assured of substantive access to legal services. This maldistribution of legal services has rendered the presumed fairness of the adversary system more myth than reality. Given our dependence upon the legal profession to provide and implement equal justice under the law, the phenomenon of an elite, stratified bar serving an elite, stratified clientele preserves and reinforces social and economic inequality.

Unequal wealth results in unequal justice.[145] Even the U.S. government can be legally outmuscled. Take, for example, the long-running antitrust suit against IBM brought by the federal government in 1969. By 1979 IBM had 243 attorneys on its staff, fully half of the total attorneys in the Justice Department's Antitrust Division. Notwithstanding this number of staff attorneys, IBM's resources enabled it to retain the powerhouse Wall Street law firm of Cravath, Swaine and Moore for its defense. According to a *New York Times* report of the trial, "Cravath brings only seasoned lawyers to the court. Several times, [the Department of] Justice has stuck a fresh-faced lawyer right out of law school in court and had him question witnesses."[146] In the same year, the highest paid Justice Department trial attorney made $47,500—less than one-third of his IBM counterpart.[147] A similar resource disparity occurred in another government-big business legal battle. In 1978, the government sued major oil companies to refund $1.3 billion in alleged overcharges to consumers. Court documents listed thirty separate attorneys representing the oil companies against just two for the U.S. government.[148]

More recently, consider the 1991 rape trial of William Kennedy Smith, nephew of U.S. Senator Ted Kennedy. According to University of Chicago law professor Stephen Schulhofer, Smith's acquittal hinged in large part on the disparity of resources and talent between the prosecution and defense. The defense team's skill contrasted sharply with the prosecution's strategic errors. Complementing its skills advantage, the defense hired a leading jury selection consultant, and spent thousands of dollars more on expert witnesses and exhibits. Writes Schulhofer:

Money made a big difference in the Smith case. It makes an even bigger difference in common criminal cases. . . . Everyday, defendants without resources are convicted on shaky evidence in our urban courts. . . . The rich will continue to get special justice because our society remains unwilling to make the constitutional guarantee of a fair trial a reality for all.[149]

Not everyone deprecates this state of affairs. Some view the inequality as integral to the "free enterprise" concept of social justice, whereby justice, like other scarce commodities, is the reward to those who *compete* the most effectively for it. The adversary system merely extends the practices of the business world to the operation of the legal system. Thus it reflects the primacy of competition in our society. The system, concludes game theorist Anatol Rapoport, is a "direct transplant of competitive economics into the apparatus of justice."[150]

Because any competitive system is held in such high regard in American culture, the failings of the adversary system and the legal profession are popularly viewed as a function of individual shortcomings, instead of structural, systemic deficiencies. Consequently, the most salient response has been promulgation and symbolic enforcement of ethical rules, notably the MRPC. It is with lawyers, this view holds, not the trial system, whither the problem lies. This micro-perspective ignores the economic verities of the adversary system—the unequal access to the system, the wealth-based mismatching of legal skills—which preclude attainment of the equal justice ideal.

The maldistribution problem is two-pronged: At one end, it implicates those situations where financially mismatched litigants are represented by commensurately mismatched legal talent; on the other end, the problem contemplates all of the less-privileged members of society who have *no* access to the civil justice system for lack of resources. (There is no civil counterpart to the Sixth Amendment's right to counsel for indigent defendants.) In the first instance, there is unequal justice; in the latter, there is no justice, at least not through the courts.

In its *Blueprint for Improving the Civil Justice System* (hereafter the ABA Blueprint), the American Bar Association assesses the societal impact upon the many groups who do not have access to civil justice. Articulating the need to provide universal access, it cites eminent jurists such as Justice Learned Hand, who believed one commandment must be adhered to if democracy is to be preserved: "Thou shall not ration justice."[151] This is not empty rhetoric. The ABA identifies government as the proper vehicle for universal access to court justice:

The first responsibility of our federal government specifically enumerated in the U.S. Constitution is to establish justice. Ever since that admirable document was adopted, primary responsibility for providing access to justice has rested with government. Whether all people are created equal becomes a moot question if access to the system that ensures that equality is available to only a selected few.[152]

The poor undoubtedly suffer most from lack of access to necessary legal assistance. According to an ABA national pilot study and numerous state studies, the poor have access to the legal system for only 15 to 20 percent of their legal problems.[153] New York surveys found that 61 percent of tenants were unrepresented in court cases with landlords.[154] Another study found that over 90 percent of debtors in New York, Chicago and Detroit lose their cases by default.[155]

In a paper delivered at the ABA meeting which established the Commission on Legal Aid, it was stated:

If man, because of poverty, cannot secure counsel, the machinery of justice becomes unmovable, and that in turn means that rights are lost and wrongs go unredressed.

When persons are thus debarred from their day in court they are as effectively stripped of their only protection as if they had been outlawed.

No democracy can tolerate such a condition in its most essential institution, nor can it safely incur the dangerous sense of injustice, bitterness, and unrest which it inevitably engenders.[156]

Court justice is generally inaccessible to the disadvantaged as well as to the poor. Certain segments of our society are traditionally underrepresented in the justice system—the homeless, children, physically or mentally disabled, the institutionalized and those with AIDS.[157] Furthermore, our civil justice system sadly lags behind all other countries in the Western world in providing for access to justice for the middle class, a problem acknowledged by the ABA.[158] How extensive is this problem? Another ABA publication reveals the answer: "The [ABA] has long been aware that the *middle 70 percent of our population is not being reached or served by the legal profession.*"[159] (Emphasis supplied.)

Judicial Passivity and Judicial Elections

A final justice problem related to the adversary system lies with the role of the judge. Bloated court dockets impel the current movement toward greater judicial pretrial case management and control over jury selection. But this path oppugns convention. Historically, judicial passivity has been a corollary to the adversary system's fundamental tenet of judicial impartiality.[160] The passive judge remains integral to the adversary trial model. (The related problems were discussed in Chapter 3.) Not surprisingly, many if not most trial judges prefer the traditional passive standard. Compelling deterrents temper the zeal of many a judge who might otherwise be moved to intervene in the name of justice. Judges charged with "compromised neutrality" often find their decisions reversed on appeal.

Nonetheless, waxing case backlogs continue to erode the old paradigm of judicial restraint. New court reforms at the federal and state levels constrain judges to act where before they could remain aloof. The reforms prescribe that judges try to (a) induce settlement by the parties, and (b) foreshorten jury selection, discovery and other pretrial processes for those cases that go to trial. As a result, greater interventionism may be forced upon judges—not to remedy defective or decisively mismatched advocacy, but to expedite case disposition. This poses a dilemma. With more involvement in pretrial case management required, how is the judge to avoid the appearance (if not the actuality) of bias *during trial* toward litigants who failed to heed her pretrial entreaties to settle? Does not the enhanced participation in narrowing the issues and proposing compromises unalterably color the judge's judgment? This has been the stated assumption of the ABA and the most prestigious "defenders of the faith," such as Lon Fuller.[161]

Once in trial, fear of appellate reversal constrains many a judge to passivity. Perhaps a greater impetus to passivity is the judicial election. In the many states where the judiciary must stand for election or reelection, judges seek to distance themselves from the consequences of unpopular decisions. The passive judge runs less risk of political repercussions.

States use a variety of judicial selection procedures. A small number of states emulate the federal system and appoint their judges for life. Although this ensures maximum independence of the judiciary from politics, lifetime tenure is a two-edged sword. Judges who never have to answer to voters are unaccountable to the public. Thus thirty-nine states hold judicial elections in some form.[162] In some states, would-be judges run as political candidates, affiliated with a political party. These judicial candidates must run for election as well as reelection.

While infusing accountability, judicial elections create conflict-of-interest problems. As with other elections, fund-raising is a necessary evil. In judicial elections, attorneys are often the only people interested enough to donate to judicial campaigns. How can judges retain their neutrality when they must solicit contributions from attorneys who appear before them? To avoid the appearance of politically influenced judicial candidates, as well as to select judges based on merit, some states have adopted a system which seeks to strike a balance: the so-called "Missouri Plan." Under it, the governor appoints (or rejects) the nominee of an expert panel or group. Such appointees must then be periodically approved by the electorate to retain their seats. Retention elections have no opposing candidates; the only issue is whether to retain the judge.

Politics can easily erode the judicial neutrality paradigm. The harsh realities of fund-raising and responsibility to the electorate do not mix well with judicial independence. "The whole problem," notes a California presiding judge, "is we want both. We don't want judges who are totally immune and divorced from real life, and on the other hand we want them to be sufficiently independent so that they can make decisions based on principle."[163]

NOTES

1.   Speech, Feb. 11, 1851.
2.   A lengthy discussion of this case, with documents and interviews, is found in Patrick Keenan, ed., *Teaching Professional Responsibility: Materials and Proceedings from the National Conference* (Detroit, Mich.: University of Detroit Press, 1979), pp. 233-324.
3.   Dan Weikel, ""When the Prosecutor is Guilty," *Los Angeles Times*, 5/13/94, p. 1.
4.   Id.
5.   Id.
6.   Id.
7.   Id.
8.   Id.
9.   Claudia MacLachlan, "Plaintiffs See Civil RICO in Nicotine Suit," *National Law Journal*, 5/23/94, pp. 1 at 13.
10. *Estes v. Texas*, 381 *U.S.* 532, 540 (1965); *Tehan v. U.S. ex rel Schott*, 382 *U.S.* 406, 416 (1966); *U.S. v. Wade*, 388 *U.S.* 218, 256 (1967).
11. John Wigmore, *A Treatise on the Anglo-American System of Evidence in Trials at Common Law*, 3d ed., Vol. 1 (Boston: Little Brown, 1940), p. 3.
12. Geoffrey Hazard, *Ethics in the Practice of the Law* (New Haven, Conn.: Yale University Press, 1978), p. 122.

13. Philip Shuchman, *Problems of Knowledge in Legal Scholarship* (Hartford, Conn.: University of Connecticut School of Law Press, 1979), pp. 8, 15, 16, 57.

14. Id., pp. 46-49.

15. James Marshall, *Law and Psychology in Conflict*, 2d ed.(New York: Bobbs Merrill, 1980), p. 148.

16. Max Radin, "The Permanent Problems of the Law," in *Jurisprudence in Action* (New York: Baker, Voorhis, 1953), pp. 415, 419.

17. Shuchman, *op. cit.*, pp. 50-51, 56-60.

18. Peter Sperlich, "Scientific evidence in the courts: the disutility of adversary proceedings," *Judicature, 66(10)* (May 1983), pp. 472 at 474, 475.

19. Wallace Loh, "The Evidence and Trial Procedure: The Law, Social Policy and Psychological Research," in S. Kassin and L. Wrightsman, eds., *The Psychology of Evidence and Trial Procedure* (Beverly Hills, Calif.: Sage Publications, 1985), p. 16-38.

20. Empirical studies suggest that the party control feature of the adversary system contributes most to the perception of fairness and thus to litigant satisfaction. See E. Allan Lind, "The Psychology of Courtroom Procedure," in Kerr and Bray, eds., *The Psychology of the Courtroom* (New York: Academic Press, 1982), p. 19; and Laurens Walker, E. Allan Lind and John Thibaut, "The Relation Between Procedural and Distributive Justice," 65(8) *Virginia Law Review* 1401, 1416 (1979).

21. Marvin Frankel, "The Search for Truth: An Umpireal View," 123 *University of Pennsylvania Law Review* 1037 (1975).

22. Id. at 1036.

23. See related discussion in Chapter 2.

24. Monroe Freedman, "Judge Frankel's Search for Truth," 123 *University of Pennsylvania Law Review* at 1066 (1975).

25. Most of these illustrations are from Wayne Brazil, "The Adversary Character of Civil Discovery," 31 *Vanderbilt Law Review* 1319-31 (1978).

26. Id., p. 1329.

27. Wayne Brazil, "Civil Discovery: Lawyers' Views on Its Effectiveness, Its Principal Problems and Abuses," 1980 *American Bar Foundation Research Journal* 787 (1980).

28. Brazil, "The Adversary Character of Civil Discovery," *op. cit.*, p. 1331.

29. William Schwarzer, "Slaying the Monsters of Cost and Delay: Would Disclosure be More Effective than Discovery?," *Judicature, 74(4)* (December-January 1991), p. 178-79.

30. Id., p. 179.

31. Id.

32. See John Sirica, *To Set the Record Straight* (New York: Norton, 1979), for the judge's impression of the Watergate trial.

33. Quoted in W. Holdsworth, *A History of English Law*, 3d ed. (London: Methuen and Co., 1922), p. 216.

34. Jack Weinstein, "Alternatives to Present Hearsay Rules," 44 *FRD* at 375, 377 (1968).

35. Jeremy Bentham, *Rationale of Judicial Evidence* (New York: Garland Publishing, Inc., 1978), p. 593. (1827 facsimile; London: Hunt and Clark.)

36. *U.S. Department of Health, Education and Welfare, Digest of Educational Statistics* (Washington, D.C.: Author, 1964), pp. 56, 76.

37. Edmund Morgan, "Practical Difficulties Impeding Reform in the Law of Evidence," 14 *Vanderbilt Law Review* 725 (1961).

38. See Stephan Landsman and Richard Rakos, "Research Essay: A Preliminary Empirical Inquiry Concerning the Prohibition of Hearsay Evidence in American Courts," *Law and Psychology Review*, *15* (1991), pp. 65-85; and Meine *et al.*, "The Evaluation of Hearsay Evidence," paper presented to the American Psychological Association, Boston, Mass., August 1991.

39. Landsman and Rakos, *op. cit.*, p. 81.

40. Mirjan Damaska, *The Faces of Justice and State Authority* (New Haven, Conn.: Yale University Press, 1986), p. 88.

41. E. Allan Lind, John Thibaut and Laurens Walker, "Discovery and Presentation of Evidence in Adversary and Nonadversary Proceedings," 71 *Mich. Law Review* 1129 (1973).

42. Thibaut and Walker, "A Theory of Procedure," 66 *California Law Review* 541 at 547-48 (1978). They nevertheless claim that the adversary system is preferable for most lawsuits. They reason as follows: In the average lawsuit, matters of distributive justice are more important and hotly contested than issues of fact. Once the basis of the conflict is one of justice rather than truth, the adversary process is optimal because assigning maximum process control to the disputants is most likely to result in distributive justice (p. 566). Many propositions must be accepted before one subscribes to this theory, not the least of which is a workable disjuncture between truth and justice.

43. Critics of the confidentiality rule assume its impairment of the truth search occurs *after* the client has disclosed relevant information to the attorney. This is an untested and counterintuitive assumption. Withdrawal or limitation of the confidentiality privilege would more likely cause clients to withhold their confidences. Hence the actual effect of the privilege on the search for truth is probably negligible.

44. Jack Weinstein, "Some Difficulties in Devising Rules for Determining Truth in Judicial Trials," 66(2) *Columbia Law Review* 223, 237 (1966).

45. See the discussion in Chapter 3.

46. Quoted in M. Demont, *A Treatise on Judicial Evidence Extracted from the Manuscripts of Jeremy Bentham, Esq.* (Littleton, Colo.: Fred Rothman and Co., 1981), p. 37.

47. The comment to MRPC Rule 3.4 says, in part: "Fair competition in the adversary system is secured by prohibitions against destruction or concealment of evidence, improperly influencing witnesses, obstructive tactics . . . and the like."

48. Abraham Ordover, "The Lawyer as Liar," 2 *American Journal of Trial Advocacy* 305 at 314 (1979); Wayne Brazil, "The Attorney as Victim: Toward More Candor About the Psychological Price Tag of Litigation Practice," *Journal of the Legal Profession*, 3 (1978), pp. 107, 111.

49. Rule 3.3 states in part:

    (a) A lawyer shall not knowingly:
    (1) make a false statement of material fact or law to a tribunal;

    (2) fail to disclose a material fact to a tribunal when disclosure is necessary to avoid assisting a criminal or fraudulent act by the client;

    (3) fail to disclose to the tribunal legal authority in the controlling jurisdiction known to the lawyer to be directly adverse to the position of the client and not disclosed by opposing counsel.

50. *In re Mascolo*, 505 *F.2d* 274, 278 (5th Cir. 1974).

51. *Quality Molding Co. v. American National Fire Insurance Co.*, 287 F2d 313, 316 (7th Cir., 1961).

52. *U.S. v. Burnette-Carter Co.*, 575 *F.2d* 587, 589 n.4 (1978).

53. This is contrary to the practice in inquisitorial system countries and in England, where attorneys take no part in the preparation of witnesses for trial.

54. Rule 1.2(d) says, in part: "A lawyer shall not counsel a client to engage, or assist a client, in conduct that the lawyer knows is criminal or fraudulent."

    Rule 3.4 says, in part: "a lawyer shall not . . . (b) falsify evidence, counsel or assist a witness to falsify evidence, or offer an inducement to a witness that is prohibited by law."

55. Disciplinary Rule 7-102 (A)(6) provides: "(A) In his representation of a client, a lawyer shall not: . . .(6) Participate in the creation or presentation of evidence when he knows or it is obvious that the evidence is false."

56. *State v. McCormick*, 298 *N.C.* 788 (1979).

57. *In re Stroh*, 97 *Wisc.2d* 289 (1982).

58. *Wigmore On Evidence*, Vol. 3 (Boston: Little, Brown and Co., Chadbourne rev., 1970), sec. 788.

59. *Lawrence v. Texas*, 457 *S.W.2d* 561 (Texas App. 1970).

60. T. R. Caretta and R. L. Moreland, "The direct and indirect effects of inadmissible evidence," *Journal of Applied Social Psychology*, *13* (1983), pp. 291-309; W. C. Thompson *et al.*, "Inadmissible evidence and juror verdicts," *Journal of Personality and Social Psychology*, *40* (1981), pp. 453-63.

61. Wigmore, *op. cit.*, p. 3.

62. Id., sec. 983, at 841.

63. *Commonwealth v. Rooney*, 313 *N.E.2d* 105, 112-113 (1974).

64. Francis Wellman, *The Art of Cross-Examination* (New York: MacMillan, 1936), pp. 194-95.

65. *People ex rel. Department of Public Works v. Lillard*, 219 *Cal. App. 2d* 368, 33 *Cal Reptr.* 189, 196 (1963).

66. Lewis Lake, *How to Cross-Examine Witnesses Successfully* (Englewood Cliffs, N.J.: Prentice-Hall, 1957).

67. Saul Kassin *et al.*, "Dirty Tricks of Cross-Examination: The Influence of Conjectural Evidence on the Jury," *Law and Human Behavior*, *14(3)* (August 1990), pp. 373-385.

68. R. Hopper, "The taken for granted," *Human Communications*, Vol. 7 (1981), pp. 195-211.

69. MRPC Rule 3.4(e).

70. R. H. Underwood and W. H. Fortune, *Trial Ethics* (Boston: Little, Brown and Co., 1988).

71. See, e.g., *U.S. v. Brown*, 579 *F.2d* 1368 (1975).

72. *Draper v. Airco, Inc.*, 580 *F.2d* at 96 (1976).

73. Ordover, "The Lawyer as Liar," *op. cit.*, p. 314.

74. James McElhaney, "Dealing With Dirty Tricks," 7 *Litigation* 45 (1981).

75. John Wilkes, "Life in the Fast Lane: The Adversary Ethics of an Ex-Lawyer," 7 *Criminal Defense* 11-12 (March-April 1980).

76. MRPC Rules 3.4(c) and (e).

77. See, e.g., Abraham Ordover, "Why 'Dirty Tricks' are Taught at Emory College," *National Law Journal*, 6/14/82, at 14.

78. For an expansive discussion on this, see Philip Shuchman, "The Question of Lawyers' Deceit," *op. cit.*

79. Richard Burke, "Truth in Lawyering: An Essay in Lying and Deceit in the Practice of Law," 38 *Arkansas Law Review* 1 at 2 (1984).

80. Samuel Thurman, "Limits to the Adversary System: Interests That Outweigh Confidentiality," 5 *Journal of the Legal Profession* 5 at 19 (1980).

81. R. J. Gerber, "Victory vs. Truth: The Adversary System and its Ethics," 19(3) *Arizona State Law Journal* 3, 19 (1987).

82. Sissela Bok, *Lying* (New York: Parthenon Books, 1978), pp. 25, 163-64.

83. Charles Curtis, "The Ethics of Advocacy," 4 *Stanford Law Review* 9, 15 (1951).

84. Freedman, *Lawyers' Ethics in an Adversary System* (Indianapolis: Bobbs-Merrill, 1975), p. 27.
85. MRPC Rule 3.4(a)(4).
86. MRPC Rule 3.4(a)(1).
87. MRPC Rule 3.3(a)(2) and (3).
88. FRCP, Rule 11. However, such sanctions are rare in the absence of an egregious omission of clearly controlling cases.
89. MRPC Rule 3.3(a)(4).
90. Rule 3.3 comment 5.
91. 475 *U.S.* 157 (1986).
92. Id., p. 177 (Justice Harry Blackmun, concurring).
93. Id.
94. MRPC Rule 4.1.
95. Samuel Williston, *Life and Law: An Autobiography* (Boston: Little, Brown and Co., 1940), pp. 271-72.
96. Curtis, *op. cit.*, pp. 9-10.
97. Stephen Gillers and Norman Dorsen, *Regulation of Lawyers: Problems of Law and Ethics,* 2d ed. (Boston: Little, Brown and Co., 1989), p. 506.
98. Anthony Amsterdam, *Trial Manual for the Defense of Criminal Cases*, 2d ed. (Philadelphia: Joint Committee on Legal Education of the American Law Institute and the American Bar Association, 1972), sec.370 at 2-327; David Bress, "Professional Ethics in Criminal Trials: A View of Defense Counsel's Responsibility," 64 *Michigan Law Review* 1493, 1494 (1966); Warren Burger, "Standards of Conduct for Prosecution and Defense Personnel: A Judge's Viewpoint," 5 *American Criminal Law Quarterly* 11, 14-15 (1966); and M. Freedman, *Lawyers' Ethics in an Adversary System, op. cit.*, pp. 79-80.
99. *U.S. v. Wade*, 388 *U.S.* 218, 257-58 (1967), (White, J., dissenting and concurring in part.)
100. Thomas Steffens, "Truth as Second Fiddle: Reevaluating the Place of Truth in the Adversarial Trial Ensemble," 1988(4) *Utah Law Review* 799, 817 (1988).
101. Gerald Miller and F. Joseph Bolster, "Three Images of the Trial: Their Implications for Psychological Research," in Bruce Sales, ed., *Psychology in the Legal Process* (New York: Spectrum Books, 1977), pp. 23, 24, 28.
102. Id., pp. 33, 34.
103. Id., p. 34.
104. Peter Sperlich, "The Evidence on Evidence: Science and Law in Conflict and Cooperation," in S. Kassin and L. Wrightsman, eds., *The Psychology of Evidence and Trial Procedure* (Beverly Hills, Calif.: Sage Publics, 1985), pp. 343-46.

105. Michael Saks and Charles Baron, eds., *The Use/Nonuse/Misuse of Applied Social Science Research in the Courts* (Cambridge, Mass.: Abt Books, 1980), pp. 37-38, 79, 158, 176.
106. Id., pp. 12, 152-53.
107. Id., pp. 34, 37, 100.
108. 293 *F.* 1013, D.C. Cir.
109. Fed. R. Evid. 702.
110. *Daubert v. Merrell Dow Pharmaceuticals, Inc.*, 113 *Supreme Court* 1245 (1993).
111. *Graham v. Wyeth Laboratories*, 906 *F.2d* 1399 (1990), discussed in Peter Huber, *Galileo's Revenge: Junk Science in the Courtroom* (New York: Basic Books, 1991), p. 156.
112. Huber, *op. cit.*, pp. 79-85.
113. Id., at pp. 95-98.
114. S. Golding, "Increasing the Reliability, Validity and Relevance of Psychological Expert Evidence," *Law and Human Behavior*, *16(3)* (1992), pp. 253 at 255.
115. David Luban, *Lawyers and Justice: An Ethical Study* (Princeton, N.J.: Princeton University Press, 1988), p. 70. More likely a system employing independent investigators, whose compensation was directly tied to their effectiveness, would produce a greater approximation of the unadulterated truth. Severing the search for truth from the attorney's need to win is the key feature.
116. See, e.g., John Thibaut and Laurens Walker, *Procedural Justice: A Psychological Analysis* (Hillsdale, N.J.: Lawrence Erlbaum Associates, 1975), pp. 39, 40.
117. See, e.g., Gerry Spence, "Questioning the Adverse Witness," 10 *Litigation* 13 (Winter 1984).
118. Kenneth Milelli, "Prosecutorial Discretion in an Adversary System," 1992 *BYU Law Review* 669, 695 (1992).
119. R. J. Gerber, "Victory Versus Truth: The Adversary System and its Ethics," 19 *Arizona State Law Journal* 3, 4 (1987).
120. Charles Wolfram, *Modern Legal Ethics* (St. Paul, Minn.: West Publishing, 1986), p. 585.
121. Richard Wasserstrom, "Lawyers as Professionals: Some Moral Issues," *Human Rights*, *5* (1975), p. 10.
122. Kenneth Pye, "The Role of Counsel in the Suppression of Truth," 1978 *Duke Law Journal* 921, 935-37 (1978).
123. Shuchman, "The Question of Lawyers' Deceit," *op. cit.*, p. 102.
124. Wasserstrom, *op. cit.*, p. 14.
125. William Simon, "The Ideology of Advocacy: Procedural Justice and Professional Ethics," 1978 *Wisconsin Law Review* 29 at 36 (1978).
126. Id., p. 116.

127. Thomas Morgan and Ronald Rotunda, *Problems and Materials on Professional Responsibility*, 4th ed. (Mineola, N.Y.: Foundation Press, 1987), p. 188, quoting George Hill, ed., *Boswell's Life of Johnson* (Oxford: Clarendon Press, 1887), p. 47.

128. Simon, *op. cit.*, p. 36, 37.

129. Id., p. 117.

130. J. Nightingale, ed., *Trial of Queen Caroline*, 3 vols., Vol. 2 (London: J. Robins & Co., Albion Press, 1820-21), p. 8.

131. 1908 *ABA Canons of Ethics*, Canon 15; 1969 *ABA Model Code of Professional Responsibility*, DR 7-101(A)(1); 1983 *ABA Model Rules of Professional Conduct*, Preamble and Comment, Rule 1.3.

132. Under the MRPC, zealous advocacy is mentioned only in the Preamble and in a Comment (which is not binding) to one of the rules, perhaps as a concern to the drafters who argued for substantial restrictions on the duty. See *The Legislative History of the Model Rules of Professional Conduct: Their Development in the ABA House of Delegates* (Chicago: Center for Professional Responsibility of the American Bar Association, 1987), p. 6. (The American College of Lawyers withdrew a motion to substitute "zeal" for "diligence" in Rule 1.3.)

133. In addition to the duties to the court described in Rule 3.3, the attorney must avoid conduct prejudicing the administration of justice. Rule 8.4.

134. Stephen Gillers, "What We Talked About When We Talked About Ethics: A Critical View of the Model Rules," 46 *Ohio State Law Journal* 242, 245 (1985).

135. Simon, *op. cit.*, p. 38.

136. Id.

137. Kenney Hegland, "Moral Dilemmas in Teaching Trial Advocacy," *Journal of Legal Education*, 32 (1982), p. 71-74.

138. Id., p. 72, 74-75.

139. Id., pp. 70, 72, 75-77.

140. John Flynn, "Professional Ethics and the Lawyer's Duty to Self," 1976(3) *Washington University Law Quarterly* 429, 442 (1976).

141. Wasserstrom, *op. cit.*, p. 12.

142. See, e.g., the Californian State Bar Act: "It is the duty of an attorney to counsel or maintain such actions . . . only as appear to him legal or just, except the defense of a person charged with a public offense." See also MRPC 3.1, which exempts criminal defense from the requirement that attorneys have a "not frivolous," good faith basis for the litigation.

143. Wasserstrom, *op. cit.*, p.13.

144. Jerold Auerbach, *op. cit.*, pp. 12-13.

145. Id., pp. 3, 4, 10, 12, 308.

146. Quoted in Philip Stern, *Lawyers on Trial* (New York: Times Books, 1980), p. 9.

147. Id.
148. Id., p. 10.
149. Stephen Schulhofer, "An Indigent Willie Smith Might Be In Jail," *L.A. Times*, 12/17/91, p. B7.
150. Anatol Rapoport, "Theories of Conflict Resolution and the Law," in M. Friedland, ed., *Courts and Trials: A Multidisciplinary Approach* (Toronto: University of Toronto Press, 1975), p. 29.
151. *Blueprint for Improving the Civil Justice System* (Chicago: ABA, 1992), p. iv.
152. Id. at pp. 22, 29.
153. Id., p. 21.
154. City of New York, Office of the Comptroller, *Performance Analysis of the New York City Housing Court* (New York: Author, January 7, 1977), p. 9.
155. David Caplovitz, *Consumers in Trouble* (New York: Free Press, 1974), p. 221, Table 11.8.
156. *ABA Blueprint*, p. 19.
157. Id., p. 24.
158. Id., p. 22.
159. *Revised Handbook on Prepaid Legal Services: Papers and Documents Assembled by the Special Committee on Prepaid Legal Services* (Washington, D.C.: ABA, 1972), p. 2.
160. Canon 3 of the ABA's *Judicial Code of Conduct* (1987), is entitled, "A Judge Should Perform The Duties Of His Office Impartially And Diligently."
161. See, e.g., Lon Fuller and John Randall, "Professional Responsibility: Report of the Joint Conference," 44 *ABA Journal* 1160 (1958).
162. Cheryl Stolberg, "Politics and the Judiciary Coexist, but Often Uneasily," *Los Angeles Times*, 3/21/92, pp. A1 at A24.
163. Id.

CHAPTER 6

ALTERNATIVE DISPUTE RESOLUTION, THE EXPANDED VERSION

*Over the next generation, I predict, society's greatest opportunities will
lie in tapping human inclinations towards collaboration and
compromise rather than stirring our proclivities for competition and
rivalry. If lawyers are not leaders in marshalling cooperation and
designing mechanisms that allow it to flourish, they will not be at the
center of the most creative social experiments of our time.*

—Derek Bok[1]

Attorney-dominated dispute resolution can be prohibitively expensive,
protracted, and may provoke even greater hostility between the disputants.
Should the dispute proceed to trial, it can become a public spectacle. Moreover,
there is no assurance that a decision so arrived at will address the real needs of
the parties. As individuals, businesses and governments become disaffected with
this approach to dispute resolution, they turn increasingly to alternative methods.

Alternatives to adversary (trial) dispute resolution fall into two categories.
One is the group of domestic, nontrial dispute resolution mechanisms usually
referred to in the United States as Alternative Dispute Resolution, or ADR.
Domestic ADR includes private and court-annexed arbitration, private and court-
referred mediation, mini-trial, summary jury trial, early neutral evaluation,
private judging, specialized courts, administrative tribunals, ombudsmen,
factfinding, conciliation, diversion and negotiated settlement. This list is not
exhaustive. For example, there are hybrids, such as "med/arb," (mediation
arbitration). Use of one method does not preclude later use of another.

Disputants may attempt several alternative dispute resolution mechanisms before resolving their problem or going to trial.

Over 90 percent of cases filed in American courts are resolved out of court, most by negotiated settlements. Unlike other ADR mechanisms, negotiated settlement has no distinct form, procedure or philosophy. Typically, the attorneys are the sole interlocutors. Once represented by attorneys, the parties do not directly communicate with each other. Negotiated settlements are said to be bargained "in the shadow of the courthouse" or "in the shadow of the law." This means they tend to be influenced by the probable outcome of a trial should the disputants fail to settle. Of course, this milieu induces brinkmanship and other adversarial characteristics of trial.

The other ADR category discussed in this chapter is the inquisitorial system of trial justice, used in most nonEnglish-speaking postindustrial nations. ADR, as the term is used in the United States, doesn't include foreign courtroom procedures; domestic ADR mechanisms and foreign trial procedures are treated separately. Nevertheless, several reasons militate in favor of breaking new ground by aggregating foreign trial procedures with domestic ADR mechanisms: First, the procedures of inquisitorial system trials and domestic ADR mechanisms have as much in common with each other as they have with adversary trial procedure; second, both domestic ADR and inquisitorial system procedures serve to demarcate our adversary trial procedures as but one limited means to third-party dispute resolution; finally, both categories contain specific features which could be adopted by U.S. courts.

This chapter examines both kinds of ADR, as broadly defined here, and evaluates their pros and cons vis-a-vis traditional adversarial litigation. These alternative procedures reappear in the next and final chapter. I recommend there that jurisdiction over several kinds of disputes be removed from the trial court to domestic ADR fora. For those disputes remaining in the trial system, adoption of various foreign trial procedures is the recommendation. Although this chapter discusses only inquisitorial system procedures among foreign systems, the final chapter also recommends several practices of the English trial system for adoption by U.S. courts.

GROWTH OF THE ADR MOVEMENT

ADR growth in the United States has been explosive. "Twenty years ago," observes a law professor, "alternative dispute resolution was primarily the concern of a few academics. A decade ago, it was the province of a few idealistic practitioners. Today, it is an integral part of law practice."[2] The ADR movement is now an institution driven by associations, journals and agencies which fund applied ADR research.

The movement dates to colonial times, impelled in part by dislike and distrust of the colonial courts controlled by the king's governors. Another stimulus to growth was the need for special treatment in certain cases, for example, commercial disputes. Probably the most compelling reasons for the development of alternatives were the desires to avoid the cost and delay associated with trial court dispute resolution.[3]

Arbitration is the oldest ADR mechanism. It first arose in the 1920s as an effort by business to replace the complex, costly and lengthy trial with simple, cheap and speedy procedures.[4] Federal and state legislation in that period legitimized arbitration. Congress passed the Federal Arbitration Act in 1925 to encourage commercial arbitration as an alternative to court adjudication. This effectively halted the widespread practice by courts of refusing to enforce agreement-to-arbitrate provisions found in many commercial contracts. All fifty states now have similar statutes.[5]

In 1977, the American Bar Association boosted the ADR movement with an important conference at Columbia University. Its purpose was to review various ADR techniques and evaluate the results of ADR programs nationwide. Prepatory to the conference, the ABA Special Committee on Resolution of Minor Disputes reviewed 141 dispute resolution programs. The committee found: (a) most disputants believed they had a fair opportunity to tell their side of the story; and (b) most cases were processed within one month, including follow-up.[6]

A 1982 article by former Chief Justice Warren Burger in the *American Bar Association Journal*[7] lent his support to the movement. Citing court congestion and "excessive litigiousness," Burger declared the need for nonjudicial routes to dispute resolution, and then called for a systematic reevaluation of ADR mechanisms:

Obviously two of those "nonjudicial routes" are arbitration and negotiation. . . . A third approach is greater use of the techniques of the administrative process exemplified by the traditional workmen's compensation acts. The adversary process is expensive. It is time-consuming. It leaves a trail of stress and frustration. . . . We need to consider moving some cases from the adversary system to administrative processes like workmen's compensation, or to mediation, conciliation, and especially arbitration. Divorce, child custody, adoptions, personal injury, landlord-and-tenant cases, and probate of estates are prime candidates for some form of administrative or arbitration processes. . . .[8]

What we must have, I submit, is a comprehensive review of the whole subject of alternatives, with special emphasis on arbitration. It is now clear that neither the federal nor the state court systems are capable of handling all the burdens placed upon them.[9]

To institute this reorientation to ADR, Burger placed primary responsibility on the law schools. He said the schools have carried adversarial training too far. Instead, he urged them to provide more training in the skills which resolve human conflict.[10]

Spurred by Burger's clarion call, interest in ADR by law schools continues apace. A 1988 article in *Dispute Resolution* chronicled the expansion:

Ten years ago, there were no law school courses on dispute resolution. Today, over one-half of the law schools in the United States have an identifiable program in dispute resolution. There were very few attorneys who classified themselves as professional mediators. Today, it is estimated that over 2,000 attorneys include mediation as a vital part of their practice. No bar association had a dispute resolution committee. Today, over 100 bar associations have created such committees.[11]

ADR is particularly popular in the business world, where chronic litigation costs suppress profits, expansion and job creation. In response, business schools have joined law schools in the creation of ADR courses and programs. A University of Colorado survey found 334 conflict resolution courses offered in business programs.[12]

Advocacy organizations sponsor myriad activities promoting ADR. In 1983, for example, the American Arbitration Association's National Task Force on Law and Business Schools sponsored conferences at New York University and the University of California at Berkeley on teaching ADR in business and law schools. Grants to underwrite ADR research and encourage the development of ADR teaching materials in business and law schools come from the National Institute for Dispute Resolution.[13]

Many state governments and the federal government passed legislation in the past ten to twenty years establishing *neighborhood justice centers*.[14] Increased court filing fees fund the centers. Consumer complaints, landlord-tenant disputes and minor criminal matters constitute the bulk of center cases. The centers are community-based resources where a variety of ADR mechanisms are applied by local citizens employing community standards. The centers receive many cases from the courts. If there is no resolution, the cases may be referred back to the trial court for review, or serve as the basis for the court's judgment.[15]

California's program is illustrative. Passage of The Dispute Resolution Programs Act in 1986 allowed counties to increase court filing fees by $1 to $3 in order to fund neighborhood resolution centers. Pursuant to the legislation, twenty of the most populous counties developed programs. Centers in the adopting counties handled over 7,000 disputes over a six month period in 1989. Of these, it is estimated that over 5,000 would have ended up in formal litigation were it not for the programs. Arbitration, mediation or conciliation successfully settled approximately two-thirds of the disputes. Resultant savings were substantial. In Los Angeles County alone, the dispute resolution program saved taxpayers $1.7 million in court costs during 1988.[16] Since its inception, the state program has raised over $10 million in revenues for dispute resolution programs.[17]

Federal mandates too have spurred ADR growth. Federal district courts (plus courts in at least sixteen states) now require some litigants to submit to nonbinding arbitration before proceeding to trial.[18] ADR even has a presidential imprimatur. A 1991 presidential executive order authorized the use of ADR methods in claims by or against the United States.[19] And under the Administrative Dispute Resolution Act of 1990, Congress mandated that every federal agency prepare policy reports on how they intend to implement ADR techniques. In response, the Labor Department established pilot projects in five states and the District of Columbia. The results proved ADR can produce speedy, fair and effective results.[20]

The Civil Justice Reform Act of 1990 (CJRA) gave significant impetus to ADR. The act constitutes a blueprint for future dispute resolution in the federal courts. It invites ADR and consensual outcomes. At the same time, it announces clear preferences for avoiding trial or changing its form. Conspicuous by the absence of any mention is the jury trial. Indeed, trial is mentioned only in the context of trial preparation, date-setting and bifurcation of issues.[21] By contrast, ADR and settlement figure prominently in the CJRA's dispute resolution scheme.[22]

The CJRA and parallel state statutes reflect a growing distrust of adjudication by the polity. Undoubtedly, the cost and time of trial account for much of this sentiment. But other and perhaps more profound failings of trial adjudication may be implicated. As the King I trial demonstrated, trial factfinding, particularly jury factfinding, is suspect. The frequent mismatch of resources (and commensurate mismatch of legal talent) in adjudication often arouse public cynicism.[23]

AN ADR TAXONOMY

Both traditional and newer forms populate domestic ADR. Arbitration and mediation (with or without factfinding) are traditional. Newer forms include diversion and mini-trials. As contrasted with trial, ADR proceedings are generally faster, simpler, cheaper, more private and less formal with regard to both presentation and investigation of evidence. There is more direct discussion between and among the parties and the third party facilitator. And unlike a trial where the litigants passively accept the judge assigned to their case, ADR disputants commonly *choose* a mutually acceptable third-party facilitator. ADR mechanisms, however, have clear and substantive drawbacks (vis-a-vis trials) to which I recur later in the chapter. But first, thumbnail descriptions of the most common ADR procedures are offered.

Arbitration is the most prevalent ADR mechanism. The disputants allow an impartial party, called the arbiter or arbitrator, to resolve their quarrel. Arbitration is adjudication in that it is a decision imposed by a third party. Arbitrators are often experts in the matter being contested. Hence businesses frequently look to them for authoritative opinions on how best to settle complicated commercial disputes. Many businesses insert an arbitration clause in their contracts. The arbitrator's decision may be binding or challengeable in court, depending upon the agreement between the parties and the particular circumstances. Disputes involving construction, computer software, insurance, labor and securities constitute the bulk of commercial arbitration cases,[24] but the scope of arbitration-governed disputes grows.[25]

A growing number of states require arbitration as a prerequisite to trial if the amount in controversy is relatively small. California, for instance, requires all civil suits for damages not exceeding $15,000 be referred to mandatory arbitration.[26] Because it is done by court referral and has many of the trappings of a trial, it is called *court-annexed arbitration*. Either party may reject the arbitrator's decision and request a trial. Relatively few parties opt for trial, however. Financial disincentives offer at least a partial explanation. If a party who rejects the arbitrator's decision and litigates the dispute does not improve his or her position at trial, some of the court-annexed arbitration programs require that party to pay all arbitration costs, including often-expensive expert witness fees and other penalties.

In addition to arbitration, other types of adjudication less formal than trial are available. The *small claims court*, for example, is an adjudication forum whose simple and informal rules were designed to make the justice system accessible to many who otherwise could not afford it. Absent are juries and the traditional, rigid rules of evidence common to the typical trial court. Many small claims courts forbid legal representation. Even where attorney representation is permitted, it is nevertheless rare because the small amount in dispute make legal fees too small to be attractive to attorneys, but too large for the client vis-a-vis the potential award. Small claims courts have limited jurisdiction. Restrictions limit both the amount in controversy and the subject matter of the dispute. Texas, for example, has a $1,500 cap on the amount of the dispute, and only debts and contract disputes can be heard.

Another alternative adjudicatory process less formal than trial is the *specialized court*. Traffic, housing, juvenile, landlord-tenant and family courts fall into this category. In each, a legally trained judge with experience in the area or an expert layperson preside. Evidence rules are greatly relaxed. Consonant with the overriding policy goals inherent in each type of court, a larger range of sanctions are available than in litigation. In the juvenile court, for example, sanctions are informed by the concern for the safety and welfare of the child, the statutorily prescribed hallmark of the court.

Along similar lines fall *administrative tribunals*, such as those hearing workers' compensation claims. One of the administrative tribunal's objectives is reducing or eliminating fees to lawyers and expert witnesses. Procedures are accordingly less formal than those followed by regular courts. An administrative law judge or a hearing examiner who is independent of the agency involved presides over the tribunal. Legal representation is allowed but usually unnecessary, particularly because there are no juries. Although disputants generally can get court review of administrative hearings, a court will not overturn an agency decision unless the agency has acted without substantial evidence to support its decision; has been arbitrary, capricious or discriminatory; has violated procedural due process or other constitutional safeguards; or has taken action that exceeds its statutory authority.

A growingly popular ADR form is *private judging*, commonly referred to as "rent-a-judge." As the name implies, the disputants hire a mutually agreeable referee to informally adjudicate their spat. The referee is usually retired from the bench and experienced in the disputed matter. Confidentiality is ensured: The proceeding is completely private, often held in the judge's home. If the parties so stipulate, the judge's decision can be binding, in which case it is adjudicatory. More often, however, the judge functions much like the neutral expert in a mini-trial: She tries to induce the parties to take reasonable positions and to fashion consensus on a solution. Proponents say private judging is an effective dispute resolution mechanism which provides relief to overcrowded court dockets.[27] Opponents criticize it as a luxury available only to the rich.[28]

Most ADR is nonadjudicatory. Unlike a judge or arbiter, the third party's role is not to impose a decision. Instead, she tries to facilitate a negotiated settlement. *Mediation* is the most popular form of nonadjudicatory domestic ADR. The mediator clarifies the parties' areas of disagreement, helps them understand each other's viewpoint, ameliorates lines of communication, suggests settlement options and reminds the parties of the potential costs if they fail to reach agreement. Perhaps the most valuable service of the mediator is in providing the parties a realistic assessment of the strengths and weaknesses of their respective cases.

Like arbitration, mediation can be court-annexed.[29] But court-annexed mediation bears only passing resemblance to mediation programs independent of courts. In the latter (independent) context, the mediator plays a passive, facilitative role.[30] Court-annexed mediation, on the other hand, refers to something quite different. Bargaining takes place "in the shadow of the law," that is, with an eye toward the probable outcome of the trial. In this regard, the mediator typically plays an active role in helping the litigants assess their chances and predicting the costs of proceeding further.[31]

Mediation is far more informal than arbitration, especially court-annexed arbitration. The confidentiality of communications and the absence of rules of evidence allow the parties to air their grievances freely. Mediation is always voluntary and nonbinding. Labor-management disputes supply the wellspring of experience in mediation. When the collective bargaining process breaks down (assuming that labor is unionized), the parties often obtain the assistance of the Federal Mediation and Conciliation Service.

A hybrid of arbitration and mediation is known as *med-arb*. The third party acts initially as mediator, trying to facilitate a resolution of the dispute. If mediation is unsuccessful, the mediator turns arbitrator, rendering a decision. The most extensive use of the process has been in public sector contract negotiation disputes.[32] Another variant is used in child custody cases.

When litigation is contemplated or already begun, disputants increasingly turn to the *mini-trial*. It is an abbreviated, non-binding hearing on the issues. A neutral expert or panel of experts jointly selected by the parties hear all sides and render a confidential opinion on the strengths and weaknesses of each party's case. The goal is to induce settlement. Attorneys for businesses with ongoing relations developed the mini-trial to reduce the delay and cost of the inevitable settlement. Therefore the panel sometimes includes key executives from each business with authority to settle.

The jury equivalent of a mini-trial is a *summary jury trial*. When the parties appear headed for a jury trial, the trial judge may refer them to a summary jury trial. A mock jury is selected by procedures resembling those used for real trial juries. An attorney for each side presents a precis of his arguments. The evidence is limited to that admissible in a trial. At the conclusion of the presentations, a judge or magistrate gives abbreviated legal instructions to the jury. Ordinarily, the jury's decision is advisory only. Again, the purpose is to encourage settlement by giving the parties a quick and relatively inexpensive insight into their chances at a real trial.

Along the same lines as the mini-trial and summary jury trial is *early neutral evaluation*. Acting under its inherent power to appoint special masters, the court appoints a respected private attorney to hear summary presentations of each party's case. The evaluator then renders a frank, realistic assessment of the relative strengths of their evidence and arguments, and predicts the likelihood of liability and probable damages, if any.

By serving as a reality check for attorneys and their clients, all three techniques—mini-trial, summary jury trial and early neutral evaluation—facilitate settlement. The need to prepare case presentations forces them to confront difficult decisions about their case they might otherwise defer.[33] Salutary effects follow. First, client involvement increases. By telling their stories to a neutral third party, clients have the opportunity for a measure of catharsis often absent in the trial. Also, client involvement serves as a source of economic discipline on the actions of their attorneys. Conversely, neutral assessment helps attorneys with unrealistic clients. If no settlement is ultimately reached, the sessions can still reduce the scope of the dispute and related discovery in the trial which follows.

Perhaps the most valuable benefit of any form of neutral evaluation is the use of the evaluator to act in another capacity, one that the trial courts cannot or do not: problem solver. ADR, after all, is about more than reducing the time and cost of dispute resolution. It is a means to a fresh approach to problems, to helping parties recast their goals and seek alternative solutions.

In factually complex disputes, resorting to *factfinding* frequently expedites resolution. The factfinder has no power to impose a decision or sanction. But the intervention of a jointly chosen neutral expert who offers an authoritative finding of the disputed facts often encourages early settlement. State governments and public unions often use factfinders to expedite stalled collective bargaining sessions.

The *ombudsman* concept is a form of factfinding often used by institutions. An ombudsman is a nonpartisan official who investigates complaints and even has the power to publicly criticize—but not reverse—institutional action. Various federal and state agencies, universities and large businesses have successfully adopted the ombudsman approach. So have other countries.[34] The ombudsman and the adversary procedures use antithetical means to arrive at due process. Thus ombudsmen flourish in settings where the adversary system is not entrenched. Disputes over public interests involving privileges, benefits and rights are better resolved by an ombudsman than by adversary procedures geared to the resolution of private conflicts. Ombudsmen have effectively overseen public programs and interests without adding substantially more government control and bureaucracy.[35]

Conciliation in the United States was originally modeled after the conciliation courts of Norway and Denmark as a means of providing accessible and inexpensive court justice to small claimants. Later it became associated with voluntary proceedings to be used before resort is had to litigation in the courts.[36] Akin to shuttle diplomacy, the conciliator contacts the disputants separately to facilitate an agreement. Proponents touted it as a superior form of dispute resolution which could supplant and obviate adversary litigation.[37] Today, conciliation is frequently used as a generic term for a variety of nonadjudicatory ADR mechanisms, such as mediation.

Civil diversion acts as a safety valve by relieving particular cases from turgid court calendars. No-fault car insurance and no-fault divorce illustrate: They obviate litigation by removing, as a matter of policy, particular disputes from the need for a factfinding inquiry as to fault. Instead, they substitute prescribed remedies. In no-fault divorce, for example, the state may decide it has no compelling reason to insinuate itself into what is essentially a personal and inherently private matter between spouses. This removes the nonsensical requirement of perjuring oneself by publicly claiming to be the "wronged" party in order to justify relief.

Most ADR applies to civil cases. But criminal law also has ADR mechanisms. One with new-found appeal is *criminal diversion*. In the criminal law context, diversion suspends proceedings before conviction if the accused agrees to a course of remedial action specified by the court, such as a rehabilitation program, psychiatric treatment or certain employment. "Diversion programs use the threat of possible conviction to encourage the accused to participate."[38] Simply stated, diversion offers an accused treatment rather than risking conviction. It represents an application of the court's prerogative (in criminal cases) to act occasionally as problem solver rather than dispute settler. A celebrated criminal diversion program was the Manhattan Court Employment Program begun in 1968 by the Vera Institute of Justice in New York. The program postponed and ultimately dismissed charges against criminally accused individuals who made progress toward rehabilitation.[39] Explaining the premise of criminal diversion, Boston judge and Harvard law professor John Cratsley writes:

Many violations of the criminal law are, in fact, more indicative of illness (e.g., drug addiction or alcoholism) or other disabilities (lack of employment, schooling, or job skills) than of purposeful, dangerous criminality. The availability of treatment, counseling, education and similar options is therefore of greater value to the individual and the larger society in which he or she lives than the symbolic act of his or her conviction.[40]

Broadly conceived, criminal ADR also includes the widespread negotiated settlements of criminal cases, commonly known as the *plea bargain*. The negotiated plea has become a fixture of the criminal justice system. It is a classic illustration of party control of the case: The prosecution and defendant negotiate a deal in which the defendant pleads guilty in return for certain concessions, typically the reduction of charges and/or the promise of a more lenient sentence. In 1970, the U.S. Supreme Court articulated the "mutuality of advantage" rationale for the plea bargain. The state was "extend[ing] a benefit to a defendant who in turn extends a substantial benefit to the state and who demonstrated by his plea that he is ready and willing to admit his crime and to enter the correctional system in a frame of mind which affords hope for success in rehabilitation over a shorter period of time than might otherwise be necessary."[41] Such guilty pleas, the Court said, were not involuntary because they were "motivated by the defendant's desire to accept the certainty . . . of a lesser penalty rather than . . . [a trial that might result in] conviction and a higher penalty."[42]

The civil counterpart of the plea bargain is the negotiated settlement. American judges today facilitate settlements as never before. Changes in procedural rules empower and induce judges to pursue settlements so aggressively as to revise the traditional passivity of the trial judge.[43] Judges have always used the pretrial conference to eliminate undisputed issues and correspondingly reduce the scope of discovery and evidence to be introduced in trial. Prompted by reinforced procedural rules, judges now integrate a wide array of ADR mechanisms into their pretrial case management. Under their expanded powers, judges make referrals both to court-administered programs and privately funded programs administered by non-court personnel. In court-administered programs, magistrates, judicial colleagues, practicing lawyers or others with no regular connection to the court may nonetheless function as court-appointed agents of settlement. Indeed, "the development and application of innovative case management has become a source of prestige and distinction among judges."[44]

Although settlements are negotiated out of court, they remain adversarial because they are conducted "in the shadow of the law,"[45] that is, affected by the probable outcome if the case went to trial. Several new books and many new courses, however, suggest a growing preference for *nonadversarial negotiation*.[46] Perhaps the most influential of the new publications is *Getting To Yes*, by Professors Roger Fisher and William Ury of the Harvard Negotiation Project.[47] Their message is simple: Eschew false bargaining positions and focus instead on mutually beneficial solutions; choose win-win bargaining instead of the win-lose (zero-sum) environment characteristic of adversary procedures. Fisher and Ury cite the example of two sisters debating over which should get the only orange in the house. The problem is solved through an approach called principled negotiation, whereby the sisters discover that one wants the orange for its juice, while the other wants the rind to flavor a cake. In other words, full and candid exposition of interests may reveal the existence of many more interests that are shared and compatible than ones that are opposed.[48]

However helpful, this approach is not a panacea. Many situations remain where interests will conflict because the disputants desire the same thing and for the same purpose. No amount of brainstorming or Solomonic intuition will avail; a zero-sum distribution pattern may be inevitable. Given this outcome, adversarial bargaining will be harder to avoid.[49]

PROS AND CONS

Domestic ADR mechanisms vary widely. For purposes of comparison with court adjudication, however, proponents claim these common advantages:

1. the relative nonadversariality of the proceedings allows for continuing relations between the parties,

2. greater participation by the parties and less reliance on attorneys promotes party satisfaction with the results,

3. speedier resolution,

4.   cheaper resolution,

5.   expert factfinder/facilitators,

6.   more flexible remedies, and

7.   more privacy.

But these are generalizations. A closer look at a specific type of ADR, mediation, best illustrates ADR-versus-trial differences. Two mediation programs used in Colorado child custody and landlord-tenant disputes exemplify mediation in action. In both types of cases, a continuing relationship between the disputants is desired or necessary.

Resolving child custody issues through the traditional adversary system trial is laden with pitfalls. A trial frequently polarizes the parents, who want to maintain a long-term relationship with each other because of the children. Preferable is an informal, off-the-record forum where parents can arrive at a mutually agreeable solution. David Ebel, an experienced Denver litigator, reports that this type of environment has been enthusiastically received by domestic relations judges.

Judges frequently lament the difficulty of deciding such intensely human questions on the basis of hired expert testimony, and the angered, hostile testimony of the parents. Much better, they say, to have a solution that is mutually agreeable to all the parties and with which both spouses are prepared to live.[50]

To this end, the Child Custody Mediation Project works as follows. If child custody or visitation is a contested issue for parents dissolving their marriage, the court encourages them to try reaching agreement via mediation. Any agreement resulting from the mediation sessions must be approved by the court. On the other hand, if mediation fails, the parents return to the court for a traditional judicial determination.[51] The mediation team has one attorney plus either a social scientist, counselor, psychologist, psychiatrist or pediatrician. Both members of the mediation team must have had substantial child custody experience; both will be given intensive training. Eight to ten mediation sessions are scheduled. The format varies from case to case: Some sessions have parents only, some children only, some a combination of both.

Recognizing that failed mediation may end up in litigation, parents may use the sessions to posture in anticipation of a trial. To deter this, certain rules apply. The sessions are not transcribed. Mediators cannot make reports to the judge nor testify unless they believe the child's health or welfare are in jeopardy. As a result, parents focus on the child's interests rather than establish a strategic base for subsequent judicial action.[52]

This procedure improves upon trial as a system for resolving child custody disputes in several ways. First, compliance is more likely because the parties jointly develop the resolution rather than having the decision of a judge—who has no knowledge of the parents or children—unilaterally imposed upon them. Second, the resolution is apt to be more enlightened; each parent will have gone through multiple iterations of his or her story, giving the other ample time to reflect and consider the spouse's perspective. Third, the resolution is reached freed of the constraints of formal rules of evidence, which often inhibit deep analysis and constructive thinking. Finally, the mediation sessions are almost always cheaper and quicker than a fully contested custody hearing.[53]

The Colorado Bar's Landlord-Tenant Mediation Program is similar. Again, the program emphasizes guiding dialogue and facilitating a mutually acceptable agreement. (If unsuccessful, the parties can always resort to trial.) The process focuses on creative and flexible alternatives not available in trial. For example, where the tenant's right to remain in possession is disputed, the mediator may conclude that the optimal solution is to allay the tenant's anxiety over locating suitable alternative housing. In return, the tenant promises to vacate the premises on a specified date. The landlord may prefer this arrangement to an eviction action which could be more expensive, protracted and risky. Similarly, the landlord may prefer a mediator's determination of the specific damages which the tenant must repair, rather than resorting to a damages action which may ultimately be uncollectible.[54]

Two assumptions antithetical to the adversary system underlie mediation. First, mediation approaches each conflict as unique. In contrast with the trial, the solution is not automatically derived from application of a general principle.[55] The mediation case is neither to be governed by a precedent nor to set one.[56]

A second assumption behind mediation is that positive-sum results are obtainable through creative solutions, that is, the gain of one disputant is not at the expense of an equal loss to the other disputant. Individual circumstances matter. In divorce mediation, for instance, a spouse's need for continuing emotional support and the other spouse's willingness to provide it could become important. In essence, the parties decide what is relevant. Contrarily, in a trial, rules determine what is relevant.[57] In short, the whole notion that the disputants can synergistically work together contravenes the adversary system's presumption of party adversariness.

The attorney's philosophical map—adversary relationship between the parties; rule-solubility of the dispute—blinds him to solutions available through mediation. Attorneys are oriented towards linear thinking about problems: rights, duties and prescribed types of remedies. Problem solving is a creative enterprise. A mediator is trained to be sensitive to *all* of the circumstances of a dispute, including the idiosyncracies of the parties and their collective and individual needs. Conversely, rigidity and predetermined rules characterize the attorney's methodology when operating in an adversarial environment. When the adversary paradigm is unavailing, the attorney's instincts may be counterproductive, his skills useful only in advising the parties of the probable outcome should the dispute go to trial.

From the individualized nature of the mediated solution and the parties' participation in its construction redounds the primary, overarching benefit of mediation: continuation of the relationship. Mediation is a more global process than adversarial adjudication. The latter distributes economic interests through prescribed rules and principles. On the other hand, the mediation process can touch all aspects of a relationship between people, addressing noneconomic interests (e.g., emotional needs) as well as economic ones. It conduces the healing of interpersonal rifts. In addition, it can avoid the nastiness and aggravation common to adversarial proceedings.[58] Thus mediation has special utility in the wide array of situations where a continuing relationship is desired or needed.

Other advantages of mediation are privacy, convenience and independence in the choice of mediator.[59] As noted earlier, communications made during mediation are confidential.[60] Coupled with its voluntary and nonbinding nature, this makes mediation virtually *risk-free*. Mediation is usually conducted in an informal setting. The parties can choose a mutually agreeable time and place for meetings, such as a law office. Informality also helps build consensus on basic issues. In contrast, the sheer momentum of the civil adjudication process often irreversibly polarizes parties long before they have an opportunity to consider compromise and reconciliation.[61]

The ability to choose the mediator is an especially attractive feature. Parties who select their dispute resolution facilitator are more likely to abide by and be satisfied with her guidance. To do otherwise, in a sense, is to contradict one's own judgment. After all, the mediator is chosen for her reputed fairness and expertise in the disputed area. Parties will have more confidence in such a person than one randomly assigned to them whose expertise in the area is serendipitous—the trial scenario. Both the mediator's expertise and the confidence the parties have in her induce efficient sessions which, in turn, hold down costs. When attorneys represent the parties, attorney posturing and histrionics are minimized, partly due to the absence of a jury, before which such tactics often succeed, and partly because of the expertise of the mediator, before whom such tactics are often ineffective.

Another ADR mechanism commonly sponsored by the courts is arbitration. Surprisingly few useful empirical studies have investigated the effectiveness of such programs. One exception is the Rand Corporation's review of the Pittsburgh program.[62] In general, the study found a high degree of litigant satisfaction. Almost three-fourths of all litigants (winners and losers) were either very or somewhat satisfied. Most did not miss having a judge or jury, preferring instead the informality and privacy of arbitration. Two-thirds believed they received a fair hearing. Of those who did not feel they received a fair hearing, most were *pro se* litigants—representing themselves without counsel. These individuals were frustrated by their unfamiliarity with the arbitration process and their inability to present their case as well as opponents represented by counsel.[63]

Whatever else may be said of court-annexed arbitration, it substantially reduces the courts' caseloads by sharply increasing settlement rates. According to a Federal Judicial Center survey, cases going to trial were reduced by up to 50 percent in those federal district courts which adopted court-annexed arbitration.[64] The need could not be more timely. Case filings in state courts are reaching record levels according to a new study by the National Center for State Courts. 1990 court filings in state courts exceeded 100 million for the first time since the Center began reporting this data in 1984. Since that year, the study says, civil caseloads have increased by 30 percent and criminal caseloads have risen by 33 percent, while the population has grown by only 5 percent. Court backlog is even more grim in the federal courts. The National Center for State Courts survey found that state courts were three time more efficient than the federal courts in processing cases: State courts handle 48 times as many cases with only sixteen times as many judges.[65]

Despite its putative advantages, ADR has its critics. Being informal forums, ADR mechanisms do not provide the constitutional safeguards found in formal trials. Unreliable and even prejudicial evidence can be introduced. In criminal ADR, the privilege against self-incrimination and other constitutional rights are not provided. In short, there is no guarantee of due process.[66] The lack of procedural safeguards has led some to denounce ADR as "second class justice."

Furthermore, because the goal of ADR is settlement, not the assertion of principles, the thrust of ADR is toward the surrender of legal rights. Take, as illustration, the consumer who sues in small claims court after being victimized by a merchant. The small claims court refers the case to mediation, where it is settled by having the vendor make a modest recompense, in essence, a "buy-off." But the consumer remains victimized because of not being apprised of his or her right to treble damages under the applicable consumer protection law. By focusing on accommodative solutions of individual disputes, ADR leaves many wrongs effectively unredressed.[67]

Some fear that the loss of such protections in ADR processes does more damage to "weaker" parties. By general agreement, mediation is unsuitable when the disputants are of decidedly unequal power. For example, mediation between a child abuser and victim would be completely inapt. Whether involving individuals or institutions, mediation is viable only if sufficient leverage can be developed to equalize the power of disputants.[68]

Similarly, ADR can be coercive, which tends to benefit wealthier litigants at the expense of their poorer opponents. Mentioned earlier was the financial disincentive to seek a trial for litigants unhappy with a decision under court-

annexed arbitration. At the federal level, the same disincentive to litigate applies
to any litigant rejecting an offered settlement. If the rejecting litigant does not
best that offer in trial, he or she must pay the other party's expenses, including
attorney's fees.[69] Many poorer litigants will not risk becoming liable for the
other side's costs and attorney's fees. As a result, wealthier contestants may
"lowball" the settlement offer if acting as defendants, or reject a settlement offer
if acting as plaintiffs. Why? Simply this: The threat of additional costs is less
ominous to them. When an institutional litigant opposes an individual in a
lawsuit, these inequalities are exaggerated. Because businesses can deduct their
legal fees and associated costs on their tax returns, the tax law bestows upon
them the equivalent of a government subsidy for litigation costs.[70]

A more fundamental concern is that ADR undermines the legitimating role
of the courts. In a crisp and powerful article in the *Yale Law Journal*,[71] Owen
Fiss criticizes ADR because it substitutes settlement for adjudication. Only
through adjudication, he argues, can courts fulfill their duty to enunciate legal
principles. In his view, articulation of rights and duties, not dispute resolution,
is the central function of the courts. Being nonrecord fora, ADR mechanisms
preclude the state from exercising its responsibility to identify legal principles,
develop new law, set standards and shape conduct through precedent. Fiss
voices concern over the resulting danger of settlement:

Settlement is for me the civil analogue of plea bargaining: Consent is often coerced; the
bargain may be struck by someone without authority; the absence of a trial and judgment
renders subsequent judicial involvement troublesome; and although dockets are trimmed,
justice may not be done. Like plea bargaining, settlement is a capitulation to the
conditions of mass society and should be neither encouraged nor praised. . . . [T]he
purpose of adjudication should be . . . to explicate and give force to the values embodied
in authoritative texts such as the Constitution and statutes: to interpret those values and
bring reality into accord with them. This duty is not discharged when the parties
settle.[72]

In addition to the foregoing general critiques, specific forms of ADR suffer
their share of adverse commentary. As illustration, take the small claims courts.
Unexpected and untoward results accompanied their growth. One of the
predominant goals of the small claims concept was access to justice by relatively
powerless private citizens for claims where the small amount of money involved
did not justify the time and expense of formal litigation. Yet experience has
corrupted this intent: Small claims courts are used more frequently by
institutional creditors against private citizens than the other way around.[73]

Another frustrated goal of small claims court reformers is that the court
should be a true alternative to the adversary model: Attorneys should be
unnecessary; the judge should be an active participant working toward a flexible
settlement of the dispute; adversary advocacy and winner-take-all remedies
should be avoided. Instead, most small claims hearings continue to follow the

adversary model. A review of the small claims literature indicates that the reformers' objectives have been sorrowfully undercut by the continuing influence of lawyers and corollary adversariness.

In spite of the goal that lawyers should be unnecessary, they are present in most courts, a factor which seems to increase rather than reduce complexity. In spite of the goal of a radical change in the role of the judge, he remains a judge in the traditional sense in most courts, although this role is unsuited to proceedings in which one or both parties may be unrepresented and may need judicial assistance. . . .

The mistaken premise [was] that parties to small claims were not viewed as engaged in a traditional adversary contest, and courtroom skills were not considered an advantage. The judge, not counsel, . . . was to elicit the facts and effect settlement of a dispute, rather than deciding on a winner or loser.

In spite of these assumptions . . . many litigants behave as though they *are* engaged in a contest. . . . This puts some unrepresented litigants . . . at a disadvantage.[74]

Med-arb is another ADR mechanism receiving mixed reviews. Proponents believe it has distinct advantages. The parties are less likely to resort to posturing before a mediator—even one with ultimate decisional power—than they would be before an arbitrator. They should, however, agree more readily than they would before a mediator without decisional authority. And should mediation fail to end the dispute, the med-arbitrator's familiarity with the circumstances of the case leave her particularly well-suited either to suggest solutions or adjudicate.[75]

Yet involvement in the dispute is at once med-arb's most profound innate weakness as well as its major advantage. For the mediator's participation in the case contradicts the arbitrator's role neutrality. A dual capacity renders the third party neither fish nor fowl; her failed efforts at mediation seriously compromise the integrity of her subsequent adjudication role. So argues Lon Fuller in his evaluation of a collective bargaining mediator serving dually as ultimate arbitrator.

Mediation and arbitration have distinct purposes and hence distinct moralities. The morality of mediation lies in optimum settlement, a settlement in which each party gives up what he values less, in return for what he value more. The morality of arbitration lies in a decision according to the law of the contract. The procedures appropriate for mediation are those most likely to uncover that pattern of adjustment which will most nearly meet the interests of both parties. The procedures appropriate for arbitration are those which most securely guarantee each of the parties a meaningful chance to present arguments and proofs for a decision in his favor. Thus, private consultations with the parties, generally wholly improper on the part of an arbitrator, are an indispensable tool of mediation.[76]

In the criminal law arena, the plea bargain is not without its critics. They note that the crime plead too often has little or nothing to do with the crime the defendant was accused of committing. If we accept the premise that one of the paramount objectives of the criminal justice system is to determine whether the defendant was guilty of committing the alleged crime, and then to either exonerate him or her or impose an apt penalty, the plea bargain effectively negates that value in favor of what is essentially a private bargain between the prosecution and the defense.

Plea bargaining obviously relieves overloaded courts. But equally unassailable are the untoward consequences: It coerces some innocent defendants into a guilty plea, while allowing guilty defendants to mitigate their guilt and sentence by pleading to a lesser crime. Desiring faster case processing, judges rarely invoke their power to reject the deal.

Lastly, even the Zeitgeist of judicially induced pretrial settlements has been deprecated. Although judges generally appreciate the opportunity to expedite their cases, and litigants and their attorneys report a fairly high level of satisfaction with the new judicial role in case management, detractors of the new judicial role say we need also consider the legitimacy of such judge-induced settlements. Specifically, what assurance do we have that judges are not placing expediency and efficiency (perhaps unwittingly) over fairness? In "Managerial Judges," a widely-cited article in the *Harvard Law Review*, Judith Resnik decried the shift in judicial role:

[B]ecause managerial judging is less visible and usually unreviewable, it gives trial courts more authority and at the same time provides litigants with fewer procedural safeguards to protect them from abuse of that authority. In short, managerial judging may be redefining *sub silencio* our standards of what constitutes rational, fair and impartial adjudication.[77]

Fuller's concern that dual roles ultimately corrupt the judgment of the dual role player applies equally to judicially induced settlement through aggressive pretrial case management. It was Fuller who adduced this argument in criticizing the judge's role in the inquisitorial system. Writing a signal report for the American Bar Association, Fuller maintained that the only way to counteract the judge's natural tendency to prejudge was to remove her from any responsibility for developing the facts or arguments of the dispute.[78] And, as just noted, Fuller also decried the inconsistent roles of mediator and arbitrator in med-arb. But would not the same argument obtain when the judge who aggressively encourages settlement during a pretrial conference is the same judge who hears the case if there is no settlement?[79]

CONTRASTING THE INQUISITORIAL AND ADVERSARY SYSTEMS

Although somewhat simplistic, we can plot dispute resolution procedures on a scale of relative adversariness. On one end is the most adversarial and attorney-controlled procedure, the traditional court trial. Even within this grouping, there are differences: Bench trials (cases tried without a jury) are commonly believed to be less adversarial because there is less to be gained by many adversary tactics which would influence a jury but not a judge. Moving down the scale we have arbitration and other adjudicatory ADR mechanisms, such as private judging. Next we come to mediation and other nonadjudicatory forms of ADR. At the opposite end of the scale would be the somewhat amorphous area of nonadversarial negotiation, in which disputants seek positive alternatives before turning to compromise. Also at this end of the scale would be the inquisitorial system. Here, the attorney's role is decidedly ancillary to that of the judge. The perception of justice changes here, a change which dictates that control of the trial devolve to the judge.

The recent trend in domestic pretrial case management also shifts power from attorney to judge in jury selection, discovery and pretrial negotiation conferences. The new judicial activism is even beginning to creep into the trial phase: More judges now question witnesses, or call their own witnesses; the judicial practice of summary of and commentary upon the evidence has also increased.[80] To some, this heralds a movement away from the attorney-control adversary model to the inquisitorial system model popular in continental Europe.

The musings of seers prophesying ineluctable movement toward the inquisitorial system may be more fanciful than realistic. But it nonetheless behooves us to view the inquisitorial system with an eye toward eclectic adoption of those trial practices which we could beneficially import. In so doing, we will broaden our perspective by examining the procedures and governing philosophy of most other postindustrial nations. Looking abroad reveals that the American adversary model is not the inevitable means of legal dispute resolution. Most cultures have used other methods. Among industrialized countries, the inquisitorial system is far more prevalent. The inquisitorial system refers generally to the trial procedures in continental Europe and the trial systems modeled after them in other countries.

The history of each system reveals how disparate events impelled the adoption of separate trial systems. After the Norman Conquest, legal changes took place on the European continent divergent from those occurring in England. Each informed the development of discrete trial procedures. From the eleventh to the fourteenth centuries, European scholars revived the Roman civil law. The prestige which they enjoyed made a distinct impression, as students trained in Italian schools spread Roman law throughout the continent. But that which flourished on the continent was anathema in England. Civil law was characterized by emphasis on strong central authority—statutory law and judges—and rife with rules regulating relations and disputes between individuals. Nothing could have been more infelicitous to England, whose very foundation was dependant upon commercial transactions by private entrepreneurs. England needed a legal environment conducive to freedom of contract and maximum individual control over mobile private property. Hence pragmatic English kings, attorneys and merchants all gravitated to the trial form which maximized party control—the personal battle model of feudal times.[81]

In the United States, entrepreneurs were attracted to the English common law system because it emphasized law developed by court cases rather than statute. With its precedent, rigorous rules and the passive neutrality of the state's representative (the judge), this system gave American entrepreneurs maximum predictability of outcome and even more individual control of the proceedings. Thus, due process, jury trial and other constitutional rights were intended by the commercial interests of the middle class merchants to strengthen the adversary system.

A trial in an inquisitorial system is a state inquest, thus the name "inquisitorial." Although applications of the system differ from country to country, they share certain fundamental features which distinguish them from the adversary system. The most prominent distinctions are in the roles of the judge and attorney. In accord with its nature as a state inquest (rather than merely a conflict resolution), the inquisitorial system trial is conducted by the state's representative, the judge. The attorney's role is limited primarily to suggesting to the judge additional questions for the witnesses. In marked contrast are the roles of their counterparts in the adversary system, where the judge is a relatively passive party who basically referees the investigation conducted by the attorneys.

Before moving to comparisons of the particular characteristics of the two systems, a caveat should be made. In large measure, many adversarial versus nonadversarial distinctions made between the systems are generalizations which serve heuristic purposes. In fact, both systems are mixed, each containing elements of both adversariality and nonadversariality. Plea bargaining and the grand jury proceedings of the U.S. criminal system, for example, are virtually nonadversarial activities; the grand jury only hears the prosecutor's case, and plea bargaining is consensual.

Specific features of the adversary system include party-controlled procedures, a dialectic paradigm for truth-seeking, decision making by jurors, reliance on oral testimony, adjudication by party conflict resolution, parties' right to waive procedural requirements by mutual agreement, emphasis on procedure over substantive result, and a traditionally passive, neutral judge concerned only with the integrity of the process. Philosophically, the state is reactive and laissez-faire about social and civic matters. That is to say, the procedure is intended as a resolution of the parties' dispute, as defined and limited by them, with no additional or alternative state agenda.

Specific features of the inquisitorial system include state-controlled procedure, a scientific paradigm for truth-seeking, no juries but a career judiciary (trained specifically for the bench rather than the American model of selecting judges from the ranks of practicing attorneys), reliance on official documentation, adjudication as a vehicle for the enforcement of state policies, and activist judges who will intervene to ensure a solution based on the merits of the case. The state also plays an activist role regarding social and civic matters. Damaska describes how the activist state ideology behind the inquisitorial system affects trial procedure:

Requiring a controversy as a general prerequisite for the institution of the legal process clearly make no sense to an activist government. Disputes do not miraculously arrive whenever a social event suggests the need to enforce the law and thus realize a policy goal in the concrete circumstances of a case. . . .

Divorced from dispute resolution, activist justice is also free from the controlling image of a lawsuit as a symbolic contest—two sides pressing discordant claims before a decision maker in the classic triadic relation. . . . In lieu of privately controlled contest, the idea of officially controlled *inquest* epitomizes the procedural style.[82]

Thus inquisitorial system trial proceedings serve to implement the state's goals. In the process, the ultimate morphology of the trial may bear little resemblance to its original incarnation. Damaska expounds:

[T]he state may want to use a narrow controversy as an exemplum for which to drive home a lesson to a larger audience: citizens may be invited—or required—to assume a variety of roles that have nothing to do directly with the resolution of the original dispute. They may become a chorus in the forensic drama. . . .

[A]ctivist government has little reason to tailor a lawsuit to the precise contours of an interpersonal controversy: indeed, . . . prayers for relief may have to be disregarded, since plaintiffs do not always know what is best for them.[83]

In short, the inquisitorial system trial becomes a pretext for the realization of state policy. "To imagine that such proceedings are devoted to the resolution of a dispute," says Damaska, "is to smuggle ideological assumptions of the reactive state into a hostile environment."[84] The table on the following page summarizes Damaska's analysis of the contrasting features of the two systems.

The key distinction between the two systems bears repetition. Under the adversary system, adherence to procedure legitimates the result. Under the inquisitorial system, use of the legal process to enforce state policies transcends resolution of the particular dispute. The result should conform to policy.

Given their disparate orientations, the two systems are not true alternatives for achieving the same prime objective: The adversary system serves to resolve conflict; the inquisitorial system serves to implement state policy. Because the

A COMPARISON OF THE FEATURES OF THE ADVERSARIAL AND INQUISITORIAL SYSTEMS BASED ON THE UNDERLYING PHILOSOPHIES OF EACH

ADVERSARY SYSTEM	*INQUISITORIAL SYSTEM*
-contest	-state inquest
-juror decision making	-career judiciary
-reliance on oral testimony documentation	-reliance on official
-party-controlled procedure	-nonpartisan (state)- controlled procedure
-*state* is reactive and laissez-faire re social and civic matters	-*state* is activist, inter- ventionist re social and civic matters
-*society* is distrustful of government problem solving problems and formulation of social policies	-*society* looks to state for resolution of social policies
-*adjudication* is party conflict resolution	-*adjudication* is vehicle for enforcement of state policies
-*parties* are free to *waive* most of their procedural rights by mutual agreement	-*parties* are subject to rigid state regulation of the legal process
-*procedure*: deviation of verdict from result required under law is unimportant; emphasis on procedure over substantive result	-*procedure*: deviation of verdict from result required under law is inconsistent with intent of the proceeding
-*judge* remains neutral, concerned only with integrity of the process	-*judge* can intervene to ensure solution based on the merits

inquisitorial system is geared to providing the best policy response to a given situation, the proceeding must be state controlled. Otherwise, private interests might thwart realization of state programs, and information other than that offered by the litigants might not be introduced.

Bearing in mind variations among countries using each type of trial system, both criminal and civil cases in the inquisitorial system can be contrasted with their counterparts in the adversary system. In discussing inquisitorial procedure, most writers use the French or German systems as models. The French criminal system uses an investigating magistrate who takes a proactive role in discovering all evidence.[85] Although the police are delegated some responsibility, neither prosecutors nor judges have discretion over the magistrate's activities. It is expected that if the magistrate sends a dossier (the investigative record) forward, conviction will follow. Once the dossier has been forwarded, the prosecutor and judge take over the investigation. By contrast, in the U.S. system, the investigation and administration of the case are left to police and counsel.[86]

No plea bargaining is allowed in the inquisitorial system because the state is obliged to ensure that the facts support the charge. (This requirement is tempered by a fair measure of reliance on confessions.) Plea bargains reflect underlying systemic philosophy. Ours is a system which prioritizes conflict resolution. In inquisitorial system countries, adjudication is seen more as a vehicle for policy implementation, which requires a determination of facts.[87] Therefore, plea bargains are not accepted.

The American and French systems have similar inquisitorial elements for pretrial investigation of criminal cases: *ex parte* investigation (by the grand jury in the United States) and persuasion of the accused to plead guilty. The American prosecutor's file, complete with witness statements, documentary evidence and expert witness reports, is similar to the European dossier.[88] As noted earlier, American judges no longer assume the traditionally passive, umpireal role. Rather, they exercise considerable control and supervision over the pretrial phase of the case. This is particularly so in criminal cases with regard to decisions about police and prosecutor evidence (e.g., eavesdropping, entrapment), regulating plea bargaining and guilty pleas, and issuing warrants.[89] When courts are badly backlogged, however, American judges commonly rubber stamp search warrant applications and only minimally supervise the process. They are usually too busy to do otherwise, and are not equipped with adequate staff to carry out administrative duties. Further, the adversary system model prescribes that they react to parties' counsel, not initiate actions.

As in France, there is no jury under the German criminal system. Instead, a mix of lay and professional judges decide cases. The mix is expected to have a broadening impact on the professional judges' perspectives. Further, the absence of a jury removes the need for almost all exclusionary evidence rules. Hearsay evidence, for example, can be admitted and the court must judge its value.[90] The same applies to opinions, character evidence and evidence of prior convictions. All must be admitted unless better evidence is available. Under the German system of "free proof," almost all facts and inferences from facts must be set out in detail. The court has an obligation to ascertain the truth for itself.[91] No such obligation exists in American courts.[92]

Interrogation of the German defendant is conducted by the judge, although the prosecutor and defense counsel can ask supplemental questions. Cross-examination does not exist. The underlying reason why judges conduct the inquisitorial trial is to safeguard against partisan distortion of the facts by advocates. Judges can clarify ambiguities by requiring relevant evidence not previously requested by the parties. In contrast, American juries are often not permitted to hear relevant evidence because of possible misunderstandings, yet are often expected to make difficult distinctions among uses of admitted evidence.[93]

Also in accord with the French practice, German prosecutors have no discretion to plea bargain. Prosecution is compulsory in all but minor cases. Guilty pleas are simply not permitted, although confessions are allowed in nonpetty crimes.[94] Continental procedure is geared to truth-seeking, which is inconsistent with plea bargains. On the other hand, plea bargaining is consistent with dispute resolution, the adversary system's primary objective. The adversary system casts litigation as between parties, who should be allowed to limit or settle their dispute without court adjudication.[95] It is basically private. Conversely, inquisitorial proceedings are public: The prosecution is even more strongly obliged than under the adversary system to present *exonerating* as well as inculpating evidence in an impartial manner because the prime objective is the discovery of truth.[96] Compulsory prosecution in the inquisitorial system stands in bold relief to the extensive prosecutorial discretion permitted in the adversary system.[97] Similarly, the inquisitorial prosecutor cannot emulate the tactic commonly used by his adversary system counterpart: manipulating the outcome of a case by overcharging the defendant. Under the inquisitorial system, for example, a defendant accused of manslaughter may end up being convicted of murder.

Differing values translate to differing procedures. Because American procedural law is based on a distrust of public officials, greater consideration is given to so-called nontruth values: individual dignity, privacy and integrity. This leads to higher evidentiary barriers to conviction than are found in continental countries. In order for a procedure to legitimate adversary system verdicts, it must be perceived as fair—each side must have an equal chance of winning. Where the parties are unequal, as in criminal cases, it is believed fair to handicap the state as the litigant with superior resources in order to *balance the advantages*. That is why the prosecution must prove its case beyond a reasonable doubt even if this reduces the symmetry of procedural rights. Our system has much greater concern over the erroneous conviction of innocents than it does over the acquittal of the guilty. Evidentiary barriers which are erected to protect individual liberties against the state can severely impede the truth and effectively defeat the substantive criminal law. Given the distrust of state overreaching, the trial procedure is more properly a "battle" or "contest," whereas in inquisitorial system countries an "inquiry" is conducted by the paternalistically viewed state.

Looking at civil cases, American and German trial procedures differ markedly in their perspectives of procedural justice and efficiency. This is generally reflected in the roles of the trial participants. Yet the roles of the American and German trial attorneys are not as antipodal as one might expect. Except for factfinding, the German trial attorney is active in every phase of the trial from pleading to final arguments. His role includes:

- suggesting legal theories and lines of factual inquiry;

- supplementing the judge's examination of witnesses;

- nominating additional witnesses;

- urging inferences of fact; and

- discussing and distinguishing precedent.[98]

Hence adversariality is still a generally viable characteristic of the German trial. The significant exception is factfinding. There, advocacy is believed to distort evidence.

As in criminal cases, no evidence is automatically excluded. German law exhibits expansive notions of testimonial privilege.[99] Evidence shortcomings that would affect admission in the adversary system only affect *weight* in the inquisitorial system. Hearsay, for example, is admitted, but given a relatively low probative value.

Written findings of fact and reasoned application of the law accompany the German court's judgment. This serves general and specific purposes. Generally, it protects against arbitrary and eccentric adjudication. Specifically, it acts as a basis for judicial evaluation and facilitates appellate review.[100] Contrast this with the American practice. No rationale for the decision or findings of fact need be offered in most state court trials. Except for the rare instances where the judge requests a special verdict or general verdict plus interrogatories, the general verdict shrouds the jury's decision making process in secrecy. In a bench trial, the judge usually provides a brief verbal explanation of her decision, but ordinarily with little depth or analysis.

Unlike the unitary (continuous) trial of the adversary system, inquisitorial trials are noncontinuous and issue-separated. Proof-taking is episodic and marked by great flexibility. The presiding judge decides what evidence to hear at particular sessions. Because the trial is segmented, the court is free to return to issues raised in earlier sessions; even pleadings can be subsequently amended. The court focuses its initial inquiry on those issues most likely to narrow or dispose of the factual investigation. An analogue in American trials is found in criminal procedure. Sentencing in capital cases is separated from the guilt or innocence phase of the trial. A finding of not guilty, of course, obviates sentencing deliberations. Although such separation of issues is permitted in civil cases,[101] it is used only infrequently. Our evidence-gathering thus suffers from self-imposed constraints. Harvard law professor Benjamin Kaplan assessed the possible causes and some important consequences.

With us in this country jury trial must be carried out as a single continuous drama, for a jury cannot be assembled, dismissed and reconvened over a period of time. We tend toward concentrated trial *even when a judge sits alone*, perhaps by magnetic attraction to jury trial as the historic centerpiece of civil procedure, perhaps because the system puts a high value on the trier's fresh impression of live proof, perhaps for other reasons. Hence the opposing sides must appear in court knowing the precise issues and fully armed and prepared to meet them. To these ends we have our pleadings and amendments and motions, our discovery devices, our pretrial conference. Concentrated trial forces accommodations in many rules and practices and has no doubt profoundly affected the character and role of the American lawyer and judge.[102] (Emphasis supplied.)

A key distinction between the systems lies in the allocation of attorney expenses. The loser pays the winner's attorney's fees in the inquisitorial system, subject to statutory or court-imposed fee limits. Under the adversary system, each side requests, but is typically denied, reimbursement of attorney's fees as part of the court's award. Interestingly, England follows the practice in inquisitorial courts. In fact, "loser pays" is known in the United States as the "English Rule."

Central to either system is "proof-taking" (evidence gathering). Divergent techniques for collecting information from witnesses reveal fundamental systemic differences. Continental witnesses begin by giving a narrative account of their knowledge of the events in question. Only the judge can interrupt these stories, and then only to ask questions for clarification or to return the witness from "the labyrinth of utter irrelevancy,"[103] but she usually refrains from doing so until the witness has finished testifying. Following the witness' narrative, the presiding judge poses questions. These tend to be more conversational than the adversary system practice of questions and short answers. Afterwards, the attorneys can request supplemental questions to add emphasis to earlier evidence or reveal omitted evidence, but the bulk of information comes from the judicial investigation. In contrariety, testimony in adversary trials is filtered through the attorneys by direct-and cross-examination (punctuated by frequent interruptions), in conformity with the party-control model.

Continental witnesses are typically called and questioned by the court. When witnesses are called by the parties, there are financial and other inducements to be biased.[104] Inquisitorial system theory holds that cross-examination is ineffective to undo the consequences of *witness-coaching*. This potential distorting effect is avoided when witnesses are those of the court. In fact, inquisitorial system attorneys usually do not even meet the witnesses before the trial. In the rare circumstances when they do, the court assigns a commensurately low probative value to their testimony.

Few trends have marked major civil litigation in the United States more than the increased incidence of partisan expert testimony. In the inquisitorial system, expert witnesses are almost always those of the court, and are called "judges' aides," not witnesses. This avoids the "battle of the experts" which so confounds many American juries. Written opinions of inquisitorial system experts are first reviewed by the attorneys, whose comments may prompt the court to hold a hearing where counsel can directly question. Alternatively, the court may seek a second expert.

The composition of the factfinding body is one of the more prominent differences between the systems. No parallel to our lay jury is used. Germany employs a mixed lay-professional bench instead of the single presiding judge in cases of serious crimes or civil cases heard before specialized courts in labor, tax, administrative, family and commercial disputes.[105] Other cases have no lay component. Instead, they are tried before a single judge or a presiding judge plus two or more associate judges.

The German court's duty to discover the truth is matched by a cognate responsibility to ascertain and apply the law without prompting from the parties. In essence, the court seeks to ensure a decision based on the merits of the case. A contrary dynamic obtains in the adversary system. The general premise of adversary procedure is that the court has no independent knowledge of the law and must therefore be informed of it by argument.[106]

Appellate review of both law and fact is allowed; in the inquisitorial system proceeding, there is no presumption of lower court accuracy. Usually just a summary of the trial is read by the appellate court. But witnesses can be recalled when the record is deemed insufficient, and parties can offer new proof and invoke new legal theories.[107] Consonant with the judicial obligation to independently make the right decision, the court is not confined to the grounds urged by counsel.[108] In contrast, appellate courts in the adversary system review only the law. Witnesses are not heard because their testimonies relate only to factual matters.

Despite these paradigmatic differences, actual practices in the two systems move toward convergence, most evidently during pretrial proceedings. In this phase, judges in both systems attempt to reduce issues, minimize discovery and induce settlement. Although substantial pretrial judicial supervision is routine now only for complex cases in the United States, the incidence of such litigation increases. And the trend toward greater judicial involvement appears inexorable.[109]

Ethical codes of the two systems have significant similarities and differences. Instead of looking to France, Germany or other continental European countries for comparison, however, the authoritative source is a multinational code. In line with the rapid integration of Europe, The Council of the Bars and Law Societies of the European Community—known in Europe by the multi-lingual acronym CCBE—adopted the Code of Conduct for Lawyers in the European Community in 1988. For the adversary system, the most representative code is the ABA's MRPC (Model Rules of Professional Conduct) adopted in 1983.

Taking the similarities first, we see that the CCBE shares the American principle of lawyer confidentiality. CCBE Rule 2.3.2 states, "A lawyer shall . . . respect the confidentiality of all information . . . received by him . . . in the course of rendering service to his client." Ethical codes of both systems preserve the confidentiality obligation after the conclusion of the attorney's representation. The European attorney has a duty of competence and diligence in handling the client's affairs and maintaining communication with the client. If the attorney wishes to withdraw, the CCBE tracks the MRPC in enjoining the attorney to do so in a way that does not prejudice the client. Other similarities include rules on avoidance of conflicts of interest, the use of lawyer trust accounts and permissible advertising.

Among the differences, the most salient relate to the lawyer's duties. The preeminent duty of the adversary system attorney is to his client. Under the inquisitorial system's CCBE, that duty rises no higher than the attorney's duty to the courts and the public. This, in turn, translates to a higher duty of candor than is found in the MRPC. For instance, MRPC Rule 3.3 proscribes knowingly offering false evidence, whereas CCBE Rule 4.4 prohibits knowingly offering information which is false *or misleading*. Other differences under the CCBE include a ban on contingency fees, regulation of fees and a requirement that the lawyer maintain liability insurance coverage for professional negligence.[110]

INQUISITORIAL VS. ADVERSARY SYSTEM: PROS AND CONS

"Which system is better?" is an expectable but largely unanswerable question. That is because the question itself begets another question, "Better at what?" Each system pursues its own set of values—not all of which are shared, nor are they given the same priorities.[111] The disparate roles of the judge and attorney under the two systems reflect the relative value each places on truth-seeking. Under the inquisitorial system, the judge, a neutral party, continues to search the facts until satisfied that there is enough to render a correct decision. Under the adversary system, the partisan attorneys introduce only as much evidence as will help their cases.

Each system has advantages and disadvantages with respect to factfinding. Adversary system proponents contend that the self-interest of the attorneys better motivates them than the neutral judge to find evidence. Without financial or professional motivations, the argument goes, a judge does not have the same incentive as an attorney to probe deeply into the facts. Inquisitorial system proponents counter that irrespective of the *quantity* of evidence produced in an adversary system trial, its *quality* is tainted by the self-serving manner in which it is chosen and the garnished form it is presented. Moreover, partisan incentives endemic to the adversary system lead to attorney excesses that confound truth and justice.

Three specific arguments collectively rebut the claim that a neutral judge will lack the partisan attorney's factfinding diligence. First, empirical studies support this contention only as to the attorney who finds the facts to be decidedly unfavorable. Second, an inquisitorial system judge cannot refuse without stated reason to investigate party-nominated proofs, so little relevant evidence is excluded. Finally, the inquisitorial system contains professional incentives to qualitative judicial performance which are absent from the adversary system. In contrast with American judges, continental judges are chosen after rigorous examination and specially trained for career appointments. The judiciary is a prestigious, well-paying career not sustained by political appointment or reelection, but by meritocracy. Advancement depends, in part, on factfinding efficacy.

Intractable problems inhere in the adversary factfinding model. Somewhat like an infant's diet, information flow to the factfinders in an adversarial trial is first selectively limited, then that which is allowed through is carefully strained or predigested. Limitations occur because one or both of the opposing attorneys may want to keep relevant information from the factfinder. The hearsay rule and other evidence exclusions enable the attorneys to effectuate this information blockade. And unlike the narrative style of testimony in the inquisitorial system, the adversary system strains testimony through narrow "yes" or "no" type responses. Consequently, the factual basis for the ultimate decision is frequently incomplete.

Another unfavorable aspect of the adversary trial is its tendency to corrupt witness testimony. Coaching may unconsciously fill gaps in a witness' memory that correspond with the coaching lawyer's expectations and theses. Further distortion lies in cross-examination tactics, which can easily obfuscate otherwise clear information.

The nonadversarial inquisitorial system avoids these problems. Interparty arrangements concerning facts are prohibited. The court's investigatory duty extends to all relevant facts. Inasmuch as information gathering is the province of the state, there are no difficulties in exchanging information between parties. Hearsay and other grounds for inadmissibility do not apply. Finally, the state's neutrality precludes coaching or abuse of witnesses in cross-examination.[112]

An extrinsic consideration strongly indicates the innate factfinding weakness of the adversary system. Adversarial procedure is rarely used for other (nontrial) types of investigations in the United States. We usually appoint an individual or board to conduct the inquiry instead of having two competing versions presented to a judge. Even advocates of the adversary system typically use nonadversary procedures to find something out. Gordon Tullock, author of *The Logic of the Law*, writes: "Altogether, it does not seem likely that the adversary system would long survive if individuals were permitted to choose their own procedural rules."[113]

Candid advocates of adversary procedure concede the shortcomings of the system, but say, "If you want adversary safeguards, you're stuck with adversary excesses." This is an erroneous, all-or-nothing contention. As the German experience demonstrates, eliminating party control during factfinding leaves adversarial safeguards substantially intact but without the problems attending witness-coaching and other forms of partisanship.

Adherents of the inquisitorial system claim that evidence produced by neutral investigation results in more reliable factfinding. We have more to learn from psychology and the other social sciences before we can confirm or reject this conclusion. More certain is that the two systems employ antithetical cognitive roles for their factfinders: the active inquiry by the inquisitorial judge versus the passive role of the adversary system's judge and jury. One thing is certain: Virtually the entire factual basis for the adversary trial factfinder's decision is presented by biased advocates.

The distribution of resources invested in a trial provides a clue to the relative reliability of trial factfinding. A lawsuit finds the court and one side seeking the correct result. The other side seeks the incorrect result. Since the court's share of the factfinding (independent investigation) is far greater under the inquisitorial system, a correspondingly higher share of the total resources invested in the case are applied to reaching the correct conclusion. Therefore, a higher degree of accuracy should be expected. Conversely, the parties control most of the resources invested in the adversarial suit. As a result, a great deal of the resources spent in the adversary trial are contributed by the side seeking to mislead.[114] Tullock explains:

Assume, for example, that in the average American court case 45 percent of the total resources are invested by each side and 10 percent by the government in providing the actual decision making apparatus. This would mean that 55 percent of the resources used in the court are *aimed* at achieving the correct result, and 45 percent at reaching an incorrect result. Under the inquisitorial system, assume that 90 percent of the resources are put up by the government which hires a competent board of judges (who then carry on an essentially independent investigation) and only 5 percent by each of the parties. Under these circumstances, 95 percent of the resources are contributed by people who are attempting to reach the correct conclusion, and only 5 percent by the saboteur.

Normally, we would anticipate a higher degree of accuracy with the second type than with the first.[115]

We can also compare systems by the level of decision maker bias. American critics of the inquisitorial system argue that the judge's involvement in the case makes it difficult for her to evaluate the evidence fairly. Although the judge's familiarity with the case (through the dossier) enables her to be an effective interrogator, Fuller contends that the same familiarity may lead to the formation of a tentative hypothesis before trial and more receptivity to information confirming that hypothesis. By contrast, the adversary model decision maker can suspend judgment longer.

Inquisitorial advocates maintain that their system satisfies Fuller's concerns. Necessary safeguards prevent judicial prejudgment. For example, the German system addresses this issue in criminal cases by dividing the initial investigation and final adjudication between prosecutor and court.[116] Moreover, the constant input of the inquisitorial system attorney inhibits, at least to some degree, the premature formulation of opinion.

The influence of attorney performance on case outcome has long been the subject of conflicting discussion and speculation among theorists and empiricists alike. One related point, however, is less debatable: The adversary system's presumption of roughly equal representation is implausible. Nothing in the adversary system is designed to match attorneys of comparable skill or litigants of comparable resources. Inquisitorial procedure, on the other hand, lessens forensic theatrics, dirty tricks and the advantages of superior forensic skills by one side's attorney. This is critical. Diluting the impact of disparate attorney skills in large measure frees inquisitorial system decisions from that which has little or nothing to do with the merits of the case. Under the adversary system, says Tullock,

the greater importance of the lawyers means that the relative excellence of those hired by the two parties is of much greater importance. . . . Since a case in which two lawyers are of exactly equal ability must be very rare, it would seem that the inaccuracy introduced by this factor alone would more than offset the possible inaccuracy resulting from giving the judge the dominant role.

A further advantage of the inquisitorial system is a reduction of the importance of courtroom strategy. . . . [T]he smaller the role played by the lawyers, the more likely it is that the outcome will be in accord with the facts.[117]

Trial flexibility is another inquisitorial advantage. As discussed earlier, the adversarial trial litigates all issues in one continuous trial. Inquisitorial trials are noncontinuous and issue-separated. This is far less onerous on attorneys, who can offer additional proof during later stages of the trial. More important to accurate factfinding, the court need only consider at any given time evidence related to the specific issues under inquiry.

Witness testimony dominates evidence; it is the warp and woof of the trial. The inquisitorial system trial is much friendlier to witnesses. They can begin their testimonies with uninterrupted narratives. No such freedom is afforded the adversary system witness, whose testimony, when not limited to "yes" or "no" answers, must commonly endure a plethora of scattershot strategic disruptions by opposing counsel. A witness' testimony, otherwise impeccable, may be remembered by the decision maker for a single flawed response which the opposing attorney pounced upon like a ravenous piranha and mercilessly belabored.

A final advantage of the inquisitorial system issues from its broader view of the role of the courts. If, as Tocqueville observed, every important issue in America is eventually litigated, we must compare the two systems in their respective facilities for engaged discourse and debate over pivotal social problems. In this role, Robert Bellah and the other authors of *The Good Society* found American courts grievously lacking. In their critique, Bellah *et al.* inferentially endorsed a process far more descriptive of the inquisitorial system.

Because the courts sustain debate about fundamental principles of how Americans live their lives in common, they are an arena where we can address central social questions. . . . But the courts as an institutional system have grave weaknesses in this regard: they have no independent fact-gathering ability . . . and they respond to adversaries in cases brought before them rather than framing a debate about what is best for the common good.[118]

Are the courts rather than the legislatures the appropriate fora for these broad-gauged debates? Arguably not. But the legislatures have evinced a reluctance bordering on pusillanimity to tackle thorny and intractable public problems such as adequate funding of legislated programs. For instance, courts have had to order allocation of funds for court operations and prisons. So it is that many basic governmental responsibilities and related discourse devolve from the legislatures to the courts. While this state of affairs obtains, it is a purely academic issue whether or not courts are the proper vehicles for the realization of governmental policies. To the extent our courts have this *de facto* responsibility thrust upon them, they should have the facility to hear broader and more dispassionate views than they currently do. (Rarely, for example, is every potentially affected interest represented in a trial.) In this regard, the inquisitorial system trial is clearly superior—in design and experience.

NOTES

1. Derek Bok, quoted in the *California State Bar Bulletin*, *1(12)* (October 1991), p. 3.
2. Robert Cochran, "Take Care This Suit Isn't Yours," *National Law Journal*, 3/30/92, p. 13.
3. Paul Nejelski and Larry Ray, "Alternatives to Court and Trial," in F. Klein, ed., *The Improvement of the Administration of Justice* (Chicago: ABA Press, 1981), p. 264.
4. Charles Rosenberg, "Alternatives to Litigation: Long-Term Solutions or Short-Term Fad?" *Management* (Fall 1983), p. 7.
5. G. Richard Shell, "The Role of Public Law in Private Dispute Resolution: Reflections on *Shearson/American Express, Inc. v. McMahon*," 26 *American Business Law Journal* 397, 398 (1988).
6. Nejelski and Ray, *op. cit.*, p. 272.
7. Warren Burger, "Isn't There A Better Way?" *ABA Journal, 68* (1982).
8. Id. at 275,276.
9. Id. at 277.
10. Id. at 275.
11. Larry Ray and Judy Devonshire, "Dispute Resolution in the Law Schools: Extracurricular or Essential Activity?" *Dispute Resolution* (Summer 1988), at 18.
12. Paul Wehr, "Conflict Resolution Studies: What Do We Know?" *Dispute Resolution Forum* (April 1986), at 3, 4.
13. George Seidel, "Present and Future Directions in ADR Research," 26 *American Business Law Journal* 387, 388 (1989).
14. The federal program was established by the 1980 Dispute Resolution Act.
15. Nejelski and Ray, *op. cit.*, p. 264.
16. Carla Rivera, "Bad Blood Flows For Neighbors," *Los Angeles Daily Journal*, 3/14/91,p. 1 at 20.
17. State Bar Report, "Promoting Dispute Resolution to Lawyers and the Public," reported in *California Lawyer* (March 1992), p. 56.
18. Patricia Ebener and Donna Betancourt, *Court-Annexed Arbitration: The National Picture* (Santa Monica, Calif.: The Rand Corporation, 1985).
19. Claudia Carver, "Proposals to Increase ADR Use in Court System, State Agencies," reported in *California Lawyer* (March 1992), p. 58.
20. Marshall Breger, "Labor Department Leads Way On ADR," *National Law Journal*, 2/15/93, p. 16.
21. 28 *United States Code* sections 473(a)(1), (a)(2)(B), and (a)(2)(B)(i) and (II), respectively
22. See, e.g., section 475(b)(5) which allows courts to require that parties' representatives "with the authority to bind them in settlement be present or available by telephone during any settlement conference."

23. See Judith Resnik, "Failing Faith: Adjudicatory Procedure in Decline," 53 *University of Chicago Law Review* 494 (1986).

24. Roger Meiners *et al.*, *The Legal Environment of Business*, 4th ed. (St. Paul, Minn.: West Publishing, 1991), p. 106.

25. In *Shearson/American Express, Inc. v. McMahon*, 107 *Supreme Court* 2332 (1987), the U.S. Supreme Court affirmed the public policy favoring arbitration by enforcing a provision in brokerage contracts which requires customers to arbitrate their claims against broker-dealers.

26. For a discussion and evaluation of the California program, see Deborah Hensler, Albert Lipson and Elizabeth Rolph, *Judicial Arbitration in California: The First Year* (Santa Monica, Calif.: Rand Corporation, 1981).

27. See Robert Coulson, "Rent-A-Judge: Private Settlement for the Public Good," *Judicature, 66* (1982), p. 7.

28. See Robert Gnaidza, "Rent-A-Judge: Secret Justice for the Privileged Few," *Judicature, 66* (1982), p. 6.

29. California, for example, mandates mediation of child custody issues in divorce cases before adversary proceedings. California Civil Code sec. 4607.

30. See Susan Silbey and Sally Merry, "Mediator Settlement Strategies," 8 *Law and Policy* 7 (1986) for an analysis of strategies pursued by mediators to encourage settlement.

31. D. Marie Provine, "Managing Negotiated Justice: Settlement Procedures in the Courts," *The Justice System Journal, 12(1)* (1987), p. 91 at 95.

32. See Stephan Goldberg, "The Mediation of Grievances Under a Collective Bargaining Contract: An Alternative to Arbitration," 77 *Northwest University Law Review* 270 (1982).

33. Wayne Brazil *et al.*, "Early neutral evaluation: an experimental effort to expedite dispute resolution," *Judicature, 69(5)* (February-March 1986), p. 279 at 283.

34. Walter Gellhorn, *Ombudsman and Others: Citizens' Protectors In Nine Countries* (Cambridge, Mass.: Harvard University Press, 1966).

35. Paul Verkuil, "The Ombudsman and the Limits of the Adversary System," 75 *Columbia Law Review* 845 at 847, 851-853 (1975).

36. Reginald Smith, "The Place of Conciliation in the Administration of Justice," 9 *ABA Journal* 747 (1923).

37. Marc Galanter, "The emergence of the judge as mediator in civil cases," *Judicature, 69(5)* (February-March 1986), p. 257 at 258.

38. Comment, "Pretrial Diversion: The Threat of Expanding Social Control," 10 *Harvard Civil Rights-Civil Law Review* 180 (1975).

39. Nejelski and Ray, *op. cit.*, p. 264.

40. John Cratsley, "Community Courts: Offering Alternative Dispute Resolution Within the Judicial System," 3 *Vermont Law Review* 1 at 10 (1978).
41. *Brady v. U.S.*, 397 *U.S.* 742 (1970), at 410.
42. Id. at 412.
43. See, e.g., FRCP 16(b).
44. D. Marie Provine, *op. cit.*, pp. 95-96.
45. Robert Mnookin and Lewis Kornhauser, "Bargaining in the Shadow of the Law," 88 *Yale Law Journal* 950 (1979).
46. G. Bellow and B. Moulton, *The Lawyering Process: Negotiation* (St. Paul: Foundation Press, 1978); Robert Axelrod, *The Evolution of Cooperation* (New York: Basic Books, 1984); Carol Gilligan, *In A Different Voice* (Cambridge, Mass.: Harvard University Press, 1982); Harold Raiffa, *The Art and Science of Negotiation* (Cambridge, Mass.: Harvard University Press, 1984).
47. Roger Fisher and William Ury, *Getting To Yes* (Boston: Houghton Mifflin, 1981).
48. Id. at 43.
49. James White, "The Pros and Cons of 'Getting to Yes,'" *Journal of Legal Education, 34* (1984), pp. 115-117.
50. David Ebel, "Bar Programs—Other Ways to Resolve Disputes," *Litigation, 6* (1908), pp. 25, 26.
51. Id.
52. Id.
53. Id., p. 27.
54. Id., p. 52.
55. M. L. Marasinghe, "The Use of Conciliation for Dispute Settlements: The Sri Lanka Experience," 29 *International and Comparative Law Quarterly* 389 at 400-403 (1980); F. S. C. Northrop, "The Mediational Approval Theory in American Legal Realism," 44 *Virginia Law Review* 347 at 356 (1958).
56. Northrop, *op. cit.* at 353.
57. Leonard Riskin, "Mediation and Lawyers," 43 *Ohio State Law Journal* 29 at 34 (1982).
58. See Marvin Frankel, *Partisan Justice* (New York: Hill and Wang, 1980), pp. 62-63, for a discussion of the nasty and aggravating effects characteristic of judicial adversary adjudication.
59. This would not be the case in court-annexed mediation.
60. See, e.g., California Evidence Code Sec. 1152.5, which states that mediation settlement discussions are deemed confidential if the parties sign an agreement to that effect.

61. Bruce Edwards and Vivien Williamson, "Mediation: Effective Alternative," *Los Angeles Daily Journal (State Bar Bulletin Supplement)*, 4/2/91, pp. S1, S3.
62. Jane Adler, Deborah Hensler and Charles Nelson, *Simple Justice: How Litigants Fare in the Pittsburgh Court Arbitration Program* (Santa Monica, Calif.: Rand Corporation, 1983).
63. Id., pp. 72-75.
64. John Shapard, *Updated Analysis of Court-Annexed Arbitration in Three Federal District Courts* (Washington, D.C.: Federal Judicial Center, 1983).
65. Randall Samborn, "State Court Filings Hit New Highs," *National Law Journal*, 5/4/92, p. 7.
66. Stephen Goldberg, Eric Green and Frank Sander, *Dispute Resolution* (Boston: Little Brown, 1985), p. 491.
67. Id.
68. Linda Singer, "Nonjudicial Dispute Resolution Mechanisms: The Effects on Justice for the Poor," 13 *Clearinghouse Review* 569, 575-579 (1979).
69. FRCP Rule 68.
70. J. Marks, E. Johnson and P. Szanton, *Dispute Resolution in America: Processes in Evolution* (Washington, D.C.: National Institute for Dispute Resolution, 1984), p. 18.
71. Owen Fiss, "Against Settlement," 93 *Yale Law Journal* 1073 (1984).
72. Id. at 1075-1078.
73. Barbara Yngvesson and Patricia Hennessy, "Small Claims, Complex Disputes: A Review of the Small Claims Literature," *Law and Society Review*, *9* (1975), pp. 219 at 268.
74. Id. at 256-270.
75. Goldberg, Green and Sanders, *Dispute Resolution*, *op. cit.* , pp. 246-247.
76. Lon Fuller, "Collective Bargaining and the Arbitrator," Proceedings, Fifteenth Annual Meeting, National Academy of Arbitrators (1962), p. 8.
77. Judith Resnik, "Managerial Judges," 96 *Harvard Law Review* 376 at 380 (1982).
78. Lon Fuller, "Professional Responsibility: Report of the Joint Conference," *ABA Journal, 44* (1958), 1159 at 1160.
79. Resnik, "Managerial Judges," *op. cit.*, 426-427.
80. Stephan Landsman, *The Adversary System: A Description and Defense* (Washington, D.C.: The American Enterprise Institute, 1984), p. 30.
81. Neef and Nagel, "The Adversary Nature of the American Legal System From a Historical Perspective," *op. cit.*, p. 123 at 147-48.
82. Mirjan Damaska, *The Faces of Justice and State Authority* (New Haven, Conn.: Yale University Press, 1986), pp. 84-87.
83. Id.
84. Id.

85. Contrary to the practice in other continental European countries, in Germany the public prosecutor conducts the investigation. Thus among inquisitorial system countries, the German system is closest to the American. John Langbein, *Comparative Criminal Procedure: Germany* (St. Paul, Minn.: West Publishing, 1977), p. 2.

86. Abraham Goldstein, "Reflections of Two Models: Inquisitorial Themes in American Criminal Procedure," 26 *Stanford Law Review* 1009 at 1019 (1974).

87. Mirjan Damaska, *op. cit.*, pp. 112-113, 119, 224.

88. Id. at 1020-21.

89. Id. at 1022-24.

90. Hans-Heinrich Jescheck, "Principles of German Criminal Procedure in Comparison with American Law," 56 *Virginia Law Review* 239 at 243-45 (1970).

91. A. Goldstein and M. Marcus, "The Myth of Judicial Supervision in Three 'Inquisitorial' Systems: France, Italy and Germany," 87 *Yale Law Journal* 240 at 247-49 (1977).

92. Karl Kunert, "Some Observations on the Origin and Structure of Evidence Rules Under the Common Law System and the Civil Law System of 'Free Proof' in the German Code of Civil Procedure," 16 *Buffalo Law Review* 122 at 123-25, 153-56, 160-64 (1967).

93. Id.

94. Informally, processes comparable to plea bargaining occasionally take place by tacit understanding between prosecutor and defendant.

95. Thomas Volkmann-Schluck, "Continental European Criminal Procedures: True or Illusive Model?" 9 *American Journal of Criminal Law* 1 at 4-5 (1981).

96. Id., p. 26.

97. Some comparativists maintain that inquisitorial systems avoid the extreme prosecutorial discretion which leads to plea bargaining in the United States. Strong judicial supervision and control of the process allegedly keep it in check. John Langbein and Lloyd Weinreb, "Continental Criminal Procedure: 'Myth' and Reality," 87 *Yale Law Journal* 1549, 1567 (1978). To others, the claim that continental procedures adhere to a rule of law more strictly than ours is based less on fact than on ideology, and the assumption that the officials adhere to the ideology. Under this view, prosecutors and police are as dominant in continental Europe as they are here; judicial responsibility is mostly reactive to the primary roles played by the police and prosecution. Thus, we should be skeptical and cautious about conclusions drawn from constructional differences. Given the high degree of prosecutorial discretion in both systems, "the usual debate about whether an adversarial or inquisitorial system more fairly and

accurately searches out the truth hardly seems relevant." Goldstein and Marcus, *op. cit.*, pp. 240, 282, 283.

98. John Langbein, "The German Advantage in Civil Procedure," 82(4) *University of Chicago Law Review* 822 at 824, 829 (Fall 1985).

99. Id.

100. Id. at 829,856.

101. See, e.g., FRCP 42(b).

102. Benjamin Kaplan, "Civil Procedure—Reflections on the Comparisons of Systems," 9 *Buffalo Law Review* 409 at 419 (1960).

103. Damaska, *op. cit.*, p. 137.

104. Langbein, *op. cit.*, pp. 833-34.

105. Id. at 864-65.

106. W. Zeidler, "Evaluation of the Adversary System: Some Remarks on the Investigatory System of Procedure," 55 *The Australian Law Journal* 390 at 394 (July 1981).

107. Langbein, *op. cit.*, p. 857.

108. Kaplan, *op. cit.*, at 413.

109. Resnik, "Managerial Judges," *op. cit.*

110. Geoffrey Hazard, "Ethics," *The National Law Journal*, 3/30/92, p. 13, 14.

111. Of course, one could say they both seek "justice" as their first priority. But that begs the question because justice is often defined tautologically: Justice results from adherence to prescribed trial procedure; the procedures are used because they are just.

112. Mirjan Damaska, "Presentation Of Evidence And Factfinding Precision," 123 *University of Pennsylvania Law Review* 1083, 1093-94 (1975).

113. Gordon Tullock, *The Logic of the Law* (New York: Basic Books, 1971), p. 93.

114. Gordon Tullock, "On the Efficient Organization of Trials," *Kyklos*, **28** (1975), pp. 745 at 756.

115. Id.

116. John Langbein, *Comparative Criminal Procedure* (St. Paul, Minn.: West Publishing, 1977), pp. 150-51.

117. Tullock, *The Logic of the Law*, *op. cit.*, p. 92.

118. Robert Bellah *et al.*, *The Good Society* (New York: Alfred A. Knopf, 1991), p. 130.

CHAPTER 7

A BLUEPRINT FOR REFORM

The courts of justice are the visible organs by which the legal profession is enabled to control democracy. The judge is a lawyer who works with lawyers to maintain the status quo—and aggressively denounces and works against legal reform that would strengthen the Constitutional rights of the American people. Lawyers are united in their common interests and intent to maintain the status quo at all times.

—Alexis de Tocqueville[1]

We are captive to the notion of a proper trial as an adversarial one. Our servitude comes at a high price. The adversary system produces a procedure-laden trial, where process often outweighs substance, and the relative skills of the opposing attorneys determine outcomes. Moreover, rancor frequently prevails and comity is sacrificed at the altar of victory.

Despite its institutional status and cultural appeal, the adversary trial has major problems, as delineated in earlier chapters. These problems beggar our judicial system and impede us from realizing our potential to be a more just society. This chapter proposes specific meliorative reforms. Because most of the proposed reforms contemplate a greater role for the trial judge, the chapter also provides a rationale and guidelines for judicial intervention.

The core problem lies within the attorney's role of zealous advocate. Although mandated by ABA ethical codes[2] and public expectations, zealous advocacy frequently results in adversary excess. Stories are legion of adversarial dirty tricks, witness-coaching, discovery abuse and hardball tactics. But with generally vague and typically unenforced restraints in federal and state bar ethical codes, adversarial mischief is limited only by the often fertile imaginations of trial attorneys. Many jurors notice the tactics. In the Los Angeles survey, about two-fifths of the jurors thought the attorneys were trying *harder* to distort or hide the facts than reveal them.[3]

None of this pathology occurs in a vacuum. The public nourishes and sustains the adversary system. While media critics commonly censure pettifoggery and litigator tricks, it is clear that many clients expect their attorneys to use every potentially gainful forensic device—no matter how ethically or morally questionable—and to exploit every partisan advantage available. And although prosecutors are supposed to "do justice" by disclosing exonerating evidence, there is no limitation on their zeal. Indeed, an incumbent's win/loss record is a material factor in elections for public prosecutors. Thus several of the proposals offered here seek to diminish the attorney's extensive powers to affect case outcomes through tricks and adversarial excess during the pretrial and trial stages.

Juries exacerbate the problem of attorney domination of trials. Attorneys would not be as consequential without the widespread use of juries. The peculiar combination of inherent lay juror limitations and imposed restrictions on jury functioning render the jury the unwitting accomplice to attorney manipulation. A distinct set of proposed remedies would mitigate the affects of jury inadequacies, adversarial excess and mismatched attorney skills. These measures would empower juries when they are used, and substitute bench trials or ADR in other cases. Irrespective of attorney influence, the use of juries should be reevaluated in a variety of cases. Certainly when lay juries cannot comprehend the facts or law of complex cases, and jury empowerment measures are either not implemented or unavailing, logic and justice militate in favor of replacing juries with more capable decision makers.

Some cases should be removed not only from juries, but from litigation altogether. The American courtroom is badly overextended as a panacea for multifarious social, economic and political problems. Many disputes now brought to trial are clearly ill-suited to adversarial resolution. This chapter identifies those instances when the best trial reform is simply to refer the disposition of certain classes of conflicts from the jurisdiction of the courts to alternative fora.

Problems of trial justice do not end neatly within the parameters of the adversary system. We cannot look at the trial in a vacuum, blissfully ignorant of cognate problems which do not fit purely within a discussion of trial methodology. Issues peripheral to trial procedure can be weighty, and must be addressed in any larger scheme to overhaul the trial system. Therefore, remedies to such trial-related problems are offered as well.

FOREIGN MODELS

Selective importation from both the continental and English trial models can inure to our benefit. But first we must disabuse ourselves of antediluvian canards about the inquisitorial system. "Inquisitorial" refers to inquest. The inquisitorial system trial is regarded primarily as a search for truth rather than a dispute resolution. It does *not* refer to the barbaric practices of the thirteenth century Inquisition, involving judicially-imposed torture and presumption of guilt. Our aversion to the inquisitorial system arises from a failure to distinguish between its ancient and modern incarnations. After the French Revolution, France and other European countries abolished judicial torture and secret proceedings. Nevertheless, there still exists an erroneous impression by Americans (including some U.S. Supreme Court justices) that the inquisitorial system presumes guilt instead of innocence, provides criminal defendants no rights of silence or counsel, and establishes a standard of prosecutorial proof less rigorous than "beyond a reasonable doubt." Another misimpression is that the common citizen has no role in the inquisitorial trial. Although the all-lay jury is found only in Anglo-American courts, lay participation in inquisitorial trials continues with the mixed lay-professional bench.

Continental (inquisitorial) systems even provide criminal defendants protections absent in our system: absolute and full disclosure of the prosecutor's case; the opportunity to give uninterrupted narrative opening and closing statements; and written reasons explaining the factfinder's decision. Viewed collectively, the inquisitorial system arguably affords greater due process to the defendant.

If we must hew to an adversarial system, the English system is instructive. Despite the common (adversarial) label, there are significant differences. The English trial is adversarial, but not as excessively so; we are at the extreme end of the adversarial spectrum. Yet the English system is generally viewed as efficient and vigilant in safeguarding criminal defendant rights.

England gives its judges more power over the proceedings, while reigning in the role and thus the power of the barristers. (The barrister is the counterpart of our trial attorney.) After final arguments, English judges comment on and summarize the evidence for the jury. Solicitors (attorneys who do not try cases) investigate and prepare the case; barristers try it. The barrister's primary obligation is to the court, not the client. In England, it is assumed that the merits of the case, not forensic skills or tricks, determine outcome. There is far less identification with the client. Rules of ethics restrict the responsibilities of barristers. They are never alone with the client; solicitors do all the work preparatory to the trial.[4] No opportunity for witness-coaching arises because the barrister does not meet with the client before the trial. And since barristers cannot interview witnesses, they are not considered responsible for the performance of their witnesses, further reducing the pressure to win.

Prosecutors are under greater constraints to be administrators of justice rather than advocates. Defense barristers must accept referrals from the solicitor. All this contributes to a greater detachment of the barrister from the client, reduced commitment to victory at all costs, and far less adversarial excess. Additionally blunting excessive adversariness is the practice of allowing barristers to do both prosecution and defense work. Overall, the independence of the barristers, along with their ethical restrictions on interviewing witnesses, permits barristers to maintain a restrained but purer form of the art of advocacy without the pressure to win. England's barrister system demonstrates that a trial can be adversarial without that feature detracting from what should be its primary goals: trials and justice.[5]

In short, labels by which other systems are characterized are best avoided. Instead, we can *eclectically borrow* from other systems after due consideration of political and philosophical differences. Accordingly, foreign practices inspire and inform several of the reforms proposed herein.

Many of those now clamoring for tort reform in the United States point to systems of foreign countries as models for emulation.[*] But these would-be reformers have no interest in adoption of foreign trial procedures *per se*. Rather, they seek the benefits of certain rules prevalent in foreign courts regarding civil case damage awards and attorney fees. The identities of the reformers betray their interests: the defense bar, doctors, insurance carriers and large manufacturers who are often defendants in products liability suits. All seek measures which reduce potential liability or deter potential lawsuits. Thus they advocate adoption of the "loser pays" rule followed in almost all court systems outside of the United States, whereby the losing plaintiff pays the attorney's fees of the successful defendant. They similarly favor foreign rules which limit damage awards: no punitive damages; established limits on other damages, including pain and suffering; and mitigation of the award to the extent of plaintiff's insurance.

Contrast this with our tort system. Damage awards—especially those of juries—are generally unbridled. Awards are so much higher in the United States because the scope of recoverable damages is much larger. American plaintiffs can ask for punitive damages which far exceed compensatory damages (actual out-of-pocket and projected losses). Many juries oblige. For example, a jury recently added $101 million in punitive damages to $4 million in compensatory damages to the family of a driver killed when the side-mounted gas tank of his General Motors pickup truck exploded in a collision. Conversely, very few other countries recognize punitive damages; none to this size.

---

[*]   Most of these countries are in Europe, but they also include Japan, Canada, Australia and New Zealand. For brevity, I refer to them as the "model countries" or with the adjective "foreign."

Also contributing to the larger "damages pot" in the U.S. is the relative lack of government entitlements and other alternative sources to compensate the injured. Social security and other government benefit programs are far more extensive in Europe.[6] Universal health care, for example, leaves few with uncovered risks. Disabled workers receive replacement income higher than our workers compensation awards. And model country workers compensation systems cover risks typically not covered in the United States.[7] Hence there is far less pressure on their tort systems to compensate injured parties.

Our collateral benefits rule further induces lawsuits. Under this rule, plaintiffs do not have to reduce their compensable damages by insurance recoveries. This permits plaintiffs a double recovery. Other countries do not have the collateral benefits rule, reflecting public policy against undue enrichment.[8]

Foreign legal expenses are kept low by U.S. standards, mainly because damage awards are much smaller. Two factors contribute to the disparity. First, judges, not juries, make the awards. Unlike our juries, their judges must give written explanations of their findings of fact and law. Second, awards hew to written and unwritten guidelines set by statute, regulation or the judiciary, depending upon the country.[9] Consequently, foreign damage awards are more predictable as well.

Model country judges add a second constraint: They consider it their role to contain litigation costs. Thus they impose various procedural economies, such as limitations on witnesses and discovery to that strictly necessary. (Contrast the United States practice of "piling on.") An important additional curb on foreign legal costs is the widespread availability of cheap legal expense insurance.[10] Foreign regulations also circumscribe attorney fees. The contingent fee system for plaintiff's attorneys, so popular in the United States, does not apply. Defense attorneys bill by the service instead of the hour. Judges further limit attorney fees to "reasonable and necessary" amounts. This combination results in significantly lower legal costs. So when tort reformers call for adoption of the "loser pays" rule, we must appreciate that the attorney fees which the loser pays in the model countries are materially lower than in the United States, with a commensurately lower deterrent effect on prospective plaintiffs.

What this means is that the prize to shoot for is much larger in the U.S. tort suit. All of these factors combine to enhance the fecundity of U.S. tort litigation as a source of compensation: unpredictable juries with increasingly pro-plaintiff bents; larger and more frequent damage awards,[11] more uninsured and thus recoverable damages. As the pot grows bigger, more and better attorneys enter the field, along with their supporting corps of experts-for-hire. The result: Litigation rates and expenses climb.[12]

A final ingredient to this legal soup is the disparity of attitudes towards litigation among citizens of different countries. Comparative law expert Werner Pfennigstorf and University of Maryland Law School Dean Donald Gifford compared the tort liability systems of ten foreign industrialized countries with that of the United States. Their findings tell us much about our cultural preferences in resolving disputes.

> [I]n the countries surveyed here both claimants and defendants (or their insurers) are more reluctant to go to court than their counterparts in the U.S. and indeed regard litigation as an undesirable complication. In other countries, following disasters or other incidents affecting large numbers of persons, conscious efforts are made on all sides to bring about a speedy resolution through negotiation, often involving government. Settling all or nearly all claims without litigation is considered an achievement.[13]

To recap, lower damage awards, lower attorney fees and widespread, cheap legal insurance considerably moderate the effect of the loser pays rule in the model countries. Moreover, extensive government entitlements clearly moderate reliance on foreign tort systems to compensate injured parties. Given this "big picture" perspective, the call for tort reform takes on a decidedly different cast. Would business and other politically conservative interests at the core of the tort reform movement in the United States favor a similar expansion of government entitlements and government regulation of the attorney-client relationship? An alternative to tort litigation stemming from unsafe products, workplaces and professional services is stepped-up government regulation. Would the tort reform proponents alacritously pay the taxes to fund enhanced administrative regulation of business?

If the answer to both questions is "No," a reasonably safe assumption, then we must rethink the tort reform proposals. The question of whether adopting the foreign rules mentioned above would improve America's economic competitiveness, as proponents claim,[14] must be evaluated in light of the entire legal and regulatory mechanism for compensating the injured. The ultimate decision is more political than legal, more philosophic than economic. Prevalent notions of American justice ostensibly dictate that injured victims be compensated more through the victim's individual initiative (a lawsuit) than government programs, with awards usually determined by juries (instead of judges) unencumbered by any predetermined limits on damages. Until these values change—as they may—proposals for wholesale adoption of the model country liability rules must be viewed guardedly. Before acting, lawmakers should consider the tort reform proposals in the proper context. What the proponents fail to mention is substantial.

On the other hand, little such external, gestalt-type referencing need accompany selective adoption of foreign trial procedures. The changes discussed below either save money or have no economic impact. Because they are primarily procedural and not economic, they do not have the same societal resonance as the tort reform proposals. Yet they hold far greater promise for trial justice.

REFORM OBJECTIVES

If we want to cleave to some form of the adversary system so as to retain its perceived benefits while sanitizing its untoward aspects, we have two basic options. One is to change the *incentives* to attorneys. That is, trial attorneys would be compensated based on something other than conventional performance measures—primarily economic booty for the client in civil cases; conviction or acquittal in criminal cases. How to do this without radically restructuring legal practice and education escapes me. Further exhortations or ethics code prescriptions of greater courtroom civility and less adversarial zeal will continue to be nugatory, as will the occasional judicial sanction.

Rather, I advocate a second path: Reconfigure the allocation of procedural power in the lawsuit. The initial steps facilitate jury functioning by removing unnecessary hindrances and empowering jurors to perform their roles more effectively. If we are to continue using juries, we should do so intelligently. Accompanying the jury's responsibility should be the reasonable means to fulfill it.

The judge's role should also be expanded. She should be more than a passive referee. As nonpartisans, the judge and jurors are the logical participants in which to repose more power to seek trial justice. Conversely, attorney powers should be curtailed where they have the greatest potential for mischief. But unlike court remedies, this is not a zero-sum game. Every recommended empowerment of the judge or jury is not perforce at the expense of an equal loss of power by the attorneys. Most proposals follow more of a shared power model.

Other objectives are to authorize more creative and flexible court remedies and rationalize the current jurisdictional parameters of the trial. But no matter how much we tinker with an adversarial means of dispute resolution, it will remain unsuitable, even harmful, for numerous problems. Therefore, we should designate the courthouse as the central community resource for dispute resolution, complementing trial with a rich variety of ADR mechanisms.

To recap, the general objectives of the reforms proposed here are:

1. Facilitating the search for truth by empowering and improving juries.

2. Mitigating the consequences of adversarial excesses (e.g., delay and truth distortion) and mismatched attorneys.

3. Outlining solutions to other, trial-related problems while expanding the scope of courthouse justice.

Many of the reforms proposed below serve more than one objective. That which mitigates the consequences of adversarial excess and attorney mismatching (objective 2) also tends to facilitate jury factfinding (objective 1). Consider, for example, having the judge summarize and comment upon the evidence. This provides jurors a framework for their deliberations as it supplements the partisan adversarial presentations with a neutral, expert perspective of the relevant facts.

What is *not* proposed herein is as important as what is. One might expect a book advocating trial reform to urge: (a) changes in law school curricula—to inculcate prospective attorneys during the formative stages of their careers to the new gospel, and (b) a new government regulatory body, with members of unmistakable cachet drawn from multiple disciplines, to oversee the proposed reforms. I propose neither.

I seek changes in the way trials work, specifically in the disproportionate influence attorneys have on trial outcomes. But that will come about through profound systemic transformation, not by appealing to the law student's sense of fair play or rectitude. To be effective, the reforms proposed must be changes in the rules of the game, not merely changes in the attitudes of the players. Those most likely to be influenced by "high road" exhortations are least in need of moral or ethical suasion. Besides, what good would come of placing more emphasis on nonadversarial problem solving in law school when the legal world the new law school graduate enters remains an ethical miasma infested with hardball-playing sharks?

Establishing regulatory bodies to monitor implementation of far-reaching programs is a time-honored tradition. Often these bodies symbolize change more than effectuate it. Worse still are many of the "study commissions" offered as anodyne sops to mollify public constituencies demanding action. Any such body would be extraneous to the realization or oversight of the reforms proposed here. The best check on adversarial excess and injustice is a revitalized, fortified judge and jury. They are closer to the action and can provide immediate melioration specific to the case being heard. Most importantly, they can best counteract attorneys' power to distort and undermine trial justice.

REFORMS

Jury Empowerment and Improvement

Jury competence can be improved in two basic ways: (1) help the jurors, and (2) use better jurors. Regardless of the sophistication level of the particular juror, jury functions—factfinding, deliberation, understanding and application of the law—can be facilitated by various cognitive aids and changes in procedure. A discrete but compatible path to enhanced jury competence is to upgrade the quality of the jury's composition. Illustrations of both categories follow.

Juror Orientation

Better juror orientation could enhance jury competence. Current programs—which are now haphazard, varying from state to state, county to county and court to court—could be enlarged to more substantive training sessions. Courts may choose from a wide range of training and education programs to elevate juror sophistication.

Orientation programs can introduce and educate prospective jurors to basic legal concepts and trial procedures. Handbooks, lectures and audio-visual presentations ordinarily provide some of this information. Handbooks are available to jurors on their first day of service in most courts, but vary markedly in size, coverage and content.[15] Typical topics are jury selection, the functions of the attorneys, judge and jury, trial procedure, jury deliberations and desired conduct of jurors. Covered trial procedures may include: the difference between criminal and civil cases, challenges for cause and peremptory challenges during jury selection, what is evidence, what is meant by an inference and when jury sequestration is necessary. Discussion of jury deliberations may address the deliberation procedure, limitations on discussing the case, the meaning of the rule that the case must be decided on the evidence only, and the role of the foreperson.

Orientation lectures vary as much as the handbooks. Lectures may be given by a judge or a jury clerk. Whether the lecture will be lengthy or brief, comprehensive or sketchy, administratively or legally oriented, detailed or abstract depends on the identity of the lecturer and the time available.[16] The most effective lectures are those given by judges, and emphasize the importance of jury duty, explain the basic nature of the trial (while avoiding sophisticated concepts), indicate the inherent uncertainties of the trial process and do not reiterate information given in the handbook or audio-visual presentation.

The handbook and audio-visual presentation have certain advantages over the in-person lecture. They provide uniform information to all prospective jurors. They also usually speak to the most frequently-asked questions, and they do not take the time of court personnel. Overall, well-executed orientations can convey essential information to prospective jurors while mitigating any apprehensions they may have about jury service. This translates to better prepared jurors who perform their duties more effectively, often to the satisfaction of the jurors themselves.

Juror Aids

Judges can enhance jury competence by eliminating all unnecessary restrictions on jury factfinding and decision making. Permitting certain cognitive aids could improve both functions. Subject to judicial supervision, jurors can expressly be empowered to do the following:

a. take notes.

b. ask questions.

c. obtain a daily transcript or videotape of the testimony, and copies of all other evidence.

d. obtain a written copy or audiotape of understandable instructions once in deliberation.

e. hear the judge's instructions before (as well as after) the evidence is presented.

Studies assessed the effects of juror note-taking[17] and question-asking [18] on actual[19] and mock[20] juries. The bases for opponents' concerns failed to materialize. Moreover, jurors reported increased satisfaction from both privileges.[21]

As noted in Chapter 4, every argument against juror note-taking is either refutable or addresses a potential drawback which can easily be rectified. By the same token, courts which continue to deny this aid to jurors or, what is tantamount, fail to advise jurors of a note-taking privilege confound the opportunity for improved jury performance. At the least, the empirically-proven satisfaction jurors experience from note-taking merits adoption. As long as jurors cannot avail themselves of transcripts of the testimony, every juror should be allowed to take notes and should explicitly be informed of the privilege. A connatural aid is to provide jurors with a *notebook of all exhibits*. When witnesses are being examined as to documents, the jurors frequently have no idea of the nature of the document or its contents. Providing exhibit notebooks allows jurors both to better follow the related testimony and to have a copy of the exhibit during deliberations.[22] Further assistance should be supplied in complex cases. Providing jurors with *decision trees or algorithms* in such cases might immeasurably facilitate their deliberations.[23]

Another constraint which, on balance, is insupportable is the prohibition of juror questions. Juror questioning is rarely permitted. The opposition to juror questions was discussed in Chapter 4 and found wanting in light of the incalculable benefits foregone. Questioning allows jurors to clarify confusing evidence and fill in gaps in the evidence. Further, the active participation of the jurors should improve their overall performance. This process can also help the attorneys. Questions reveal areas of juror confusion or ignorance which the attorneys may want to remedy.

The issue is not whether jurors should be allowed to ask questions. They should. Rather, the issue is how best to implement this factfinding tool with the proper precautions. At the outset of the trial, jurors should be advised of their right to ask questions. If at the end of a witness' testimony a juror has a question, the juror can submit to the judge a note containing the question. This avoids the problem of an improper question reaching the ears of the other jurors. If neither counsel nor judge object to the question, it can be put to the witness. If an objection is registered, the judge may revise or reject the question. In some instances, the judge may forestall the question if it is likely to be answered by subsequent evidence; if not, the juror may reiterate the question later. Judges should also moderate the juror disappointment and potential prejudice which may result from a rejected question by explaining why certain questions cannot be voiced.[24] In sum, the absence of insurmountable objections and the lost opportunity for improved jury factfinding compel adoption of what should be an intuitively obvious practice. Furthermore, this was the reform most desired by the jurors in the Los Angeles survey.

Testimony in lengthy trials can easily exceed the ineluctable limits of human recall. This is particularly evident in some of the civil megatrials. For example, the paperwork at the pretrial stage of *In re U.S. Financial Securities Litigation*[25] reached 150,000 pages in depositions and over five million documents, roughly equal to the height of a three story building. Access to a transcript or videotape of the testimony plus copies of all other evidence of record would permit jurors to review the evidence without relying on human memory, which is notoriously fallible and varies from juror to juror.[26]

Barring use of videotaped testimony denies two possible benefits: It precludes potentially significant enhancement of jury factfinding, and it eliminates the opportunity to substantially foreshorten the trial. Videotapes could complement or replace transcripts by allowing jurors to also review witness behavior and other nonverbal evidence. Besides being more realistic, videotape is infinitely more interesting for jurors than dry transcripts.

Videotaping also allows a prerecorded trial. Ohio judge James McCrystal, who presided over the first prerecorded videotaped trial, and James Young, Director of the Ohio Legal Center Institute, identified twenty-one additional advantages to this use of videotape. Those that specifically facilitate jury functioning are as follows:

- the trial flows without interruptions from objections, bench conferences, delays for witnesses, counsel's pauses, client conferences and chamber retreats;
- maximum utilization of juror time is achieved;
- the time required for a given trial is shortened considerably;
- the trial can be scheduled, with certainty, for a specific day;
- there is no need to recess for the preparation of instructions;
- testimony on location is facilitated;
- elimination of live trial impediments give the jury a comprehensive related view of the entirety of the case;
- extrajudicial judge influence through reactions to witnesses and comments to counsel is reduced;

- the court need no longer resort to the fiction that a juror can disregard what he has heard in accordance with the judge's instructions.[27]

Another benefit of the prerecorded trial is that it would restrict attorney tactics such as asking questions or posing objections known to be doubtful but intended for effect.[28] Note, however, that the major virtue of videotaping is increased trial efficiency. Indeed, enumerating the advantages of videotaping illuminates how ponderously slow the present jury trial is. In short, resistance to using videotape technology prolongs trial delay and impedes more effective and efficient jury performance.

Chapter 4 explained the pressing need to aid jury understanding of the judge's instructions on the law. Although research indicates distinct advantages to providing jurors with written copies of the instructions,[29] many judges resist. Their reasons include more work, resulting delay, and apprehensions that blind or illiterate jurors will be put at a disadvantage. All of these concerns are either groundless or easily remedied.[30] Moreover, surveys indicate that attorneys[31] and jurors[32] overwhelmingly favor juror access to a written copy of the instructions during deliberations.

Another difficulty many jurors have with the judge's instructions is the time of their receipt—after all the evidence is heard. This problem can be rectified by giving the jurors a preliminary version of the instructions before (in addition to after) the evidence is heard. Judge William Schwarzer, Director of the Federal Judicial Center, calls these instructions "the logical corollaries to the lawyers' opening statements."[33] Studies consistently show that preinstructing jurors with a preliminary charge before hearing the evidence would greatly facilitate various aspects of jury performance, such as integration of law and facts.[34]

Research also indicates that the vast majority of jurors cannot suspend their decision until the end of the trial.[35] Hence a concern was that preinstruction would further predispose the jurors to prejudge. But a recent study found to the contrary: Preinstructed jurors were more likely to *defer* judgment.[36]

The best way to accomplish preinstruction without prejudice to either party is by requiring attorneys to submit proposed instructions to the court at the outset of the trial. So informed, the judge can apprise the jury of the basic uncontested legal doctrines involved. Despite the favorable empirical findings of behavioral science, courts have yet to adopt this sensible reform.

As if the delayed receipt of instructions and their lack of written form were insufficiently problematic, juries commonly have considerable difficulty understanding the *language* of the instructions. They can be highly jargonistic and complex.[37] Yet all the received wisdom of the ages contained in the law is fruitless without jury comprehension of the judge's instructions. Curiously, those same jurors who, in the words of a judge, have been "treated like children while the testimony is going on [are] then . . . doused with a kettleful of law, during the charge, that would make a third year law student blanch."[38] The history of this unfortunate state of affairs was noted earlier: Seeking to avoid the many appellate reversals ordered due to faulty instructions, trial judges opted for a misguided nostrum. Almost universally, they adopted time-tested, reversal-proof, standardized *pattern instructions*. But these are often so devoid of clarity and simplicity as to defy comprehensibility.[39] Appellate courts exacerbate the problem by failing to provide trial courts with simple, nontechnical instructions which will withstand scrutiny. Clearly, the prospect of a non-clarifying appellate reversal deters trial judge temerity in seeking to improve instructions. An intolerable situation thus persists.

Unfortunately, those in the position to rectify this problem prefer instead to immerse themselves in fine tuning the subtle niceties and arcana of the instructions. Left unresolved is an unpleasant reality: The appallingly low level of jury comprehension of instructions dictates their wholesale revision. After extensive investigation, a team of University of Michigan jury researchers found that actual jurors understood *fewer than half* of the jury instructions they receive at trial. They concluded:

> Jury instructions are constantly being rewritten to reflect more precisely the nuances of the law, but legal policymakers and courts rarely concern themselves with jurors' comprehension of the law. Unless some attention is paid to the jurors' *use* of the instructions they are given, the never-ending, intensive solicitude for the wording of the law is pedantry in fantasyland: The law as spoken by the judge is of the utmost consequence; the law as understood by the jurors, moments later, is not a matter of concern. Either this implies the assumption that jurors do understand what the judge says, or it implies that judicial instructions are magical incantations, in which the perfect utterance is not a means to understanding but an end in itself.[40]

(As a university professor, I understand the appeal of this self-delusion by the courts. In the classroom it is infinitely more satisfying to dwell solely in the intellectual stratosphere of your subject—presuming near-perfect understanding by the students of the banal but necessary fundamentals—than to contemplate the grim likelihood that half of your audience is not sure it is in the right classroom and the other half is sure but has not yet bought the textbook.)

Research shows that significant improvement in juror comprehension can be obtained by *rewriting the instructions in simpler language*.[41] In a welcome heterodoxy, a recent California Supreme Court decision offers hope. Rejecting as too confusing the state's pattern instruction on proximate cause, the court banned further use of the instruction in favor of clearer ones.[42]

Importantly, some of the law's resistance to reform here may be politically based. That is, instructions may be obfuscatory by design. For example, studies indicate that improved clarity reduces conviction rates.[43] The interests served by clearer instructions are those of criminal defendants, not law enforcement.

Assuming that the clarity can be calibrated, the degree of comprehensibility of drafted instructions becomes an issue of policy rather than science. If clarity were the preeminent value, judges (or court law clerks) could give jurors comprehensive lectures on the instructions before and after evidence, together with the opportunity to ask questions.

More Evidence to the Factfinder

A great deal of relevant evidence is hidden from juries.[44] Our exclusionary rules impair factfinding accuracy, particularly in criminal cases. With no detectable uniformity in case-by-case application nor objective guidelines for future applications, otherwise probative evidence can be excluded by judges if they feel its admission would prejudice, confuse or mislead the jury.[45] Evincing distrust of jury competence, judges now occasionally use this power to exclude expert testimony in technical and complex cases. Exclusionary rules flagrantly contradict the fundamental belief that lay jurors are competent to hear and decide upon *all* evidence.

"Blindfolding" is another questionable American evidentiary practice. Fearing wrongful inferences, our courts intentionally deny jurors access to certain evidence. The existence of a defendant's insurance coverage, which party pays attorney fees, the taxability of damage awards, the treble damages feature in antitrust cases, settlement offers and settlements of the other parties are all excludable from the jury's purview. The problem is that jurors go ahead and make their own assumptions anyway, often erroneously, thereby exaggerating the problem.

Judges can and should allow more information to reach the jury. Exclusionary rules should be reevaluated to ascertain whether their premises remain cogent. Judges could be more flexible in allowing admission—or judicial instructions—of social science findings relevant to the evidence. Legal or court rules denying jurors access to such information are often based on untested assumptions about the jury's true cognitive abilities and decision making processes.[46] Given the value our society places on scientific information, the law's obduracy in this regard is anomalous. The blindfolding rule should also be reevaluated. It too is based on untested assumptions about how jurors make decisions.[47]

Preferable is the inquisitorial system method of "free proof." Under it, the court must admit virtually all relevant information until satisfied of the truth or falsity of a propounded position. When evidence is questionable or potentially prejudicial, the court accords it a commensurately low weight rather than excluding it.[48] Continental courts, therefore, do not exclude hearsay—the kind of information individuals, businesses and governments use daily to make decisions.

The arguments for severely limiting the hearsay exclusion were discussed in Chapter 5. We should adopt Bentham's proposed liberalization of the rule: Hearsay should be excluded only when more direct proof is available.[49] Bentham's proposal was actually incorporated into the Model Code of Evidence,[50] and has empirical[51] and scholarly support. One such scholar, University of Chicago law professor Albert Alschuler, decries our retention of the hearsay rule: "The common law's system of proof remains essentially intact—a circumstance that may reflect the self-interest of lawyers and their deep attachment to the familiar, for rules of evidence make only a little more sense today than they did in 1800."[52]

Unlike American courts, continental courts make no automatic exclusion of the fruits of an illegal search. This exclusionary rule is one of many in the United States intended as a police control mechanism, not a bar of unreliable evidence. In implementing it, our system does not weigh the loss of probative evidence against the extent of official lawlessness. Continental courts choose a more moderate path by weighing the seriousness of the offense against the strength of the police's suspicion. Our courts could easily adopt a form of this practice by providing jurors with *cautionary instructions* on the appropriate weight to be given each item of evidence.

An area with potential for increased evidence to the factfinder is the pretrial statements and trial testimony of criminal defendants. Our rules discourage the defendant's statements, thereby precluding evidence from the most important witness. The continental and English practices supply two desirable alternatives to our rules. After a Miranda-type warning, the continental criminal defendant's refusal to speak is made known to the court (contrary to U.S. practice). In accord with the privilege against self-incrimination, the court cannot draw an inference of guilt from the defendant's silence.[53] English procedure induces the defendant's testimony by providing that it will usually *not* open the defendant's testimony to impeachment by evidence of prior convictions. In the search for truth, it is usually better to hear defendants' testimonies than their prior convictions, especially given the historic difficulty jurors have in applying the apposite evidentiary rule: Consider prior convictions only as to the defendant's credibility, not his or her culpability for the crime charged.

Ironically, measures to alleviate swollen court calendars may strongly dilute the impact of the exclusionary evidence rules. The trend toward nontrial dispute resolution means more disputes will be resolved in fora where the strict rules of evidence do not obtain. In all of these fora, factfinding is more informal than in trial, and not encumbered by the exclusionary evidence restrictions applicable in court. The new emphasis on nontrial factfinding suffuses the Civil Justice Reform Act.

Sequential (Issue-Separated) Litigation

An inquisitorial system procedure with great potential for simplifying American jury factfinding is greater use of the noncontinuous, issue-separated trial. In an issue-separated trial, the court focuses initially on the issue(s) most likely to be dispositive. The litigation of other issues may be obviated. For instance, in a toxic product liability suit, the court could begin by considering only evidence on causation (e.g., whether defendant's product caused plaintiff's injury). If issue-separation is combined with special verdict use (discussed below), a finding of no causation would end the suit. Issues of liability and damages need never be litigated.[54] When used in the United States, issue-separated trials are typically bifurcated into liability first; then, if necessary, damages. Issue-separated trials offer these potential benefits:

1. Great economies of time and expense are made possible. In the Harris survey, the judges overwhelmingly supported the principle and practice of bifurcation. Judges who used it reported expedited settlements and trial process, reduced transaction costs and improved fairness of outcome.[55]

2. Limiting issues could also limit discovery abuse. If judges limited discovery to the specific issues being tried at the time, all obviated issues would have no discovery counterpart.[56] The less discovery, the less opportunity for discovery abuse.

3. Separation of issues could greatly facilitate juror comprehension, recall and decision making.[57]

4. Separation of issues reduces juror tendency to apply evidence on emotional issues such as damages to less emotional issues such as causation or liability.[58]

5. When opposing experts testify on specific issues, the bases for their differences can be crystallized for the benefit of the jurors. After their testimonies, the experts would respond to questions from the judge, attorneys or jurors. This back and forth questioning would create in essence a confrontation of experts with expectable salutary effects on juror comprehension.[59]

Although American judges have the power to order issue-separated trials,[60] they rarely exercise it.[61] However, a distinct trend in judicial administration is toward more pretrial managerial judging,[62] which includes eliminating and narrowing the scope of issues and corresponding discovery. Use of issue-separated trials to limit discovery is a logical extension of this trend.

Juror Discussions During Trial

Traditional trial procedure forbids jurors from engaging in discussions about the trial before final deliberations, no matter how lengthy or difficult the evidence. Two concerns underlie this restriction. One is premature formation of juror positions. The other is giving early testimony disproportionate attention or credibility.

But two arguably stronger reasons militate against the restriction on preliminary juror discussions. First, during lengthy or complex trials, discussions allow jurors to correct misconceptions and handle information in a far more normal process. Second, discussions alleviate juror stress. Psychiatrists conducting post-verdict sessions in cases involving difficult decisions and/or heinous testimony (primarily in criminal cases) say prohibiting discussion of this evidence greatly contributes to stress and post-verdict trauma.[63]

We simply do not know whether or not, on balance, midtrial deliberations facilitate and/or enhance jury performance. They may, as feared by some, unacceptably prejudice the final deliberations. The proscription against midtrial deliberations, as with most other rules of trial procedure, implements untested assumptions about human behavior.

This is an area ripe for experimentation by behavioralists. If the concerns underlying the rule are empirically validated, the restriction should be retained, or the judge could allow some preliminary deliberations after admonishing jurors to withhold judgment until all the evidence was heard. Conversely, if the presumption is wrong, jurors, litigants, and the justice system all stand to gain.

Special Juries

A distinct but compatible approach to enhancing jury competence is to improve the quality of jurors. Two means are available. One would eliminate the many hardship exemptions from jury duty routinely afforded professionals and other well-educated individuals in half the states. Fewer professional exemptions would fortify and diversify juries. States can do much to soften the economic hardship of jury service upon which the exemptions are based. They could limit the term of service, pay more and/or require employers to pay employees the first few days on jury duty.[64] Greater use of the issue-separated trial and videotaped testimony could also decrease jury service time, and with it, the basis for the hardship exemption.

Jury performance can also be improved where most needed by using specially qualified jurors. In complex litigation, for example, the jury could be limited to individuals with superior potential for comprehending the evidence and instructions, such as college graduates. Specifically, every juror in particularly complex cases could be required to hold a bachelor's degree from an accredited school.

Let us evaluate the major premise of the educated juror proposal: The discipline and experience gained from college education should render one better equipped to execute the juror's factfinding and application-of-law tasks in complex cases. Responses from the Los Angeles survey suggest support for the hypothesized advantages of college-educated juries.[65] Take, for example, the capacity to understand judicial instructions. College-educated jurors apparently had far greater comprehension. Perceived comprehension of the judge's instructions was tested by two questions, one specific and one general. The specific inquiry—the number of words, terms and concepts the juror found difficult to understand—elicited especially pronounced differences favoring the college-educated. The general question asked whether the instructions were sufficiently comprehensible to apply to the evidence. Here too the survey found a clear correspondence between education and the utility of the instructions. The results confirm a study suggesting that higher levels of education result in superior understanding and application of jury instructions.[66]

Several writers suggest that inclusion of more educated jurors would enhance the jury's capacity to deal with different issues.[67] Regarding evidence comprehension, college graduates have usually taken courses in math, economics and (physical and natural) science—the very subjects which frequently give jurors difficulty in complex cases. Not to be overlooked, however, is the discipline gained by learning from college lectures and class discussions which finds application as a juror. Students can rarely devote full attention for an entire class; they must learn to selectively focus their attention when critical material is being discussed, and then relax their concentration somewhat during teacher digressions. Similarly, during evidence presentation—when juror lapses of attention are notoriously commonplace—college graduates' conditioning should better prepare them to pay most attention to critical testimony, rather than to oratorical flourish and attorney diversions. The college experience, at least in part, makes students more educable as well.[68] They must assume responsibility for learning and applying new and sometimes sophisticated concepts introduced, in large measure, by verbal presentation with occasional visual support. Again, the parallels to the juror's courtroom experience are clear.

At least one study indicates that college-educated jurors have greater and more accurate retention of detail.[69] It is not surprising then that when jurors in the Los Angeles survey were asked to respond to suggestions for making the evidence clearer and more judicable, only the noncollege-educated showed a marked preference for reordering the proceedings so that all of the evidence on the same subject was presented at the same time, that is, issue-separation.[70] Processing fragmented information is a skill one ordinarily must bring to or acquire in college in order to succeed. In elementary and high school pedagogy, information is fed the students in neatly packaged bundles; a perceptible thread typically runs through the material given the students. Conversely, college instruction often presents information desultorily, so that the instructor can ask the students to find the common thread as a heuristic exercise. In similar fashion, trial attorneys are free to present evidence in any order, however scattered, which most effectively redounds to their benefit. College-educated jurors may have less need than their lesser educated counterparts to simplify this presentation process. Their college education probably stimulated and honed the very skills employed in synthesizing diffuse evidentiary information. By the same token, the less educated juror may be overwhelmed by the task.

In addition to their reactions to the attorneys and judges, the Los Angeles survey sought the jurors' reactions to their own performance. Specifically, did they think their decision making process, as a jury, was in any way faulty or improper?[71] The college-educated expressed more confidence in the soundness and propriety of their jury's decision making process. Inasmuch as juror orientation is the same for all jurors, disparity of formal education may bear upon the perception of proper jury decision making. One mock jury study found that more educated jurors tended to participate more actively during jury deliberation; they also gave more attention to procedural matters than did the lesser educated.[72] Intellectual and emotional investment in an activity can certainly imbue the participant with a sense of its rectitude. If the college-educated jurors in the Los Angeles survey in fact played more active roles in jury deliberation, it is easy to see how they would have had a higher regard for the validity of their decision making process.

The jury's role is central to our justice delivery system. Why entrust it to people who may have never performed any similar task?[73] Mandating a college education for jurors in the increasing number of complex cases could effect a signal improvement of the jury system. While avoiding the time and expense of individual testing, we could obtain better qualified laypersons more familiar with the type of cognitive exercises required of all jurors. A college-educated jury, having the potential for better understanding and ordering of the relevant facts and law, should typically render better informed and thus more just verdicts. This is not elitism; it is merely functionalism.

A minimum education rule would admittedly invite court challenge involving federal and state jury selection statutes. The Federal Jury Selection Act (the model for most states) requires that the procedures used to create the jury pool be designed to obtain a "fair cross section of the community," that is, be representative of the population.[74] In a *Virginal Law Review* article, professors William Luneberg and Mark Nordenberg cogently argue that a bachelor's degree requirement for the jury in complex civil cases would not violate that injunction.[75] The proposal here endorses that argument and extends it to complex criminal cases.[76]

Along the same lines, greater use could be made of court-appointed special masters for factfinding in complex civil cases. Some have even suggested establishment of a "science court."[77] Actually a board of scientists, the science court would be used for certain kinds of scientific factfinding. Expert case managers from each side of a controversy would argue their positions before a three-member board.[78] But is this expertise necessary in complex cases? A majority of judges in the Harris survey thought so. They reached these agreements regarding complex civil cases:

- A serious study should be made of alternatives to jury trial.

- Jurors need more guidance than they usually get.

- It is difficult for jurors with different educational levels to be effective.

- *Trial before a panel of experts would be preferable to jury trial.*[79]

Using specially qualified juries or factfinding bodies will undoubtedly strike some as tantamount to defiling a sacrosanct icon. But a great deal of distrust of the jury coexists with its veneration. This is an explainable paradox. Recall that the jury's popularity rose dramatically under King Henry II, who used it as a political tool against the competing baronial and ecclesiastical courts. Jury popularity later surged in the American colonies, where the jury was regarded as a check on the authority of royal judges.[80] The notion of the jury as a redoubt against an arbitrary and overreaching government persists, despite the advent of representative government and all the other protections we enjoy under the Constitution. Contrast this wellspring of public good will for the jury in the U.S. with the harsh judgments of other countries. As an enduring institution in both criminal and civil cases, the all-lay jury has failed in every country except the United States. Even so, we shore up its presumed shortcomings with numerous "fixes": excluding relevant evidence it cannot be trusted to accurately process; immunizing it from any obligation to account for its decisions or rationale. Indeed, if juries were required to explain their decisions, they would quickly lose their legitimacy and support. Judge Learned Hand mused that we "trust [jurors] as reverently as we do, and still surround them with restrictions which, if they have no rational validity whatever, depend upon our distrust."[81]

Juries may still work well in simple tort, contract and criminal cases, although their notorious receptivity to emotional appeal and other attorney stratagems render every jury case undivinable. Unpredictability, however, is the lesser of its problems. In complex modern cases, juries are demonstrably ill-equipped. Antitrust, high-technology patent, securities, products liability, environmental and medical malpractice litigation are but a sampling of areas where it is increasingly clear that the apotheosized lay jury is a malfunctioning anachronism.[82]

Mixed Juries

The problems of the jury are many. But its underlying premise, lay participation in the administration of trial justice, need not be abandoned. A number of inquisitorial system countries employ a variant of the jury called a mixed court. On it, lay and professional judges sit together as a single panel in cases of serious crimes and certain civil disputes.

The mixed court holds many potential benefits for use in the United States. One is speedier trials. Inquisitorial trials are considerably shorter than their adversarial counterparts.[83] The reason is clear. Jury selection in the United States usually takes more time than do entire trials elsewhere in the world.[84] If we adopted the mixed court, time consuming jury selection would be unnecessary—at least for the professional component of the court. Also obviated would be elaborate jury instructions and other evidentiary procedures designed to address the inexperience of an all-lay jury.

Use of the mixed jury expands the scope of admissible evidence. The presence of professional judges eliminates the need for exclusionary evidence rules such as hearsay. During deliberations, the professional judges can advise the lay judges against consideration of extra-legal factors, such as attorney opinions, and focus instead on relevant matters.

Mixed courts also issue written, reasoned opinions explaining their findings of fact and law. This requirement is absent under our general verdict. If written statements of findings were adopted by American courts, two consequences would follow. First, it would expose court judgments to deeper-reaching appellate review.[85] A second consequence is more controversial. It would virtually eliminate jury nullification of the law.

Those opposing an American experiment with the mixed court may fear that professional judges will dominate their lay counterparts. Experience has not validated this concern. The authors of an extensive study of the German mixed court in criminal cases concluded that lay judges "exercise independent judgment...and do serve a societal purpose comparable to that of American juries—namely, injecting the values, experiences, and judgments of the lay community into the adjudication process."[86]

Not the least of its virtues is that the mixed court comes closer to serving many of our justice system policies than does the vast majority of our case dispositions. For example, mixed court lay judges fully participate in criminal sentencing, which, except for capital cases, is relatively rare in common law countries, and of course totally absent in the many cases plea-bargained or tried without a jury. Because it is assumed that professional judges will caution their lay counterparts against wrongful inferences and other misuses of evidence, far less relevant evidence is excluded. Courts would enjoy a corollary saving of time typically spent in adversarial trials arguing about exclusions. Despite all our time-consuming safeguards against jury error (during jury selection, judicial

admonitions in trial, complex instructions), stories are legion of egregious and
grave jury mistakes. In a Washington, D.C., case, for example, three-fourths
of the jury intended to acquit the defendant based on his claim of self-defense.
They nevertheless convicted him for manslaughter. Both the trial and appellate
courts refused to set aside the verdict.[87] In 1977, a former president of the
ABA suggested experimenting with the continental mixed court.[88] The time
may be ripe to take up the cudgel for this reform.

Suggesting a Deliberations Model

One suggestion which could easily be imparted (during orientation or during
the judge's instructions) is the ideal method of deliberations. Contemplate the
situation jurors confront when they first begin jury deliberations. Twelve people
who have never met before the trial are sequestered in a room. Most have no
comparable experience at group decision making. Nevertheless, they must
collectively decide on matters often complex and weighty, including life or
death. For this task, possibly the most consequential of their lives, they find
absolutely no guidance from the vast majority of courts.

Yet there is clearly an optimal model for jury deliberations, that is, one that
conduces the type of deliberations the legal ideal favors. Jury researcher Reid
Hastie found that jurors tend to adopt either of two distinct deliberation
structuring models or styles. One is "evidence-driven," the other "verdict-
driven."[89] Hastie found that evidence-driven juries begin their deliberations
with general discussions about the case. They tend to engage each other
cooperatively and open-mindedly about accepting new points of view regarding
the evidence. The process is more inquisitorial in appearance. Balloting
functions mainly to confirm agreements already reached informally.

In stark contrast, the verdict-driven jury begins with an open ballot. This
profoundly affects the dynamics of deliberation. Having taken a position, jurors
become more close-minded and militant in their arguments. Battle lines are
drawn and the deliberations become distinctly adversarial. Jurors act like
advocates instead of impartial factfinders, referring only to the evidence that
supports their verdict. Evidence analysis and deliberation time shrink decidedly.
There is less discussion of the applicable law.[90] In addition to rigidifying
positions, early ballots tend to deter jurors with nonassertive personalities from
contributing.[91]

Thus adversariness is suboptimal for jury deliberations as well as dispute
resolution. Indeed, the weakness of adversarial, verdict-driven deliberations is
a metaphor for the deficiencies of the adversary system. Some courts recognize
this and have placards in their jury rooms advising the panel to discuss the
evidence before voting.[92] But this is a rare exception to the customary hands-
off approach on deliberations. Ever fearful of being viewed as interfering with
the jury, judges remain silent. Given the virtues of the evidence-driven model,

this should change. The justice system would not fall from a mere *suggestion* to the jurors that they defer their initial vote until they have had the opportunity to discuss the issues without commitment to a position.

Guidance on Damages Awards

Unpredictable jury damages awards have become a *bete noire* of civil litigation and a putative cause of lost American competitiveness in the international market. Various responsive proposals address the problem. A commonly one is placing a cap on award amounts, particularly punitive damages. Another is removing the determination of damage awards from juries after they find liability. A minority of the Harris judges, albeit a substantial one (46 percent of the federal and 39 percent of the state), agreed with this suggestion in some or all civil cases.[93] Far more popular was the suggestion that judges provide guidelines to the juries about the amount of damages to be awarded. Large majorities supported this proposal in some or all civil cases.[94]

The guidelines proposal should be adopted. It behooves the judiciary to provide juries with some paradigm for damages calculations. The present practice of simply advising jurors to arrive at a figure which will make the plaintiff "whole" will not do. It leads to wildly inconsistent awards which, in turn, encourage parties not to settle. Damage awards today are more a function of the identity and financial condition of the parties than of the actual damages sustained. To those who condone or even applaud this state of affairs, it should be pointed out that the favorite targets of juries—insurance companies and governments—pass on much of the resulting expenses to policyholders and taxpayers. Anyone who pays premiums or taxes bears the additional burden. Consequently, this kind of justice causes the many to pay for the windfalls of the few—a reverse utilitarian solution.

The more moderate approach, judicial guidelines, is better. Jury damage award decisions could greatly be facilitated with more relevant information to guide the jurors. For example, the jury should be allowed to know what the last offers of the parties were during pretrial negotiations. The alternative is to perpetuate their ignorance.

Judicial guidelines would also minimize the frequent appellate court retrenchments of jury awards. This absurd dance of "excessive" jury awards, followed by appellate modifications is largely unnecessary and a waste of valuable court time. After a finding of liability, giving the jury the appropriate range for the damages award will save a lot of time and legal fees. When past appellate reviews of similar cases indicate that the final (post-appeal) award will fall within a certain range, obfuscating that datum only serves to line the pockets of litigation attorneys. A recent case illustrates the problem. A Los Angeles jury tacked a cool $25 million punitive damage award onto compensatory damages of $100,000—a multiplier of 250—against an insurance company it found to have defrauded a policyholder.[95] Experience suggests the insurance company will succeed in getting an appellate court to reverse most of the punitive damages. In the meantime, awards like this reinforce the popular image of a civil case tried before a jury as a wholly unpredictable crapshoot. The consequences: higher insurance premiums, fewer settlements, more court congestion.

Guidelines are simple to implement. The jury's findings enable the court to classify the injury according to an established damages schedule. Within each such classification, the jury would retain some discretion as to the award. One of the reasons litigation costs so much less in continental European countries is their use of such schedules for both damage awards and attorney fees.[96]

Damages schedules have other benefits. Limiting—not eliminating—the jury's discretion would result in similar treatment for similar cases. Outcomes would be more predictable. On these values, there should be harmony.

Special Verdict Forms

A direct way for judges to control jury incompetence—particularly in complex cases, where it is most likely—is to make more use of special verdict forms: the special verdict or the general verdict plus interrogatories.[97] Both would reveal some obvious errors in jury factfinding and deliberation, and avoid other mistakes. Using the special verdict, the judge asks the jury to make specific findings of fact to which the judge applies the law in rendering a verdict. This has clear advantages. By allowing the judge to monitor the jury, its inconsistent findings and consideration of irrelevant factors become conspicuous. It is therefore more scientific than the commonly used general verdict, and would lead to fewer appellate reversals. It also saves time. Judges are relieved of delivering lengthy and complex instructions on legal doctrine. Similarly obviated is the need for the jury to ponder the meaning and application of legal jargon and concepts. Instead, the jury confines itself to that for which it is better suited: factual issues.

We can reasonably expect the jury to perform creditably if we limit it to such jobs as determining whether the plaintiff purchased the defendant's product and used it as specified. It is an entirely different prospect if we add to that task a crash course on products liability law—complete with nuances and jargon—and then application of that law to the facts as found. The more legally complicated the case, the more improbable become instant juror mastery and application of the law.

In a recent survey of 160 actual trials in thirty-three states, the use of the special verdict was found consistently beneficial. When special verdict forms were used, the jurors reported feeling more informed, better satisfied and more confident that their verdict reflected a proper understanding of the judge's instructions. Furthermore, the jurors found the special verdict most helpful in dealing with large quantities of information.[98]

One caveat qualifies the potential benefits of the special verdict. It denies the jury its traditional power to ignore the law in the interest of justice: jury nullification.[99] The debate over whether to allow jury nullification rages unabated.[100] Courts should recognize that jury nullification is a howling anomaly in the law. It begets inconsistent results in like cases, improbable in an institution where consistency is a touchstone for justice. For example, *stare decisis*, the policy that courts will apply the same legal precedent to similar cases, is one of the polestars of adjudication. Continued allowance of the inherently random and unstructured incidence of jury nullification wreaks havoc with this principle. To resolve the inconsistency of nullification, courts should either *inform* juries of their power to ignore the law under conditions which the court describes, or expressly advise the jurors that any intentional deviation from the judge's instructions defeats the intent of the law and is therefore a breach of their obligation. A third alternative is to condition nullification on a written explanation by the jury of the rationale for its use in the particular case. This accountability requirement would convey the gravity and caution which should attend nullification, while keeping the power intact.

Proponents argue that the nullifying jury serves as a minilegislature against unjust laws or harsh, inequitable application of law in individual cases. But jury nullification is a sorry means to legal reform for several reasons. First, it is applied inconsistently. Second, it leaves bad laws on the books. Third, it gives jurors the power to disregard the law without accountability; at least legislatures are accountable to the people. Lastly, "jury sympathy does not always favor the angels."[101]

Perhaps the most judicious alternative to the general verdict is another special verdict form, the general verdict plus interrogatories. Under this procedure, the judge requests responses to specific questions to see whether the verdict rendered by the jury is consistent with its findings of fact. If not, the judge has several remedies. Federal rules permit the judge to order a new trial, return the case to the jury for further consideration, or enter a verdict consistent with the specific answers, even if contrary to the verdict.[102]

Limiting Jury Jurisdiction

Any discussion of jury reform must consider one of its most important issues: What is the desirable scope of civil jury jurisdiction? A serious critical inquiry of this topic is long overdue. As prologue, we need to distinguish the criminal and civil juries. The former has unique and entrenched historic moorings. As noted earlier,[103] the criminal jury provided essential protections against government abuse during the colonial period. No such special historical significance attends the civil jury.

Besides loyalty to the Constitution—the Seventh Amendment right to jury trial in "suits at common law," an increasingly vague standard when applied to current litigation—the primary justifications for the civil jury are its roles as conscience of the community and as a lightning rod for criticism in controversial cases.[104] Assume for the sake of argument that we accept these as legitimating justifications. In the many cases where these justifications are inapt, continuation of the civil jury is difficult to defend. Controversial cases are rare. That leaves cases where the jury's role of bringing community values to bear is desirable. Professor George Priest of Yale Law School breaks these down into two main groups:

1. Cases requiring the application of complex societal values, especially where the application is problematic because the values are conflicting or inherently difficult; and

2. Cases having a political dimension.[105]

Priest analyzed jury cases processed in the Cook County, Illinois, civil courts between 1959 and 1979. He found the vast bulk of these cases to be routine injuries and accidents: 63 percent involved auto collisions; 53 percent of the cases involved determining damages in which the most serious injury was a cut, fracture, strain or bruise.[106] These cases present no complex societal issues or political ramifications which justify bringing community values—via juries—to bear. Rather, *they are simply matters ordinarily capable of widely-accepted formulaic resolution.* As such, they lend themselves to predictable outcomes and, therefore, a very high level of out-of-court settlements. Predictability smoothes the way for settlement. It does so by decreasing the disparities between each party's expectations of (a) prevailing at trial and (b) the likely size of the award.[107]

Then why do so many routine accident and injury cases go to trial? The answer is unequivocally clear: Juries generate uncertainty. Says Priest:

This method of choosing trial versus settlement presents a much different picture of delegation to the civil jury than might be imagined from the literature justifying the institution. . . . [D]isputes are delegated to civil juries for decision not on the ground that the jury is the most appropriate decision making institution because the disputes implicate complex societal values or political issues. Instead, disputes are delegated to civil jury because the parties' settlement offers diverge. In turn, parties' settlement offers diverge because the underlying uncertainty over the outcome overwhelms the potential savings in litigation costs.[108]

Several characteristics of the jury explain the bases for the uncertainty. None are more responsible than the jury's unaccountability for its decisions or awards. The secrecy of its general verdict leaves the jury totally unaccountable. This is antithetical to how power is generally exercised in American democracy. And with its power of nullification, the jury can even contravene one of our fundamental precepts of justice. Frank wrote, "Proclaiming that we have a government of laws, we have, in jury cases, created a government of often ignorant and prejudiced men."[109] Nowhere else in our government can significant authority be wielded without the obligation of explaining and justifying important public decisions.[110]

Swollen urban court dockets can result in delays of several *years* between filing and trial. (A five year delay is not uncommon in southern California courts.) This dictates that we opt for means of dispute resolution which facilitate and conduce settlements that would naturally eventuate were jury trial decisions more predictable. To this end, we could require juries to supply explanations justifying their decisions—as is done in inquisitorial courts. This would likely improve jury decision making. It would certainly eliminate quotient balloting, coin flipping and other substitutes for reasoned deliberations.[111] And juries would surely be reluctant to ignore the law (jury nullification) if they had to publicly explain the exercise of the power. A requirement of explained decisions would increase out-of-court settlements while reducing the costs and delay incident to jury trials. Moreover, our equal justice axiom also militates in favor of requiring explained jury decisions. The need for consistency among similar cases is consonant with justified decisions.

Nevertheless, the traditional unaccountability of the jury is unlikely to change. If lay jurors were required to justify their decisions, it would behoove the judiciary to provide some paradigm for deliberations—a task it has shunned. Even more resistant to change would be the jury's historic power of nullification.

Given the apparent perduration of the general verdict, the more realistic proposal is to limit the jurisdiction of the lay civil jury. It should be retained only in cases where its use is philosophically and rationally justified. Complexity is an overriding consideration. When a highly complex or technical case clearly beyond the ken of the average lay jury falls within the identified scope of traditional jury jurisdiction, it should instead be resolved by a specially qualified jury, or removed for a hearing before an expert administrative tribunal. This is admittedly a radical proposal. That is why I cannot understate that implementation of the contracted jury jurisdiction proposal should be *specifically conditioned* on the occurrence of the following two events. First, there must be conducted extensive *actual case* experimentation testing the effects of jury aids and the other jury empowerment reforms proposed herein. Ideally, courts would welcome the attempt to improve jury functioning and allow appropriate bodies such as the Federal Judicial Center and the National Center for State Courts to monitor and assess the findings. Secondly, the clear findings from these experiments should be that the proposed measures either did *not* significantly improve jury competence, especially in complex cases, or did so but not without appreciable and insurmountable drawbacks.

Many cases should be bench trials—tried by judges alone. I concur with the majority of judges in the Harris survey who favored a limitation on the use of juries for minor civil cases involving small sums of money.[112] Other adversarial system countries provide precedents. Canada confines jury trials to disputes for which the jury's decision making characteristics are more felicitous. England has eliminated civil juries in all but defamation, malicious prosecution and false imprisonment cases.

Certain criminal cases should be removed from juries as well. In fact, they should not be tried at all. Drug cases are now the bane of the American criminal justice system. Its preoccupation with drugs has reached obsessive proportions. The "war on drugs" frenzy produced irrational minimum sentence laws at the federal level. Some examples: Anyone convicted of possessing (including possession for private use only) more than five grams (about one-fifth of an ounce) of crack cocaine must get five years without parole; ten years without parole for having any role in the distribution of more than fifty grams (about two ounces) of crack. (The latter far exceeds the specified guideline range for solicitation of murder.) These sentences must be doubled to ten and twenty years respectively for defendants with any prior drug convictions.[113] The new federal laws removed all judicial discretion to divert some or all of the sentence when there are mitigating circumstances, for example, a nonviolent first offender who appears to be a good candidate for rehabilitation. Predictable results followed. Federal drug cases increased almost 200 percent from 1982 to 1992. In 1992, over one quarter of the federal criminal case load was drug cases.[114] A recent Justice Department study found that fully one-fifth of federal inmates committed mostly nonviolent, first-time drug offenses.[115] Consequently, overcrowded prisons now release violent offenders—who ordinarily are not subject to minimum sentences, and who in any event rarely do ten years—to make room for drug offenders, many of whom are young, nonviolent and just made one bad mistake. This state of affairs is not just perverse, it is dangerous. By creating it, the government fails of its most fundamental obligation: protecting the safety of its citizens.

Many members of the federal judiciary excoriated the drug sentencing scheme, both for its severity and its disallowance of judicial discretion. Several prominent judges announced they will refuse to hear drug cases when they take senior status. Their voices were amplified by U.S. Supreme Court Justice Anthony Kennedy. In Congressional hearings, Kennedy said: "I am in agreement with most judges in the federal system that mandatory minimums are an imprudent, unwise and often unjust mechanism for sentencing."[116]

The inconsistency of the government's drug policy further reveals its irrationality. Marijuana is illegal. Yet alcohol and tobacco, far more deleterious to health, are legally available in unlimited quantities. The government even subsidizes their manufacture with price supports.

Alcohol policy is particularly troubling. Alcohol overconsumption not only harms the user, but often leads to injury and death of others. No drug contributes more to the pathology of domestic violence, especially the battering of women and children. An enormous amount of rape is undoubtedly facilitated through salutary inhibitions eradicated by liquor. This does not even consider traffic deaths and injuries attributable to alcohol. How can we reconcile the legality of alcohol (and indirectly the alcohol-related death and violence visited on innocent people) with the criminalization of simple possession or use of other drugs, a victimless crime? Remember, we are talking about mere drug possession or use, not drug-related violent crime.

No one denies that drug abuse is a problem. Heavy users become dysfunctional. They deteriorate and burden friends, family, neighbors, fellow employees and employers. Eventually we all have to pay for their infirmities in higher health insurance premiums and taxes. But this describes the sequela of heavy smokers and drinkers at least as much as that of illegal drugs.

Other countries and some pilot programs in the United States recognize the problems excessive use of illegal drugs creates. They treat it in a more enlightened and humane way, however. Instead of deeming it a crime and clogging up the courts and jails beyond their capacities, they treat it as a behavioral problem requiring treatment. Nonviolent drug users receive therapy and counseling rather than stigmatization and punishment. The benefits of taking this approach would be inestimable. We spend over one billion dollars annually on a drug interdiction program which by clear consensus has not staunched the flow of illegal drugs from other countries, predominantly Mexico. Legalization and regulation of these same drugs by the government—just as we do for alcohol and tobacco—would not only save the waste in unavailing interdiction, but also reap substantial additional revenue in sales taxes. The courts would realize immense savings from the elimination of drug cases, and worthier cases would be processed more expeditiously.

Another type of case which should be removed from litigation is capital punishment, that is, all the litigation which comes *after* the defendant in a capital punishment state has been convicted of murder in the first degree: the sentencing phase of the trial and all subsequent appeals. (The jury plays an especially prominent role here; unlike other criminal cases where the sentence is typically left to the judge, jury sentencing is the rule in capital cases.) Many of the arguments against capital punishment are now familiar to the general public: The death penalty has not been shown to deter murder; some innocent defendants are killed; a higher proportion of minority defendants receive the death penalty; the state should not be killing people; life imprisonment with no chance of parole sufficiently incapacitates the murderer. Put aside these positions for the moment. Considerations of economy and efficiency, standing alone, make compelling arguments against capital punishment.

The cost of legally killing people has become phenomenally expensive—five times greater than life imprisonment without chance of parole.[117] Using California figures as a base for comparison, housing the average prisoner (not on Death Row) costs about $20,000 per year.[118] Contrast that with the expenses of litigating a death sentence. Charles Lindner, a California attorney who has been counsel of record in numerous capital cases breaks them down as follows:

A Courtroom costs the taxpayer about $6,500 a day to run, including salaries for the judge, staff, security, overhead, depreciation, maintenance, etc. If the average death-penalty trial runs 50 days (counting motions, most do), the baseline cost is $325,000. Adding the salaries of one or two prosecutors, two investigating officers, support staff, coroners, laboratories, law clerks and "indirect costs" that the police and county spend to support the prosecution—and you easily have another $400,000 to a half million (which the prosecution always understates to the press). The defense team consists of an attorney (occasionally two), an investigator, a pathologist, psychiatrist or psychologist, forensics and other costs, depending on facts. Cost: $300,000-$500,000, depending on the case.[119]

Bear in mind this only describes the costs of the trial phase of the litigation. Say the defendant is given the death sentence. Before the defendant can be executed, appeal costs will be incurred which are much higher. The case will be reviewed by the state's Supreme Court, then the U.S. Supreme Court (this first time on direct appeal is usually denied), then a federal district judge under federal *habeus corpus*, then a three-judge panel of the federal Circuit Court of Appeals, the Circuit Court again on rehearing *en banc* (all the judges), and finally back to the U.S. Supreme Court. Lindner estimates this cost to be between $3.5 million and $4.5 million per Death Row defendant.[120]

The time factor is equally stupefying. In California, it takes between four to six years before the state Supreme Court will hear the appeal. In the meantime, death penalty cases occupy *half* of the state Supreme Court's time.[121]

Drug cases and death penalty litigation combine to grievously overload the criminal court system. This, in turn, directly impacts civil trials. The Sixth Amendment of the federal Constitution, applicable to the states, requires that criminal defendants receive a fair and *speedy* trial. Accordingly, courts give scheduling preference to criminal cases. The result: Important civil disputes involving billions of dollars languish unresolved.

Mitigating the Consequences of Adversarial Excesses and Mismatched Attorneys

The theme of the reforms proposed in this section is that a reallocation of procedural power can retain the benefits of the adversary system while improving the quality of trial justice. Some attorney prerogatives and skill mismatches which often distort and corrupt the fairness and rationality of the trial should be moderated. A corollary of this change would be an increase in the discretion and control of the judge who, as a nonpartisan official, seeks a just result. Wholesale importation of the inquisitorial system is not suggested, that is, the judge's role would not be to implement state policy. Rather, eclectic adoption of specific procedures, some drawn from foreign countries (including other adversary system countries), are recommended where promising. As with the jury improvement measures, the intent is to preserve the basic trial mechanism, replacing those specific practices which do not work well, retaining those which do.

Judicial Expedition of Pretrial and Trial Procedure

Experimentation with judicial expedition of pretrial procedure is being conducted in New York, California and other states, as well as at the federal level per the Civil Justice Reform Act of 1990 (CJRA). The Act requires creation of expense and delay reduction programs in each of the ninety-four federal districts. Experiments include differing procedural tracks (fast-track for simpler cases, slower tracks for standard and complex cases), early judicial control, setting firm trial dates and mandatory disclosure. Many states are now urging parallel changes in their procedures, with the emphasis on inducing settlements via judicial intervention.

One proposal, juror questionnaires, can produce substantial time savings during jury selection. Prospective jurors (simultaneously) answer the written questions, obviating much of the lengthy individual questioning. Other benefits follow. For example, responses to the questionnaire may better disclose grounds for challenges for cause—which, unlike peremptories, are unlimited—because prospective jurors might be more forthcoming in confidential written answers than they would in open court in the presence of others.[122]

Once in trial, attorneys with weak cases often attempt to compensate by inundating the court with marginally relevant or uncontested evidence, a practice sometimes referred to as "siege litigation." This prolongs litigation, needlessly confusing and tiring jurors while limiting court access for more meritorious claims. Seeking attorney self-restraint would be folly. Only judicial intervention can rectify the problem. As the U.S. District Court for the Eastern District of Kentucky observed, "If [attorneys] believe [they] can win cases by proliferating the evidence of the favorable, but relatively uncontested matters so that the weaker aspects of the case will be camouflaged, it is asking too much of our fallen nature to expect [them] voluntarily to do otherwise."[123]

We can reduce trial delay by having the court *set apt limits on the number of witnesses and the time spent on their interrogation*. Courts experimenting with this have had little difficulty complying. Limiting the number of expert witnesses is especially useful. This comports with the objectives of the CJRA in the federal courts, and parallel efforts by the states to expedite litigation. Authority for this kind of judicial intervention also inheres in Rule 611 of the Federal Rules of Evidence.[124] It provides, "The court *shall* exercise reasonable control over the mode and order of interrogating witnesses and presenting evidence so as to avoid needles consumption of time." (Emphasis supplied.) The word "shall" arguably connotes a duty to set appropriate time limits to trials. More generally, Rule 403 sanctions the exclusion of relevant evidence to avoid "undue delay, waste of time, and needless presentation of cumulative evidence." Similar authority is found in state rules. Under the California Evidence Code, for example, the judge can "exclude evidence if its probative value is substantially outweighed by the probability that its admission will necessitate undue consumption of time."[125]

Given the potential benefits, judges should not shy from exercising their authority. By setting apt time limits, judges force attorneys to prioritize their most important evidence. The results: Cases become simpler; jury factfinding becomes more tolerable; court backlog is eased. A rule like 611 is, as Justice Holmes commented, a mere "concession to the shortness of life."

Discovery Reform

Of all the discovery reforms proposed, the most consequential would be mandatory disclosure of core information. In a seminal 1975 law review article, Frankel called for prioritizing truth in trials by requiring attorneys to disclose material relevant evidence.[126] Recent amendments to Rule 26 of the FRCP take up this call by requiring the parties to exchange core information, including name, address and phone number of all people having knowledge bearing upon claims and defenses, plus the location of relevant documents. In great measure, mandatory disclosure would supplant discovery, perhaps the greatest single source of trial delay, expense and adversary abuse.[127] About forty federal districts now experiment with mandatory disclosure in pursuance of the CJRA.

Intense controversy surrounds the mandatory disclosure proposal. Opponents cite some legitimate complaints. Because each side would determine what information within its control meets the disclosure standard, the proposal suffers a certain measure of ambiguity which will inevitably lead to disputes. Another claim is that mandatory disclosure contravenes the attorney-client privilege and the confidentiality of the attorney's work product.

Leading the bogus arguments is the one complaining that the proposal creates "a dramatic departure from the adversarial model."[128] If so, it promises to be a salutary trip. The very aspects of the adversary system which the proposal seeks to reform are the discovery excesses and resultant time and costs now plaguing the trial courts. If facilitating the search for truth and reducing the time and cost of trials can be achieved at the expense of an incursion into the adversary system, even a "dramatic" one, so be it.

Some form of mandatory disclosure—if not the current one—should be adopted. The potential gains far exceed the potential problems. A rule with more specificity can certainly be drafted. And the courts should be able to develop an acceptable standard which does not unduly encroach upon attorney-client privilege or the attorney's work product. (This will have to be fleshed out on a case-by-case basis.) Given the magnitude of the projected benefits, this reform cannot afford to be aborted by "what-ifs" and cries of ambiguity. Implement. If the new rule proves unworkable in practice, it can be revised or abandoned. Few advances grace civilization with iron-clad guarantees of perfection from their inception.

Although the ABA and former President Bush's Council on Competitiveness (formed to mitigate the detrimental impact of litigation on business) agreed on the general thrust of needed discovery reform, they undeniably differed as to the specific recommendations for implementation. The disagreement was clear: The Council wanted codified and quantified standards; the ABA preferred judicial discretion. For example, while the ABA supports the concept of limiting discovery, it opposes the Council's recommendation of setting quantitative limits on discovery after the exchange of core information.[129] Another difference which belied the surface agreement was with respect to the Council's recommendation that the Federal Rules of Civil Procedure (FRCP) be amended to establish clear standards for sanctioning attorneys who abuse the system. The ABA's position that it supports the "concept" of the recommendation was largely betrayed with this appended commentary: "Proper judicial control of the proceedings, including discovery limits, should be sufficient."[130] Inasmuch as the views of the ABA and the Council represented opposing factions, this ostensibly innocuous one-sentence comment marked the future battleground over discovery reform: If discovery reforms are to have teeth, judges must have and be willing to impose special sanctions for violations. History teaches us that judicial control over trial proceedings, particularly as regards imposing sanctions on miscreant attorneys, will be desultory and anemic without distinct and special standards.

Eliminate Peremptory Challenges

During jury selection, the peremptory challenge allows attorneys to remove a limited number of prospective jurors without stating any reason. This encourages a view of jurors as pawns to be manipulated by the attorneys, not as responsible decision makers. Theoretically, peremptories are used to challenge jurors who are biased, but not so overtly as to justify a challenge for cause. In practice peremptories are used to obtain favorably biased jurors. Advising on the strategic use of peremptories, a Dallas County prosecutors manual says, "You are not looking for a fair juror, but rather a strong, biased, and sometimes hypocritical individual who believes that Defendants are different from them in kind, rather than degree."[131]

Peremptory challenges should be eliminated because disparities in the attorneys' jury selection skills probably skews the final jury more in a particular direction than the full panel from which it was drawn. A study making the most serious attempt to gauge the effect of peremptory challenges on juries and verdicts found considerable variability of performance among attorneys. Writing in the *Stanford Law Review*, the study's authors state: "Lawyers apparently do win some of their cases, as they occasionally boast, during or at least with the help of, voir dire . . . thereby frustrating the law's expectation that the adversary allocation of challenges will benefit both sides equally."[132]

Attorneys most often use their peremptory challenges based on crude stereotypes and assumed prejudices. Supreme Court decisions have made it nearly impossible to use peremptories to remove jurors for racially discriminatory purposes.[133] Most recently the Court extended the ban to gender.[134] Eventually all peremptory challenges may have to be justified, essentially eliminating the distinction from challenges for cause.

Peremptories have another drawback. They allow attorneys to dilute the quality of juries when they remove educated and professional individuals whom they fear will be too influential. Instructively, England has banned peremptory challenges in the few types of cases where there still are civil juries—defamation, malicious prosecution and false imprisonment. We should follow suit. All too often the peremptory challenge is used to select a favorably incompetent jury rather than eliminate potential jurors whose prejudice escaped the sieve of the challenge for cause. Of this practice, jury expert Richard Lempert of the University of Michigan Law School declares: "The tactical desire to gain a jury that can be fooled deserves no legal respect."[135]

Judge-Conducted Voir Dire

The arguments for and against judge versus attorney *voir dire* were presented in Chapter 4. Those states which have not already done so should adopt the practice of the federal courts, which leaves *voir dire* entirely within the judge's discretion. Two persuasive arguments impel judge-conducted *voir dire*. The first is pragmatic. Judge-conducted *voir dire* is dramatically more expeditious. According to a Federal Judicial Center study, the average judge-conducted *voir dire* took one hour.[136] In contrast, a study of attorney-conducted *voir dire* in

New York found the average *voir dire* took 12.7 hours.[137] In California, a 1990 initiative limited attorney *voir dire* to questions "in aid of the exercise of challenge for cause." Average jury selection time dropped from days to hours.

The second argument against attorney *voir dire* is theoretical. Attorneys take longer to conduct *voir dire* in large part because they seek to indoctrinate and sway prospective jurors, rather than merely probing for bias. As noted in Chapter 4, studies indicate that the vast majority of attorneys' efforts during *voir dire* constitute illicit extensions of the adversary process to (what is supposed to be) a nonadversary exercise. The presumed, sanctioned function of *voir dire* is to enable counsel to descry and eliminate prejudiced prospective jurors in order to achieve the ideal of an impartial jury. That this is honored more in the breach is not exactly a state secret. By their stratagems to ingratiate themselves with, and indoctrinate prospective jurors during *voir dire*—a tactic urged in trial advocacy courses and texts—attorneys flagrantly subvert the impartial jury ideal. Many litigators believe that trials are won or lost during *voir dire*. The trial becomes a game whose booty goes to the attorney most adept at selecting and/or creating a favorably biased jury, or to the attorney who prevails in a beauty contest of personalities. With the advent of "scientific" jury selection, the process is skewed further toward the side with the greater resources. For jury selection services are nothing if not expensive. Unrestricted attorney *voir dire* conduces the triumph of personality and tactics over the merits of the case. As widely practiced, it corrupts the intended purpose of *voir dire* and exacerbates preexisting inequalities between the parties.

Minimum Skills

Perhaps prodded by well-chronicled criticisms of trial counsel ineptitude,[138] some states are considering minimum skills training for attorneys. In addition to raising the quality of court representation, it is hoped such measures would mitigate the potential injustice when opposing attorneys are of significantly disparate competence. Mismatching sabotages the condition upon which optimal functioning of the adversary system is predicated: roughly equal competence of opposing counsel.

Alternatively, we should consider the advantages of the English barrister system. Barristers are litigation specialists. Adopting a barrister system thus obviates minimum skills training. The barrister system meliorates three of the stated problems of our trial system. First, it eliminates witness-coaching and the evils associated therewith. Second, it minimizes the likelihood of attorney mismatching of the sort found in U.S. courts. Using specialists on both sides potentiates the functioning of the adversary system, and with it, the chances of a just result. Third, the professional independence of barristers and their freedom to take any kind of case—criminal prosecution and defense cases as well as civil representation—tends to moderate adversarial excess. Detachment from the client does not mean weaker or less persuasive case presentation. Rather, it translates to one free of histrionics, irrelevant verbiage and misplaced emotionalism.[139] The introduction to the ABA Standards Relating to the Prosecutorial Function notes the efficacy of the barrister system:

Many qualified observers of our system of criminal justice who have also studied the British system have commented on the importance of the professional independence enjoyed by the barrister assigned on an ad hoc basis to represent the prosecution. Since he is also likely to appear for the defense . . . traditions have grown which *blunt excessive zeal without impairing, and which indeed improve, the quality of advocacy.* (Emphasis supplied.)[140]

A 1976 pilot program undertaken in Yuma County, Arizona, augurs well for further experimentation with the barrister system. Funded by a grant from the Law Enforcement Assistance Administration, the Yuma County Model Barrister Program was established with the following objectives:

- To increase professionalism on the part of the criminal trial bar, both prosecution and defense.

- To increase respect in the community for the criminal trial bar.

- To promote better relations between criminal defense attorneys and prosecutors, resulting in a better understanding by both of the criminal justice system, which will promote a more efficient and more just system.[141]

Under the grant, the county attorney hired established members of the criminal defense bar to prosecute selected cases. Although the sample size was small, the responses of the participating attorneys indicated that the objectives were met and an American barrister system is workable.[142] Using the Yuma County program as a model, future barrister programs should also authorize the public defender's office to hire prosecutors for selected cases on an as-needed basis. Both prosecutor and public defender offices should take steps to avert conflicts of interest. As it does in England, an American barrister system can heighten the professionalism of the criminal trial bar and raise its standing in the community. And by allowing the participants to also practice civil litigation, the high incidence of burn-out among criminal trial attorneys would be reduced.[143] The time has arrived for a suitable experiment with the barrister approach in a large metropolitan area.

Judicial Questioning

Whatever the merits of the minimum skills approach, it still leaves control of the trial to the attorneys. In the Los Angeles survey, the most common suggestion to counteract the effects of mismatched attorney skills was, "Allow the judge to ask supplemental questions."[144] Accordingly, another alternative to the mismatching problem is to place more responsibility for evidence-taking with the judge. In many inquisitorial system countries, a common justification given for increasing the authority of the judge is the need to equalize the parties.[145] The inquisitorial system procedure for witness selection and interrogation provides an instructive model. Under this procedure, witness-coaching is virtually absent.[146] Any contact with prospective witnesses is frowned upon, and the probative value of such witness' testimony would be downgraded. Witnesses are called and questioned by the judge. During evidence-taking, attorneys reserve the right to nominate additional witnesses, suggest additional questions and, at least in Germany, submit closing arguments. In the periods between evidence-taking hearings, attorneys suggest further proof, discuss and distinguish precedent, interpret statutes and develop adversarial positions on the significance of the evidence.[147] In this manner, partisan advocacy is preserved while factfinding control shifts to the judge.

Several potential advantages flow from judicial questioning. Freed of the distorting effect of partisan preparation (coaching) and trial interrogation, the testimony of court-called witnesses is arguably more reliable.[148] Another benefit is the reduced influence of lawyer theatrics and dirty tricks. Lastly, the judicial interrogation tempers the skewing effect which occurs when the advocacy skills of opposing counsel are decisively mismatched.[149]

To gain the benefits of independent, judicial questioning during trial, we need not replace purely adversarial evidence-gathering with the judge-dominated model of the inquisitorial system. An acceptable middle ground could be the same allocation of interrogating power employed during our *voir dire*, where questioning is frequently shared by judge and attorneys.[150] The *voir dire* model of shared control can be adapted to evidence gathering. That is, the judge might conduct the initial interrogation, after which the attorneys would be free to probe for additional details. But the judge could always ask supplemental questions which an incompetent or marginally competent attorney neglects to pose. The occasional need for this judicial "safety net" protection escapes few who are familiar with adversary system trials.

Albert Alschuler declared, "[T]he American legal system probably makes the kind of justice that a defendant receives more dependent on the quality of the lawyer he is able to hire than any other legal system in the world."[151] Alschuler's conclusion is a disturbing commentary about American trial justice. Consider: Ours is a country whose legal system, above all, honors equality of treatment—or, as it is sometimes characterized, equal justice. Yet we adopted a trial mechanism which, more than any other, skews trial outcomes in favor of the side with the better attorney. And in the freest of all free market economies, wealth commands the best legal representation. Consequently, equal justice through the court system is but a chimera, an ennobling standard whose correspondence with reality is barely discernible.

This is certainly not what most American litigants want or deserve. The evidence-taking scheme proposed here substantially mitigates attorney-dictated trial justice by permitting questions from three distinct kinds of sources—judge, attorneys and jurors—instead of one. In a case with a twelve-person jury, this means questions could come from fifteen people (twelve jurors, two attorneys and the judge) instead of just the two attorneys. Juror questions, being the most potentially problematic, would be permitted subject to the checks specified earlier; further, juror questions should be forestalled until the judge and attorneys have asked all of their initial and follow-up questions.

Anything more than an occasional question from the trial judge would be perceived as a dangerous deviation from current trial procedure (and a commensurate threat to the litigation bar). Let us then address some of the expressed reservations. *Would judicial questioning lead to too many questions?* Perhaps. But it is better to have too many than too few questions, especially if they are in fact different questions. When a trial attorney elicits an advantageous response from a witness, a favored tactic is to ask the same question of the same witness multiple times over the course of the interrogation so as to reinforce and reemphasize the answer in the jurors' minds. The attorney creates the impression that one question is many by asking it at discrete intervals over the course of his interrogation, and using slightly different wording. I watched a murder case where the state's key witness was a prostitute who had accused the defendant, her pimp, of killing the victim, another prostitute in the defendant's employ. During the defense counsel's cross-examination, the witness admitted lying about her identity when she called the police (for obvious reasons). Several times over the course of his interrogation of the witness the wily defense counsel returned to that phone call, each time phrasing his question differently, but nonetheless eliciting each time an admission of lying to the police. He would then quickly move on to another line of questioning, thereby impairing the jurors' ability to note the essential identity of all the questions about the phone call to the police. By the end of the trial he apparently had the jury believing the witness to be an inveterate liar: The defendant was acquitted.

With judges making such a radical departure from their traditionally passive role, wouldn't they lose their (actual or perceived) impartiality? To some extent, a more engaged judicial role is already a widespread *fait accompli.* I refer to the earlier discussion of the marked increase of judicial activism in the pretrial phase. Some of this new activism is spreading incrementally to evidence-taking. I suggest this is a trend presaging greater judicial participation at all levels of the trial, although not to the extent proposed here. As to the concern over the loss of judicial impartiality from the more active role proposed here, nonpartisan evidence-taking could still be accomplished through a *neutral investigator.* If either attorney objected to the judge's enhanced evidence-taking responsibility, one or more individuals appointed by the court and approved by the attorneys would review the available evidence, using subpoenas if necessary, and conduct the court's questioning during the trial. Here again, the inquisitorial model is instructive. Some continental cases have a presiding judge who conducts the investigation and two associate judges. This dilutes the effect of any bias the presiding judge may acquire by virtue of her investigative role.

Likewise, if the judge believed greater involvement would compromise her neutrality, she could order the court's interrogation be done by the neutral investigator. Under this proposal, however, this should be the exception rather than the norm. The notion that the third party adjudicator must remain near-totally passive in order to retain her impartiality is peculiar to American jurisprudence. Foreign trial systems and domestic ADR mechanisms show this to be a myth. In a bench trial (no jury), it is ludicrous for the judge to refrain from asking questions out of fear of self-corruption. No scientific findings suggest that inquiry intended merely to clarify induces a fatal loss of discipline. The same conclusion follows in jury trials. Case after case indicates that jurors seek and need judicial guidance in factfinding, particularly in complex trials. However, that does not translate to a willing relinquishment of their decision making authority. I find it of no small significance that the Los Angeles jury survey, the largest in American history, found that questioning by both jurors and judge were the two most popular juror suggestions to improve juror functioning.

What will judicial questioning cost? Judges must be present during questioning, so their trial time costs would be unaffected. But they (or their staffs) would have to devote more time to pretrial investigation in order to pose the best questions during the trial. Alternatively, neutral investigators would also increase the public component of trial costs. Two countervailing factors should neutralize these incremental costs. First, the continental experience is testament to the fact that judge-run trials are substantially shorter and less costly than their adversarial counterparts. Second, many would-be litigants will eschew litigation whose outcome will be more the product of neutral investigation—not for sale—than of litigation determined by the high-priced legal representation they can buy. With that realization, litigation rates should decline dramatically, easing court caseloads and more than compensating for the additional costs.

Court-Called Expert Witnesses

Court-called expert testimony would counteract many of the problems posed by the testimonies of partisan experts. But conforming to adversarial precepts of party control and judicial passivity, American judges rarely exercise their prerogative to call expert witnesses.[152] No question exists as to the judge's authority to do so. According to an advisory committee note to the Federal Rules of Evidence, "The inherent power of the trial judge to appoint an expert of his own choosing is virtually unquestioned."[153] Because they are called and paid by the court, court-called witnesses are neutral, a feature of inestimable value when experts testify. Judges should select acknowledged experts holding views representative of the scientific community.

If judges exercised their authority to call expert witnesses, jurors could be spared the exasperation of choosing whom to believe in the notorious "battle of the experts." Here again, the continental practice is educative. Continental courts rely almost exclusively on court-called experts. The written opinion of the court's expert is circulated to the attorneys. Their responsive comments may lead the court either to hold a hearing where the attorneys can interrogate the expert, or to get the opinion of a second expert. Witness expertise is thereby kept impartial, but with the opportunity for attorney confrontation and rebuttal to protect against error or caprice.[154] In complex civil cases, a majority of the Harris survey judges favored the use of neutral expert witnesses in addition to those called by the parties.[155]

Witness Narratives

Another practice of the inquisitorial system could improve the value of witness testimony to the factfinder: Allow witnesses to begin their testimonies with an uninterrupted narrative. Objections to the narrative could be deferred until the narration's completion so as to preserve its pristine flavor. If the objection is sustained, the jury would be appropriately cautioned.

Two salutary consequences from this proposal can be projected: First, more (and arguably better) information would go to the factfinder than that elicited from "yes" or "no" responses to attorney questions; second, the testimony-corrupting impact of strategic attorney disruptions during the initial narratives would be eliminated. Such tactics are commonplace. In the Los Angeles survey, jurors rank-ordered the perceived frequency of attorney obfuscation tactics. "Repeated interruptions and disruptive tactics" ranked second, just behind "Appeals to the emotions of jurors."[156]

Commenting/Summarizing the Evidence

As mentioned earlier, in England judges comment upon the evidence and summarize the issues and facts after the final arguments by the attorneys. Judges also suggest the proper inferences for the jury. The presiding judge in the inquisitorial court also summarizes the evidence in the dossier before deliberations. Our judges do not,[157] despite comparable authority in the federal courts and many state courts. Yet such commentary affords the opportunity to rescue the case from the false gloss of powerful advocates. Moreover, it is particularly helpful to jurors in long and complex cases. Judge Schwarzer advocates its use whenever explanation of complex evidence will ensure its fair consideration. Schwarzer's only admonition is that the judge does it in a way that does not improperly influence the jury.[158]

The judge's evidence summary and commentary is most usefully given with the instructions. If so, the judge must carefully distinguish for the jurors evidence interpretation from legal instructions. The latter must be followed, whereas jurors are free to draw their own conclusions regarding differing evidentiary analyses by the judge and attorneys.

Other Measures to Improve Courthouse Justice

Taking a more global view of courthouse justice, several other problems related to trial procedure remain unresolved. Three are discussed here. First, many people cannot afford attorney representation in civil disputes. Additional public funding for civil representation and stepped-up *pro bono* work are only partial answers. The balance must come from lawyerless tribunals, ADR, and the licensing of paraprofessionals to assist in all dispute resolution outside of litigation. Second, in numerous civil and even some criminal cases, trial court dispute resolution is a suboptimal means to justice. Those seeking other vehicles find, to their dismay, a disconnected patchwork of alternatives. Finally, many litigants discover that narrow court remedies poorly serve their underlying needs. All of these concerns are addressed in the following section on improving courthouse justice. As used here, "courthouse" is a much broader term than "courtroom." "Courthouse" contemplates the entire panoply of dispute resolution resources which could be available to the public under the court's auspices.

Greater Access to Civil Representation

Chapter 5 discussed the maldistribution of legal services for the poor and middle class in civil disputes. The ideal of equal justice is unattainable without equalizing access to representation. Although impressive gains have been made in publicly subsidized legal representation for the poor, the quality of such representation is generally inferior to the high-priced talent available in the private market. A small gain toward the equal representation goal is realized through *pro bono* (voluntary) work of quality attorneys. But until *pro bono* service is mandated for the entire profession, and made accessible to middle income litigants as well as the poor, the goal will remain a chimera.[159] Equal justice for all is impeded by two problems: unequal representation, and no representation. Remedies such as greater judicial intervention and minimum skills training for trial attorneys address the first problem. The second problem is a higher priority. Many poor and middle class citizens cannot afford legal representation in civil disputes. Increased funding of the Legal Services Corporation enhances the accessibility of legal representation. Yet funding for the Corporation has dropped. Adjusted for inflation, the 1991 appropriation was $173 million less than the 1980 appropriation.[160] In 1975, the Legal Service Corporation articulated a "minimum access" goal of two attorneys for every 10,000 poor persons. The 1991 appropriation of $350 million would have to be doubled to reach that goal today.[161] When the LSC requested a 50 percent budget hike in 1992, Congress responded with a whopping 2 percent increase.[162]

Greater access to legal representation will also materialize if the private bar increases its *pro bono* work for the poor. According to the MRPC, this is a "professional responsibility."

A lawyer shall render public interest legal service. A lawyer may discharge this responsibility by providing professional services at no fee or a reduced fee to persons of limited means or to public service or charitable groups or organizations, by service in activities for improving the law, the legal system or the legal profession, by financial support for organizations that provide legal services to persons of limited means.[163]

Once again, however, the true meaning of the legal profession's language is cryptic. The true meaning is revealed by an accompanying official Comment. It states that this "responsibility" rule expresses a "policy but is not intended to be enforced through disciplinary process."

This is not to condemn the entire bar. Its good works should be accorded their due. *Pro bono* participation has been substantial—the ABA cites several state surveys indicating that *pro bono* participation may involve 50 to 70 percent of the bar.[164] That is nonetheless insufficient to meet the needs of a growing population of poor and disadvantaged. For that, more aggressive measures are required. One can argue that the modern version of the social contract implies an obligation of the state to fund civil representation for basic social needs (in addition to criminal defense). Absent legislation or a landmark court ruling to that effect, attorneys might be compelled to perform *pro bono* work as a condition of their license to practice. After all, that license is a state-sanctioned monopoly. Other state approved monopolies, such as utilities, must serve the public on a nondiscriminatory basis at rates set by the state. Attorneys bear no such obligation.

Mandatory *pro bono* programs have been proposed or considered in New York, West Virginia, Texas, Connecticut, Arizona, Maryland, Hawaii and Florida.[165] But the tendency has wisely been to allow voluntary programs to succeed before resorting to mandatory service. The most successful prods to *pro bono* work are those by the state supreme courts which reaffirm the ethical obligation of every attorney to serve the civil legal needs of the poor, and which articulate an expectation of a specific number of hours.[166]

A promising movement is the adoption by a small but growing number of law schools of mandatory *pro bono* activity by their students as a prerequisite for graduation. Tulane was the first school requiring it. Now joining it are ten more. In these communities, the availability of free student help also leads to increased *pro bono* activity among local practicing attorneys.[167]

Often ignored in the identification of groups with inadequate access to representation is the working middle class. By the ABA's own admission, a broad majority of the population is underrepresented: "The [ABA] has long been aware that the middle 70 percent of our population is not being reached or served adequately by the legal profession."[168] Two measures will help—one specific, the other general. The specific measure would maintain the favorable tax status of employer prepaid legal plans which now serve an estimated 17 million employees. They use these plans for assistance with such problems as divorce, child support and child custody, landlord-tenant disputes, consumer complaints and traffic offenses.[169]

The general measure contemplates a broad-scale public education program designed to inform citizens not only of some of their basic rights, but where and how to redeem those rights. Otherwise the law operates in a vacuum, unusable to all save the cognoscenti and the wealthy. (Experts retained by wealthy individuals and corporations commonly advise their clients in a proactive fashion of significant changes in the law.) Government should promulgate major changes in the law not just in the specialized publications for attorneys where they now appear, but in the general media. And the changes should be explained in nonjargonistic, comprehensible language. Equally important, the public should be apprised of free or low cost legal assistance available in the community.

To be sure, the major print media carry pieces on major legislative changes. Radio and television would reach far more. As a condition of their FCC licenses, broadcast stations are expected to deliver a certain amount of public affairs programming. The FCC has been spectacularly toothless in implementing this mandate, as evidenced by the subject matter of most television and radio shows. (News programs have deteriorated to little more than entertainment; reportage of crime, fire, accidents, weather and sports dominate.) Without any additional legislative authorization, the FCC could direct broadcast licensees to devote a little more of their program schedules to informative public service programming. For starters, synopses and brief discussions of important legal changes might occasionally replace some of the time now dominated by music, sitcoms and soap operas. (I elide mention of Oprah, Phil, Geraldo and their stylistic clones from my "hit list" in recognition of the epithets such tampering of sacred turf would surely evoke.)

There is a quick and cheap way to provide low cost legal assistance to the poor and middle income who cannot afford an attorney: Break the bar's monopoly on the practice of law. Paralegals could be trained and licensed in specialized areas to perform numerous standardized services for which many states now require an attorney. Included would be probating an uncontested will, obtaining an uncontested divorce, real estate title searches and purchase contracts, forming a small corporation, license applications and other routine government compliance work. Besides paralegals, other professionals could perform legal services in their respective areas of expertise. A bank officer, for instance, could easily be trained to handle the probate of an uncontested will. Similarly, a real estate broker could provide and help fill in a standard, preprinted real estate purchase contract form, while a title company could do the title search (both are now done in California and other states).

These nonattorney legal experts would not represent clients in court. But the services they provide would, in myriad circumstances, obviate the need to sue. As business attorneys know, practicing preventive law—by tailoring transactions to avert potential legal problems—is the most effective way to avoid litigation. Should it be necessary, however, the client of the paralegal or other nonattorney expert will have the proper documentation to support claims or defenses in court.

One notable exception to the bar's stranglehold on legal services is tax law. CPAs and other tax accountants commonly file tax returns and advise clients on the tax consequences of past and proposed transactions. CPAs can even represent clients before the Internal Revenue Service. Attorneys retain the exclusive right to draft tax-related legal documents and issue advisory opinions on certain proposed transactions, but in all other respects tax accountants commonly practice law, broadly defined, without a license. Yet the bar's remonstrations have been desultory and half-hearted for at least two good reasons. First, business attorneys and tax accountants have a symbiotic relationship. Accountants often refer their clients to attorneys for the drafting of documents (such as trusts and partnership agreements) necessary to implement the accountant's tax plan. Quality is the second reason. For all but the highest level of statutory or case law interpretation (or for litigation), the best tax CPAs are as qualified as their legal counterparts and generally cost less.[170] Moreover, much of the public knows this, so the bar's expostulations that accountants lack the requisite competence in tax law would be perceived as rank, self-serving canards.

Incompetent service is not the sole source of the bar's fixation regarding the unauthorized practice of law. Abject greed, not concern over incompetent representation, also causes the bar to jealously forfend the sharing of legal services. That is one reason why all paralegal work is done under the auspices of attorneys. Paralegals must be complaisant, even obeisant, for the work thrown them by their benefactors. After a cursory review of the paralegal's work—if indeed there is any review—the attorney bills the client at multiples of the rates paid the paralegal. The bar's monopoly over quotidian legal needs thereby benefits attorneys to the detriment of the public. Qualified, licensed paralegals could perform a plethora of legal services at a fraction of the prices charged by attorneys, whose fees are based on recovering large overheads plus the cost of years of expensive schooling. The paralegal's bailiwick could be carefully circumscribed, with an obligation to refer the client to an attorney if there is a reasonable expectation of litigation or other services requiring an attorney. As added insurance, the state could also require paralegals to carry performance bonds.

The same greed which drives the bar's monopolization of legal services also perpetuates the mystification of the law, primarily through abstruse legal jargon. Self-help law advocate Jake Warner offers this disconcerting report:

In most states, documents for routine actions such as simple probate or child support modification to adjust for inflation must be typed on a weird sort of paper used no place else in the world, following a bizarre format. Much of the language required (which, incidentally, legal secretaries slavishly copy from legal form books or, if they are current, download from computerized form generators) has so little real meaning that it has scarcely changed since the death of (or, for that matter, the birth) of Queen Victoria.[171]

Indeed, attorney avarice may motivate not only the impenetrable language of most legal instruments, but their prolixity as well. Some experts believe the typical wordiness of legal instruments stems from the former practice by British lawyers of charging by the word.[172] The wording of many common transactions can be simplified so as to be within the pale of the average person's ability to effect.

It is time to chip away at the bar's monopoly on legal services. The competence argument by which the bar has arrogated to itself the exclusive authority to practice law does not withstand scrutiny when it comes to routine, common transactions. Despite exorbitant fees for simple services, there is no guarantee against attorney incompetence. Moreover, if attorney counsel on such matters is, in fact, indispensable, the bar should be willing to permit the educating impact of the free market to take effect. The public would soon sort out which transactions are unacceptably risky without attorney involvement. Where there is negligence by the nonattorney professional, several remedies would be available, including lifting the professional's license and/or damages.

Paramedics can treat many simple injuries without extensive training in human anatomy and pathology. By the same token paralegals and other licensed professionals can render adequate legal services on simple, common transactions without law school training in constitutional law, evidence and other courses in law school curricula usually irrelevant to the poor or middle-income client's needs. Monopoly produces this kind of inefficiency. A freer market in legal services would enable a more felicitous matching of customer needs and the service-provider's breadth of expertise.

The multi-door courthouse

Justice is not limited to the courtroom. For many, the real problem is not trial representation, but access to means of justice. In this regard, public ADR via the multi-door courthouse is the most promising solution for those who cannot afford private counsel or private ADR.

No single method of resolution is ideal and just for all disputes. Common sense dictates multiple methods, some nonadversarial. Selecting the most appropriate method for the particular dispute is the linchpin. For this, few devices are better than the multi-door courthouse. The multi-door courthouse is a gestalt approach designed to encourage public perception of the court as an all-purpose resource for dispute resolution. It works by using an intake specialist who refers disputes to the appropriate "door," that is, dispute resolution mechanism. This approach consolidates dispute resolution mechanisms of varying adversariness in one location, and incorporates them into the existing court system, permitting parties to choose (or be referred to) the form and forum most felicitous to the resolution of their dispute. After successful pilot projects in Houston, Tulsa and Washington, D.C., the multi-door concept was adopted in several cities. Only disputes requiring immediate court action would be referred to trial following screening.

Integral to operation of the multi-door courthouse is the removal of appropriate cases from full-blown adversarial dispute resolution, i.e., trial. There are two ways to accomplish this. One is by simply removing either a cause of action or a defense by legislative fiat. The cause of action route was accomplished in the many states which abolished the right to sue for breach of promise to marry, alienation of affections, adultery and similar causes—the so-called "heart balm" statutes.[173] Adoption of strict liability in the products liability field exemplifies the elimination of defense approach, effectively eliminating the defense of due care.

The other way to remove a class of cases from adversarial dispute resolution is to effect a change of forum from a trial court of general jurisdiction to a more informal, less adversarial specialized court or administrative body. States have increasingly diverted the resolution of certain disputes to less or nonadversarial fora. A prime illustration is the workers compensation hearing, which supplanted industrial accident suits against employers. Along similar lines are the many cases now referred by the courts to court-annexed arbitration or mediation.[174] In these situations, the disputants can only get full adversarial (trial) review after submitting to ADR, and even then subject to certain disincentives.[175] Problems particularly unsuitable to adversarial dispute resolution are family matters, especially child custody, and other instances where continuing relations are needed, such as partnerships and landlord-tenant relationships. Adversarial dispute resolution is also entirely unsuitable when there is no real controversy, for example, uncontested divorces.

Additional constraints militate in favor of diversion of certain cases to nontrial fora. Not the least is the bloated court docket. Moving all minor civil and criminal disputes (minor traffic violations, for example) to magistrate courts, small claims courts, administrative tribunals or other alternative fora may soon be widely mandated to relieve court caseloads.[176] The time and cost of these cases usually render trial court adjudication impracticable. This would leave full-blown adversarial litigation to major cases.

To fulfill its promise as an all-purpose resource for dispute resolution, the multi-door courthouse should offer expansive services. By that is meant a more global vision of meliorating disputes, with emphasis on their root causes. Holistic problem solving and an overall treatment-centered approach to resolution would prevail. Family courts, for example, would hear all disputes arising in the family as broadly defined, from marriage dissolution and child custody to prosecutions involving domestic violence between family members. Social service counselors would be available to meet specific needs of certain individuals, such as drug addicts or illiterates, and to advise judges and other decision makers.[177] Ideally, law schools would complement this vision of the court. Students can be educated about the multi-door system and the types of cases that are best resolved—at least initially—with less adversarial and nonadversarial alternatives.

Court-mandated ADR plus aggressive judicial settlement and pretrial case management will continue under federal law (the FRCP, the CJRA) and comparable state legislation. Before wholesale implementation, however, certain realities must be addressed. In the same manner that the medical system can worsen illnesses—iatrogenic problems—so the legal system can aggravate interpersonal problems—juridogenic problems. Mass integration of trial and ADR, including judicially facilitated settlement, is an unnatural process. If judges and attorneys carry the baggage of their adversary system training and instincts into nonadversarial dispute resolution processes, the multi-door courthouse experiment, and indeed all of public ADR (that is, court-mandated as opposed to voluntary private ADR, such as that found in neighborhood justice centers) will ineluctably yield to adversarial corruption. The more that attorneys participate in ADR proceedings, the more adversarial they become. Clear indications of this distortion of purpose already appear in the language employed. Many mediation programs, for example, now label one party the complainant and the other the respondent, rather than "the parties." Further, the procedural rules have begun to mimic those of the trial: opening statements, cross-examinations, rebuttals and closing "arguments."[178] Thus mediation, one of the "softest" ADR forms, comes to look and sound like adversarial litigation.

Settlement activity in the courts is, to a great degree, a clash of two cultures.[179] Skills suitable to settlement frequently controvert those useful in litigation. Judges and attorneys seeking negotiated settlement must be reoriented to problem solving in order to be effective in reaching quality solutions. By the same token, too much pretrial mediative conduct by judges may seriously impact their ability to adjudicate those disputes which go to trial. Pretrial "managerial judging" may risk some loss of impartiality central to the trial judge's role. Moreover, the revelation of evidence inadmissible in trial may taint the judgment of the person who is later charged with finding the facts and making judgment. For this reason, it is advisable to use a different judge if the case is ultimately tried.[180] This conflicting roles problem can be resolved by the use of magistrates or a rotation of judges to supervise all pretrial activities.

Another answer lies in emulating the English masters practice. Linda Silberman, who authored a detailed study of the English separation of trial and pretrial functions, had these observations: "The English . . . see an advantage in insulating their judges from the parties' contests over interlocutory [temporary] or other collateral matters; keeping trial proceedings away from the presiding trial judge prevents matters arising at a preliminary stage from influencing or prejudicing the judge when he presides in the context of a full trial."[181] Adoption of the English masters system, opines Alschuler, could be salutary on two counts: "Rather than seek an accommodation of conflicting values, our legal system could pursue both values more effectively. A clear division of labor would also eliminate the danger that a 'pretrial' judge might deliberately or inadvertently coerce settlement through an explicit, implicit or even misperceived threat of retaliation at trial."[182]

One inference is compelling. A separate class of settlement facilitators—be they judges, magistrates or masters—would be specially trained more easily than trial judges. It would require remarkable flexibility and discipline for the ideal pretrial case manager—informal, active, conciliatory and innovative—to abruptly transmogrify into the conventionally ideal trial judge—formal, passive, rule-bound and aloof.

The first consideration of would-be ADR users should be their goals. ADR mechanisms vary. They should be distinguished by their nature and primary advantages. Their degrees of adversariality differ markedly. Some, like the summary jury trial, mimic the trial, whereas others, like mediation, contemplate the articulation of views and feelings leading to eventual accord. Another consideration is purpose: What beneficial characteristic is the potential user seeking? Commercial users tend to favor ADR because of its relative speed and inexpensiveness. Yet many look to ADR for a better, not a quicker solution. UCLA law professor Carrie Menkel-Meadow, who teaches and facilitates ADR, writes, "Caseload management and docket-reduction may suggest entirely different processes than a search for a better quality solution which might be costly and time-consuming."[183] At this crossroad—selection of the optimal dispute resolution method—the intake specialist's skill comes to fruition.

More Diverse Remedies

Limited breadth of remedies is one of the great deficiencies of our trials. Court remedies reflect binary legal thinking, resulting in clearly polarized models: right/wrong, win/lose and rights/duties. In this world of absolutes, decisions are typically of an either-or, all-or-nothing nature, commonly known as winner-take-all, or WTA. Another deficiency is that adjudication only provides a zero-sum solution: One party's gain is only at the expense of an equal loss to the other party. Further, the media of the remedies themselves are few and predetermined. Absent are creative, case-specific remedies, whether fashioned by the judge or the parties, which could permit variable or positive-sum alternatives.

So long as the judge must choose a zero-sum, WTA, predetermined remedy, the law does not achieve optimal adjudication in hard cases. Instead, it obscures the realities of particular existential situations. The absence, for instance, of judicial compromise in trial is peculiar in light of its high incidence in out-of-court settlement, by which 90 percent of cases are resolved. Northwestern University law professor John Coons writes:

Judicial activism in chambers is matched only by judicial paralysis on the bench. The "fair" decision promoted in private is one unattainable in law. That which the judge thinks just he cannot order. That which in chambers he calls "unjust" he orders and defends with thirty pages of rhetoric.[184]

Traditionalists would balk at compromise as a Pandora's Box waiting to be opened. But confining it to narrowly circumscribed situations could make it sufficiently predictable to mollify those fearful of a material increase in judicial discretion. Coons describes two types of situations in which court-ordered compromise would be fairer and more appropriate than WTA. Coons calls the first type of case "factual indeterminacy." This arises when either side's version of the facts is equally probable, and no policy issue is involved. Assume both disputants claim ownership to a disputed item and neither side has a preponderance of the evidence. A court ordinarily would resolve the dispute by ruling against the party who had the "burden of persuasion." Burden of persuasion, however, is often just an artifice to facilitate the WTA result by arbitrarily preferring one litigant over another. Instead, the desired item could be split equally between the litigants; if it is indivisible, then it could be sold and the proceeds split equally. This is a more rational approach in its greater approximation of the factual probabilities. And it better serves the legal principle of equal treatment under the law.

The other type of case Coons describes as apt for compromise he calls "rule indeterminacy." This would be the policy counterpart of fact indeterminacy: cases involving conflict of equally significant policies. An example would be a suit between A, the owner of stolen property, and B, the bona fide purchaser of same. Each side is equally deserving; neither is at fault. Why should one, because of some arbitrary preference in the law, suffer the entire loss? Ensuring a WTA result is not a sufficient reason. If the property were not unique, it could be sold and the proceeds split between A and B. If it were unique, the person who is awarded possession under current law could compensate the other with an amount approximately half the property's worth.[185]

Precedent exists for compromise. Apportionment remedies are now awarded in civil cases. Comparative negligence has largely displaced the WTA rule of contributory negligence. In some states liability is apportioned among industrial polluters on a market share basis when it cannot be shown which company's discharge actually caused the complainant's injury. It is not that large of a step to import the same logic in cases of fact and rule indeterminacy. No compelling argument dictates retention of the draconian WTA remedy.

Another unattractive feature of our court remedies is that they are zero-sum. Potential for breaking the zero-sum bind lies in situations where the parties do not place equal value on the item(s) in dispute. Trade-offs should be possible because the parties do not have absolutely antipodal positions on all the issues.[186] For example, say A is court-ordered to pay B $1 million. A does not have this in cash or liquid assets, but does own a highly successful business whose operating assets could fetch $600,000. If the court ordered A's business assets to be sold (the standard remedy), A loses his or her business and the ability to pay B in full. Result: Neither party is satisfied. Alternatively, B, a wealthy individual, may be amenable to receiving deferred installment payments for tax purposes. This allows A to retain his or her business and pay B the full award (plus interest) over the course of a mutually acceptable time schedule.

Court remedies are remarkably inflexible. It is an obtuse perversion of the equal justice principle to contend that all litigants are restricted to the same predetermined forms of relief, irrespective of the utility of those forms to the particular dispute and disputants before the court. Litigants would reap greater satisfaction if courts structured remedies responsive to their real needs. (Chapter 6 discusses the flexible remedies possible using ADR, particularly mediation.) Consider another example.[187] Ms. Brown puts a down payment on a used car sold to her by Mr. Snead. Shortly thereafter, the car ceases to work. Repeated attempts to repair it are to no avail. Brown sues for rescission of the contract or, alternatively, money damages. Snead counterclaims for the balance due on the car,[188] claiming the warranty period had expired and insufficient time to cure the defects. Although Snead would probably prevail under the law (if all the claims were factual), his actual recovery could be diminished by Brown's lost income from losing time at work (to get the car repaired) and the cost of the repairs. Snead's reputation is bound to suffer too. None of the remedies meet the real needs of either party: Brown wants a functioning car to transport her to work; Snead wants his full profit plus the goodwill value of a satisfied customer. But if, after considering the inadequacy of the remedies to either party, the court instead ordered Snead to *substitute* a reliable car from his large inventory, both parties emerge in a better position. Brown gets her car, Snead gets his full profit and no damage to his reputation.

Menkel-Meadows lists alternative remedies which, in apt situations, would be superior to those typically ordered by courts in civil cases:

- Apologies.[189] UCLA law professor Richard Abel contends that part of the pain and suffering multiplier by which tort claims are commonly computed is based on compensation for apologies and other recompense which a court cannot directly award.[190]

- Joint custody is a classic example of an alternative to WTA, but at least one court has gone further and ordered divorced spouses to alternate living in the marital residence in order for the children to remain at home.[191] Application can be to disputes involving unique property.[192]

- Plaintiff might be provided with a job instead of money.[193]

- Buyer and seller in a real estate transaction may break an impasse by getting the broker to take a reduced commission.[194] The broker is likely to agree if this will salvage an otherwise doomed deal.

The point is that when the actual needs of the parties are ascertained—rather than converted by their attorneys to impersonal demands for money and/or an injunction—the possible means to mutually acceptable and ultimately more satisfying dispute resolution rise dramatically. By appointing attorneys to represent them in the most adversarial, hard-nosed fashion, disputants forfeit their humanity and individuality vis-a-vis each other. Lost are all the solutions which the natural human sentiments of sympathy and understanding would engender. Also precluded is the capability to discern shared interests and bases for the reconciliation of differences.

A statutory illustration of alternative remedies can be found in business reorganizations under the Bankruptcy Act. Judgment creditors can always force a liquidation of the debtor business. By doing so, they would ordinarily receive only a fraction of their claims, and the business would terminate. Under the Act, creditors of a legally bankrupt but going concern often agree to forestall enforcement of their claims so that the business can continue, possibly under receivership. If the company prospers, more or even all of the creditors' claims will be satisfied. On the other hand, if the business falters, the receivers can always liquidate the company.

Remedies offered by the criminal justice system are similarly deficient. Again, this is because the tunnel vision nature of the adversarial trial ignores the real causes of the problems between victim and offender. Rather, the adversary system superimposes an artificial battle model which precludes any actual analysis of the relationship. The criminal trial further distances victim and offender by substituting the state for the victim as the complainant. Consequently, the victim loses any significant contact with the case other than as a witness for the state if the case goes to trial.

The origin of this disassociation of victim and offender is revealing. It dates to early English history, when crimes were redefined as being against the state rather than against the victim. King Henry II used the ancient Anglo-Saxon concept of a breach of the "King's Peace" to expand the jurisdiction of the royal courts at the expense of the competing ecclesiastic and manorial courts. Prior to Henry, the concept applied only to offenses actually committed in the king's sight or on the highways he controlled.[195] Henry's genius was to broaden it to include almost any kind of criminal offense. Not only was this a political victory, but an economic one as well. Crimes that breached the king's peace were punishable by fines.

How long and to what sacrifice must our present criminal justice system rigidly conform to this hoary model? Chapter 3 noted how the criminal trial alienates and polarizes victim and offender. This precludes any possibility of reconciliation. The result, complains a legal reformer, is the development of attitudes antithetical to responsible social living.

Social responsibility depends upon a capacity to see an identity of interest with a potential adversary, to know how to compromise, to give a little and take a little. If parents taught children how to relate to other children in the way in which the criminal process teaches victims and offenders to respond to one another, social life would become impossible.[196]

Rather than creating artificial barriers between them, victims and offenders should be recognized as the real parties to the conflict. Telling the victims of fraud or theft that these are offenses "against the state" will neither mitigate their injuries nor blunt their sense of personal violation. Distinctions between criminal and civil offenses are often tenuous and legalistic, not based on substantive differences. Frequently, the subject matter of a criminal case and a civil case arises from the same disputes and acts. An assault and battery, for example, is grounds for both criminal and civil actions.

A profoundly different approach may prove preferable in many cases. In recognition of the preexisting relationship between many (if not most) victims and offenders, they should be given the right of first refusal to deal with their problem. Emphasis would be on reconciliation instead of adversarial battle. Government and defense counsel would be encouraged to seek reconciliation instead of confrontation. Their incentives would be based on solving problems instead of winning cases. The criminal justice system as it now operates would be viewed as a back-up. The traditional adversarial trial would be used only when the seriousness of the crime (most likely those involving violence) makes settlement impossible, or when either party feels threatened by less formal mechanisms.[197] Voluntary participation of the parties is most important.

Offenders would have a duty of *restitution* under this approach. (As an equitable counterweight, the victim's role, if any, in contributing to or participating in the crime would be examined.) There is much to recommend a system which obligates offenders to restore their harmed victims rather than spend time in prison.[198]

Not all offenders would be eligible for this victim-offender reconciliation program. Where offenders pose continuing threats to the community, they should be incarcerated. The gravity of the offense is relevant. A burgeoning ADR movement in criminal cases is now afoot in several states, but the cases referred for mediation or arbitration are primarily misdemeanors (more precisely, offenses otherwise eligible for prosecution as misdemeanors). Statutes in California, New York, Connecticut, Florida and Indiana authorize the use of victim-offender reconciliation programs.[199] Misdemeanor-type offenses are most appropriate for these programs because the parties involved are often acquainted, and the difference between victim and offender may be "who gets to the phone first."[200]

Proponents of this concept cite several advantages. The nonadversariality of the process affords the parties the opportunity to work out the underlying problems in a way that would be impossible in a typical trial. Conflicts can be resolved before they escalate into problems more fit for the present criminal justice system. Victims may regain a lost sense of control, restitution and/or an agreement governing future behavior. "Typically, victims feel excluded and ignored," says the director of one program. "We give them a chance to take ownership of the justice process. They feel like someone's listening, and they can get some closure on the offense, both emotionally and in a practical way."[201] The program also offers the offender the opportunity to avoid a criminal record and a chance to right a wrong. As with its civil counterpart, criminal ADR is expeditious and convenient because it occurs outside the courtroom and outside normal business hours. It is free to the users. Taxpayers realize cost savings and the courts experience a needed and welcome workload reduction.

Reforms with inestimable potential benefit to the American criminal justice system issue from the inquisitorial system. None are more valuable than as the model to *mitigate or even eliminate the need for plea bargaining.*[202] I infer "need" rather than preference because the arguments typically justifying plea bargaining are time and cost savings. Although this is not the place to become embroiled in the debate over plea bargaining,[203] its use undeniably subverts the Sixth Amendment right to trial. Eclectic implementation of inquisitorial procedures promises substantial savings of time and money which could be applied toward full adjudication of deserving cases rather than plea bargaining them. Adoption of the mixed jury, for example, would eliminate the extensive time needed for *voir dire*, often longer than the trial.[204] Moreover, the mixed jury removes the need for drafting and reading judicial instructions, as well as the associated time spent by the jurors discussing the meaning of the instructions.

The adoption of other inquisitorial practices could realize even more time and cost savings. Attorney-judge discussions and debates over most evidentiary exclusions would be obviated. Evidence rules would be simpler. Issue-separated trials and judicial ordering of proof and witnesses would allow the consecutive testimonies of opposing witnesses, at once enhancing jury comprehension and facilitating witness scheduling. Issue-separation would truncate many trials and avert time-consuming discovery and discussion of precluded issues. Enhanced juror comprehension would expedite jury decisions. When supplemented by the other time-saving proposals suggested above, such as videotaped testimony and the diversion of minor crimes to alternative fora, adoption of these inquisitorial measures can revivify the dream of full trial for all criminal defendants.

The all-or-nothing, zero-sum, formalistic, procedure-dominated style of the adversary system is antithetical to reaching agreements between disputants. An alternative approach is needed which emphasizes conciliation and compromise. As the dynamics of business and personal relations evolve, the use of adversarial dispute resolution will depend on its adaptability to meet the needs of tomorrow. When circumstances dictate consensus between disputants rather than vindication or victory, two consequences follow: First, more unique solutions will be found; and second, the attorney's role must change dramatically in order to remain useful in these situations. The new Los Angeles Drug Court, for example, charges the prosecutor and defense counsel with the responsibility of working together in a nonadversarial manner. Law schools and the bar are attempting to meet this challenge by teaching nonadversarial dispute resolution. Will this suffice? Can the leopard change its spots simply by changing its hat? (Please forgive the mixed metaphor.) The prognosis is extremely guarded.

We ignore the utility of our remedies unless we periodically reexamine them. Such an inquiry must raise questions which focus on the consequences of trial outcomes. Does the trial remedy in fact approximate a reasonable resolution of the dispute to which it is applied? Mere mechanical observance of prescribed procedure usually will not. Are the litigants satisfied? Money damages, after all, are but substitutes for that which was lost. Many litigants would rather a process which provided the option of mitigating or even eliminating the actual loss itself. The most significant question is, Did the trial remedy (a) ameliorate, (b) worsen or (c) leave unaffected the underlying problem(s)? If answers (b) and/or (c) predominate, the system should be changed.

Law is the handmaiden of justice. But substance, in the sense of substantive trial results, cannot be relegated to being the handmaiden of procedure. The adversary system is just a procedure which all too often rewards those with the most adroit, cunning and ruthless advocates, irrespective of the actual merits and equities of their cases. The battle of the champions thus perseveres. As long as we measure trial justice *solely* by adherence to procedure we perpetuate a profoundly flawed construct of justice. Worse still, we inhibit constructive engagement of our intellects and sensitivities toward more satisfying and salutary dispute resolution.

I do not suggest wholesale adoption of the inquisitorial philosophy that a trial is the vehicle for the implementation of state policy. Instead, I prescribe a departure from our self-imposed enslavement to the principle that (except for the relatively rare jury nullification) procedure is all-important in trial and outcome is irrelevant. We will not compromise the integrity of our trial system if we occasionally drop the blindfold of Justice to avert gross inequities. If we do not, if we continue to abide by a blind, quasi-religious faith in adversary procedure, then the means to justice will have swallowed the ends.

JUDICIAL INTERVENTION: WHY AND HOW

Implementing many of the specific reforms proposed here will clearly require greater judicial involvement. Can, or more properly, should the judge intervene to prevent an injustice created by the way the case is being conducted by one or both of the advocates? Many eminent jurists think so.[205] One of them, Lon Fuller, (a prominent proponent of the adversary system), concludes:

It is the culmination of the efforts of many of our greatest legal thinkers to induce the judges to abandon the passive role of referees at a sporting match and take an active part in the control of litigation. . . . I believe that it is impossible to consider seriously the vital elements of a fair trial without concluding that it is the *duty of the judge*, and the judge alone, as the sole representative of the public interest, to step in at any stage of the litigation where his intervention is necessary in the interests of justice.[206] (Emphasis added.)

Additional authority for judicial intervention exists. After noting that "the adversary process should not be regarded as sacred," the Comments to the ABA's Standards Regulating Special Functions of the Trial Judge urge judicial action "to give the jury the opportunity to decide the case free from irrelevant issues and appeals to passion and prejudice. This includes questioning witnesses to elicit important facts when the case is not being presented intelligibly or when cross-examination appears to be misleading the jury."[207]

Even more extensive measures may be warranted. An illustration arises when a cross-examining attorney uses an especially insidious dirty trick: the presumptuous question loaded with unsupported insinuations. Research mentioned earlier[208] shows that these questions severely diminish the witness' credibility, even when the witness denies the allegation and the judge sustains an objection to the question. By asking presumptuous questions, the cross examining attorney may well be playing a tactical game. Why shouldn't the judge let the jury in on the rules of this game? If so disposed, the judge can partake of several options. Opposing counsel may be given leave to call the cross-examining attorney to the stand to inquire into the "good faith basis" for a specific line of questions.[209] Another approach is to directly caution the jury. The judge can do this during instructions or, if she exercises this authority, when commenting on and summarizing the evidence. Through either, the message is the same: Attorney questions are not evidence; in fact, presumptions contained in their questions may have no factual basis whatsoever.

The adversary system is said to work well only when the presumption of roughly equal competent counsel obtains. But the daily rough-and-tumble of litigation belies this premise. No less a legal personage than former U.S. Supreme Court Justice William Brennan expressed skepticism over its plausibility. He concluded that we "traditionally have resisted any realistic inquiry into the competence of trial counsel, preferring instead to indulge the comfortable fiction that all lawyers are skilled or even competent craftsmen in representing the fundamental rights of their clients."[210] When trial counsel is so incompetent that the client's rights are prejudiced, the adversary process ceases effective functioning. At that point, the judge must choose: She can take over from counsel, or revert to passivity while the case stumbles toward, at best, serendipitous justice. To some judges, the choice is clear. Writes Judge Alfred Gitelson:

One party may be represented by counsel of greater ability, resourcefulness, diligence, salesmanship, and prestige than the other party. One party may be possessed of greater economic means to enable a better biased presentation and preparation than the other party. The only possible equalizer, the only assurance that justice may be done, whether desired by either of the parties, is the trial judge. . . . To aid in seeing that justice be done, he must, even upon his own motion, participate in presenting evidence and determining the facts and the applicable law.[211]

Many stalwarts of the adversary system have advocated judicial intervention to *improve* it.[212] Professor Fleming James explains how judicial intervention can minister to the objectives of the adversary system: "Anything that the law of procedure or the judge's role can do to equalize opportunity and to put a faulty presentation on the right track *so that disputes are more likely to be settled on their merits*, will . . . bolster up rather than destroy the adversary system, and will increase the moral force of the decisions."[213] (Emphasis supplied.)

The best argument for greater judicial intervention may be the lack of acceptable alternatives. When an attorney is incompetent, the injured client can either seek appellate review or sue the incompetent counsel for malpractice. Either requires the services of another attorney; both are inadequate remedies. In neither instance is the court present at the original trial to observe the problems. Furthermore, errors of omission, such as failing to raise a defense, are not reviewable absent a showing of "plain error." As for malpractice suits, they are very difficult to win, especially those spawn from civil cases. The complainant must prove he or she probably would have won, which, in the absence of obvious procedural mistakes like failure to appear, is almost impossible.

One caveat to judicial intervention is that judges can become cynosures. Hence they risk appellate reversal and even censure unless they act with circumspection, forethought and purpose. (Indeed, this is probably why judges do not summarize or comment upon the evidence in jurisdictions which allow it.) To ensure due process, judges must carefully monitor attorney performance, particularly of criminal defense counsel, during the pretrial and trial stages of criminal cases. In pretrial discussions, the judge might guide incompetent counsel by informing them of their obligations, noting deficiencies in the evidence and considering possible defenses. If necessary, the judge can advise the defendant of the right to change counsel or, in extreme cases, appoint substitute counsel. To a lesser degree, judges can also monitor and advise the prosecution. Once in trial, the judge should raise questions of counsel's conduct in chambers or sidebar conferences so as not to prejudice the jury. In sidebar, for example, the judge can ask if counsel intends to question a witness. In some cases, judges should call their own witnesses or declare a mistrial.

Unlike criminal cases, there is no constitutional right to effective counsel in civil cases (and no case has found a Fourteenth Amendment due process right to appointed counsel). It is nevertheless accepted that a judge can intervene when egregious deficiencies appear.[214] The means of intervention are similar to those for criminal cases.

JUDICIAL SELECTION AND RETENTION

If trial judges are to exercise the discretion advocated here, they should be competent and free from political pressure. The system of selection and retention of judges used by most states fosters neither condition. In the vast majority of states, judges must either be elected, stand for retention election, or both. The necessary politics and fundraising of campaigning create a conflict of interest and a loss of judicial independence. Judicial elections require candidates to lobby bar associations and other attorney groups, some of whose members appear before the candidates. These constituents have disproportionate influence, as they are usually the only ones with enough knowledge of or interest in judges to vote in high percentages. But this is hardly the most important drawback of judicial elections. Without lifetime tenure, judges are too sensitive to the pressures of retaining their positions. The ever present danger is that such anxiety may affect their decisions. When cases are tried without a jury, the state judge has no "lightning rod" protection. Public criticism following an unpopular decision may result in a loss of the judge's seat in the next confirmation election, or even a mid-term recall.

All too often, initial judicial appointments are the products of cronyism. As a corollary to greater judicial activism, we should replace the appointment process and judicial elections with merit-based selection, retention and advancement of judges. The ABA supports merit selection of judges at the state level for the initial term because "the elective process . . . is almost completely useless in ensuring adequate judicial qualifications. Far too few members of the electorate have any, let alone substantial, contact with the judiciary to have any reasoned opinion as to whether a judge should be elected, and consequently their vote seldom has real meaning."[215]

Our federal judges and England's judges are appointed for life. Both are usually more respected than our state judges. Continental countries also appoint their judges, but not from the bar. Instead they use a career judiciary, specially trained for the bench. Judges are appointed and promoted through merit evaluations. Thus states have two alternative models (federal and continental) from which to raise the respect, independence and integrity of their judiciaries. If lifetime appointment is necessary to secure the best people for the bench and protect them from possible political fallout from assuming greater leadership roles, then it is a cheap price.

An adjunct to a merit-based judiciary and lifetime appointment would be a continuing education requirement, similar to the continuing legal education requirement of attorneys. These courses would not only focus on procedural law, but judicial administration as well. For example, the National Judicial College trains judges on such diverse subjects as use of contempt power and other sanctions, caseflow and calendar management, and computer uses for judges.[216]

Of all the trial participants, only the judge has an obligation to ensure a fair trial. If we expand the concept of courtroom justice beyond mere adherence to prescribed procedure, judicial intervention becomes justifiable to avoid a miscarriage of justice. If done discreetly, it would preserve rather than undermine the integrity of the adversary process.

CONCLUSION

Public discontent will eventually sow the seeds of reform. This is suggested by the national (Yankelovich) survey discussed in the introductory chapter. It found the public willing to back its high level of concern about court problems with tax dollars. Topping the survey's list of proposed improvements to the justice system for which the public is willing to use taxes are three advocated in this chapter: getting the best possible people to serve as judges (74 percent); making good lawyers available to anyone who needs them (71 percent); and developing ways to settle minor disputes without going through formal court proceedings (66 percent). The study also reported popular support for greater judicial discretion, at least with regard to sentencing. Contrary to expectations, only 11 percent favored determinate sentencing, which requires judges to give the same sentence for the same crime. On the other hand, over 80 percent favored judicial discretion. According to the survey's authors, this suggests a basic confidence in judges.[217]

Reform cannot come too soon. Without it, current trends portend an apocalyptic vision of the court system. Technical advances and the unforeseen but inevitable complications of future life will bring more and more complex cases to juries for resolution. But without change neither the sophistication of lay jurors nor the tools at their disposal will elevate commensurately. As a result, the hiring of expert witnesses, jury consultants and, most importantly, attorneys skilled at jury manipulation will proliferate. A truly just trial may result more despite, rather than because of, the influence these players have on the outcome.

Experts disagree on whether we are experiencing a "litigation explosion."[218] However characterized, court backlog will continue mounting due to the combination of population increase, the exponential rise of drug cases, the creation of more justiciable rights, and insufficient allocation of resources to the courts. Overlaying all this is the historic American propensity to litigate some of the most common disputes rather than conciliate, compromise or seek nonjudicial dispute resolution alternatives. Concomitantly, trial court adjudication will be available to a dwindling portion of civil disputants. The growing time and cost necessary for litigation will ensure that. Few but the wealthy and powerful will have access to the courts.

The adversarial trial and its conventional remedies will become patently unsuitable for a growing number of disputes and problems. Businesses and individuals will look increasingly to alternative forms of justice. But any such alternatives will lack the cherished traditional virtues of trial court dispute resolution—constitutional due process protections and precedent developed through judicial reasoning.

What is prevalent is not necessarily what is functional or fair. We must be chary of a misplaced complacency that our trial procedures are optimal, and therefore inviolable. The adversary system is not sacrosanct. By eschewing labels, we can bring to our table the option to adopt the best features of foreign systems. Several other reforms—some founded on social science empiricism, others on common sense—hold great promise for improved trial dispute resolution.

With all its flaws, the adversary system endures relatively unreconstructed because of vested interests in maintaining the *status quo*. It would betray great naivete to deny that. Most saliently, the litigation bar staunchly resists any fundamental change in a system it regards as hallowed ground. Prosperity, prestige and power are reluctantly relinquished. Walter Olson warns:

[T]he litigation industry has not simply sat back to enjoy the billions that have rolled in from its extraordinarily lucrative trade. It has shrewdly invested its newfound wealth and power in the currency of political and ideological influence. . . . [Attorneys'] profound and wide-ranging power can no longer be denied. In state legislatures across the country, as well as in the U.S. Congress, they sit astride key committees that determine whether and how the legal system will be reformed. . . . The power of the litigation industry is likewise felt strongly in the realm of ideas and ideologies. Plaintiff's lawyers swarm into movements for social reform of all sorts. . . . And although these lawyers claim to be the tribunes of all the put-upon underdogs of the world, they have every motive to sabotage proposals, however advantageous to those underdogs in other respects, that threaten to shut down their own cash machine.[219]

Trial attorneys profitably control the adversary system from within. We cannot expect them, individually or collectively, to change their behavior or reform the system which serves them so well. That, in large measure, would be asking them to fall on their swords. We ask few others to make such sacrifice—even for the common good. Hence exhorting trial attorneys to be less adversarial or more forthcoming or to seek justice even at the expense of their own interests is ill-conceived and inevitably futile.

Nevertheless, to do nothing is a most consequential choice. It is to perpetuate a costly and dysfunctional system whose ancient moorings have been partly or totally discarded by all other advanced nations. Lincoln said that when the dogmas of the past are inadequate to the present, it is time to think and act anew.[220] That wisdom was never more apt than now. Lasting change requires vision and leadership. It remains mainly for courageous judges, but also legislators and community spokespersons to break with tradition and reform the trial system in the interests of justice and efficiency.

In 1984, Warren Burger, then Chief Justice of the United States, said: "Trials by the adversarial contest must in time go the way of the ancient trial by battle and blood. Our system is too costly, too painful, too destructive, too inefficient for a truly civilized people."[221] Burger was right. We deserve better.

NOTES

1. Quoted by V.Corsetti, *Nolo News*, Spring 1987, p. 10.
2. ABA, *Model Rules of Professional Conduct* (Chicago: Author, 1989), pp. 5, 15.
3. Franklin Strier, "Through The Jurors' Eyes," *ABA Journal, 74* (October 1988), p. 80.
4. Continental attorneys have the same restriction on witness interviews.

5. In practice, there is no "pure" adversarial or nonadversarial system. Much of the continental system is adversarial, while much of ours in nonadversarial, e.g., plea bargaining.

6. Werner Pfennigstorf and Donald Gifford, *A Comparative Study of Liability Law and Compensation Schemes in Ten Countries and the United States* (Oak Brook, Ill.: Insurance Research Council, 1991), p. 158.

7. Id., p. 158.

8. Id., p. 132.

9. Id., pp. 27, 157.

10. Id., p. 80.

11. See the related discussion in Chapter 4.

12. The data are somewhat inconsistent, but civil litigation rates have increased steadily in recent years. Pfennigstorf and Gifford, *op. cit.*, p. 46. Whether we are experiencing a "litigation explosion," as many claim, continues to be the subject of spirited debate.

13. Id., p. 150.

14. See the related discussion in Chapter 3.

15. G. Thomas Munsterman *et al.*, *Methodology Manual for Jury Systems* (Williamsburg, Virg.: National Center for State Courts, 1981), p. 5-3.

16. Id., p. 5-5.

17. Victor Flango, "Would Jurors Do a Better Job if They Could Take Notes?" *Judicature, 63(9)* (1980), pp. 436-443.

18. Michael Wolff, *"Juror Questions: A Survey of Theory and Use,"* 55 *Missouri Law Review* 817 (1990).

19. Leonard Sand and Steven Reiss, "A Report on Seven Experiments Conducted by District Court Judges in the Second Circuit," 60 *New York University Law Review* 423 (1985); *Wisconsin Judicial Council, Committee on Improving Jury Communications, Final Report* (Madison: State of Wisconsin, Judicial Council, 1985).

20. Larry Heuer and Steven Penrod, "Increasing Jurors' Participation in Trials," *Law and Human Behavior, 12(3)* (1988). pp. 231-259.

21. Id., pp. 233, 252.

22. L. Sarokin and T. Munsterman, "Recent Innovations in Civil Jury Trial Procedures," paper presented at the Brookings Institute/ABA Symposium on the Future of the Civil Jury System in the United States, Charlottesville, Virginia, June 18-21, 1992, p. 20.

23. David Strawn and G. Thomas Munsterman, "Helping Juries Handle Complex Cases," 65 *Judicature* 444, 445 (1982); *Manual For Complex Litigation Second*, Sec.22.433 (New York: C. Boardman, 1986).

24. Stephen Saltzburg, "Improving the Quality of Jury Decisionmaking," paper presented at the Brookings Institute/ABA Symposium on the Future of the Civil Jury System in the United States, Charlottesville, Virginia, June 18-21, 1992, pp. 38-40.

25. 609 *F.2d* 411 (1979).
26. This was allowed in *SCM Corp. v. Xerox Corp.*, 77 *F.R.D.* 10, 15 (D. Conn. 1977) (pretrial ruling). See also Rule 53(d) of the *Uniform Rules of Criminal Procedure*.
27. James McCrystal and James Young, "Pre-Recorded Videotape Trials—An Ohio Innovation," 39 *Brooklyn Law Review* 560, 663-64 (1973).
28. Marvin Frankel, "From Private Fights Toward Public Justice," 57 *New York University Law Review* 516, 534 (1976).
29. See, e.g., Sand and Reiss, *op. cit.* Also suggesting the value of written jury instructions are the findings of educational and cognitive psychological research. Several researchers found that students comprehend and retain material much better when given written texts than when simply given lectures. Kenneth Beighly, "An Experimental Study of the Effect of Four Speech Variables on Listener Comprehension," *Speech Monographs, 19* (1952), p. 249; Stephen Corey, "Learning From Lectures and Learning From Reading," *Journal of Educational Psychology, 25* (1934), p. 459; Howard Siegal, "McLuhan—Mass Media—And Education," *Journal of Experimental Education, 41* (1973), p. 68.
30. Robert Forston, "Sense and Nonsense: Jury Trial Communication," 1975 *Brigham Young University Law Review* 601 (1975).
31. *New York State Bar Association Report of the Committee on Federal Courts—Improving Jury Comprehension in Complex Civil Litigation* (Albany, N.Y.: New York State Bar Association, 1988), p. 28.
32. *Ninth Circuit Judicial Council Survey of Jurors' Attitudes* (1986), p. 9.
33. William Schwarzer, "Reforming Jury Trials," 132 *F.R.D.* 575 at 583 (1991).
34. Phoebe Ellsworth, "Are Twelve Heads Better Than One?" *Law and Contemporary Problems, 52(4)* (Autumn 1989), pp. 205-224.
35. Forston, *op. cit.*, p. 612.
36. Vicki L. Smith, "The Psychological and Legal Implications of Pretrial Instruction in the Law," (doctoral dissertation, Stanford University, 1987) in *Dissertation Abstracts International* (1987), p. 48.
37. See the related discussion in Chapter 4.
38. Curtis Bok, *I, Too, Nicodemus* (New York: Alfred A. Knopf, 1946), pp. 261-62.
39. See the related discussion in Chapter 4.
40. Alan Raifman, Spencer Gusick, and Phoebe Ellsworth, "Real Jurors' Understanding of the Law in Real Cases," *Law and Human Behavior, 16(5)* (October 1992), pp. 539, 553.
41. Amiram Elwork, Bruce Sales and James Alfini, "Juridic Decisions: In Ignorance of the Law or in Light of it?" *Law and Human Behavior, 1(2)* (1977), pp. 163-189; Amiram Elwork *et al.*, *Making Jury Instructions Understandable* (Charlottesville, Virg.: Michie Co., 1982).

42. *Mitchell v. Gonzalez*, 819 *P.2d* 872 (1991).
43. L. Severance and E. Loftus, "Improving the ability of jurors to comprehend and apply criminal jury instructions," *Law and Society Review, 17* (1982), pp. 153-197.
44. See the related discussion in Chapters 3 and 4.
45. Federal Rules of Evidence, Rule 403.
46. Lisa Eichhorn, "Social Science Findings and the Jury's Ability to Disregard Evidence Under the Federal Rules of Evidence," *Law and Contemporary Problems, 52(4)* (Autumn 1989), p. 341; S. Diamond, J. Casper and L. Ostergren, "Blindfolding the Jury," *Law and Contemporary Problems*, *52(4)* (Autumn 1989), p. 247.
47. S. Diamond *et al.*, *op. cit.*, p. 267.
48. Evidence admitted is subject to appeals for "factual error." Mirjan Damaska, *The Faces of Justice and State Authority* (New Haven, Conn.: Yale University Press, 1986), p. 55.
49. Jeremy Bentham, *Rationale of Judicial Evidence* (New York: Garland Publishing, Inc., 1978), pp. 407-410 (1827 facsimile; London: Hunt and Clark.)
50. Model Code of Evidence, Rule 503(a) (1942).
51. See the related discussion in Chapter 5.
52. Albert Alschuler, "Implementing the Criminal Defendant's Right to Trial: Alternatives to Plea Bargaining," 50(3) *University of Chicago Law Review* 931, 1020-21 (1983).
53. In England, however, the judge may invite the jury to give less weight to an account the defendant gives for the first time at trial, and to give special weight to prosecution evidence that the defendant failed to answer questions before. While the same proscription against adverse inferences applies in continental courts, there is no principle analogous to the Anglo-American privilege not to take the stand. As with the English caveat, this also acts as a disincentive to silence.
54. There is always the possibility that an appellate court would reverse and remand, necessitating trial of the issues not presented to the jury. The relatively low likelihood of this, however, should not preclude terminating deliberations once the jury made a dispositive decision.
55. Louis Harris and Associates, *Judges Opinions on Procedural Issues* (April 1986), p. 6.
56. John Langbein, "The German Advantage in Civil Procedure," *82(4) University of Chicago Law Review* 821, 831 (Fall 1985).
57. D. Hensler *et al.*, *Asbestos in the courts: The challenge of mass toxic torts* (Santa Monica, Calif.: Rand Corporation Institute for Civil Justice, 1985).
58. I. Horowitz and K. Bordens, "An Experimental Investigation of Procedural Issues in Complex Tort trials," *Law & Human Behavior, 14(3)* (June 1990), pp. 269 at 271.

59. Schwarzer, *op. cit.*, p. 595.

60. FRCP, 42(b).

61. Harris, *op. cit.*, p. 6. Earlier research found a 20 percent savings by separating liability and damages into separate trials. Hans Zeisel and Thomas Callahan, "Split Trials and Time Savings: A Statistical Analysis," 76 *Harvard Law Review* 1606, 1619 (1963).

62. Judith Resnik, "Managerial Judges," 96 *Harvard Law Review* 376-445 (1982).

63. T. Feldman and R. Bell, "Crisis Debriefing of a Jury After a Murder Trial," *Hospital and Community Psychiatry*, Vol.79 (1991).

64. Massachusetts requires employers to pay jurors for the first three days.

65. A review of prior research yields little comparable data. Studies of both mock and actual jurors commonly measure juror education level and other demographic variables. For example, both mock (see, generally, Ruth Simon, *The Jury and the Defense of Insanity* [Boston: Little, Brown and Co., 1967]) and actual (J. P. Reed, "Jury Deliberations, Voting and Verdict Trends," *The Southwestern Social Science Quarterly* [1965], pps. 45, 361-370) trials found that better-educated jurors were more likely to vote guilty than poorer-educated jurors. Other studies have examined the effect on jurors (irrespective of education level) of various aspects of attorney performance, including jury selection strategy (Hans Zeisel, *American Jury System* [Washington, D.C.: Roscoe Pound Foundation, 1971], p. 78 ff; Wallace Loh, *Social Research in the Judicial Process* [New York: Russel Sage Foundation, 1984], p. 505), opening speeches (a frequently cited statistic from the University of Chicago Jury Project is that 80 percent of the time jurors do not change their mind after hearing the opening statement. David Shrager, *Opening Statement on Behalf of Plaintiff* [Washington, D.C.: Roscoe Pound Foundation, undated], p. 1; contra, John Guinther, *The Jury in America* [New York: Facts on File, 1988], p. 61), closing speeches (Malthon Anapol, "Behind Closed Doors," *The Barrister*, *4(4)* [1973], p. 10), interruptions and other trial tactics (Harry Kalven, Jr. and Hans Zeisel, *The American Jury* [Chicago: University of Chicago Press, 1971], p. 114; William O'Barr, *Language, Power and Strategy in the Courtroom* [New York: Academic Press, 1982], pps. 79-81; Amiram Elwork, Bruce Sales and David Suggs, "The Trial: A Research Review," in Bruce Sales, ed., *The Trial Process* [New York: PLenum Press, 1981], p. 36). Only one major survey of actual jurors tested various attorney performance factors by juror education level, but the results were inconclusive (Guinther, *op. cit.*, p. 61).

66. R. Charrow and V. Charrow, "Making legal language understandable: A psycholinguistic study of jury instructions," 79 *Columbia Law Review* 1306, 1320 (1979).

67. See, e.g., Lee Sutton, "A More Rational Approach to Complex Civil Litigation in the Federal Courts: The Special Jury," *University of Chicago Legal Foundation* (1990); Joe Cecil, Valerie Hans and Elizabeth Wiggins, "Citizens' Comprehension of Different Issues: Lessons From Civil Jury Trials," 40 *American University Law Review* 727, 773 (1991).

68. See Robert Gagne, *The Conditions Of Learning*, 2d ed. (New York: Holt, Rinehart & Winston, 1970), pp. 333-334.

69. See James Marshall, *Law and Psychology in Conflict*, 2d ed. (New York: Bobbs-Merrill, 1980), pp. 59-100.

70. Franklin Strier, "Is Your Jury Smart Enough?" *Barrister, 18(2)* (Summer 1991), p. 9.

71. This issue takes on special significance in light of the secrecy of the general verdict. Jurors do not have to explain their findings or reasoning, however questionable either might appear upon scrutiny.

72. R. M. James, "Status and Competence of Jurors," *The American Journal of Sociology* (1959), pp. 64, 563-570.

73. Outside of the United States and England (where, as noted, civil juries have all but been abolished), there are no lay jury parallels with other major industrial countries. That is not to say lay participation in factfinding is not valued. In continental Europe, it is felt that factfinding is too important to entrust to a *fully* lay jury; thus laymen participate as part of a mixed professional and lay bench. See Karl Kunert, "Some Observations on the Origin and Structure of Evidence Rules Under the Common Law System and the Civil Law System of 'Free Proof' in the German Code of Civil Procedure," 16 *Buffalo Law Review* 122, 163 (1967).

74. 28 *United States Code* Sec.1861.

75. W. Luneberg & M. Nordenberg, "Specially Qualified Juries and Expert Nonjury Tribunals," 67 *Virginia Law Review* 887 (1981).

76. Although most technically complex cases are civil, there is no reason to distinguish them from equally difficult criminal cases. For an illustrative discussion of the jury's confusion over medical and legal terminology which led to a mistrial of the last McMartin Preschool molestation case, see Carol McGraw, "In the End, Jury Gave In to Confusion," *Los Angeles Times*, 7/28/90, pp. 1, 30. It should be noted also that the jury trial requirement for criminal cases under the Sixth Amendment is completely distinct from its Seventh Amendment civil counterpart. Consequently, no similarity of treatment can be inferred from court pronouncements interpreting the Seventh Amendment.

77. T. Markey, "A Forum for Technocracy: A Report on the Science Court Proposal," *Judicature* 60 (1977), pp. 365-371.

78. Id., p. 367.

79. Harris, *op. cit.*, pp. 76-82.

80.   See the related discussion in Chapter 4.

81.   Learned Hand, "The Deficiencies of Trials to Reach the Heart of the Matter," in *Lectures on Legal Topics, 1925-1926*, Vol. 3 (New York: MacMillan Company, 1929), p. 89.

82.   See, e.g., Mark Brodin, "Accuracy, Efficiency, and Accountability in the Litigation Process—The Case for the Fact Verdict," 59 *Cincinnati Law Review* 15-16 (1990) ("the jury has become part of the national folklore" although concerns remain "regarding decision-making by amateurs").

83.   See, generally, National Center For State Courts, *On Trial: The Length of Civil and Criminal Trials* (Williamsburg, Virg.: Author, 1988).

84.   Alschuler, *op. cit.*, p. 999.

85.   John Langbein, "Mixed Court and Jury Court: Could the Continental Alternative Fill the American Need?" 1981 *American Bar Foundation Research Journal* 195, 203 (1981).

86.   Gerhard Casper and Hans Zeisel, "Lay Judges in German Criminal Courts," 1 *Journal of Legal Studies* 135 *et seq.* (1972). But cf. Mirjan Damaska, "Structures of Authority and Comparative Criminal Procedure," 84 *Yale Law Journal* 480 (1975), where studies suggest a limited influence of lay judges on decision making in mixed panels.

87.   *Sellars v. U.S.*, 401 *A.2d* 974 (1979).

88.   Justin Stanley, "The Resolution of Minor Disputes and the Seventh Amendment," 60 *Marquette Law Review* 963 (1977).

89.   Reid Hastie, Steven Penrod and Nancy Pennington, *Inside the Jury* (Cambridge, Mass.: Harvard University Press, 1983), pp. 163-65.

90.   *Id.*, p. 165.

91.   Secret ballots would lessen the coercion. However, there is no agreement on how often juries employ the secret ballot. Moreover, it tends to be abandoned when there is continuing disagreement. C. Hawkins, "Interaction rate of jurors aligned in factions," *American Sociological Review*, *27* (1962), pp. 38-56.

92.   Guinther, *op. cit.*, p. 85.

93.   Id., p. 84.

94.   Id., p. 88.

95.   Penelope McMillan, "Jury Awards Man $25 Million in Health Insurance Fraud Case," *Los Angeles Times*, 10/2/93, B1.

96.   Pfennigstorf and Gifford, *op. cit.*, pp. 26, 76, 78.

97.   Both are authorized under FRCP Rule 49.

98.   Larry Heuer and Steven Penrod, "Trial Complexity: A Field Investigation of Its Meaning and Its Effects," *Law and Human Behavior, 18(1)* (February 1994), pp. 29 at 50.

99.   For a historical review and discussion of jury lawlessness, see A. Scheflin and J. Van Dyke, "Jury nullification: The contours of a controversy," *Law and Contemporary Problems*, *4* (1980), pp. 52-115; Mortimer Kadish and

Sanford Kadish, *Discretion to Disobey* (Stanford, Calif.: Stanford University Press, 1973); and C. Rembar, *The Law of the Land* (New York: Simon and Schuster, 1980).

100. See the related discussion in Chapter 4.

101. Langbein, "Mixed Court and Jury Court," *op. cit.*, p. 213.

102. FRCP, Rule 49(b).

103. See related discussion in Chapter 4.

104. See the related discussion in Chapter 2.

105. George Priest, "Justifying the Civil Jury," paper presented at the ABA/Brookings Institute Symposium on the Future of the Civil Jury System in the United States, Charlottesville, Virginia, June 18-21, 1992, p. 15. If within either of these categories Priest would include multidimensional, multiparty cases involving complex public policy or program issues, then I beg to differ with the good professor. I think these cases are unsuitable for adversarial dispute resolution, and thus for jury determination. Priest also included de Tocqueville's justification that jury service provides an involuntary civic education to citizens. That is omitted here because changed conditions render it largely obsolete. For example, civics is traditionally taught in elementary schools, a phenomenon undoubtedly inconceivable to de Tocqueville, in whose time democracy remained mostly a theory in a country with few sources of formal education.

106. George Priest, *op. cit.*, p. 34.

107. See the related discussion in Chapter 4.

108. Priest, *op. cit.*, pp. 40-41.

109. Jerome Frank, *Law and the Modern Mind* (Garden City, NY: Doubleday, 1930), p. 187.

110. Priest, *op. cit.*, p. 5.

111. See the related discussion in Chapter 4.

112. Harris, *op. cit.*, p. 83.

113. "Will the Real Janet Reno Please Stand Up?" *Los Angeles Times*, 3/21/94, p. B6.

114. Don Edwards, "Federal Courts Are Casualties in War on Drugs," *L.A. Times*, 10/25/93, B7.

115. "Will the Real Janet Reno Please Stand Up?" *op. cit.*

116. Id.

117. Charles Lindner, "Cost of Death: A Billion Dollars and Counting," *Los Angeles Times*, 8/29/93, M1, M3.

118. Id.

119. Id., M1.

120. Id., M3.

121. Id.

122. Saltzburg, *op. cit*,. p. 14.

123. Quoted in Howard Cabot, "Judges Can Break the Siege Through Rule 611," *Los Angeles Daily Journal*, 9/12/91, p. 7.
124. Howard Cabot, "Breaking the Siege: Protecting the System Through Rule 611," *Arizona Attorney*, 5/27/92, p. 18.
125. California Evidence Code, section 325.
126. Marvin Frankel, "The Search for Truth: An Umpireal View," 123 *University of Pennsylvania Law Review* 1031 (1975).
127. For an informative discussion of discovery abuse, see Wayne Brazil, "The Adversary Character of Civil Discovery: Critique and Proposals for Change," 31 *Vanderbilt Law Review* 1295 (1978).
128. Alfred Cortese, Jr., and Kathleen Blaner, "A Change In the Rules Draws Fire," *National Law Journal*, 10/18/93, pp. 25 at 26.
129. *ABA Blueprint for Improving the Civil justice System* (Chicago: ABA, 1992), p. 70.
130. Id., p. 71.
131. Quoted in J. Rosen, "Jurymandering," *The New Republic*, 11/30/92, p. 15.
132. Hans Zeisel and Shari Diamond, "The Effect of Peremptory Challenges on Jury and Verdict," 30 *Stanford Law Review* 491 at 519, 529 (1978).
133. *Batson v. Kentucky*, 476 *U.S.* 79 (1986) (prosecutors violate a defendant's equal protection rights when they strike potential jurors solely because of their race); *Powers v. Ohio*, 113 *Sup. Ct.* 1364 (1991) (criminal defendants can challenge race-based strikes of potential jurors not of the same race as the defendant); *Edmonson v. Leesville Concrete Co.*, 111 *Sup. Ct.* 2077 (1991) (race-based peremptory challenges in civil cases are prohibited); *Georgia v. McCollum*, 112 *Sup. Ct.* 2348 (1992) (criminal defense lawyers as well as prosecutors cannot use race-based strikes).
134. *J.E.B. v. Alabama*, 92-1239 (1994).
135. Richard Lempert, "Civil Juries and Complex Cases: Taking Stock After Twelve Years," paper presented at the Brookings Institute/ABA Symposium, The Future of the Jury System in the United States, June 18-21, 1992 (Charlottesville, Virg.), p. 74.
136. Gordon Bermant and John Shepard, *The Voir Dire Examination, Juror Challenges, and Adversary Advocacy* (Washington, D.C.: Federal Judicial Center, 1978), reprinted from Bruce Sales, ed., *The Trial Process* (New York: Plenum Publishing, 1981), p. 87.
137. Irving Kaufman, "Verdict on Juries," *New York Times Magazine*, 4/1/84, p. 48.
138. In a famous critique, former Chief Justice Warren Burger decried the lack of skills among trial advocates. Among other inadequacies, he scored the lack of skill in direct and cross-examination, and the time wasted in developing irrelevant facts. Warren Burger, "The special skills of

advocacy: Are special training and certification of advocates essential to our system of justice?" 1973 *Fordham Law Review* 42, 227 (1973).

139. Daniel Meador, *Criminal Appeals: English Practices and American Reforms* (Charlottesville, Virg.: University Press of Virginia, 1973), p. 112.

140. *ABA Standards for Criminal Justice: The Prosecution Function* (Washington, D.C.: ABA, 1971), p. 20.

141. LEAA Discretionary Grant No. 75DF-99-0054, Project Narrative, at 1.

142. James Cameron, "The English Barrister System and the American Criminal Law: A Proposal for Experimentation," 23 *Arizona Law Review* 991, 1008 (1981).

143. Id., p. 1002.

144. Strier, "Through The Jurors' Eyes," *op. cit.*, p. 80.

145. Neil Brooks, "The Judge and the Adversary System," presented at the Conference on the Canadian Judiciary (Toronto: Osgood Hall Law School of York University, 1976), p. 111.

146. The adversarial palliative to witness-coaching, cross-examination, is often nugatory. Even proponents of the adversary system concede that cross-examination may be inadequate to undo the effects of coaching. Stephan Landsman, "Reforming the Adversary Procedure: A Proposal Concerning the Psychology of Memory and the Testimony of Disinterested Witnesses," 45 *University of Pittsburgh Law Review* 547, 570-71 (1984). Moreover, cross-examination may be the source of fresh distortion.

147. Langbein, "Mixed Court and Jury Court," *op. cit.*, p. 835.

148. Id., p. 833.

149. Id.

150. According to figures compiled in 1980 by the National Center for State Courts, the breakdown was as follows. In criminal cases, nineteen states gave the attorneys primary control subject to judicial control only for abuse, 12 states gave the judge unfettered control and 19 states divided control between judge and attorneys. In civil cases, 21 states had attorney-controlled voir dire, 17 gave complete control to the judge and 12 used mixed control. John Riley, "Voir Dire Debate Escalates Over Lawyers' Participation," *National Law Journal*, 12/24/84, pp. 23-24.

151. Alschuler, *op. cit.*, p. 1005.

152. Jack B. Weinstein and Margaret Berger, *op. cit.*, p. 706-12 ; S. Feinberg, ed., *The Evolving Role of Statistical Assessments as Evidence in the Courts* (New York: Springer-Verlag, 1989); T. Willging, *Court-Appointed Experts* (Washington, D.C.: Federal Judicial Center, 1986).

153. *Federal Rules of Evidence,* Rule 706, advisory committee note.

154. Langbein, "Mixed Court and Jury Court," *op. cit.*, pp. 835-839.

155. Harris, *op. cit.*, pp. 44, 52, 53.

156. Strier, "Through The Jurors' Eyes," *op. cit.*, p. 80.

157. For a discussion of the possibilities in detail, see Jack Weinstein, "The Power and Duty of Federal Judges to Marshall and Comment on Evidence in Jury Trials and Some Suggestions on Charging Juries," 118 *F.R.D.* 161 (1988).

158. William Schwarzer, "Reforming Jury Trials," 132 *FRD* 575,585 (1991).

159. It is not altogether clear that redistribution of legal services will achieve either formal or social justice. See Richard Abel, "Socializing the Legal Profession: Can Redistributing Lawyers' Services Achieve Social Justice?" *Law and Policy Quarterly, 1* (1979), pp. 5-51.

160. *ABA Blueprint, op. cit.*, p. 21.

161. Id. Of course, any proposal to reallocate public funds is ultimately a political issue not well served by brief discussion. I leave that to another time and forum.

162. Charley Roberts, "LSC Board Votes to Seek a Large Budget Increase," *Los Angeles Daily Journal,* 2/1/93, p. 1.

163. MRPC, Rule 6.1.

164. *ABA Blueprint, op. cit.*, p. 23.

165. Talbot D'Alemberte, "Lawyers Have a Duty to Serve the Poor," *The Judges Journal, 31(3)* (Summer 1992), pp. 19 at 21.

166. Id., p. 37.

167. J. C. Monks, "Toward Justice For All," *Los Angeles Daily Journal,* 3/24/93, p. 6.

168. ABA, *Revised Handbook on Prepaid Legal Services: Papers and Documents Assembled by the Special Committee on Prepaid Legal Services,* 2d edition (Chicago: ABA, 1972), p. 2.

169. *Id.*, p. 28.

170. This conclusion is drawn from my experience in both capacities—first as a CPA in the tax departments of two of the "Big Six" CPA firms; later as a corporate tax counsel.

171. Jake Warner, "More Access, Not More Lawyers," *Nolo News* (Winter 1987), p. 9.

172. See, e.g., David Hapgood, *The Screwing of the Average Man* (New York: Doubleday, Bantam ed., 1982), p. 82.

173. The enactment by a few states of no-fault car insurance is another illustration of legislative preemption of litigation. So too is the federal statute which bars veterans from court review of Veterans Administration decisions.

174. See the related discussion in Chapter 6.

175. See the related discussion in Chapter 6.

176. See the related discussion in Chapter 5.

177. Ira Pilchen, "The future of the courts: a perspective from Illinois," *Judicature, 76(3)* (October-November 1992), p. 137 at 144.

178. See Carrie Menkel-Meadow, "Pursuing Settlement in an Adversary

Culture: A Tale of Innovation Co-opted or 'The Law of ADR'," 19(1) *Florida State University Law Review* 1, 17 (1991).

179. Id., p. 32.

180. For a more elaborate disquisition on the use of different judges for pretrial conciliation and trial adjudication, see Albert Alschuler, "Mediation With a Mugger: The Shortage of Adjudicative Services and the Need for a Two-Tier Trial System in Civil Cases," 99 *Harvard Law Review* 1808, 1836-38 (1986).

181. Linda Silberman, "Masters and Magistrates: The English Model," 56 *New York University Law Review* 1070, 1079-1105 (1975).

182. Alschuler, "Mediation With a Mugger," *op. cit.*, pp. 1838-39.

183. Menkel-Meadow, *op. cit.*, p. 40.

184. John Coons, "Approaches to Court-Imposed Compromise—The Use of Doubt and Reason," 58 *Northwestern University Law Review* 750 at 751 (1964).

185. Id.

186. Menkel-Meadow, "Toward Another View of Legal Negotiation," 31 *UCLA Law Review* 754, 758 (1984).

187. Id., pps. 772-775. This example, based on teaching materials from the Legal Services Corporation, is used by Menkel-Meadow to demonstrate nonadversarial *negotiation* techniques. Application to trials is the next logical step.

188. He would also be entitled to additional expenses incurred to obtain payment, such as attorney and collection fees.

189. Menkel-Meadows, "Toward Another View of Legal Negotiation," *op. cit.*, p. 805.

190. Richard Abel, "A Critique of American Tort Law," 8 *British Journal of Law and Society* 199 (1981).

191. *Church v. Church*, 8 *Family Law Reporter* 2252 (Mich. Cir. Court, 1981).

192. Menkel-Meadow, "Toward Another View of Legal Negotiation," *op. cit.*, p. 806.

193. Id., p. 810.

194. Id., p. 811.

195. Sir Frederick Pollock and Frederic Maitland, *The History of English Law*, Vol. 2 (Cambridge: Cambridge University Press, 1895), pp. 44-45.

196. John Hogarth, "Alternatives to the Adversary System," in *Studies on Sentencing* (Ottawa, Canada: Law Reform Commission of Canada, 1974), p. 56.

197. Id., pp. 82-83.

198. Ordinarily, the two are mutually exclusive. Too often prisons are graduate schools of applied criminal behavior, not places of rehabilitation. Whatever their benefits, prisons have two drawbacks: They are expensive, and they inhibit or prevent the prisoner from making restitution.

199. State Bar of California, "Criminal Mediation: A Concept Whose Time Has Come," *California Lawyer*, *12(12)* (December 1992), pp. 68-70.

200. Id., p. 69.

201. Id., p. 70.

202. Plea bargaining is virtually absent in inquisitorial system countries. See the related discussion in Chapter 6. Even in common law countries, it is used far more sparingly. See Alschuler, "Implementing the Criminal Defendant's Right to Trial, " *op. cit.*, pp. 972-76.

203. For a brief discussion of the pros and cons, see Chapter 6.

204. Skeptics contend that the mixed jury might be unconstitutional. But it has been cogently argued from U.S. Supreme Court dicta that adoption of mixed courts at the *state* level would not contravene the right to jury trial; indeed, it would provide greater constitutional protection than now afforded from plea bargaining and bench trials. See Alschuler, "Implementing the Criminal Defendant's Right to Trial," *op. cit.*, pp. 995-98.

205. See the authorities cited in Brooks, *op. cit.*

206. Lon Fuller, "The Adversary System," in Harold Berman, ed., *Talks on American Law* (New York: Vintage Books, 1961), p. 45.

207. "Special Functions of the Trial Judge" comment to Standard 6-1.1(a) in *ABA Standing Committee on Association Standards for Criminal Justice*, 2d ed. (Boston: Little, Brown, 1986). But it goes on (schizophrenically) to warn against judicial intervention which intrudes upon the traditional adversary process: "The judge should be aware that there may be a greater risk of prejudice from overintervention than underintervention. . . . The judge should avoid trying the case for the lawyers." *Id.*

208. See the discussion in Chapter 5.

209. *U.S. v. Pugliese*, 152 *F.2d* 497 (1945); *U.S. v. Cardarella*, 570 *F.2d* 264 (1978).

210. *Wainright v. Sykes*, 433 *U.S.* 72, 117-18 (1977) (Justice William Brennan, dissenting).

211. Alfred Gitelson and Bruce Gitelson, "A Trial Judge's Credo Must Include His Affirmative Duty To Be An Instrumentality of Justice," 7 *Santa Clara Lawyer* 7 at 8 (1966).

212. See Chapter 3.

213. Fleming James, *Civil Procedure* (Boston: Little, Brown, 1965), p. 7.

214. In some cases, there is an express obligation to do so, e.g., cases involving minors or absent parties, such as members of a class suit.

215. *ABA Blueprint*, *op. cit.*, p. 9.

216. Id., p. 10.

217. Yankelovich, Skelly and White, Inc., *The Public Image of the Courts: Highlights of a National Survey of the General Public, Judges, Lawyers,*

and Community Leaders (Williamsburg, Virg.: National Center for State Courts, 1978), pp. 2, 29.

218. For a view contending we are in the midst of a litigation explosion, see Walter Olson, *The Litigation Explosion* (New York: Dutton, 1991); contra, see Marc Galanter, "Reading the Landscape of Disputes: What We Know and Don't Know (and Think We Know) About Our Allegedly Contentious and Litigious Society," 31(4) *UCLA Law Review* 4 (1983).

219. Olson, *op. cit.*, pp. 300-301.

220. Second annual message to Congress, December 1, 1862.

221. Burger's remarks were given at the 1984 midyear meeting of the ABA. See J. Carnaham, "What Chief Justice Burger Had to Say," in *Ohio Bar Association Report* (1984).

SELECTED BIBLIOGRAPHY

Auerbach, Jerold, *Unequal Justice* (New York: Oxford University Press, 1976).

Brazil, Wayne, The Adversary Character of Civil Discovery: Critique and Proposals for Change," 31 *Vanderbilt Law Review* 1295 (1978).

Brooks, Neil, "The Judge and the Adversary System," presented at the Conference on the Canadian Judiciary, Toronto (1976), p. 89.

Cratsley, John, Community Courts: Offering Alternative Dispute Resolution Within the Judicial System," 3 *Vermont Law Review* 1 (1978).

Damaska, Mirjan, *The Faces of Justice and State Authority* (New Haven: Yale University Press, 1986).

Fisher, Roger and William Ury, *Getting To Yes* (New York: Penguin Books, 1983).

Fiss, Owen, "Against Settlement," 93 *Yale Law Journal* 1073 (1984).

Frank, Jerome, *Courts On Trial: Myth and Reality in American Justice* (Princeton: Princeton University Press, 1949).

Frankel, Marvin, *Partisan Justice* (New York: Hill and Wang, 1978).

————————, "The Search for Truth: An Umpireal View," 123 *University of Pennsylvania Law Review* 1031 (1975).

Freedman, Monroe, *Lawyers' Ethics in an Adversary System* (Indianapolis: Bobbs-Merrill, 1975).

Galanter, Marc, "Reading the Landscape of Disputes: What We Know and Don't Know (And Think We Know) About Our Allegedly Contentious and Litigious Society," 31 *UCLA Law Review* 4 (1983).

Goldberg, Stephen, Eric Green and Frank Sander, *Dispute Resolution* (Boston: Little Brown, 1985).

Guinther, John, *The Jury in America* (New York: Facts on File, 1988).

Kadish, Mortimer and Sanford Kadish, *Discretion to Disobey* (Stanford: Stanford University Press, 1973).

Kalven, Harry, Jr, and Hans Zeisel, *The American Jury* (Chicago: University of Chicago Press, Midway Reprint, 1980).

Kassin, Saul and Lawrence Wrightsman, *The American Jury On Trial: Psychological Perspectives* (New York: Hemisphere Publishing, 1988).

Landsman, Stephan, *The Adversary System: A Description and Defense* (Washington, D.C.: American Enterprise Institute, 1984).

Langbein, John, "Mixed Court and Jury Court: Could the Continental Alternative Fill the American Need?" 1981 *American Bar Foundation Research Journal* 195 (1981).

Lieberman, Jethro, *The Litigious Society* (New York: Basic Books, 1981).

Luban, David, ed., *The Good Lawyer* (Totowa, N.J.: Rowman and Allanheld, 1983).

Luneberg, William and Mark Nordenberg, "Specially Qualified Juries and Expert Nonjury tribunals: Alternatives for Coping with the Complexities of Modern Civil Litigation," 67 *Virginia Law Review* 887 (1981).

Marshall, James, *Law and Psychology in Conflict*, 2d ed. (New York: Bobbs-Merrill, 1980).

Menkel-Meadow, Carrie, "Toward Another View of Legal Negotiation: The Structure of Problem Solving," 31 *UCLA Law Review* 754 *(1984)*.

Pfenigstorf, Werner and Donald Gifford, *A Comparative Study of Liability Law and Compensation Schemes in Ten Countries and the United States* (Oak Brook, Ill.: Insurance Research Council, 1991).

Pound, Roscoe, "The Causes of Popular Dissatisfaction with the Administration of Justice," 40 *American Law Review* 729 (1906).

Resnik, Judith, "Managerial Judges," 96 *Harvard Law Review 376* (1982).

Riskin, Leonard, "Mediation and Lawyers," 43 *Ohio State Law Journal* 29 (1982).

Rosenthal, Douglas, *Lawyer and Client: Who's in Charge?* (New York: Russell Sage Foundation, 1974).

Simon, Ruth, *The Jury: Its Role in American Society* (Lexington, Mass.: Lexington Books, 1980).

Simon, William, "The Ideology of Advocacy: Procedural Justice and Professional Ethics," 1978 *Wisconsin Law Review* 29 (1978).

Strick, Anne, *Injustice For All* (New York: Putnam, 1978).

Strier, Franklin and Edith Greene, *The Adversary System: An Annotated Bibliography* (Littleton, Colo.: Fred Rothman, 1988).

Strier, Franklin, "Through the Jurors' Eyes," *ABA Journal, 74* (October 1988), p. 78.

Thibaut, John and Laurens Walker, *Procedural Justice: A Psychological Analysis* (Hillsdale, N.J.: Erlbaum Associates, 1975).

Wasserstrom, Richard, "Lawyers as Professionals: Some Moral Issues," *Human Rights, 5* (1975), p. 1.

Wolfram, Charles, *Modern Legal Ethics* (St. Paul, Minn.: West, 1986).

Zeisel, Hans and Shari Diamond, "The Effect of Peremptory Challenges on Jury and Verdict: An Experiment in a Federal District Court," 30 *Stanford Law Review* 491 (1978).

INDEX

ABA (American Bar Association),
36, 180, 181, 261, 271, 286
ABA Code Of Judicial Conduct, 83
ABA Special Committee on
Resolution of Minor Disputes,
193
ABA Standards Regulating Special
Functions of the Trial Judge,
283
ABA Standards Relating to the
Prosecutorial Function, 264
Abortion and Western Law, 71
Adams, George, 29
Adams, John Quincy, 6
Administrative Dispute Resolution
Act of 1990, 195
Administrative Office of the United
States, Report of, 88
ADR (Alternative Dispute
Resolution), domestic forms:
administrative tribunals, 197,
arbitration, 196, 209;
arbitration, court-annexed, 196,
204-205; civil diversion, 199;
conciliation, 199; criminal
diversion, 199-200; early neutral
evaluation, 198; factfinding,
199; med-arb, 198, 207;
mediation, 197-98, 202-4, 209;
mediation, court-annexed, 197;
mini-trial, 198; nonadversary
negotiation, 201; ombudsman,
199; plea bargaining (*see* Plea
bargaining); private judging,
197; small claims court, 196,
206-7; specialized courts, 196;
summary jury trial, 198
ADR, domestic, growth of movement, 192-95
ADR, domestic, versus trial, pros
and cons, 201-8
ADR, foreign: English system (*see*
English system); inquisitorial
system (*see* Inquisitorial
system); inquisitorial system
versus adversary system, pros